Studies in European Economic Law and Regulation

Volume 19

This series is devoted to the analysis of European Economic Law. The series' scope covers a broad range of topics within economics law including, but not limited to, the relationship between EU law and WTO law; free movement under EU law and its impact on fundamental rights; antitrust law; trade law; unfair competition law; financial market law; consumer law; food law; and health law. These subjects are approached both from doctrinal and interdisciplinary perspectives.

The series accepts monographs focusing on a specific topic, as well as edited collections of articles covering a specific theme or collections of articles. All contributions are subject to rigorous double-blind peer-review.

More information about this series at http://www.springer.com/series/11710

Csongor István Nagy
Editor

World Trade and Local Public Interest

Trade Liberalization and National Regulatory Sovereignty

Springer

Editor
Csongor István Nagy
Department of Private International Law
University of Szeged
Szeged, Hungary

ISSN 2214-2037 ISSN 2214-2045 (electronic)
Studies in European Economic Law and Regulation
ISBN 978-3-030-41919-6 ISBN 978-3-030-41920-2 (eBook)
https://doi.org/10.1007/978-3-030-41920-2

This Springer imprint is published by the registered company Springer Nature Switzerland AG.
The registered company address is: Gewerbestrasse 11, 6330 Cham, Switzerland

Contents

1 **World Trade, Regional Economic Integrations and Local Public Interest: Comparative Perspectives** 1
Csongor István Nagy

Part I

2 **Benefits and Costs of International Trade** 11
Zombor Berezvai

3 **The EU in the Mirror of NPE: Normative Power Europe in the EU's New Generation Trade and Investment Agreements** . . . 33
Jessica C. Lawrence

4 **Acquis Communautaire+ The Copyright Aspects of the EU's Free Trade Agreements** 51
Péter Mezei

Part II

5 **Addressing Environmental Protection in the United States-Mexico-Canada Agreement (USMCA)** 67
David A. Gantz

6 **Member State Capitalism(s) and EU Law: Protecting Local Varieties in the Single Market** 95
Marton Varju and Mónika Papp

7 **South American Trade Policies Reconsidered: The "Convergence While Diversity" Mantra** 117
Valentina Delich

Part III

8 **The Supreme Court's Attempts Via Its Dormant Commerce Clause Jurisprudence to Navigate State Police Power and National Free Trade: Potential Lessons for International Trade** 137
Lee J. Strang

9 **The Judicial History of the Federal Market of Australia: Free Trade Versus Free Enterprise** 155
Gonzalo Villalta Puig

10 **India's Tryst with Free Trade: Overcoming the Inherent Challenges of Federalism** 173
Wasiq Abass Dar

Part IV

11 **Foreign Investors and Greater Transparency in Investor-State Dispute Settlement: Reevaluating Confidentiality Expectations in International Investment Arbitration** 187
Rebecca E. Khan

12 **Investment Protection and Sustainable Development in International Investment Agreements: Building Bridges Instead of Walls** 205
Begaiym Esenkulova

13 **New Model of Investment Protection Under CETA** 243
Zoltán Víg and Gábor Hajdu

14 **Screening of Foreign Investments: Promises and Perils of Technological Sovereignty** 253
Marcin J. Menkes

Chapter 1
World Trade, Regional Economic Integrations and Local Public Interest: Comparative Perspectives

Csongor István Nagy

Trade liberalization has featured international economic relations since the conclusion of the GATT in 1947. The club it established served as a platform for a series of trade rounds, which have been remarkably successful in diminishing tariffs, and became a truly universal system with the creation of the World Trade Organization in 1994 and the extension of its membership (currently WTO members account for 97% of world GDP).[1]

The last couple of decades have seen a significant shift in the focus of this process.

First, multilateralism seems to have reached its limits, giving room to bilateralism and plurilateralism (or regionalism). While the Doha Trade Round has fallen into a stalemate, new generation free trade agreements have been gaining ground. By today, it became clear that the about-face of US foreign trade policy did not block the internationalization of free trade. Although the US put the EU-US free trade agreement (TTIP) aside,[2] backed down from the trans-pacific free trade agreement (TPP) and renegotiated NAFTA, the last decade of international trade has featured numerous success stories. The TPP, renamed as Comprehensive and Progressive Agreement for Trans-Pacific Partnership (CPTPP), was signed in March 2018, without the US. The Canada-EU free trade agreement (Comprehensive Economic and Trade Agreement, CETA) entered into force in September 2017, followed by the Economic Partnership Agreement between the EU and Japan in February 2019 and the EU-Singapore Free Trade Agreement in November 2019.

Second, it is generally accepted that although customs duties are still an issue, especially in industries hit by tariff peaks, they are no longer the major hurdle faced by cross-border trade. As a corollary of this recognition, the focus of trade

---

[1]Nagy (2019), p. 88.

[2]For an analysis on the TTIP's controversial issues, *see* Martonyi (2018).

C. I. Nagy (✉)
University of Szeged, Department of Private International Law, Szeged, Hungary

C. I. Nagy (ed.), *World Trade and Local Public Interest*, Studies in European Economic Law and Regulation 19, https://doi.org/10.1007/978-3-030-41920-2_1

liberalization shifted to non-tariff barriers. States, in the name of the public interest, may introduce standards, develop regulations, shape taxation, impose regulatory burdens or maintain monopolies in a way that restricts trade. As a general experience, at times, these measures are influenced by disguised protectionism. In response to this, a new generation of free trade agreements emerged that are comprehensive, cover the whole spectrum of trade items (goods, services, technology, capital etc.) and extensively target non-tariff barriers. These agreements adumbrate a new governance for international economic relations and, not surprisingly, have incited a good deal of criticism for encroaching, with renewed enthusiasm, on national regulatory autonomy.

While these developments have incited a good deal of attention in the scholarship, the subject's comparative perspectives have been largely neglected. Notably, trading systems—the WTO, regional economic integrations and federal systems—center around the dichotomy of free trade and local public interest: they prohibit the constituent parts (states) from restricting trade and release them from this duty if the restriction is warranted by a local legitimate end. These free trade laws concentrate in four layers: the global framework (WTO), regional economic integrations, as well as the EU as a one-of-a-kind system, and federal markets, that is, federal states with strong local regulatory powers (e.g. Australia, India and the United States). Although the scholarship has not completely neglected the comparative perspectives of the subject, still, a lot of work needs to be done to grasp the pervasive issues and cross-cutting questions of these systems. The limited number of works having a comparative perspective has been confined to comparing two federal systems[3] or to making comparisons as to special points.[4] With this, free trade law lags considerably behind other (more traditional) fields of law, like contracts,[5] constitutional law[6] and antitrust/competition law,[7] where the global systems have already been elaborated.

The purpose of this volume is to contribute to the filling of the above gap, through putting the central issues of regional economic integrations into a comparative perspective. It provides a general economic analysis of the measurement of the costs and benefits of trade liberalization and the role and function of normative values in commercial policy. This is followed by a comparative analysis of the approaches of different regional economic integrations (in North America, Europe and Latin-America) and federal markets (United States, Australia and India) as to the tension between free trade and local public interest. The key issues of investment

[3]For a comparison between the EU and US, *see* Barnard (2009). For Australia-EU comparisons, *see* McNaughton (2011); Kiefel (2010); Staker (1990); Puig (2008), pp. 99, 100–101 and 127–128. For an EU-WTO comparison, *see* Sørensen (2011).

[4]For a comparison of treaty provisions, *see* Bourgeois et al. (2007).

[5]To mention two notable examples from the wealth of literature: Reimann and Zimmermann (2006) and Graziano (2019).

[6]Rosenfeld and Sajó (2012) and Dorsen et al. (2010).

[7]*See e.g.* Duns et al. (2015).

law, as one of the most contentious elements of new generation free trade agreements, are also addressed.

Part I of the book deals with the general issues of international trade liberalization: the measurement of economic benefits and drawbacks and the status of normative considerations. While it is generally accepted by economists that free trade generates wealth, the empirical measurement of this still calls for further analysis. The wealth-generating effects of international economic intercourse are asymmetric and play out in a complex way. While, on the macro-level, undistorted international trade makes societies better off, on the micro-level, it leaves both winners and losers behind. Furthermore, at times, it seems that the development of trade calls for a normative structure based both on economic and non-economic considerations. International economic relations concern not only genuine economic issues but also non-economic ones that are relevant for trade.

The chapter of Zombor Berezvai ("Benefits and Costs of International Trade") gives an economic analysis of the benefits and costs of international trade. It provides an overview of the effects on consumers, enterprises and the national economy as a whole, with the use of theoretical models and empirical analyses. The chapter points out that the gains and losses of international trade liberalization emerge unequally in different segments of the society and the net positive effects are non-linear. The latter may explain why policy makers are decreasingly interested in furthering international trade liberalization. The chapter presents a set of issues that need to be addressed to grasp the likely effects of new generation free trade agreements.

The chapter of Jessica C. Lawrence, titled "The EU in the Mirror of NPE: Normative Power Europe in the EU's New Generation Trade and Investment Agreements", gives an analysis of EU trade and investment policy through the prism of "normative power Europe" (NPE), specifically the EU's use of trade and sustainable development (TSD) to incorporate social and environmental values into its bilateral trade and investment agreements. It argues that TSD chapters, instead of attempts to engage in the diffusion of EU values abroad, are better understood as performing an internal function: they allow the EU to believe simultaneously that it is a cosmopolitan, progressive power, and that it is a savvy, effective market builder.

Péter Mezei's chapter ("Acquis Communautaire+ The Copyright Aspects of the EU's Free Trade Agreements") gives an overview of how the EU has constantly modified and broadened the scope of its free trade agreements' (FTAs) copyright chapters. It argues that here the EU's chief objective was to build a TRIPS+ or *acquis communautaire+* copyright system.

Parts II and III analyze the same issue in regional economic integrations and in federal markets. All free trade systems, same as WTO law, allow states to restrict trade if justified by a local legitimate end. States may introduce standards, shape taxation, impose public service duties on enterprises or maintain monopolies in a way that restricts trade. Since the regulatory frameworks contain vague and fluid concepts and notions, states are normally afforded a wide margin of appreciation and the application of the law becomes a social and mental process, blending economic, societal and legal considerations and aspects. Free trade systems differ as to how local legitimate ends are defined, the standard on the basis of which the existence and weight of public interest are judged and the way states' margin of appreciation is conceived when comparing free trade with public interest values. Balancing free trade and local public interest lies at the heart of the social discourse on internal trade. On the one hand, facially non-discriminatory regulation and references to local public interest are frequently used (more precisely: abused) to cut out foreign trade and protect the local industry. Furthermore, experiences show that even neutral, non-protectionist and evenhanded local standards may stifle cross-border trade. On the other hand, states are afforded a certain margin of appreciation to preserve their regulatory autonomy and the system's legitimacy. The promotion of free trade may sometimes be perceived as suppressing local legitimate regulatory policy considerations and may display free trade as "unregulated trade" in the eyes of the local electorate.

Part II translates the above questions to regional economic integrations and addresses some of their key issues in North America, the EU and Latin America.

The chapter of David A. Gantz, titled "Addressing Environmental Protection in the United States-Mexico-Canada Agreement (USMCA)", analyses the environmental protection aspects of the recently renegotiated North-American free trade agreement, signed on 30 November 2018.

The chapter authored by Márton Varju and Mónika Papp ("Member State Capitalism(s) and EU Law: Protecting Local Varieties in the Single Market") analyses the EU Single Market as a multi-layered marketplace characterised by a considerable diversity among the institutional models of local capitalisms in Europe.

The chapter of Valentina Delich, titled "South American Trade Policies Reconsidered: the 'Convergence While Diversity' Mantra", discusses the discourse on trade liberalization in Latin America and addresses the current initiatives of regional economic integration.

Part III gives a structured analysis of three federal markets: the United States, Australia and India. These federal systems have developed in relative isolation from each other and have rarely been grasped from a comparative perspective.[8] Although in these federal markets courts face the very same conceptual issues, have to deal with similar (or sometimes the same) cases and suffer from the same headache-producing dilemmas, the scholarship has failed to grasp and conceptualize federal markets from a comparative perspective.

Lee J. Strang ("The Supreme Court's Attempts Via Its Dormant Commerce Clause Jurisprudence to Navigate State Police Power and National Free Trade: Potential Lessons for International Trade") gives a concise overview of the circuitous path of the United States Supreme Court's Dormant Commerce Clause case law and, from this, suggests three potential lessons for international free trade

[8]For a counterexample, see e.g. *Castlemaine Tooheys Ltd v South Australia* (1990) 169 CLR 436 (7 February 1990), para 37. As a further example, the treaty rules on the EU internal market, in particular the provisions on the free movement of goods, were modeled after GATT. For instance, both the chapeau of Article XX GATT and the last sentence of Article 36 TFEU refer to arbitrary discrimination and disguised restriction on trade.

arrangements. It demonstrates how intractable the line between legitimate and illegitimate state regulation of interstate commerce is, argues that there is a relationship between institutional competence and the efficacy of different modes of analysis to ascertain whether a state regulation is legitimate or illegitimate, and shows how different conceptions of sovereignty influenced the Supreme Court's analysis.

Gonzalo Villalta Puig's chapter, titled "The Judicial History of the Federal Market of Australia: Free Trade Versus Free Enterprise", gives an in-depth analysis of Australian constitutional law's shift from an interpretive theory of free trade as a right to an interpretive theory of free trade as a principle.

Wasiq Abass Dar's chapter ("India's Tryst with Free Trade: Overcoming the Inherent Challenges of Federalism") presents how India has coped with the challenges that a federal system encounters when engaging in trade and commerce at a multilateral level.

Part IV addresses the central issues of investment law in the context of new generation free trade agreements' investment chapters. Arguably, the purpose of the first investment protection treaties (starting with the Germany-Pakistan Treaty of 1959),[9] was to elevate certain core standards of economic constitutionalism (e.g. compensation for expropriation, protection of legitimate expectations) to the level of international obligations. With this, investment treaties overcame the shortcomings of customary international law as to the treatment of foreign property and projected certain constitutional requirements to the level of international disciplines. The most important added value of these treaties was that these requirements became internationally binding (that is, they could not be rescinded unilaterally)[10] and were backed by a dispute settlement mechanism.[11] At the outset, these treaties were concluded between developed and developing countries. Although they contained mutual (reciprocal) obligations, they were clearly led by concerns generated by the latter's legal system. Nonetheless, after a while, international investment protection law took a life of its own. Developed democracies commenced to conclude investment treaties with each other and, at times, the arbitral practice appears to have exceeded the protection afforded by developed constitutional systems.[12] This gave rise to the criticism that investor-state arbitration subjects genuine public-law disputes to a procedural pattern tailored to the needs of purely commercial disputes (arbitration) and devoid of democratic legitimacy due to its secrecy, intransparency and ad-hoc nature.[13] The above developments were topped by new-generation free

[9]Treaty for the Promotion and Protection of Investments (with Protocol and exchange of notes), Germany and Pakistan, 25 November 1959, 457 U.N.T.S. 24 (entered into force 28 November 1962), available at https://treaties.un.org/Pages/showDetails.aspx?objid=0800000280132bef.

[10]Nagy (2018), p. 206.

[11]It was not until the mid-1970s that BITs started making provision for investor-state dispute settlement. Lim et al. (2018), pp. 59 and 61.

[12]Cf. Islam (2018), p. 188.

[13]Cf. Weiler (2014) ("[T]he Bar that adjudicates them [investment disputes] is of a limited range (...), and dominated by arbitrators from private practice rather than public interest backgrounds (...); and most damning of all, the substantive provisions of the investment treaties, when it comes

trade agreements, which are blamed for reinforcing these loose standards and the attached dispute settlement mechanisms lacking democratic legitimacy into relations between developed democracies.

Rebecca E. Khan, in her chapter titled "Foreign Investors and Greater Transparency in Investor-State Dispute Settlement: Re-Evaluating Confidentiality Expectations in International Investment Arbitration", addresses a major point of criticism against investor-state dispute settlement (ISDS). It examines the tension between the two opposing requirements faced by ISDS: transparency and confidentiality.

Begaiym Esenkulova's chapter, titled "Investment Protection and Sustainable Development in International Investment Agreements: Building Bridges Instead of Walls", addresses another internal tension of investment law: the relationship between investment protection and sustainable development.

Zoltán Víg and Gábor Hajdu, in their chapter titled "New Model of Investment Protection Under CETA", provide an analysis of the EU's emerging new dispute settlement pattern (Investment Court System) proposed to address the major points of criticism against ISDS and introduced by the Comprehensive Economic and Trade Agreement (CETA) concluded between Canada and the EU.

The chapter authored by Marcin J. Menkes ("Screening of Foreign Investments: Promises and Perils of Technological Sovereignty") addresses the emerging regulatory trend of screening foreign investments and the risks involved in blurring distinctions between economic and political issues for international peace and stability.

All in all, it seems that new-generation free trade agreements are opening a new age in international economic relations and necessitate the re-thinking of our fundamental notions on global governance, state sovereignty and regulatory autonomy. The share of free trade in the global economy is becoming paramount and the emerging new-generation free trade agreements are generating a major shift from national sovereign towards international governance. Nonetheless, while these emerging international disciplines enhance wealth and development and it would be a grand mistake not to make use of them, the internationalization of national competences also raises serious questions of democratic legitimacy. The discourse on the subject calls for a conceptual lingua franca and a transsystemic understanding of the core issues and dilemmas. It is hoped that the volume's comparative approach will contribute to this process.

References

Barnard C (2009) Restricting restrictions: lessons for the EU from the US? Camb Law J 68 (3):575–606

to protecting societal interests, are woefully defective and inferior when compared with similar public interest provisions in trade agreements such as the WTO itself.").

Bourgeois J, Dawar K, Evenett SJ (2007) A comparative analysis of selected provisions in free trade agreements (2007). http://www.kamaladawar.com/userfiles/file/downloads/A%20Comparative%20Analysis%20of%20Selected%20FTAs.pdf

Dorsen N, Rosenfeld M, Sajó A, Baer S (2010) Comparative constitutionalism: cases and materials, 2nd edn. West Academic Publishing

Duns J, Duke A, Sweeney B (2015) Comparative competition law. Elgar Publishing, Cheltenham

Graziano TK (2019) Comparative contract law, 2nd edn. Edward Elgar Publishing, Cheltenham

Islam R (2018) The Fair and Equitable Treatment (FET) standard in international investment arbitration: developing countries in context. Springer, Singapore

Kiefel S (2010) Section 92: markets, protectionism and proportionality – Australian and European perspectives. Monash Univ Law Rev 36(2):1–15

Lim CL, Ho J, Paparinskis M (2018) International investment law and arbitration. Cambridge University Press, Cambridge

Martonyi J (2018) Clash of ideologies: is transatlantic trade the right battlefield? In: Martonyi J (ed) Nyitás és identitás: Geopolitika, világkereskedelem, Európa. Pólay Elemér Alapítvány

McNaughton A (2011) Integrating services markets: a comparison of European Union and Australian experiences. Aust J Int Aff 65(4):454–468

Nagy CI (2018) Free trade, public interest and reality: new generation free trade agreements and national regulatory sovereignty. Czech Yearb Int Law 9:197–216

Nagy CI (2019) World trade, imperial fantasies and protectionism: can you really have your cake and eat it too? Indiana J Global Leg Stud 26(1):87–132

Puig GV (2008) A European saving test for section 92 of the Australian Constitution. Deakin Law Rev 13(1):99–129

Reimann M, Zimmermann R (eds) (2006) Comparative contract law. The Oxford handbook of comparative law. Oxford University Press, Oxford

Rosenfeld M, Sajó A (eds) (2012) The Oxford handbook of comparative constitutional law. Oxford University Press, Oxford

Sørensen KE (2011) Removing non-discriminatory barriers to trade in the EU and the WTO: can one system benefit from the experiences of the other? Conference: Globalization: strategies and effects. http://pure.au.dk/portal/en/activities/removing-nondiscriminatory-barriers-to-trade-in-the-eu-and-the-wto(74593c79-573a-4641-a3ac-f6f7b1e81759).html

Staker C (1990) Section 92 of the Constitution and the European Court of Justice. Fed Law Rev 19:322–351

Weiler JHH (2014) European hypocrisy: TTIP and ISDS. Eur J Int Law 25(4):961–975

Part I

Chapter 2
Benefits and Costs of International Trade

Zombor Berezvai

2.1 Introduction

There is a wide consensus among economists that freer international trade is on average favorable for a society. The University of Chicago Booth School of Business surveyed its Initiative on Global Markets (IGM) Economic Expert Panel in 2012 about the overall positive effects of freer trade.[1] Ninety-five percent of the respondents agreed or strongly agreed that the benefits of freer trade significantly surpass the costs in the long run. Only two economists were uncertain, and no one disagreed with the statement. Despite this consensus, international trade is one of the most disputed part of economic theory (Krugman et al. 2018) and political voices emerge from time to time to stop or at least control international trade.

Why international trade is creating so many discussions and debates among economists and policy makers? There are three potential reasons. First, the gains and losses of freer international trade are distributed unequally in the society. The modified income distribution unfavorably impacts some citizens and/or companies. Second, the net positive effects arise in the long run, but short run problems have to be managed. Since politicians are more concerned about short run impacts (e.g., due to the next election), they might oppose a new free trade agreement. Third, the positive effects of freer international trade are not linear. After World War II, tariffs and other restrictions were much higher than today. Current tariff rates are rather small, especially in the developed part of the world (Fig. 2.1). Only in some developing countries were average tariff rates higher than 10% in 2016. Removing

I would like to thank the precious comments of Klára Major on the previous versions of this chapter.

[1] http://www.igmchicago.org/surveys/free-trade. Accessed 30 September 2018.

Z. Berezvai (✉)
Corvinus University of Budapest, Budapest, Hungary
e-mail: zombor.berezvai@uni-corvinus.hu

C. I. Nagy (ed.), *World Trade and Local Public Interest*, Studies in European Economic Law and Regulation 19, https://doi.org/10.1007/978-3-030-41920-2_2

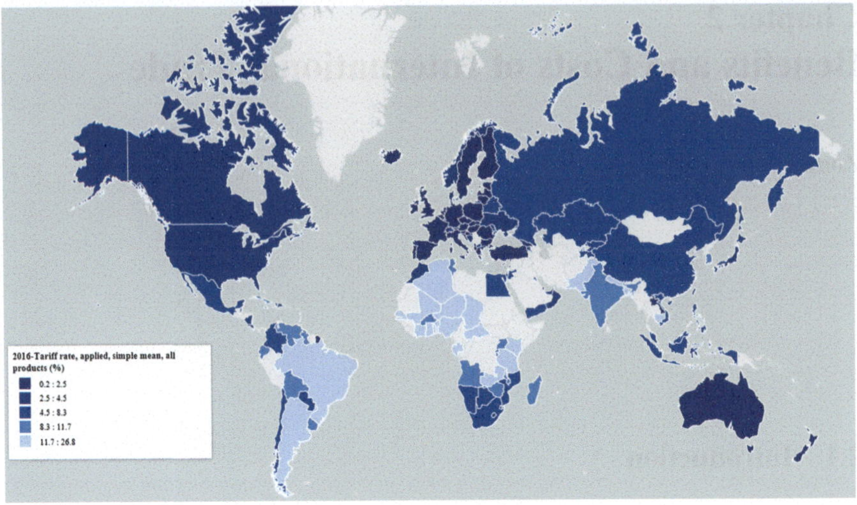

Fig. 2.1 Average tariff rates in 2016. Source: World Development Indicators (The World Bank Data Bank)

high barriers (e.g., reducing the tariff rate from 40% to 5%) provided much higher benefits and less costs than removing the remaining smaller barriers (e.g., further reducing the tariff rate from 5% to 0%) would provide. Lower potential benefits, higher costs and larger income distribution effect are less tempting, therefore, there are less motivation to freer international trade. This is one reason why newer free trade agreements are more about investment rules, intellectual property rights, environmental regulation, anti-competitive business practices than older ones were (Rodrik 2018).

There are several models to analyze the effects of international trade. Different models focus on different aspects and might provide different implications. However, the basic concept is that international trade provides access to different and more efficient production processes. This is beneficial for some consumers and firms as they can get access to these products that can mean lower prices, increased product variety, etc.

On the other hand, costs are arising from two sources. First, the effects on income distribution are hurting some specific groups. Even worse, these groups can consist of unskilled low-wage workers, therefore, it might cause severe social problems. However, industrial tycoons can also be negatively impacted that is less of a concern from a societal point of view. Second, the given country has to adjust its economy to the new circumstances. This adjustment can also be costly and requires time to get executed. Furthermore, a general observation is that losers of international trade are more organized and have better lobbying power (Viscusi et al. 1998) than the beneficiaries. This can be one reason behind national regulations, quotas, tariffs and other restrictions.

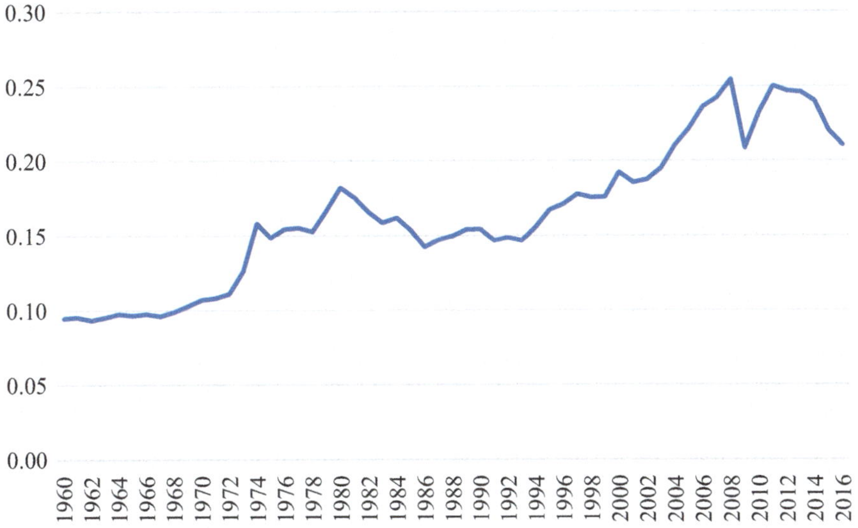

Fig. 2.2 Global export-to-GDP ratio. Source: Calculation based on WTO and World Bank data

Despite the concerns against freer trade, in the past several decades, but especially after 1972, the expansion of international trade was enormous (Fig. 2.2). Compound annual growth rate of global export and GDP in current prices between 1960 and 2016 was 9% and 7%, respectively. International trade was growing faster than GDP, and the export-to-GDP ratio more than doubled globally in 50 years.

The aim of this study is twofold. First, to provide a comprehensive picture about the advantages and disadvantages of international trade and to show empirical studies that verified these impacts. Second, to create a list of questions that should be considered to evaluate the potential effects of a new free trade agreement. The latter one is getting more and more important as the barriers against international trade are rather low today, therefore, further reduction is causing potentially lower benefits, but higher costs (Rodrik 2004). The study is organized across three main topics: effects on consumers, effects on firms and effects on economic growth.

2.2 Effects of International Trade on Consumers

As it was outlined in the previous section, international trade can provide access to different production processes. Consumers can benefit from this by paying lower prices for the same or very similar products. Lower prices mean a direct increase in consumer surplus as consumers will have the same products but have to pay less. This means that the budget constraint of the consumers is allowing more products to buy. Consumers are, therefore, always better off due to lower prices (keeping all other factors constant).

International trade is feasible in this setting if the relative price of the product in the local market is higher than adding up production cost in the exporting country and trade costs (transportation cost and tariffs). It means that the relative cost advantage of the foreign country has to be high enough to exceed trade costs.

The effect of international trade on consumer surplus was estimated by Buongiorno et al. (2017). The authors analyzed the global forest sector to identify the winners and losers of international trade. They calibrated a model to the current situation and estimated the impact of full autarky. Their analysis clearly shows that consumers are gaining due to lower prices and higher consumption compared to autarky. The increase of consumer surplus due to international trade was estimated to be around $140 billion that was distributed across consumers located both in developed and developing countries. Kersten (1995) showed that the more restrictive EU regulation on bananas caused a loss of $1.14 billion to the European consumers. The source of this loss is again price increase and consumption reduction.

Following this logic, countries should trade with different products and commodities. However, international trading data indicate a high level of intra-industry trade. Intra-industry trade refers to the case when a country is exporting and importing very similar goods. Several researchers (e.g., Krugman 1979; Brander 1981) concluded that increasing returns to scale and imperfect competition is present in reality and these are causing the observable international trading patterns.

The basic models of international trade assumed perfect competition both on the import and export sides. This is rarely the case. Taking market power of the companies into consideration, freer international trade provides another advantage, it can be a way to limit market power as more companies can enter the local market. Since the reduction of market power often lowers prices, this is also favorable for the consumers.

In this case, no technological or other differences were assumed among the trading partners, this is the reason why intra-industry trade can happen. International trade will decrease prices, but trade costs will occur. It means that it would be theoretically better to avoid trade costs by forcing local companies to act like being in a perfectly competitive market. If a regulator could force local companies to decrease prices, import could be eliminated, and trade costs could be saved (Brander 1981). This would be a better solution, however, not feasible as governments cannot force companies to sell their products on fixed prices (in market economies).

The basic model of Brander (1981) was extended by several researchers. Markusen (1981) showed that trade between identical countries is welfare improving even if companies are competing imperfectly. Nevertheless, if small and large countries are trading with each other, the large country may sustain a welfare loss.

Marjit and Mukherjee (2015) extended the analysis to the long run and showed that unilateral trade cost (transportation cost and/or tariff) reduction is often neutral or negative for the consumers located in the importing country. If domestic and foreign firms are producing exactly the same products, trade cost reduction has no effect on consumer welfare. If the products are not perfect substitutes, production costs matter. If foreign firms are producing more expensively (adding up production and trade costs) than the local ones, then trade cost reduction is welfare decreasing.

On the contrary, trade cost reduction is favorable if foreign companies can produce cheaper than the domestic ones. However, the model of Kosiec (2016) illustrated that consumers are always better off due to international trade, but this is not the case with companies. The latter can cause a decrease in welfare.

Trade cost reduction can mean both transportation cost and tariff reduction. The major difference between transportation costs and tariffs is that tariffs generate income for the importing country. Therefore, tariff cuts reduce government income. As Marjit and Mukherjee (2015) showed, further decreasing an already low tariff can cause a reduction in government expenses that can make the welfare effects even worse.

Until this point, only price changes were assessed. Imported products are, however, often not exactly the same as local ones. Higher product variety is another benefit of international trade. Imported products enlarge the consumption opportunities by making a wider portfolio of goods available. Theoretically, increasing variety cannot impact consumers negatively as they always have the opportunity to choose those products that were also available before.

Two cases need to be distinguished: new products and wider product selection. New products are mainly connected to specific resources (e.g., special climate characteristics or patents) that are not present in the country of importation. These products would not be available in the market without international trade. For example, in the Middle Ages, spices and luxury products made up the majority of long distance international trade. Trade routes originated from Africa and Asia provided products for Europe that could not be grown locally. This is still present today, and the availability of special fruits, vegetables and spices are increasing the well-being of several consumers.

Wider product selection covers products that could also be grown or manufactured domestically. The presence of imported goods adds new brands, new tastes, new packaging, new sizes, new product variants, new quality level or better price-to-value ratio to the existing product portfolio. By making these products also available in the market, consumers' selection set will increase, and this may also rise consumer surplus.

Krugman (1979) developed a general equilibrium model to verify the impacts of wider product selection. He employed the monopolistic competition model á la Dixit and Stiglitz (1977) in which consumers prefer variety: consumers' utility is increasing with the number of product varieties available in the market. Krugman (1979) showed that international trade can be a result of consumers seeking high product variety and hence, it is increasing consumer surplus.

Broda and Weinstein (2004, 2006) empirically verified the welfare consequences of increased product variety. Based on a very disaggregated database, they showed that import product variety in the United States increased by three times between 1972 and 2001. The authors estimated that this expansion in product variety caused a welfare increase equivalent to 2.6% of GDP to the US consumers.

On the other hand, increasing product variety can have potentially negative effects after the saturation point of the consumers is reached. These negative effects can come from more difficulty on choosing the right products, more frustration during selection, dissatisfaction with the final choice, etc. Some studies indicate that these are due to limited attention and bounded rationality. The meta-analysis of Scheibehenne et al. (2010) indicated that increasing the available selection of products has an average zero effect on consumers, but the results of the different studies show significant differences. The meta-analysis also showed some factors that can affect the so-called "choice overload". If the consumers are having more expertise and stronger prior preferences, they benefit more from increasing product variety. Furthermore, newer publications show that the choice overload effect is less severe compared to earlier results. This suggests that people might get used to the enlarged product selection.

Not only choice overload can cause unfavorable outcomes. Egger and Falkinger (2016) presented a different model with limited consumer attention. Companies aimed to catch as much attention from the consumers as possible and this is causing an overbidding in advertisement and diverts consumption of imported goods at an overall inefficient level.

To summarize the theoretical and empirical findings, freer international trade is welfare improving for the consumers in two channels: lower prices and higher product variety. The first benefit is always present if the exporting country can produce same or similar products cheaper than the importing country. The additional gain of further widening product selection is more likely getting lower and lower with the number of already available products on the market. The effect might be negative after the saturation point is reached. However, the saturation point varies by consumers and product categories and there is no evidence to define where it lies.

2.3 Effect of International Trade on Firms

In the previous section, only consumers were considered. In this section, we focus on companies. A company consists of both capital owners and employees. In this case, the effect of freer international trade can be either positive and negative depending on several factors. From a corporate point of view, international trade is providing access to larger markets and to cheaper (or sometimes unique) resources as well as enables global supply chains. On the other hand, competition will increase as foreign companies are granted access to the domestic market.

The main idea behind international trade is connected to the fact that countries are having different natural, human and capital resources and their production technologies are also different. These indicate that different countries can produce the same products for different prices. In case of autarky, a country has to supply all the products on its own. Even if a country is able to do it (it has all the necessary resources and technologies), it might be inefficient due to several factors:

- producing small quantities can mean that economies of scale are not exploited;
- maintaining several production technologies might be very costly;

- the country might not have the best available technology, the production system might be not efficient and productive enough;
- there is a scarcity of available natural and other resources.

The above specified problems can be grouped into two main categories: resources and technology. The Heckscher–Ohlin model focuses on the resource difference across countries and assumes similar technologies (Acemoglu 2009). The model indicates that countries are specializing based on their resource availability. As Deardorff (1982) proved, the Heckscher–Ohlin theorem suggests that there is a negative correlation between resource price in autarky and net export of the given resource. This means that countries are exporting goods that require abundant resources and importing goods that require scarce resources.

The Heckscher–Ohlin model has important consequences for companies. The model indicates a type of specialization based on the input need of the production. Companies using the abundant resources will gain from international trade as they can also sell these products abroad. Companies that are using tradable, but domestically scarce resources will also gain to get access to the global supply of these resources (Lee 1995). These companies can lower input prices, hence, increase the competitiveness and profitability of their products.

On the other hand, the scarce resources of a country are more expensive domestically than internationally. International trade can provide access to the cheaper resources; therefore, domestic producers of these resources will be adversely impacted. If the scarce resource is produced in the country (e.g., mining), then the producers will lose when the country is getting involved in international trade. If the scarce resource is not produced, but it is not tradable either (e.g., land), then the owners of these resources will be adversely impacted by freer international trade.

Bernhofen and Brown (2016) used the case of Japan to verify the predictions of the Heckscher–Ohlin model. Japan was closed from the outside world until 1859. The authors used input price, production technology and commodity trading data from the early free trade period (1865–1876) and verified that on average Japan was a net exporter of its abundant resources and a net importer of its scarce resources. This provides strong evidence supporting the Heckscher–Ohlin model at the end of the nineteenth century. Since there were significant technological differences between Japan and its trading partners,[2] the authors did not specify the abundant and the scarce resources.

Ito et al. (2016) analyzed the World Input-Output Database to verify the predictions of the Heckscher–Ohlin model in the recent years (between 1995 and 2009). According to their results, the model is valid if we analyze the added value in international trade (and not gross production value). Labor abundant countries (e.g., China) are mainly contributing to the global production with cheap (and often unskilled) workforce, while skill abundant countries (e.g., the USA or the EU) are exporting skill-intensive products.

[2]The industrial revolution did not reach Japan at that time, therefore production technologies in Japan were less efficient compared to its trading partners.

A special case of this theory is provided when some inputs are domestically not available at all. In this case, producers have no choice but to import them. It is similar to the case of new product availability for consumers. However, in case of producers, the lack of a critical resource can completely disrupt production (Ossa 2015). In some cases (e.g., for countries importing crude oil), the lack of import can hinder the functioning of the whole economy. In this case, the gain from international trade can be enormous (Ossa 2015).

The second type of models is focusing on technology and productivity differences among countries. International trade can increase global production by allowing specialization based on efficiency differences. A country can specialize on the products it can produce comparatively cheaply and trade it to other products in the international marketplace. In this way, total production cost can be decreased. The theory of comparative advantages was developed by Ricardo in the nineteenth century (Krugman et al. 2018).

The key point in this theory is that only relative production costs matter (and not nominal ones). This is rooting back to the assumption that countries are on their production frontier, i.e., increasing the production of a given good has to trigger a reduction of another good. Theoretically it is conceivable that a country can produce almost every good cheaper than other countries do. However, there is a constraint of capital and labor. For a country to produce all the products would require so many resources that no country can supply. On the other hand, the resources of other countries would not be utilized at all. This is not efficient and specializing based on comparative advantages is superior compared to this solution.

This theory presumes that there are efficiency differences among countries that can create different comparative advantages to different countries. The source of these efficiency differences can root back to several factors. First, different countries are on different levels of development and there are also differences in the complexity of the production process they can handle. Second, Belloc (2006) argued that institutional architectures are important determinants of the comparative advantages, however, the relationship is complex, not unidirectional and difficult to interpret. Costinot (2009) showed that countries with higher institutional quality and larger human capital are having comparative advantage in more complex industries. Finally, specialization can happen on purpose due to different public policies. Chatterjee (2017) proposed that there is an incentive even for similar countries to choose different policies and specializations as gains from international trade can be obtained this way.

Specialization is favorable for companies active in industries characterized by comparative advantages. However, firms operating in industries having comparative disadvantage will be the losers of international trade. In theory, these companies should leave the market and transfer their resources to a competitive industry. However, this is possible only if resources (like labor or capital) can be fully and easily allocated across industries. Resource allocation between different industries often cannot be implemented or can be done only in the long run. Industry-specific capital investments and labor skills are not easily transferable to completely different industries. Therefore, despite the favorable net effects of international specialization, some specific industries will be adversely affected and can potentially die. This is the reason behind the adjustment and income distribution effects mentioned in the introduction.

Specialization can be observed is several countries. Cadot et al. (2011) showed that there is a U-shaped relationship between export specialization and national income, i.e., low- and high-income countries are more specialized in trade than middle-income countries. This can be connected to a slow adjustment process when the country is getting more technology oriented and "old" comparative advantages are getting lost. However, "old" industries die slower than "new" industries appear. This view is also supported by Pelli and Tschopp (2017). The authors showed that after a hurricane destroyed the manufacturing sites, export decreased from industries with comparative disadvantage and increased from industries with high level of comparative advantage. The hurricane destroyed existing investments, hence, accelerated the penetration of the "new" comparative advantages.

However, international trade changed significantly in the recent period, especially after 1985. This process was enhanced by freer capital flows across nation-states that enabled companies to globalize their production processes. Baldwin and Lopez-Gonzalez (2015) called it as "denationalizing comparative advantage". This means that comparative advantages are getting more and more knowledge related, therefore, these are connected to companies rather than to countries. Large companies are building their own supply chains and are locating different activities (production, services, R&D, etc.) to locations they find the most attractive for the particular activity. The abundant resources of a given territory can be utilized by the international companies.

The presence of company-related comparative advantages caused the globalization of the production processes and supply chains. The concept of global factory indicates that large multinational companies are allocating small parts of their value chains to different countries to achieve lowest possible cost and maximum efficiency (Celo et al. 2018). In this regard, international trade is the way how a country can be part of the global factory.

The global factory phenomenon is of crucial importance today. Baldwin and Lopez-Gonzalez (2015) pointed out that in 2009 final goods accounted only for 34% of total world export, the rest consisted of intermediaries. Free trade can have two consequences on domestic firms in this setting.

First, local companies will have the opportunity to participate in the global factory. They can also dismantle the value chain and find the best locations for all their activities. Furthermore, large multinational companies are outsourcing more and more activities to other firms. Local companies can supply foreign production sites and companies if trade barriers are not preventing this. This is favorable for those companies that can connect to the global factory as suppliers. Participating in the global factory can result in higher profits, but the question is how the additional profit is distributed among the parties. Sexton et al. (2007) analyzed the agricultural product segment and found that if the market is not perfectly competitive (which is almost always the case), profits from trade liberalization (zero tariffs) flow to trading firms rather than to producers. This is lowering the benefits a developing country can obtain from international trade. However, Hoque and Schroeter (2010) showed that if ad valorem tariffs are removed, results are completely different, and producers of developing countries can get even better off compared to the perfect competition case. The perceived gain a company can obtain from trade liberalization depends therefore heavily on the market structure and the type of restriction that was eliminated.

Second, free trade implies that multinational companies can also sell their products in the domestic market without any restrictions. This is increasing competition on the domestic marketplace. Less efficient local companies will lose this competition and their sales revenue and market share will most likely decline.

Furthermore, the model of Egger and Kreickemeier (2012) indicated that companies with higher productivity tend to get involved in exporting. These companies are paying higher wages to their employees to reward the efforts they undertake. A survey of empirical literature on international trade by Wagner (2012) similarly suggests that international trade relates to higher firm productivity, however, it is mainly the result of self-selection. Namely, more competitive companies tend to present in more export markets and in more developed export markets. Similarly, there is a positive relationship between firm productivity and import activities. Wagner (2012) indicated that not international trade is making the companies more efficient, but already more efficient companies are starting to export and import products.

This means that international trade is favoring the well performing companies in two ways: they make the international market available for them and they increase competition in the domestic market that might necessitates less efficient companies to exit from the market. Both are contributing to better resource allocation. This can enhance the economic performance of a country, too. The next section deals with this question.

2.4 Effect of International Trade on Economic Growth

In the first section, we reviewed the direct effects of international trade on consumers, while in the second section we focused separately on firms. Firms and consumers are, however, connected to each other. Consumers are also gaining if domestic firms are performing well. This will create new jobs, increase salaries and foster economic growth. In this section, the focus is set on economic development and how international trade can contribute to higher economic growth and better value creation on the national level.

The link between micro-level analyses (that are focusing on particular industries and consumers) and assessing aggregated gain on a national level is not straightforward at all. Arkolakis (2012) surveyed the micro-level literature on international trade and concluded that they are not helping much in measuring the overall welfare gains of international trade. Arkolakis (2012) argued that the welfare gain of a country depends on two measures: expenditure share of domestic products (i.e., one minus import penetration) and cost elasticity of import (also known as trade elasticity).

The macro level theories, namely, the comparative advantage theory of Ricardo and the Heckscher–Ohlin theorem can be the starting points for analyzing the impact of international trade on a particular economy. Both theories conclude that international trade is favorable for the economy. However, there are two main concerns with them.

First, these theories assume that all the countries are on the border of their production possibilities and increasing the production of one good has to trigger a decrease of production of another one. In the reality, companies are often not producing on their production frontiers and are not fully utilizing their capacities. Therefore, countries can better utilize economies of scale via international trade. This is the so called "vent-for-surplus" theory. This is different from the theory of comparative advantages as it assumes that due to capacity underutilization, export can be increased without any sacrifices, i.e., simply utilizing the previously unused capacities (Myint 1958).

The main point of the "vent-for-surplus" theory is that absolute advantages matter, not comparative ones. Since developed countries often have absolute advantages for a large number of products, these countries can dominate international trade by utilizing previously unused capacities. Hence, less productive countries might be expelled from the market. This is obviously favorable for those countries having absolute advantages and underutilized capacities in several industries and bad for the rest. Freer international trade is, therefore, not mutually favorable for all the contracting parties.

A stream of empirical papers tested the "vent-for-surplus" theory by analyzing special agricultural products of Africa, like palm oil, cotton and cocoa. The idea is that Africa has underutilized land and labor that can be used to produce more agricultural products without any sacrifices (Tosh 1980). However, the "vent-for-surplus" theory not only assumes that there are available land and human resources, but also that these can be combined to produce increased export quantity. Austin (2014) examined the Ghanaian cocoa production take off between 1890 and 1936. He concluded that labor is shifted from other activities to cocoa farming, hence, the "vent-for-surplus" theory did not prove to be true.

Empirical evidences did not support the "vent-for-surplus" theory and it did not become mainstream. A further point against this theory is that there are barriers in every country and production cannot be increased only up to a certain point. Additionally, shipping and transaction costs also constitute a barrier against international trade (Pomfret 2014).

The second and more important concern regarding the macro theories is that these are static theories and the dynamic effects are not incorporated. Namely, the existing specialization can be conserved. Developing countries are often having comparative advantages in raw material production and cheap labor force (Ito et al. 2016). Exploiting these comparative advantages might not help these countries to fuel economic growth (Rodríguez and Rodrik 2000) and reach a higher stage of development. This can be one reason why developing countries are applying government policies to diversify their export portfolio (Cadot et al. 2011). This seems to be a potential way to avoid the drawbacks of specialization.

However, some examples clearly show that developing countries can also benefit from international trade. The best example is the High Performing Asian Economies[3] (HPAEs). These countries were focusing on creating internationally competitive products and incentivizing export. Furthermore, the increasing export revenues were allocated to education, research and development, capital formation and/or improving macroeconomic stability. HPAE countries were continuously developing their export goods to compete in more and more capital and skill intensive product categories. International trade was helpful for these economies to achieve exceptionally high growth rates and increase the revenue of the local companies and citizens (Krugman et al. 2018; Darku and Yeboah 2018). This example supports that international trade provides opportunities, but countries can utilize them differently. HPAEs were able to exploit the opportunities at a high extent. Empirical results of Darku and Yeboah (2018) indicated that HPEA countries were able to utilize trade liberalization the most among developing countries. The effect of trade openness on economic growth was the highest for this group compared to the rest of the developing countries.

At first glance, the survey of Wagner (2012) can be contradictory to the case of the HPAEs. The examples are, however, supporting each other. HPAEs did not start their exporting activities with state-of-the-art skill intensive products, but rather with clothes and labor-intensive mass products. They were able to identify the product categories where their companies had comparative advantage in the international marketplace. Export revenues generated by these industries were used to develop other industries; hence, they increased their productivity in more and more business segments. This productivity increase created the basis to expand the export of more and more industries and increase GDP growth through international trade.

An important element of their success was that HPAE countries exposed high tariffs on those industries that they were developing in order to avoid international competition when the industries were still in their infancies. Trade barriers were eliminated once the industries became competitive.

This overview suggests that it might be optimal for a country to restrict international free trade (Samuelson 1962). However, free trade is able to maximize world production and income. Most importantly, the heart of this problem is income allocation. Some countries gain from international trade, while others lose. This is also true within a country: consumers and exporters will have higher income, while a specific group of industry-specific resource owners will be worse off. Both can be compensated as free trade is increasing aggregate welfare (Samuelson 1962). Unfortunately, it is often not so straightforward and hardly manageable, especially among countries.

Trade liberalization has positive effects on average, but theories are mixed regarding the impact of trade openness on economic growth for particular economies

---

[3] Hong Kong, Taiwan, South Korea, Singapore, Malaysia, Thailand, Indonesia and partially China.

(Rodríguez and Rodrik 2000; Singh 2010). The differences in theories called for empirical research that also provided mixed evidences.

Balassa (1978) analyzed a group of 11 developing countries and accepted the hypotheses that export-oriented policies led to better growth performance than policies favoring import substitution. According to the calculation of Balassa (1978), South Korea (one of the HPEA countries) would have 37% lower GNP if export rate would be equal to the average of the sample. Several publications (e.g., Chang et al. 2009; Chang and Mendy 2012; Falvey et al. 2012) came to the same conclusion that trade openness is fostering GDP growth.

However, Eris and Ulasan (2013) did not find any strong evidence that trade openness is related to economic growth based on a wide dataset covering 66 countries between 1960 and 2000. Fetahi-Vehapi et al. (2015) analyzed South East European countries only and did not find robust evidence supporting the openness-growth relationship either.

A further question is the direction of causality, namely, trade openness is causing economic growth or economic growth is causing trade openness. This is not trivial to separate in empirical research. For e.g., Eris and Ulasan (2013) indicated that they estimated correlation only and did not say anything about causality. Some publications (e.g., Chang et al. 2009; Darku and Yeboah 2018) applied advanced dynamic panel model techniques and showed a positive causal relationship of international trade on economic growth.

However, without any prior assumptions, only Granger causality[4] can be tested using the data. Amadou (2013) analyzed the Granger causality between trade openness and economic growth in the West African countries. Results did not show any Granger causality among the two variables, posing questions on the existence of the relationship. Kónya (2006) executed a similar analysis for 24 OECD countries. Results are mixed, he found that export is Granger causing GDP growth in 8 countries, GDP growth is Granger causing export in 7 countries, there is a two-way Granger causality in 3 countries and no Granger causality in 6 countries.

Singh (2010) conducted a theoretical and empirical literature review on this topic to aggregate the results of several studies. According to this review, the majority of the publications support that countries can gain from international trade. Time series and panel econometric results generally indicate a positive impact. Based on the microeconomic studies, the positive impact is steaming from a self-selection, namely that already productive companies can gain from trade liberalization. Studies

[4]The idea of the Granger causality is that the future cannot cause the present or the past. Therefore, the present value of a time series can be influenced only by changes occurred in the past. Granger causality only means that something happened earlier than something else which is not a sufficient condition for causality. On the other hand, according to the opinion of the Cowles Foundation, causality cannot be examined without a priori assumptions (Maddala 2001).

supporting the learning-by-exporting hypothesis is much rare in the literature (Singh 2010).

However, some mixed evidences are arising from historical analyses (e.g., Foreman-Peck 1995; O'Rourke 2000; Vamvakidis 2002) indicating that the relationship is affected by several factors that vary in time. Important ones can be domestic regulations, policies and reforms. A further result arising from this literature stream is that implementing complementary policies can increase the benefits of trade liberalization. Chang et al. (2009) found that openness positively impact growth, and the effect is even larger if certain complementary reforms (e.g., human capital investment, financial system, public infrastructure, price stability) are undertaken. Darku and Yeboah (2018) indicated that HPAEs were able to utilize trade openness at a high extent because they executed several policies to invest in human capital and maintain economic stability.

Rodríguez and Rodrik (2000) critically assessed the openness-growth literature and indicated that they are skeptic regarding the strong negative relationship between trade barriers and economic growth. They argue that institutions and macroeconomic imbalances are more important to growth and regressions verifying the openness-growth relationship rather measure macroeconomic imbalances and bad institutions than trade barriers. This is important as countries should more focus on development strategies rather than to further opening their economies.

Falvey et al. (2012) investigated the question, when liberalization should occur. The authors compared the growth impact of trade liberalization in crisis and non-crisis periods. This is especially interesting as global financial institutions (e.g., International Monetary Fund or World Bank) often require reforms during loan agreements. Crises can serve as good times to execute reforms, therefore estimating their return is crucial. Results showed that increasing trade openness led to higher GDP growth. However, the type of the crisis impacted the size of the growth effect of trade liberalization. If the crisis was rather internal (decreasing GDP, increasing inflation, depreciating exchange rate), then trade liberalization had a lower effect on GDP growth in the subsequent years (compared to non-crisis times). However, in case of current account or debt-to-export crises (i.e., external crises), increasing trade openness enhanced GDP growth more than in non-crisis times in the short run. Falvey et al. (2012) summarized the results that since crises often have both internal and external elements, it might be more secure to execute trade liberalization measures during normal times. However, trade liberalization during crisis times might be a good idea as reforms and policy changes often take place at that time and these can enhance the positive impact of trade liberalization (Chang et al. 2009; Darku and Yeboah 2018).

2.5 Conclusions

Current economic theories and models suggest that international trade is favorable in general (Samuelson 1962), it is increasing social welfare. However, the picture is not as unambiguous as it looks at first glance. This paper reviewed several articles, theoretical and empirical analyses to show what influences whether a given country will gain or lose from freer international trade. Table 2.1 summarizes these points and provides a general overview of what kind of questions should be answered to evaluate the potential impact of trade liberalization on the social welfare of a country.

Generally, once a country is moving from autarky, it is almost absolutely sure that it will gain from freer international trade. However, once a country is already very open and applies only low trade barriers (e.g., tariffs or quotas), it is harder to assess the welfare effect of an additional trade agreement. Currently, trade barriers are already very low in the majority of the countries (Fig. 2.1). The ratification of a new trade agreement is even more difficult as the gains are distributed across several agents (consumers, firms), but the losses are almost always connected to some specific groups that are often well-organized (Viscusi et al. 1998). Additionally, current free trade agreements deal with several other issues and topics (Rodrik 2018) that make the ratification more difficult.

Ehrlich (2008) argued that an institutional change, namely delegation to the President lead to a shift from protectionism to free trade in the US. Since lobbyist had a lower number of access points to the government due to delegation, cost of lobbying increased. Lobbying is dominated by advocates of protectionism and, therefore, reduced lobbying affected them the most. Moving in the direction of free trade and reducing tariffs in the US are potential consequences of this change.

Lobbying can take various forms and the so-called "Baptists and Bootleggers" coalitions are often happening in connection with international trade. As Adler et al. (2016) summarized this type of coalition arises when an economically motivated interest group ("Bootleggers") finds support from an interest group motivated by normative justifications ("Baptists"). The normative argument can dominate the discussion about the topic and business interest can stay hidden or at least get lower attention. This way, coalitions can be more effective and can have higher influence on the final decision. For e.g., Sotirov et al. (2017) showed that the birth of the new EU regulation on timber trade was partially a result of a "Baptists and Bootleggers" coalition. Tough political discussions were about the prohibition clause of the regulation that prohibited the entry of illegally sourced timber to the EU market. Environmental organizations aimed to reduce illegal timber harvest globally and, therefore, supported the prohibition clause. On the other hand, some timber industry members were interested in higher selling prices in the EU market and banning cheap illegally sourced timber could contribute to this effort. The prohibition clause was finally accepted and is part of the timber regulation.

"Baptists and Bootleggers" coalitions can be against free trade and the normative reasons (e.g., food safety, child labor, deforestation) reveal real problems. In these

Table 2.1 Factors worth considering before a new free trade agreement

Designation	Potential positive effects	Potential negative effects	Questions to consider
Consumers			
Impact on prices	Lower prices due to availability of cheaper products or more intense competition Increasing consumer surplus	Price increase if foreign companies are less efficient and the domestic market is already competitive enough Decreasing consumer surplus	Are there large efficiency differences among the countries involved in the proposed trade agreement? Is the proposed trade agreement able to provide lower priced products to the domestic consumers? Is product market competition intense enough (number of firms, concentration, etc.)?
New product availability	Having access to new or special products	–	Does the proposed trade agreement provide new products to the consumers?
Increasing product variety	More choice opportunities for the consumers (consumers' preference for variety)	Dissatisfaction with the final choice, more difficulty on choosing the right product ("choice overload") Too many advertisements to catch the limited attention of the consumers	What is the current level of product variety in the market? In which product segment will the proposed trade agreement increase product variety? What is the marketing and advertising activities of the current market players in these product segments?
Firms			
Resource availability	Companies using domestically abundant resources will have larger market to supply Increasing the availability of domestically scarce resources for production	Local companies producing scarce resource or owning domestically scarce, but not tradable resources will lose market share and sales volume	What are the scarce resources of the given country? Will the proposed trade agreement help to supply more from these resources? How many companies are connected to the production of the scarce resources? What are the abundant resources of the given country? Will local companies

(continued)

Table 2.1 (continued)

Designation	Potential positive effects	Potential negative effects	Questions to consider
			be able to export more from those products using the abundant resources as inputs?
Access to unique resources	Companies can access to domestically not available, but necessary resources	–	Are there key resources that are not available domestically (e.g., crude oil)? Will the proposed trade agreement provide (easier) access to these resources?
Comparative advantages (technology, productivity)	Firms having comparative advantages can increase their production and sales	Firms having comparative disadvantages can lose their market share and sales volume	Which industries are having comparative (dis-) advantages relative to the countries involved in the proposed trade agreement? How many firms and employees are involved in these industries? Will local companies with comparative advantages be able to expand their production because of the proposed trade agreement?
Global factory	Enables local firms to get involved in global supply chains Local companies can easier internationalize their activities	Foreign companies can have easier access to the local market resulting a reduction in market share and sales of local companies	Is the given country currently integrated in global supply chains? Will the proposed trade agreement help domestic companies to get more involved in global supply chains? Are there domestic companies aiming to internationalize their operations? Will the proposed trade agreement help them to achieve it? What is the current presence of multinational (foreign) companies on the domestic market?

(continued)

Table 2.1 (continued)

Designation	Potential positive effects	Potential negative effects	Questions to consider
			What product segments are the most endangered by the entry of multinational (foreign) companies? Will the proposed trade agreement have an effect on these segments?
Economic growth			
"Vent-for-surplus"	Domestic production can be increased by using unexploited resources or underutilized capacities	Import can be more scale efficient and rule out domestic products from the market	What is the amount of unexploited and yet available resources? Can these resources be applied for producing internationally competitive products? Which industries might suffer from more efficient foreign competition after the proposed trade agreement will be in force?
Development	Selling internationally competitive products generates income for the country that can be used for developing new industries	International trade might conserve existing specialization that can hinder economic development	What are the most competitive industries of the given country? What industries are planned to get developed? Can infant industries be temporary secured from intense international competition?
Implementation of complementary policies	Complementary policies can enhance the positive impacts of trade liberalization	–	Is the government planning to implement any new policies to improve education, public services, public infrastructure, macroeconomic stability, etc.?

cases, several arguments need to be balanced and the final decisions are especially tough to make.

On the other hand, Rönnbäck (2015) showed that interest groups are not always protectionists, they can lobby in favor of free trade, too. This is logical if export- and/or import-dependent companies construct the interest groups. It highly depends on the given country. For large countries (e.g., the US), several firms are focusing solely on the domestic market, therefore more interest groups will potentially lobby for protectionism. This is different for small and more export-dependent countries, like Sweden (Rönnbäck 2015).

In modern democracies, not only interest groups, but also voters' interests affect policy formation. Since international trade is affecting residents' income distribution, this can create resistance. Income reallocation can be a way to mitigate this problem, but redistribution has several other disadvantages (e.g., taxation is costly, and it is hardly possible to find fair allocation rules), therefore, it is rarely happening.

Malcolm (2017) reviewed the most recent free trade agreements of the US. He found that those House and Senate members were more likely to vote in favor of the agreement, whose district was having a higher export exposure towards the countries subject to the trade agreement. Similarly, Che et al. (2016) found that those districts that are having the greatest competition with Chinese firms are more likely to vote for Democrats. This is because Democrats in general support import limitations with respect to China more than Republicans. Kagitani and Harimaya (2017) reported similar patterns from Japan.

These results indicate that not only lobbying, but also voters' preferences impact whether a country will engage in a new free trade agreement. This is favorable as potential winners are also getting influence on these decisions and not the opinion of the short run losers dominates the discussions.

The past several decades showed that the world is getting more and more open and restrictions against free international trade are getting lower and lower. Times of economic crises can disrupt this process (see Fig. 2.2 around 2008–2010), but it is unlikely that these will have a long run impact. However, a world without any trade restrictions is unlikely to arrive. Not only the potential negative effects of the free trade agreements are causing it, but also the complex political system with coalitions and lobbying. Additionally, an interesting aspect of international trade is connected to this point. International trade is riskier than domestic trade that is another factor needs to be considered. Risk averse companies and workers are, therefore, less likely to enter those industries that are open to the international market. This can cause an underproduction from these goods compared to the case of autarky. Shy (1988) showed in a general equilibrium framework that autarky can provide better outcomes (i.e., it is Pareto efficient) compared to complete free trade (i.e., zero trade barriers). However, neither is the optimal case. Shy (1988) argued that this can be an additional reason why complete free trade is never observable in the world and some restrictions are in place even in very open economies.

References

Acemoglu D (2009) Introduction to modern economic growth. Princeton University Press, Princeton

Adler JH, Meiners Roger E, Morriss Andrew P, Yandle B (2016) Baptists, Bootleggers & Electronic Cigarettes. Yale J Regul 33:313–361

Amadou A (2013) Is there a causal relation between trade openness and economic growth in the WAEMU countries? Int J Econ Finan 5:151–156

Arkolakis C, Costinot A, Rodríguez-Clare A (2012) New trade models, same old gains? Am Econ Rev 102:94–130

Austin G (2014) Vent for surplus or productivity breakthrough? The Ghanaian cocoa take-off, c. 1890–1936. Econ Hist Rev 67(4):1035–1064

Balassa B (1978) Exports and economic growth. Further evidence. J Dev Econ 5:181–189

Baldwin R, Lopez-Gonzalez J (2015) Supply-chain trade: a portrait of global patterns and several testable hypotheses. World Econ 38:1682–1721

Belloc M (2006) Institutions and international trade: a reconsideration of comparative advantage. J Econ Surv 20:3–26

Bernhofen DM, Brown JC (2016) Testing the general validity of the Heckscher-Ohlin theorem. Am Econ J: Microecon 8:54–90

Brander JA (1981) Intra-industry trade in identical commodities. J Int Econ 11:1–14

Broda C, Weinstein DE (2004) Variety growth and world welfare. Am Econ Rev: Pap Proc 94:139–144

Broda C, Weinstein DE (2006) Globalization and the gains from variety. Q J Econ 121:541–585

Buongiorno J, Johnston C, Zhu S (2017) An assessment of gains and losses from international trade in the forest sector. Forest Policy Econ 80:209–217

Cadot O, Carrère C, Strauss-Kahn V (2011) Export diversification: what's behind the hump? Rev Econ Stat 93(2):590–605

Celo S, Nebus J, Wang IK (2018) The role of internal and external complexity in global factory performance: an NKC application. J Int Manage 24:65–83

Chang C-C, Mendy M (2012) Economic growth and openness in Africa: what is the empirical relationship? Appl Econ Lett 19:1903–1907

Chang R, Kaltani L, Loayza NV (2009) Openness can be good for growth: the role of policy complementarities. J Dev Econ 90:33–49

Chatterjee A (2017) Endogenous comparative advantage, gains from trade and symmetry-breaking. J Int Econ 209:102–115

Che Y, Lu Y, Pierce JR, Schott PK, Tao Z (2016) Does trade liberalization with China influence U.S. elections? Board of Governors of the Federal Reserve System, Washington. Finance and Economics Discussion Series 2016(039)

Costinot A (2009) On the origins of comparative advantage. J Int Econ 77:255–264

Darku AB, Yeboah R (2018) Economic openness and income growth in developing countries: a regional comparative analysis. Appl Econ 50:855–869

Deardorff AV (1982) The general validity of the Heckscher-Ohlin theorem. Am Econ Rev 72 (4):683–694

Dixit AK, Stiglitz JE (1977) Monopolistic competition and optimum product diversity. Am Econ Rev 67:297–308

Egger H, Falkinger J (2016) Limited consumer attention in international trade. Rev Int Econ 24:1096–1128

Egger H, Kreickemeier U (2012) Fairness, trade, and inequality. J Int Econ 86:184–196

Ehrlich SD (2008) The tariff and the lobbyist: political institutions, interest group politics, and U.S. trade policy. Int Stud Q 52:427–445

Eris MN, Ulasan B (2013) Trade openness and economic growth: Bayesian model averaging estimate of cross-country growth regressions. Econ Model 33:867–883

Falvey R, Foster N, Greenaway D (2012) Trade liberalization, economic crises, and growth. World Dev 40:2177–2193

Fetahi-Vehapi M, Sadiku L, Petkovski M (2015) Empirical analysis of the effects of trade openness on economic growth: an evidence for south east European countries. Procedia Econ Finan 19:17–26

Foreman-Peck J (1995) A model of later nineteenth century European economic development. Revista de Historia Economica 13:441–471

Hoque MM, Schroeter JR (2010) Agricultural trade liberalization and downstream market power: the Ad Valorem case. J Agric Food Ind Organ 8(11):1–29
Ito T, Rotunno L, Vézina P-L (2016) Heckscher–Ohlin: evidence from virtual trade in value added. Rev Int Econ 25:427–446
Kagitani K, Harimaya K (2017) Electoral motives, constituency systems, ideologies, and a free trade agreement: the case of Japan joining the Trans-Pacific Partnership negotiations. J Jpn Int Econ 45:51–66
Kersten L (1995) Impacts of the EU banana market regulation on international competition, trade and welfare. Eur Rev Agric Econ 22:321–335
Kónya L (2006) Exports and growth: Granger causality analysis on OECD countries with a panel data approach. Econ Model 23:978–992
Kosiec K (2016) Liberalisation of international trade – the case of asymmetric countries. Cen Eur J Econ Model Econ 8:143–160
Krugman PR (1979) Increasing returns, monopolistic competition, and international trade. J Int Econ 9:469–479
Krugman PR, Obstfeld M, Melitz M (2018) International economics: theory and policy, 11th edn. Pearson, Essex
Lee J-W (1995) Capital goods imports and long-run growth. J Dev Econ 48:91–110
Maddala GS (2001) Introduction to econometrics, 3rd edn. Wiley, Chichester
Malcolm M (2017) Do local exports impact congressional voting on free trade agreements? Econ Lett 154:31–34
Marjit S, Mukherjee A (2015) Endogenous market structure, trade cost reduction, and welfare. J Inst Theor Econ 171:493–511
Markusen JR (1981) Trade and the gains from trade with imperfect competition. J Int Econ 11:531–551
Myint H (1958) The "classical theory" of international trade and the underdeveloped countries. Econ J 68:317–337
O'Rourke KH (2000) Tariffs and growth in the late 19th century. Econ J 110:456–483
Ossa R (2015) Why trade matters after all. J Int Econ 97:266–277
Pelli M, Tschopp J (2017) Comparative advantage, capital destruction, and hurricanes. J Int Econ 108:315–337
Pomfret R (2014) Expanding the division of labour: trade costs and supply chains in the global economy. Aust Econ Hist Rev 54:220–241
Rodríguez F, Rodrik D (2000) Trade policy and economic growth: a skeptic's guide to the cross-national evidence. NBER Macroecon Annu 15:261–325
Rodrik D (2004) Globalization and growth – looking in the wrong places. J Policy Model 26:513–517
Rodrik D (2018) What do trade agreements really do? J Econ Perspect 32:73–90
Rönnbäck K (2015) Interest-group lobbying for free trade: an empirical case study of international trade policy formation. J Int Trade Econ Dev 24:281–293
Samuelson PA (1962) The gains from international trade once again. Econ J 72:820–829
Scheibehenne B, Greifeneder R, Todd PM (2010) Can there ever be too many options? A meta-analytic review of choice overload. J Consum Res 37:409–425
Sexton RJ, Sheldon I, McCorriston S, Wang H (2007) Agricultural trade liberalization and economic development: the role of downstream market power. Agric Econ 36:253–270
Shy O (1988) A general equilibrium model of pareto inferior trade. J Int Econ 25:143–154
Singh T (2010) Does international trade cause economic growth? A survey. World Econ 33:1517–1564
Sotirov M, Stelter M, Winkel G (2017) The emergence of the European Union Timber Regulation: how Baptists, Bootleggers, devil shifting and moral legitimacy drive change in the environmental governance of global timber trade. Forest Policy Econ 81:69–81
Tosh J (1980) The cash-crop revolution in tropical Africa: an agricultural reappraisal. Afr Aff 79 (314):79–94

Vamvakidis A (2002) How robust is the growth–openness connection? Historical evidence. J Econ Growth 7:57–80

Viscusi WK, Vernon JM, Harrington JE (1998) Economics of regulation and antitrust, 4th edn. MIT Press, Cambridge

Wagner J (2012) International trade and firm performance: a survey of empirical studies since 2006. Rev World Econ 148:235–267

Chapter 3
The EU in the Mirror of NPE: Normative Power Europe in the EU's New Generation Trade and Investment Agreements

Jessica C. Lawrence

3.1 Introduction

Over the last 15 years, Ian Manners's concept of 'normative power Europe' (NPE) has become one of the most popular approaches to studying EU external policy.[1] As Sect. 3.2 of this chapter elaborates, those who support the NPE thesis—including actors at the highest levels of the EU's political infrastructure—tend to see the EU as a 'force for good' that seeks to influence global politics through the diffusion of cosmopolitan norms of good governance, human rights, and environmental protection without the use of 'hard' military or 'soft' civilian power. By contrast, critics of NPE tend to view it as a naïve re-characterization that at best oversimplifies the EU's complex institutional character and multiple foreign policy goals, and at worst simply fails to recognize or acknowledge the EU's realist pursuit of its interests.

Largely absent from this scholarship, however, is any analysis of the normative power or constructive influence of the NPE thesis itself.[2] What normative work does the NPE thesis perform? How does it portray the EU as a global actor? What subjectivity does it suggest for Europe, its institutions, and its inhabitants? And what does the rise of the NPE thesis tell us about the political rationality that guides EU external policymaking?

In order to explore these questions, this chapter examines the impact of the NPE thesis in the realm of EU trade and investment policy, an area in which the EU has prominently portrayed itself as a uniquely 'normative' actor on the global stage. International economic policy is a useful area for exploring questions about the EU's

[1]Manners (2002), p. 235.

[2]A rare example of engagement with this question can be found in: Rosamond (2014), p. 133.

J. C. Lawrence (✉)
School of Law, University of Essex, Colchester, United Kingdom
e-mail: j.lawrence@essex.ac.uk

C. I. Nagy (ed.), *World Trade and Local Public Interest*, Studies in European Economic Law and Regulation 19, https://doi.org/10.1007/978-3-030-41920-2_3

normative authority for several reasons. First, the EU has broad competences over economic policy, allowing institutional preferences to be seen more clearly. Second, the EU's position as a heavyweight in the global economy means that it has significant negotiating power in this area, and thus a great deal of leverage with which to pursue its policy goals. And third, international economic policy has lately become a contentious field in which the EU's complex and often apparently contradictory policy goals are clearly on display.

Specifically, Sect. 3.3 will examine the EU's use of so-called trade and sustainable development (TSD) chapters to incorporate social and environmental values in its bilateral trade and investment agreements. On the surface, this practice seems to broadly support the NPE thesis: the EU appears to be promoting a new norm of international economic policy that firmly incorporates non-economic values under the trade and investment umbrella. However, a closer look at the legal content of these TSD chapters raises questions regarding the value of the labor and environmental policies contained therein. Examining the primary legal mechanisms present in the EU's trade agreements (of which this chapter addresses four: commitments to international standards, 'effective enforcement' provisions, civil society consultations, and dispute settlement) reveals that in each case, the rhetoric differs significantly from the level of protection actually guaranteed by these instruments. If these provisions are of little practical value, however, then what precisely is their normative impact?

In order to address this apparent contradiction between the rhetoric and the reality of the EU's external economic policies, Sect. 3.4 returns to the constructivist question, analyzing this area of EU practice 'in the mirror' of NPE. It argues that the gap between the EU's 'market goals' and 'normative goals' can be bridged by refocusing on the political rationality underlying the EU's behavior. From this perspective, it becomes apparent that NPE is more than just an *ex post* descriptor of the EU's governmental behavior. It is (also) a discursive construct that serves to mediate the tension between the EU's market identity and its identity as a cosmopolitan polity.

In other words, this chapter argues, rather than reflecting external policy goals as the NPE thesis contends, the EU's inclusion of TSD chapters in its trade and investment agreements should be seen as serving an internal function: they allow the EU to believe simultaneously that it is a cosmopolitan, progressive power, *and* that it is a savvy, effective market builder, pursuing social and economic policy objectives in tandem.

3.2 Normative Power Europe

Ian Manners coined the term "normative power Europe" (NPE) in 2002 to describe what he saw as the EU's unique form of power in international affairs.[3] The EU's normative power stems from what Manners termed Europe's "normative

[3]Manners (2002), p. 235.

difference": its special character as a "hybrid polity" committed by reason of its history and constitution to the "core norms" of peace, liberty, democracy, the rule of law, and human rights, as well as the further "minor norms" of social solidarity, anti-discrimination, sustainable development, and good governance.[4] As a result of this normative difference, Manners argued that the EU is "different to pre-existing political forms, and that this particular difference pre-disposes it to act in a normative way."[5]

In the global realm, Manners argued that the EU's "international identity" involves a commitment to "shape conceptions of 'normal'" along the lines suggested by its normative predispositions. Accordingly, the EU exercises international power not only via the traditional, state-centric, material mechanisms of 'hard' military authority or 'civilian' economic influence, but also by means of its symbolic, normative, ideational preferences and influence on world opinion. In Manners's terms, this position can be traced to the EU's strong commitment to a neo-Aristotelian virtue ethics that pushes the EU to "lead by example" as well as a neo-Kantian drive toward "the establishment of law, including both rights and duties, in the pursuit of the common good" and a desire to be "reasonable in world politics."[6]

Manners described not only the source and content of the EU's normative authority, but also the means by which EU norms were spread to other states. Specifically, he argued that the EU's normative authority makes use of two alternate pathways. First, EU norms could be spread by means of "contagion": the "unintentional diffusion of ideas" that results from leading by example, dialogue and information sharing, and procedural relationships.[7] Second, EU norms could be spread via "transference": the exchange of "goods, trade, aid or technical assistance with third parties through largely substantive or financial means" that spread norms by means of conditionality, "the 'carrot and stickism' of financial rewards and economic sanctions," and the physical presence of the EU in international organizations and third states.[8] The combined operation of these processes, according to the NPE thesis, facilitated the global spread of the EU's values, via a novel mechanism of global governance.

[4]Manners (2002), pp. 241–243.

[5]Manners (2002), pp. 241–243.

[6]Manners (2008), pp. 57–58.

[7]Manners (2002), p. 245.

[8]Manners (2002), p. 245.

The NPE hypothesis intended to explain both the nature and the direction of EU power. That is to say, it was a theory both regarding the mechanism by which the EU exerts authority (the spread of norms via contagion and transference), and also the substance of that exercise (the substantive norms of reason, law, human rights, and the common good). Manner's original concept not only described the type of power exercised by the EU, but also cast the EU in a decidedly virtuous light, as a force for good in world affairs, non-coercively pursuing improvements in global welfare by spreading ideas and shaping the symbolic order.

NPE was criticized early on for its presumption of purity with respect to the EU's motives in international affairs. Scholars pointed out the ways in which the EU's normative and material interests often seemed to be conveniently aligned,[9] as well as how normative declarations have sometimes been used to cynically mask material motives.[10] Indeed, in light of these criticisms Manners' later (2008) work attempts to re-conceptualize NPE as a more "objective" theory, developing it into a framework for normative analysis that asks *what* norms the EU projects and *how* it does so without assuming *ex ante* the progressive character of the EU's actions.[11]

Despite such critiques, Manners's NPE thesis—in particular the original version that assumes the EU's 'normative difference' as a virtuous international actor—has been very influential. NPE has become a popular analytical framework in EU policy circles, with numerous articles reaffirming the EU's purported normative identity in international affairs. Scholars have adopted NPE as a framework for analyzing international affairs, have sought to refine or adapt NPE for use in particular legal and political contexts,[12] and have offered particular examples of the EU's normative authority.[13]

NPE has been influential outside of the academy, as well, making its way into the discourse of policy-makers at the highest levels of the EU establishment. Former President of the European Commission José Manuel Barroso, for example, commented directly on Manners's NPE article in a 2008 interview:

> [I]n terms of normative power, I broadly agree, we are one of the most important, if not the most important, normative power in the world. ... There is not another case, I'm sorry,

[9]See, e.g., Barbé and Johansson-Nogués (2008), pp. 81–96 (noting the alignment of the EU's normative and material interests in the context of the neighborhood policy).

[10]See, e.g., Goldsmith and Posner (2009) (arguing that EU is willing to abandon its commitment to international law when it suits its material interests).

[11]Manners (2008), pp. 245–252.

[12]To give just one example, a burgeoning scholarship has developed in the area of international environmental law regarding whether and to what extent the EU should be seen as a 'green normative power'. See, e.g., Baker (2007), p. 312; Harris (2005), p. 354; Lightfoot and Burchell (2005), p. 75; Vogler (2005), p. 841; Zito (2005), pp. 369–372. For a contradictory take, see Falkner (2007), p. 508.

[13]See, e.g., Björkdahl (2011), p. 103 (concluding that EU military interventions in the Congo were "guided by and in defence of some of the core values of the EU such as sustainable peace, peaceful conflict resolution and democracy"); Riddervold (2010), p. 581 (finding that the EU's human rights interests outweighed its economic interests in the negotiation of the Maritime Labour Convention).

> where the United States or China or Russia has been able to have so many other countries following their patterns. ... Look at climate change. We are the ones who are setting the benchmark. It doesn't mean that everybody is going to follow it but the reference point is now the targets that we have agreed. There was a recent analysis of accounting standards that showed the same. Why is that? It is because we have been successful in establishing norms, and applying them to different realities. In a way, we are a laboratory of globalisation. The most advanced ever. That is why I think that Europe is now much more influential than before.[14]

The popularity of the NPE hypothesis among academics and policy-makers has also made it a prime target for critique. In addition to those who dispute the purity of the EU's substantive motives, others have questioned whether the normative mechanism can really be separated from civilian/economic or military power; whether the EU as an actor can really be said to 'promote' anything at all, given its polycentricity; and whether the values the EU promotes can truly be said to be 'universal'.

As noted in the introduction, however, one area that has remained relatively unexplored is the conceptual impact of the NPE thesis itself. It is to this subject that the chapter will now turn.

3.3 Normative Power in EU Trade and Investment Policy

Trade is one of the areas in which the EU has its most extensive legal authority in foreign affairs. Managing the Common Commercial Policy, including external trade policy, is among the EU's core functions—indeed, it was the EU's very first exclusive competence.[15] Over the years, the EU's authority over international economic policy has only increased, with the EU most recently gaining competence to conclude investment agreements with the entry into force of the Lisbon Treaty on 1 December 2009.

Along the way, the EU has developed its own characteristic approach to trade and investment policy, explicitly linking its pursuit of economic growth to other values such as environmental protection, human rights, labor rights, and peace.[16] One of the primary features of the EU's trade and investment strategy has been the inclusion of TSD chapters in its agreements. TSD chapters cover environmental protection, labor, and human rights issues. Chapter 22 of the EU-Canada Comprehensive Economic and Trade Agreement (CETA), for example, covers general TSD matters; Chapter 23 addresses trade and labor; and Chapter 24 deals with trade and environment in the EU-Canada context.[17]

---

[14]Peterson (2008), p. 69.

[15]Opinion 1/75 (Draft Understanding on a Local Cost Standard) [1975] ECR 1355.

[16]European Commission (2015) Trade for All: Towards a More Responsible Trade and Investment Policy.

[17]Comprehensive Economic and Trade Agreement between Canada on the one part and the European Union and its Member States [hereinafter CETA].

Due to the inclusion of these chapters, EU representatives have argued that the new generation of EU agreements are the "most progressive ever." Commission President Jean-Claude Juncker's statement on CETA is illustrative:

> The trade agreement between the EU and Canada is our best and most progressive trade agreement and I want it to enter into force as soon as possible. It provides new opportunities for European companies, while promoting our high standards for the benefit of our citizens.[18]

EU Trade Commissioner Cecilia Malmström expressed a similar sentiment in the context of CETA:

> The agreement reached with Canada is a milestone in European trade policy. It is the most ambitious trade agreement that the EU has ever concluded and will deepen our longstanding relations with Canada. It will help to generate much-needed growth and jobs while fully upholding Europe's high standards in areas like food safety, environmental protection and people's rights at work. This is what our trade policy is all about.[19]

As comments like these indicate, the EU sees its characteristic brand of trade and investment policy as inherently progressive and uniquely sensitive to the need to balance economic and non-economic goals. The Commission's vision of EU trade policy outlined in its 2015 "Trade for All" Strategy confirms this self-characterization, citing "A Trade and Investment Policy Based on Values" as one of the five key principles guiding the EU's trade and investment negotiations.[20]

Many commentators have praised the EU's actions, seeing it as a 'force for good' in promoting a more socially responsible global economic order. Joris Larik, for example, argues that promoting "good global governance" through the use of trade policy reflects the EU's "sanguine world view," and its internal constitutional "conscience."[21] This reflects well the NPE thesis and its assertion that the EU is changing norms on the global scene through contagion and transference, promoting and incentivizing the inclusion of non-trade values not only in its own, but also in third states' trade and investment policies.

But what norms, exactly, is the EU transferring? Is it truly using its normative power to increase environmental, labor, and human rights protection levels for its trading partners? In order to answer this question, it is necessary to investigate the content of these TSD chapters somewhat more rigorously. This Section will do so by examining the four pillars of social and environmental protection in EU TSD chapters: (1) commitments to uphold international standards, (2) 'effective enforcement' provisions, (3) civil society consultations, and (4) dispute resolution procedures.

---

[18]European Commission, Press Release (2016) European Commission Proposes Signature and Conclusion of EU-Canada Trade Deal. IP/16/2371, 5 July 2016. http://europa.eu/rapid/press-release_IP-16-2371_en.htm [hereinafter CETA Press Release].

[19]CETA Press Release.

[20]European Commission (2015) Trade for All: Towards a More Responsible Trade and Investment Policy.

[21]Larik (2015), p. 44.

3.3.1 Commitments to International Standards

EU FTAs are often praised for their inclusion of language committing the FTA's parties to upholding internationally-recognized labor and environmental standards. For example, Article 13.4 of the EU-South Korea FTA affirms that the Parties "recognize the value of international cooperation and agreements on employment and labour affairs as a response of the international community to economic, employment and social challenges and opportunities resulting from globalisation," and "reaffirm the commitment[s]" that they have made under the 2006 Ministerial Declaration of the UN Economic and Social Council on Full Employment and Decent Work, as well the obligations they have undertaken under the ILO framework, specifically its Declaration on Fundamental Principles and Rights at Work and the ILO's fundamental Conventions.[22] Similarly, Article 13.5 affirms that the Parties "recognize the value of international environmental governance and agreements as a response of the international community to global or regional environmental problems" and "reaffirm the commitments" that they have made under "the multilateral environmental agreements to which they are party" as well as the "ultimate objective of the United Nations Framework Convention on Climate Change and its Kyoto Protocol."[23]

Though they provide important interpretative context to the EU's FTAs, and may be helpful in establishing dialogue and pathways for further development, these provisions are substantively weak.[24] The Parties do not agree to any new commitments beyond those that they have already undertaken and which would be in operation whether or not the FTA were concluded. These statements of purpose, intent, and affirmation are framed in the language of 'best efforts' rather than as binding legal obligations. Neither Party is obligated to accede to any additional agreement, or to increase its standards of protection.

The EU's practice in this respect should be contrasted with its approach under the GSP+ program, in which market access benefits to recipient states are made conditional on the ratification and effective implementation of 27 international

---

[22]Free Trade Agreement between the European Union and its Member States, of the one part, and the Republic of Korea OJ L 127 [hereinafter EU-South Korea FTA] at art. 13.4. See also Trade Agreement between the European Union and its member States, of the one part, and Colombia and Peru, of the other part OJ L354 (to which Ecuador subsequently acceded) [hereinafter EU-Colombia-Peru-Ecuador FTA] at art. 269; Economic Partnership between the CARIFORUM States, of the one part, and the European Community and its Member States, of the other part OJ L289/I/3 [hereinafter EU-CARIFORUM EPA] at art. 191; Free Trade Agreement between the European Union and the Republic of Singapore [hereinafter EU-Singapore FTA] at art. 13.3.

[23]EU-South Korea Art. 13.5. See also EU-Colombia-Peru-Ecuador Art. 270; EU-CARIFORM Art. 183; EU-Singapore FTA art. 13.6.

[24]Postnikov & Bastiaens find some evidence for an ex post effect of EU FTAs on labor standards due to the gradual effects of "the activity and learning of civil society actors involved in the implementation process." Postnikov and Bastiaens (2014), p. 924. However, other studies have found no positive effect, or even negative effects on labor rights enforcement. See Orbie and Van den Putte (2016); Marx (2016), p. 603.

agreements on labor standards, the environment, good governance, sustainable development, and human rights.[25] In that context, unlike with respect to its FTAs, the EU is both willing and able to make economic policy contingent on non-economic performance.

Moreover, the EU's FTA practice may be usefully compared with the US's policy of imposing pre-ratification requirements on its trading partners. The US, unlike the EU, often seeks the reform of labor and other laws prior to the signing of FTAs. Though, as Jeffrey Vogt describes, the US's success in pursuing such reforms varies by context, it is nevertheless the case that the EU has lagged behind in terms of exercising this potential pathway for leverage.[26]

Moreover, EU FTA commitments to uphold international standards are qualified by the inclusion of 'right to regulate' provisions that reaffirm the right of each Party "to establish its own levels of environmental and labour protection, and to adopt or modify accordingly its relevant laws and policies," even as they make their best efforts to "seek to ensure that those laws and policies provide for and encourage high levels of environmental and labour protection."[27] Such provisions, which seek to address developing country concerns regarding the imposition of 'external' rules without their domestic consent, push back against the normative pull of the affirmation of international standards.

3.3.2 'Effective Enforcement' Provisions

Second, the EU's TSD chapters typically include commitments to 'effectively enforce' current environmental and labor standards. The intent of such rules is to prevent a so-called 'race to the bottom', as countries compete with one another to attract investment by lowering their regulatory standards and thereby making it cheaper for investors to operate within their borders. Article 13.7 of the EU-South Korea FTA is a typical example:

1. A Party shall not fail to effectively enforce its environmental and labour laws, through a sustained or recurring course of action or inaction, in a manner affecting trade or investment between the parties.
2. A Party shall not weaken or reduce the environmental or labour protections afforded in its laws to encourage trade or investment, by waiving or otherwise derogating from, or offering to waive or derogate from, its laws, regulations or standards, in a manner affecting trade or investment between the parties.[28]

[25] Council Regulation 732/2008/EC applying a scheme of generalized tariff preferences for the period from 1 January 2009 to 31 December 2011 [2008] OJ L211/1.

[26] See Vogt (2015), p. 827.

[27] EU-South Korea FTA Art. 13.3. See also EU-Colombia-Peru-Ecuador Art. 268; EU-CARIFORUM Art. 184 & 192; EU-Singapore Art. 13.2.

[28] EU-South Korea FTA, art. 13.7.

Similar commitments can be found in other recent EU FTAs.[29] These provisions are particularly significant, as they are one of the very few legally binding (non-hortatory) obligations with respect to environmental or labor protection that are included in TSD chapters. Indeed, these 'effective enforcement' obligations are the premier 'good governance' provision included in contemporary FTAs.

These commitments to effective enforcement are, however, also quite weak. To begin with, they do not require the parties to set any particular level of environmental or labor protection. Instead, they merely state that the parties must enforce their current rules, whatever these may be. As there is no requirement to set a high level of protection or increase the levels currently in effect, these provisions thus require only that parties do not roll back their chosen level of protection after signing the FTA.

In addition to their failure to require high or improved levels of protection, 'effective enforcement' provisions are typically further qualified in three ways.[30] Again taking the EU-South Korea FTA as an illustrative example, Article 13.7 (1) requires that in order for a violation to be found, a Party must fail to uphold its environmental or labor provisions "through a *sustained or recurring* course of action," meaning that single, un-sustained, or scattered deviations, exceptions, or derogations are not prohibited. In addition, Article 13.7(2) requires that Parties not "weaken or reduce" their environmental or labor standards *for the purpose of* encouraging trade or investment. This excludes any weakening or reduction done for any other purpose, and introduces a significant evidentiary hurdle in the form of proving the party's intent. Finally, in both cases, the party must have failed to uphold or have weakened or reduced its own laws "in a manner *affecting trade or investment* between the parties." This excludes any roll-backs or enforcement failures that cannot be shown to affirmatively impact trade flows.

The arbitration concluded in 2017 between the US and Guatemala regarding the effective enforcement provision in the Dominican Republic-Central American Free Trade Agreement (CAFTA-DR) is illustrative of the significant difficulties that will hinder any attempt to enforce such provisions. Like Article 13.7(1) of the EU-South Korea FTA, CAFTA-DR's Article 16.2.1(a) prohibits each party from failing to "effectively enforce its labor laws, through a sustained or recurring course of action or inaction, in a manner affecting trade between the Parties." Following complaints by US and Guatemalan labor unions, the United States became concerned that Guatemala was failing to protect the rights of its workers and was thereby putting American workers at risk through unfair competitive practices. The US alleged that Guatemalan workers were subject to poor working conditions and had been prevented from forming unions or participating in collective bargaining processes.

---

[29]See, e.g., EU-Colombia-Peru-Ecuador art. 277; EU-CARIFORUM EPA art. 188; CETA arts. 23.4, 24.5; EU-Singapore FTA art. 13.12.

[30]The EU-CARIFORUM FTA, by contrast, is only singly qualified, prohibiting Parties from lowering or failing to enforce their standards in order "to encourage trade or foreign direct investment to enhance or maintain a competitive advantage." EU-CARIFORUM art. 188(1), 193. This omits the "continuing or recurring course of action" language present in the EU-South Korea and other FTAs.

When workers complained about these practices, the US argued, Guatemala did not investigate the claims, did not impose the penalties specified under the Guatemalan Labor Code, and did not comply with court orders requiring employers to reinstate and compensate workers wrongfully dismissed for union activities.

In this landmark decision, the Panel found that there had been no violation of Article 16.2.1. Though the Panel determined that Guatemala had indeed failed to enforce its labor laws,[31] and that this failure may have constituted a sustained or recurring course of action or inaction,[32] the failure to enforce labor laws was not done "in a manner affecting trade."[33] Essentially, this was due to the fact that while Gautemala's choice not to enforce its labor standards conferred a competitive advantage on one particular company, it did not necessarily confer a competitive advantage in a sufficient number of the cases cited, and could thus not be found to 'affect trade' on the whole.[34]

As Billy Melo Araujo argues, the Panel Report did provide some hopeful signs with respect to the interpretation of "in a manner affecting trade," as it took a broad approach in finding that the conferral of a competitive advantage (rather than a definite alteration in prices or trade flows) could be sufficient to constitute an effect on trade.[35] However, it must not be overlooked that the Panel also found that this competitive advantage must be present for the entire or a significant portion of the sustained or recurring course of action or inaction of the responding Party. The fact that some part of the action or inaction affected trade was deemed insufficient to constitute a breach of the agreement.[36] As a result, it remains clear that any action or inaction taken in contravention of an 'effective enforcement' clause must meet an extremely high threshold to be deemed a breach of the FTA.

Furthermore, as will be discussed below, even in the event that this high bar could be surmounted, there are no effective sanctions present in the EU FTAs that could be used to punish or remedy such a breach.

3.3.3 Civil Society Consultations

A third set of provisions that are often cited as evidence of the EU's 'progressive' approach to trade and investment are those that establish advisory bodies on social and environmental issues. Civil society meetings are a standard element in EU TSD chapters, which typically establish 'civil society forums' that are empowered to

---

[31] Final Report of the Panel in the Matter of Guatemala – Issues Relating to the Obligations under Article 16.2.1(a) of the CAFTA-DR, 14 June 2017 [hereinafter US—Guatemala Labor Panel Report], para. 428.

[32] US—Guatemala Labor Panel Report para. 444.

[33] US—Guatemala Labor Panel Report para. 505.

[34] US—Guatemala Labor Panel Report para. 497.

[35] Araujo (2018), p. 239.

[36] US—Guatemala Labor Panel Report para. 505.

discuss relevant issues and send reports to the European Commission for further action.[37] The EU-South Korea FTA, for example, requires that each Party establish a Domestic Advisory Group (DAG) on sustainable development.[38] The DAGs are composed of "independent representative organisations of civil society" from environmental, labor, and business organizations[39] who meet once a year at a Civil Society Forum.[40] These DAGs are charged with advising the Parties on the implementation of the sustainable development chapters of EU FTAs, and can issue communications to the Parties on relevant subjects.

These forums have been heavily criticized, however.[41] To begin with, despite being empowered to advise the Parties regarding labor, environmental, and other sustainable development issues, DAGs have no authority to initiate any further investigation or process. If a Party is inclined to act on some aspect of a DAG communication, it "may request consultations" with the other Party on the issue.[42] However, this is purely discretionary—the Party can also simply choose not to act on the DAG communication.

As an illustrative example, in 2014 the DAG constituted under the EU-South Korea FTA sent a letter to then-Trade Commissioner Karl De Gucht stating that it believed that South Korea was "in serious violation of its commitments" to uphold labor standards under the FTA and requesting that the Commission initiate consultations on this ground.[43] After the Commissioner rejected this request, the frustrated DAGs set out their continuing concerns regarding South Korea's ongoing failures to ratify and implement ILO fundamental Conventions in the Conclusions of the 2017 Civil Society Forum.[44] In December 2018 the EU formally requested consultations with the Korean government. An Expert Panel was formed in December 2019, and is expected to deliver a report in March 2020. It remains to be seen what consequences will ensue.

As Jan Orbie et al argue, the inclusion of these civil society mechanisms in EU TSD chapters may "contribute to legitimising the underlying free trade orientation of the agreement," lending the FTAs an imprimatur of social legitimacy without a significant effect on the content or conduct of trade and investment.[45] As a result,

---

[37]EU-South Korea FTA art. 13.12; EU-Colombia-Peru-Ecuador FTA art. 282; EU-Singapore FTA art. 13.15; CETA Art. 23.8.

[38]EU-South Korea FTA art. 13.12(4).

[39]EU-South Korea FTA art. 13.12(5).

[40]EU-South Korea FTA art. 13.13(1).

[41]For an overview of the potential purposes and functions of these groups, see Orbie et al. (2018), p. 135. A good overview of the criticisms of such mechanisms can be found in Orbie et al. (2016), p. 526.

[42]EU-South Korea FTA art. 13.14(1).

[43]Letter from the Domestic Advisory Group to Mr. Karl De Gucht, 13 January 2014. https://webapi.eesc.europa.eu/documentsanonymous/EESC-2014-01767-00-00-TDC-TRA-EN.doc. Accessed 25 March 2018.

[44]Conclusions of the Civil Society Forum under the EU-Korea Free Trade Agreement (20–21 February 2017). https://www.eesc.europa.eu/sites/default/files/resources/docs/eu-korea-csf-final-conclusions.pdf. Accessed 25 March 2018.

[45]Orbie et al. (2016), p. 527.

here, too, the EU's rhetorical commitment to promoting non-trade values in its trade agreements seems to be undermined by its practice in this area.

3.3.4 Dispute Settlement

Finally, even the most advanced environmental and labor provisions in the EU's trade and investment agreements are not subject to the standard dispute settlement mechanisms available for breaches of other chapters. Instead, they are subject to 'consultation' procedures and non-binding Expert Panel processes with no associated penalties for non-adherence to recommendations.

Typically, in the event of a dispute a Party may have recourse to arbitration. If a violation of the agreement is found, then a penalty in the form of a suspension of market access concessions may be imposed. By contrast, disputes regarding the environmental and labor chapters of EU agreements are subject to an alternative form of dispute resolution involving consultations and dialogue. The EU-South Korea FTA is, once more, a typical example. Under that agreement, the Parties are first entitled to enter into 'consultations' with one another by written request.[46] If the Parties fail to come to a mutually satisfactory resolution, they may request that the matter be considered by a Panel of Experts (as seen above).[47] The Panel, once convened, is entitled to seek information and to issue a report to the Parties.[48] The Parties are then obliged to "make their best efforts to accommodate advice or recommendations of the Panel of Experts," and the implementation is to be "monitored by the Committee on Trade and Sustainable Development" established by the agreement.[49]

No further judicial or quasi-judicial processes are made available for TSD matters, nor are there any further penalties associated with violation. Recourse to the 'normal' dispute settlement provisions and their associated sanctions are explicitly excluded.[50] Thus, the ultimate potential penalty for violation of the labor or environmental provisions is the issuance of a non-binding report, which Parties should make their "best efforts" to "accommodate."

The single exception to this rule is the EU-CARIFORUM Economic Partnership Agreement (EPA), which does make its sustainable development chapter subject to its dispute settlement mechanism.[51] Even in this singular case, however, there are no significant penalties available in the event of a violation: unlike with any other operative provision of the agreement, a finding that a party has breached the

[46]EU-South Korea FTA art. 13.14(1).

[47]EU-South Korea FTA art. 13.14(3).

[48]EU-South Korea FTA art. 13.15.

[49]EU-South Korea FTA art. 13.15(2).

[50]EU-South Korea FTA art. 13.16.

[51]EU-CARIFORUM EPA Art. 23(2).

sustainable development chapter cannot result in any suspension of market concessions.

The lack of effective dispute settlement mechanisms in EU TSD chapters can be usefully compared with those inserted by the United States in its FTAs.[52] US agreements such as the North American Agreement on Labor Cooperation (NAALC) (a NAFTA side agreement), CAFTA-DR, and the new USMCA create mechanisms for arbitration regarding disputes over labor obligations (as in the US—Guatemala dispute discussed above), and permit the suspension of benefits as a penalty in case of violation. The EU, by contrast, adopts what Ebert and Posthuma have termed a "promotional" approach, eschewing sanctions and instead emphasizing the use of 'soft' dialogue and consultations rather than 'hard' dispute settlement.[53]

This existence of binding dispute settlement provisions in US agreements demonstrates that the inclusion of such provisions is not merely a theoretical option for the EU. Indeed, the European Parliament has itself questioned the failure to include hard enforcement mechanisms in EU agreements, arguing that:

> [T]he chapter on sustainable development ... could be strengthened by providing for ... recourse to a dispute settlement mechanism on an equal footing with the other parts of the agreement, with provision for fines to improve the situation in the sectors concerned, or at least a temporary suspension of certain trade benefits provided for under the agreement, in the event of an aggravated breach of these standards.[54]

Some have pointed to the resistance of negotiating partners—in particular developing country partners—as an explanation for the lack of hard dispute settlement mechanisms. For example, Orbie and Khorana describe the active resistance of India to the inclusion of labor and other social provisions in the ongoing EU—India FTA negotiations, tracing this opposition to concerns regarding sovereignty, protectionism, and pride.[55] As they argue, this resistance "suggests that the EU may not always be able to promote and transfer both market liberal and cosmopolitan liberal norms through trade negotiations with India and other countries."[56] However, this response is insufficient for at least three reasons.

First, as noted, it cannot be the case that the EU is 'unable' to include such provisions in its agreements given the US's ability to do so. As one of the world's most significant traders, the EU, like the US, certainly has the negotiating power to make binding dispute settlement a part of its policy if there were sufficient political will to do so.

Second, as Billy Melo Araujo points out, the argument that the EU's failure to include binding dispute settlement provisions in its FTAs is evidence of its

[52]See Fritz (2005).

[53]Ebert and Posthuma (2011).

[54]European Parliament, 'Resolution of 25 November 2010 on Human Rights and Social and Environmental Standards in International Trade Agreements, (2009) 2009/2219(INI), 22(c).

[55]Orbie and Khorana (2015), p. 253.

[56]Orbie and Khorana (2015), p. 253.

"reluctance to engage in imperialistic practices by simply imposing its values on others through economic coercion" fails to explain "the omission of hard enforcement mechanisms in EU FTAs negotiated with trade partners that are not opposed to the enforcement of labour and environmental protection in trade agreements."[57] The EU's refusal to include such provisions in the Canada-EU Comprehensive Trade Agreement (CETA) is a case in point.[58]

Third, the failure to include sanctions in these agreements can be contrasted with the suspension clauses present in the EU's GSP+ requirements. As noted above, GSP+ makes market access benefits to recipient states conditional on the ratification and effective implementation of 27 international agreements on labor standards, the environment, good governance, sustainable development, and human rights.[59] Countries that participate in the EU's GSP+ program—unlike those that are subject to its FTA rules—are held accountable for their implementation of these conventions, as the regulation includes a suspension clause allowing the withdrawal of benefits from countries that fail to incorporate or effectively implement them.[60] The EU is thus clearly willing to require that less developed countries sacrifice their regulatory autonomy in exchange for market access in some cases, and imposes real sanctions on those that fail to comply. Why should FTAs be any different?

While the above described TSD chapters do bring the rhetoric of non-economic values into trade and investment agreements, they remain almost entirely toothless, filled with very little other than affirmations of principle and intent. Indeed, this is particularly striking when EU agreements are compared with US FTAs and the EU's own GSP+ rules. To quote Billy Melo Araujo once more, the EU's practice rather "suggests that the EU is itself against the enforceability of the sustainable development chapters."[61] In light of all this, what is the status of NPE in EU trade and investment policy?

3.4 NPE in the Mirror

The weakness of the EU's approach to including non-trade values in its agreements is puzzling from the perspective of NPE. Despite the EU's constitutional mandate for and frequent assertion of its commitment to the 'progressive' approach of incorporating non-economic policies into its trade and investment agreements, the normative vision of trade that results is one that differs little from the standard (neo)liberal

[57] Araujo (2018), p. 242.

[58] Araujo (2018), p. 242.

[59] Council Regulation 732/2008/EC applying a scheme of generalized tariff preferences for the period from 1 January 2009 to 31 December 2011 [2008] OJ L211/1.

[60] Council Regulation 732/2008/EC applying a scheme of generalized tariff preferences for the period from 1 January 2009 to 31 December 2011 [2008] OJ L211/1. at 10(2).

[61] Araujo (2018), p. 242.

model. Indeed, the TSD provisions included in the EU's new generation trade and investment agreements are, perhaps surprisingly, weaker than those of other major trading hubs such as the US.

These apparent contradictions raise many questions from the perspective of the NPE analysis. If the EU is a normative actor committed to spreading progressive values abroad, as the NPE thesis suggests, then why do its trade and investment agreements fail to include more significant protections for non-economic values? Does this mean that the EU does not actually hold these values, or that they are simply subordinate to the EU's (material) economic interests? Does it mean that the EU's external actions should be conceived as based on 'interests', specifically on the externalization of its internal market interests, as Chad Damro's 'Market Power Europe' thesis suggests?[62]

This Section suggests a different response, arguing, with Ben Rosamond, that rather than viewing the EU's practice through the lens of 'interests' versus 'norms', it is useful to approach this problem from a constructivist perspective.[63] In order to do so, it will return to the inquiry posed in the introduction: What normative work does the NPE thesis itself perform? Recontextualized in light of the particular case study analyzed in Sect. 3.3, the question might become: What does promoting the EU's trade and investment agreements as 'progressive' examples of normative leadership—despite the weakness of their content—tell us about European 'normative power'?

This exploration requires a shift in focus—directing our attention inward, toward the EU's self-construction as a 'progressive' power. As such, this chapter essentially argues that the EU's otherwise confusing practice with respect to the legal development of its new generation trade and investment agreements becomes coherent when viewed in the mirror of the EU's identity as a political order.

The EU describes itself as having (at least) two sets of preferences in the external economic realm. First, its market preferences—the desire to contribute to EU economic growth via the conclusion of FTAs. Second, its social preferences—the desire to uphold and promote high levels of environmental, labor, and human rights protection both at home and abroad. This is evident from the discourse surrounding the EU's new generation agreements. EU Trade Commissioner Cecilia Malmström's introduction to the *Trade for All* Strategy is illustrative:

> It is clear that Europeans want trade to deliver real economic results for consumers, workers and small companies. However, they also believe open markets do not require us to compromise on core principles, like human rights and sustainable development around the world or high quality safety and environmental regulation and public services at home. They also want to know more about trade negotiations carried out in their name.
>
> In this new strategy, "Trade for All," the Commission is adapting its approach to trade policy to take these lessons on board. As a result, trade policy will become more responsible,

[62]Damro (2012), p. 682.

[63]Rosamond (2014), p. 134.

> meaning it will be more effective, more transparent and will not only project our interests, but also our values.[64]

However, as can also be seen from this passage, these two sets of preferences do not simply reflect the battle of EU 'interests' versus 'norms'. In Malmström's view, Europeans do not want economic growth (interests), and, separately and in contention, social protection (norms). They want economic growth that promotes social protection (markets that do not require compromise on core principles) and social protection that promotes markets (responsible trade policy that is also more effective). This 'have your cake and eat it too' rhetoric redefines the content of its terms such that no tradeoffs are necessary—in this discourse, markets and social protection work in tandem and reinforce one another.

The idea that these 'market' and 'social' preferences can and do work together seamlessly is far from self-evident. Many critics of the EU's trade and investment policy have pointed out the ways in which the promotion of economic growth seems to come at the expense of, rather than as complementary to, non-economic policy goals. As Lucy Ford writes, "there is tension and contradiction between the creation of an economic project that is globally focused on expansion and competition and a political project that pays attention to concerns such as social justice and sustainability."[65]

The tension between these trade policy goals reflects the deeper historical tensions between so-called 'market EU' and the EU as a cosmopolitan political actor. Market integration norms were always a key—perhaps *the* key—component of EU constitutional authority (despite their absence from Manners's list of EU normative values), and these norms have sat uneasily alongside the EU's other liberal political aspirations. Both ideals—the cosmopolitan normative power EU and the market power EU—are visible in these new generation trade agreements.

It is the contention of this chapter that one of the interesting effects of the EU's efforts to include non-economic values in its trade agreements is that they help to mediate this contradiction between the different "constitutive logics of the EU."[66] Perhaps one of the reasons that the TSD chapters in the EU's new generation agreements are so disappointing from a 'hard law' perspective is that they are not really aimed at guaranteeing high levels of social or environmental protection at all, but rather at allowing the EU to believe in two stories about itself simultaneously: that it is a cosmopolitan, progressive power, *and* that it is a savvy, effective market builder.

The NPE thesis, in this sense, does a particular type of normative work for the EU: it allows it to resolve the tension between the demands of a political rationality based on market integration, and one based on the EU as a 'force for good'. The belief that the EU is a normative actor in world affairs thus supersedes the actual

[64]European Commission (2015) Trade for All: Towards a More Responsible Trade and Investment Policy 5.

[65]See, e.g., Ford (2013), p. 579.

[66]Rosamond (2014), p. 140. See also Parker (2012) and Lawrence (2018).

content of that action. In short, TSD chapters serve many purposes: perhaps most importantly, they facilitate a continued belief in the EU's normative authority on the part of participants, observers, scholars, and, ideally, the public.

3.5 Conclusion

The EU's new generation trade and investment agreements have been widely praised for their inclusion of environmental and social provisions in the form of TSD chapters. Indeed, the pursuit of non-economic policy goals within EU economic agreements has been held out as part of the EU's 'characteristic approach' to trade policy that combines 'doing well' with 'doing good'. As a result, the EU's trade policy has been proffered as a classic example of NPE, in which the EU diffuses normative commitments to labor and environmental protection through cooperation, dialogue, and economic 'carrots'.

A close examination of the content of the legal provisions included in the EU's recent FTAs, however, reveals a surprisingly toothless approach to non-economic policy diffusion. The EU's promotion of international standards, 'effective enforcement' provisions, civil society consultations, and lack of binding dispute settlement provisions or sanctions for the violation of TSD provisions seem to contradict its stated commitments to furthering environmental and social goals within its trade and investment policy. The weakness of these provisions is especially glaring in light of the stronger provisions present in the EU's GSP+ program, and similar trade agreements signed by rival trade powers like the United States.

The argument of this chapter has been that the seeming contradiction between the rhetoric of 'Normative Power Europe' and the reality of EU trade policy can be resolved by exploring NPE as a normative concept. Rather than looking outward toward structural constraints or strategic projects, we ought to look inward toward the EU's own forms of political rationality that in turn serve to construct its policy preferences in the international sphere. Viewing the EU 'in the mirror' of NPE reveals that the construction of the EU as a normative actor does something more than simply explaining the EU's policy preferences. Rather, it is (also) a way of mediating the tension between the EU's market identity and its identity as a progressive cosmopolitan polity.

References

Araujo BM (2018) Labour provisions in EU and US mega-regional trade agreements: rhetoric and reality. Int Comp Law Q 67

Baker S (2007) Sustainable development as symbolic commitment: declaratory politics and the seductive appeal of ecological modernisation in the European Union. Environ Polit 16(2)

Barbé E, Johansson-Nogués E (2008) The EU as a modest 'force for good': the European neighbourhood policy. Int Aff 84(1)

Björkdahl A (2011) Normative and military power in EU peace support operations. In: Whitman RG (ed) Normative power Europe: empirical and theoretical perspectives
Damro C (2012) Market power Europe. J Eur Publ Policy 19(5)
Ebert F, Posthuma A (2011) Labour provisions in trade agreements: current trades and perspectives. ILO International Institute for Labour Studies Working Paper
Falkner R (2007) The political economy of 'normative power' Europe: EU environmental leadership in international biotechnology regulation. J Eur Publ Policy 14(4)
Ford L (2013) EU trade governance and policy: a critical perspective. J Contemp Eur Res 9(4)
Fritz T (2005) Analysis and evaluation of the Comprehensive Economic and Trade Agreement (CETA) between the EU and Canada. Hans-Böckler-Foundation, Berlin
Goldsmith J, Posner E (2009) Does Europe believe in international law? The Wall Street Journal 25 Nov. 2009
Harris P (2005) The European Union and environmental change: sharing the burdens of global warming. Colo J Int Environ Law Policy 17
Larik J (2015) Good global governance through trade: constitutional moorings. In: Wouters J et al (eds) Global governance through trade: EU policies and approaches
Lawrence JC (2018) Governmentality in EU trade and environment policy: between rights and market
Lightfoot S, Burchell J (2005) The European Union and the world summit on sustainable development: normative power Europe in action? J Common Mark Stud 43(1)
Manners I (2002) Normative power Europe: a contradiction in terms? J Common Mark Stud 40(2)
Manners I (2008) Normative ethics of the European Union. Int Aff 84(1)
Marx LB (2016) The protection of labour rights in trade agreements: the case of the EU—Colombia Agreement. J World Trade 50(4)
Orbie J, Khorana S (2015) Normative versus market power Europe? The EU—India Trade Agreement. Asia Europe J 13(3)
Orbie J, Van den Putte L (2016) Labour rights in Peru and the EU trade agreement: compliance with commitments under the sustainable development chapter
Orbie J et al (2016) Promoting sustainable development or legitimising free trade? Civil society mechanisms in EU trade agreements. Third World Thematics 1(4)
Orbie J, Van den Putte L, Martens D (2018) Civil society meetings in EU free trade agreements: the purposes unraveled. In: Gött H (ed) Labour standards in international economic law
Parker O (2012) Cosmopolitan government in Europe
Peterson J (2008) José Manuel Barroso: Political Scientist, ECPR Member. Eur Polit Sci 7
Postnikov E, Bastiaens I (2014) Does dialogue work? The effectiveness of labor standards in EU preferential trade agreements. J Eur Publ Policy 21(6)
Riddervold M (2010) A matter of principle? EU foreign policy and the international labor organization. J Eur Publ Policy 17(4)
Rosamond B (2014) Three ways of speaking Europe to the world: markets, peace, cosmopolitan duty and the EU's normative power. Br J Polit Int Rel 16(1)
Vogler J (2005) The European contribution to global environmental governance. Int Aff 81(4)
Vogt JS (2015) The evolution of labor rights and trade: a transatlantic comparison and lessons for the transatlantic trade and investment partnership. J Int Econ Law 18
Zito AR (2005) The European Union as an environmental leader in a global environment. Globalizations 2(3)

Chapter 4
Acquis Communautaire+ The Copyright Aspects of the EU's Free Trade Agreements

Péter Mezei

> [T]he move towards bilateralism must have implication for the multilateral system as the bilateral agreements come to contain stipulations that reflect the domestic standards of the hyperpower.[1]

4.1 Development of Free Trade Agreements in Europe

National economies have historically tried to guarantee a safe and predictable internal trade order. Border impediments (customs, duties, tariffs, special taxes, quantitative restrictions, quotas etc.) and other border measures that aimed to protect the national markets against foreign goods, services, workers, investments etc. have also had an important role in maintaining the favourable balance of trade and the promotion of the domestic manufacturing. The idea of free trade has already appeared in the eighteenth century Europe.[2] Finally, in the twentieth century, regional economical collaborations as well as globalisation made closed national economies and the imperial rivalries unfeasible. The goal of the regional trading blocs was not the defence of national interest anymore. States have understood how significant and yet untapped potentials exist in the harmonization of the national trade politics, and thus in the access to large unified markets. The creation of multilateral common rules has therefore become a leading motive of regional

[1]Rickeston and Ginsburg (2006) para 4.55.

[2]On the evolution of international trade theory and the institutional history of international trade see Trebilcock and Howse (1999), pp. 1–24.

P. Mezei (✉)
University of Szeged, Faculty of Law, Institute of Comparative Law and Legal Theory, Szeged, Hungary
e-mail: mezei@juris.u-szeged.hu

C. I. Nagy (ed.), *World Trade and Local Public Interest*, Studies in European Economic Law and Regulation 19, https://doi.org/10.1007/978-3-030-41920-2_4

economic collaborations. On the one hand, these rules made members of the club equal, and—to refer to the European Economic Community's terminology—also allowed for the free movement of goods, services, workers and capital within the community. On the other hand, these rules allowed for the unified actions against those who are not members of the collaborative clubs. Regional trading blocs, like the European Economic Community (EEC), NAFTA, Mercosur, CARICOM, APEC or COMESA, have come into existence mainly for these reasons.

It is self-evident that not everybody can be a part of a given economic collaboration, even if all nations would be happy to be bound by the common rules. The geographic location of a country is such a significant limitation. In theory, a tariff union would be possible between the European Union (EU) and Australia, but it would be hard to guarantee its proper functioning. Nonetheless, geographical locations cannot fully limit the countries in finding the proper ways of collaboration. Consequently, the EU and Australia intends to conclude a free trade agreement that would eliminate tariffs and other technical and administrative limitations against each other, harmonize the definition of services, strengthen services and investments, and protect foreign direct investments.[3] Although this type of agreement is less robust than a customs union, but it seems to be robust enough to meet the economic interests of both the EU and Australia.

The acceptance and the future success of any trade agreement depend solely on whether the contracting parties can sign a mutually acceptable deal. From a European perspective, such fundamental examples are the trade with dairy products and automotive products. Eurostat's statistics indicate that in 2017 the EU has imported only 292 million € of food (excluding fish) from Japan, but exported 5.921 million € to Japan. The export of automotive products to Japan reached 9.982 million €, and imports totalled 14.038 million €.[4] These numbers indicate that the EU exports of food (including dairy products) massively surpass imports, and the import of Japanese automotive products has the most significant value within the category of machinery and transport equipment. Looking at the same categories of goods, statistics of 2017 indicate totally different trends with respect to Canada. The EU has imported 2.107 million € of food (excluding fish) from Canada, and exported 3.288 million € to Canada. The export of automotive products to Canada reached 5.089 million €, but imports totalled only 628 million €.[5]

Based on these figures, as a part of the economic partnership agreement with Japan, the EU understandably aimed to reach the elimination of e.g. the 30% tariffs applied by Japan against European cheese products.[6] At the same time, the EU

[3]Compare to http://ec.europa.eu/trade/policy/countries-and-regions/countries/australia/. Accessed 30 September 2018.

[4]European Union, Trade in goods with Japan 2017, 4. http://trade.ec.europa.eu/doclib/docs/2006/september/tradoc_113403.pdf. Accessed 30 September 2018.

[5]European Union, Trade in goods with Canada 2017, 4. http://trade.ec.europa.eu/doclib/docs/2006/september/tradoc_113363.pdf. Accessed 30 September 2018.

[6]Tabuchi and Ewing (2017).

agreed to lessen its tariffs on the Japanese car imports. Similarly, the CETA, concluded by the EU and Canada, almost failed on the protest of the Walloon dairy producers, who tried to defeat the agreement by an aggressive referendum as they believed that CETA is detrimental to their businesses. However, the Walloon referendum did not represent the overall economic interests of the EU properly. As indicated by the journalists of the New York Times,

> [t]he Wallonia region of Belgium is home to 3.5 million of the country's 11.2 million people. Yet in single-handedly blocking a trade deal produced over seven years between the European Union and Canada, it effectively determined the terms of commerce applying for 500 million Europeans. The Walloons did not relish the idea of having to compete against imported dairy products from Canada. Britain makes cars, medical devices and sophisticated parts for airplanes. It is a global leader in financial services. Somewhere in the European Union must surely lurk some other Wallonia that will seize the opportunity to slap tariffs on British goods even at the cost of broader economic interests.[7]

In sum, Jean-Claude Juncker's and Abe Shinzo's common statement perfectly mirrors why free trade agreements are generally important and useful, even if they can hinder some economic sectors on all sides:

> [a]mid widening protectionist movements, the finalisation of the negotiations on the EU-Japan EPA demonstrates to the world the firm political will of Japan and the EU to keep the flag of free trade waving high and powerfully advance free trade. (...) This EPA will create a huge economic zone with 600 million people and approximately 30 percent of the world GDP, and it will open up tremendous trade and investment opportunities and will contribute to strengthening our economies and societies. It will also strengthen economic cooperation between Japan and the EU and reinforce our competitiveness as mature yet innovative economies. We are confident that, once in place, this Agreement will deliver sustainable and inclusive economic growth and spur job creation, while at the same time confirming our commitment to the highest level of labour, safety, environmental and consumer protection standards and fully safeguarding public services.[8]

In order to secure the best available deal with its negotiating partners, the EU has signed various types of trade agreements. Some of these agreements are so-called free trade agreements. They often include chapters related to intellectual property law, including copyright law. The backbone of these rules is undoubtedly the Agreement on Trade-Related Aspects of Intellectual Property Rights (TRIPS Agreement). This is mainly due to the fact that the most important trade agreement related to intellectual property law combined (almost) all pre-existing international minimum standards of copyright law,[9] and it also introduced an international mechanism for the settlement of disputes.[10] The TRIPS Agreement is a part of the WTO law. The 162 Member States, as well as any future member, shall comply with these rules.

[7]Goodman and Kanter (2016).

[8]Joint Statement by the President of the European Commission Jean-Claude Juncker and the Prime Minister of Japan Shinzo Abe, Brussels, 8 December 2017, STATEMENT/17/5182. http://europa.eu/rapid/press-release_STATEMENT-17-5182_hu.htm. Accessed 30 September 2018.

[9]TRIPS, Art. 9–14.

[10]TRIPS, Art. 63–64. The TRIPS refers back to the general rules of GATT on dispute resolution.

Consequently, any new bilateral free trade agreement can only be signed as a TRIPS+ agreement.[11] That is, the new agreement is based on the TRIPS Agreement, however, it either complements the existing standards with stricter rules, or it eliminates the existing flexibilities.[12] In both cases, the new free trade agreement would introduce a higher level of protection for the benefit of copyright holders.

4.2 The Free Trade Agreements of the EU

The EU has a strong affect on the regional and the world trade by its economic rules, the Customs Union and the four freedoms. This is partially due to the fact that it aims to disseminate its standards on a global scale, in order to guarantee strong protection for its nationals (including copyright holders) in third countries. The EU has developed three main types of trade agreements to reach this goal. The first type is the *customs union*. It aims to eliminate customs duties in trade, as well as to establish joint customs tariffs for imports. The second group of agreements include *association agreements, stabilisation agreements, (deep and comprehensive) free trade agreements and economic partnership agreements*. They all intend to remove or reduce customs tariffs in bilateral trade. Finally, *partnership and cooperation agreements* provide "only" a general framework for bilateral economic relations, while they leave customs tariffs unaffected.[13]

The EU applies these various types of agreements partially in accordance with the geographic location of its partners. As the customs union can provide the most liberal trade for nationals and corporations of the contracting countries, the EU has rarely concluded such agreements. At the same time, the two other types of agreements have been used by the EU multiple times recently.

Intellectual property norms are mainly available in deep and comprehensive free trade agreements and economic partnership agreements. Anke Moerland noted that the agreements that the EU concluded before 2006 included only a handsome of intellectual property sections. On the contrary, the ones concluded after 2006 include approximately 33 articles on intellectual property law. This sharp change is partially due to the European Commission's "Global Europe" strategy of 2006, where the Commission declared its wish to raise the competitiveness of the EU.[14] The willingness to regulate intellectual property law through trade agreements, as well as the emergence of the new generation free trade agreements—that make bilateralism,

[11]Moerland (2017), p. 763.

[12]Acquah (2014), p. 267; Aleman (2014), pp. 62–63. Another expression is present in legal literature. "TRIPS-extra" means that countries include provisions in free trade agreements that were not regulated by TRIPS Agreement. See Aleman (2014), p. 63. On "multilateral-plus" and "multilateral-extra" see further Yu (2011a), pp. 969–970.

[13]The full list of the EU's trade agreements is available via http://ec.europa.eu/trade/policy/countries-and-regions/negotiations-and-agreements/. Accessed 30 September 2018.

[14]Moerland (2017), pp. 762–763.

rather than multilateralism, the rule—is also due to the failure of the Doha Round of WTO negotiations to further trade liberalization.[15]

The inclusion of intellectual property, including copyright norms into the EU's free trade agreements fits perfectly into the global standards. As the research paper of WTO's Economic Research and Statistics Division indicated, 71% (174 out of 245) of the still effective agreements submitted to the WTO until 2014 include provisions on intellectual property law. An even higher number, 80%, of the agreements submitted to the WTO after 2000 include such norms.[16] The presence of intellectual property norms in such new-generation free trade agreements is undoubtedly due to the fact that intellectual creations (e.g. works, inventions, trademarked goods etc.) are key elements of the new global economy. Rita Matulionyte noted that

> [o]ne of the areas where creative industries may need government support in promoting trade in creative goods and services are strong and effective intellectual property laws, including copyright. Strong IP rights have been seen by the European Commission as instrumental in ensuring remuneration for actors who participated in the creative process and who invested money into it. The EU is thus keen that its trade partners maintain high copyright protection and enforcement standards.[17]

And the EU is certainly a strong advocate for intellectual property law, as statistics have for long confirmed the importance of this sector for the European Economy. A 2016 report noted that

> [i]n the European Union (EU 28), in 2013, Cultural and Creative industries (CCIs) (excluding high-end industries) constituted 11.2% of all private enterprises and 7.5% of all persons employed in the total economy. In terms of value added, core CCIs and the fashion industry generate 5.3% of the total European GVA.[18]

As Csongor István Nagy has warned us, however,

> [t]he share of free trade in the global economy is becoming paramount and the emerging new-generation free trade agreements not merely abolish tariffs and quotas (as old-fashioned agreements did) but effectively open up national regulatory sovereignty to international governance, re-shaping regulatory autonomy, internationalizing national competences and, according to some, raising serious questions of democratic legitimacy. New-generation free trade agreements cover the whole spectrum of items (goods, services, technology, capital etc.), ambitiously, address not only traditional barriers to trade (such as tariffs and quantitative restrictions), but also, in a comprehensive manner, all trade restrictions and state acts (e.g. regulatory disparities, public procurement, certain fundamental rights issues).[19]

Likewise, Peter K. Yu noted that "[i]f the agreements are motivated by trade liberalization and are complementary to multilateral reforms, they will help achieve

---

[15] Yu (2011a), pp. 961–962; Nagy (2018), p. 199, para. 8.05; Okediji (2018), p. 2.

[16] Valdés and McCann (2014), p. 21.

[17] Matulionyte (2018), p. 2.

[18] Boosting the competitiveness of cultural and creative industries for growth and jobs (2016) Final Report, EASME/COSME/2015/003 28. (Footnotes omitted).

[19] Nagy (2018), p. 198, para. 8.03.

what developed countries cannot through traditional bargaining in the WTO or other international bodies".[20]

The research paper of the Max Planck Institute on Innovation and Competition also confirmed that such a broad application of intellectual property law norms does not generally aim to provide a high(er) level of protection for rights holders. To the contrary, they contribute to the conclusion of more robust and comprehensive free trade agreements that include intellectual property norm *as well*. As the report stated,

> [s]ince the early 1990s, the world has witnessed an unprecedented inclusion of IP provisions in trade and other agreements that are outside the traditional domain of international IP law. Those agreements cover a wide range of issues and allow for deals in which IP provisions are agreed in exchange for trade preferences and other advantages. On both sides, these deals are driven by export interests and other objectives external to the IP system rather than the common goal to achieve a mutually advantageous, balanced regulation of IP among the parties. While these agreements may pursue an overall balance of concessions, they usually do not lead to international IP rules that address the interests of all countries affected.[21]

In other words, intellectual property law is a part of the bargain, a small weight on the scale, where the ultimate goal is to reach an effective "*package deal*".[22]

4.3 Two Lessons of EU's Free Trade Agreements and Copyright Law

4.3.1 Contingent and Adaptive Refining of the Agreements

The first lesson we have learned so far is that the negotiations of the new-generation free-trade agreements and the acceptance of the original plans were "successful to varying degrees".[23] To put it differently, the final content of the agreements heavily reflected the rapid domestic and international changes in the copyright ecosystem. As Rita Matulionyte noted, the original draft of CETA mirrored the accepted text of ACTA (Anti-Counterfeiting Trade Agreement). However, following the rejection of ACTA by the European Parliament in July 2012,[24] and the acceptance of the Canadian Copyright Modernization Act of 2012,[25] the negotiations of CETA took

[20]Yu (2011a), p. 967.

[21]Max Planck Institute on Innovation and Competition (2013) Principles for intellectual property provisions in bilateral and regional agreements 1., Part One, I.1. http://www.ip.mpg.de/fileadmin/ipmpg/content/forschung_aktuell/06_principles_for_intellectua/principles_for_ip_provisions_in_bilateral_and_regional_agreements_final1.pdf. Accessed 30 September 2018.

[22]Seuba (2013), pp. 944–945; Roffe (2014), p. 23.

[23]Matulionyte (2018), p. 3.

[24]European Parliament rejects ACTA, Press Releases, 04-07-2012. http://www.europarl.europa.eu/news/en/press-room/20120703IPR48247/european-parliament-rejects-acta. Accessed 30 September 2018.

[25]Copyright Modernization Act, S.C. 2012, c. 20.

a visibly different path.[26] Similarly, the EU gave up some of its proposals during the negotiations of the EU-Korea free trade agreement (e.g. remuneration for performers and phonogram producers for the public performance of the phonograms; rules on *droit de suite*).[27]

There are other notable international examples for the purposeful reliance on Realpolitik in international trade and IP negotiations. Ruth L. Okediji correctly opined that "the shroud of secrecy enveloping both ACTA and TPP [Trans-Pacific Partnership Agreement] generated a significant political backlash".[28] The massive public resistance of European citizens against ACTA has undoubtedly led to its rejection.[29] The President of the United States of America also stepped back from the TPP on 23 January 2017 (although for purely political, rather than intellectual property related reasons). During the same year, the remaining 11 negotiating countries have concluded the Comprehensive and Progressive Agreement for Trans-Pacific Partnership (CPTPP) on 11 November 2017. They dropped some norms (e.g. on the term of protection, technological protection measures, rights management information and legal remedies and safe harbours) from CPTPP that were proposed by the USA during the original negotiations.[30]

Further, the mere fact that an international agreement has been accepted by the legislative organs of the EU does not necessarily mean that all Member States agree with all elements of these agreements. Such a notable example is the request for an opinion of the CJEU submitted by the Kingdom of Belgium.[31] By this request, Belgium seeks guidance from the CJEU, whether the CETA is compatible with the exclusive jurisdiction of the CJEU over the definitive interpretation of EU law; whether the general principle of equal treatment and the requirement that EU law is effective applies also to CETA; and whether Section F of Chapter 8 of the CETA (on the resolution of investment disputes between investors and states, in fact, the Investor Court System) is compatible with the right of access to an independent and impartial tribunal.[32] On January 29, 2019, Advocate General Yves Bot recommended to the CJEU that it should provide an answer to the affirmative in all raised questions.[33] But even if the CJEU will do so, the mere fact that the Kingdom of Belgium might be willing to halt the entry into force of the CETA shows how deep differences do exist among the Member States' views on the new generation free trade agreements.

[26]Matulionyte (2018), pp. 2–3.

[27]Matulionyte (2018), p. 2.

[28]Okediji (2018), p. 11.

[29]Geiger (2012), p. 166.

[30]Upreti (2018), p. 100.

[31]Request for an opinion submitted by the Kingdom of Belgium pursuant to Article 218(11) TFEU (Opinion 1/17).

[32]See Eckes (2018). The CJEU did not publish its opinion until the end of 2018.

[33]Opinion 1/17 - Request for an opinion by the Kingdom of Belgium, Opinion of Advocate General Bot, January 29, 2019, ECLI:EU:C:2019:72.

In sum, the final texts of the free trade agreements are constantly affected by the domestic and international politics, as well as the economic interests of and the social reactions in the contracting parties. And this also leads to the fact that the EU adaptively refines its legislative plans when concluding the ever latest free trade agreement.[34] That is, the EU aims to include an ever greater part of its *acquis communautaire* into its trade agreements, but only as long as the European or its trading partners' political, economic and social circumstances allows for that.

This is clearly visible when we take a look at the four new generation free trade agreements of the EU. The *EC-CARIFORUM Economic Partnership Agreement* includes almost no substantive copyright norms; indeed, it is focuses mainly on the transplantation of the EU's enforcement *acquis*.[35] This is partially due to the high number of contracting parties (15 out of the 16 CARIFORUM members, with the sole exception of Cuba, have signed the agreement), and the fact that these countries have significantly different copyright regimes. Many of them have not joined the most important multilateral intellectual property (and copyright) treaties. Consequently, finding the proper starting point of the negotiations looked particularly hard. This also reasons why the e-commerce *acquis*[36] did not either appear in the agreement.

The *EU-Korea FTA* includes a great number of substantive norms. South Korea did not join all relevant international copyright treaties by that time. Nonetheless, the level of copyright protection in the Asian country was much closer to the *acquis communautaire*. South Korea was also well aware of the positive effects of a strong intellectual property protection on the overall Korean economy. In sum, the negotiating parties included more substantive norms in the FTA, which have ripened since then. South Korea has signed various international treaties, it has launched the policy objective of creative economy in 2013, the *post mortem auctoris* 70 years copyright term was introduced, and the Presidential Council on Intellectual Property was also established.[37]

[34]This question has already been discussed by legal literature in great details with respect to industrial property law. See Roffe (2014), pp. 21, 24, 29; Moerland (2017), p. 764.

[35]Directive 2004/48/EC of the European Parliament and of the Council of 29 April 2004 on the enforcement of intellectual property rights.

[36]Directive 2000/31/EC of the European Parliament and of the Council of 8 June 2000 on certain legal aspects of information society services, in particular electronic commerce, in the Internal Market.

[37]Civic Consulting and the Ifo Institute (2017) Evaluation of the Implementation of the Free Trade Agreement between the EU and its Member States and the Republic of Korea Interim Technical Report Part 1: Synthesis Report 159.

The *CETA* includes only a few substantive copyright and e-commerce norms,[38] and focuses more on law enforcement.[39] This backtrack is due to the high level of copyright protection in Canada. Nevertheless, the Canadian Government has successfully resisted the EU's push to increase the term of protection to *post mortem auctoris* 70 years.[40]

The *EU-Japanese EPA* shows another minor backtrack from the adaptive refining model. As Japan has joined the vast majority of the leading international copyright treaties and agreements, the EU-Japan economic partnership agreement includes only a handsome of substantive norms. Similarly, the law enforcement measures, procedures and remedies of the agreement are expressly "complementary" to those of the TRIPS Agreement.[41] These rules are similar to the Enforcement Directive, although rules are only selectively transplanted (see below in paragraph 2). The substantive norms are much more limited compared to the *acquis communautaire.* Only the rights holders, their economic rights, the term of protection, and the three-step test are included into the text.[42] Even these rules are limited in scope, especially related to the term of protection. Namely, performers are not granted a general 70 years term,[43] and the revival of copyrights is also expressly excluded.[44] Some soft law provisions are also included in the agreement, which actually reduce the obligations of the parties. Namely, parties agreed to "continue discussion" on the use of phonograms, to "exchange views and information" on the resale royalty right, and they "recognise[d] the importance" of, agreed "to promote" and "endeavour to facilitate" issues related to collective rights management.[45]

---

[38]The CETA regulates the broadcasting and communication to the public right (Article 20.8), the protection of technological measures (Article 20.9) and rights management information (Article 20.10), safe harbours for internet service providers (Article 20.11) and the prohibition of camcording (Article 20.12).

[39]Article 20.32 to 20.42 mirror the Enforcement Directive's provisions.

[40]Roffe (2014), pp. 25–26. Although the negotiations over the amendment/replacement of NAFTA is not a part of our discussion, it is worth to note that the publicly available text of the newly accepted trilateral USMCA (United States-Mexico-Canada Agreement) intends to introduce an obligatory post mortem auctoris 70 years term of protection. See United States-Mexico-Canada Agreement Text, 20.H.7(a). https://ustr.gov/trade-agreements/free-trade-agreements/united-states-mexico-canada-agreement/united-states-mexico. Accessed 30 September 2018.

[41]EU-Japan EPA, Article 14.40.1.

[42]Article 14.8–14.11, 14.13 and 14.14 respectively.

[43]Compare Article 14.13.2 to Article 3(1) of Directive 2006/116/EC of the European Parliament and of the Council of 12 December 2006 on the term of protection of copyright and certain related rights (codified version).

[44]Article 14.17.2.

[45]Article 14.12, 14.15 and 14.16 respectively.

4.3.2 Asymmetric Rules

Such backtrack in the EU-Japan EPA, similarly to the limited scope of CETA is due to another feature, namely, the symmetry of contracting parties. More precisely, the EU is ready to adapt its trade agreements to the level of development of its contracting parties. And where the EU agrees with a country with a developed economy, intellectual property rules are much less regulated. *Vice versa*, the intellectual property chapters of the trade agreements between the EU and developing nations tend to be more detailed and require the adoption of EU's stronger or higher level of protection.[46]

As Yu noted,

> [w]hen the negotiating partners have equal bargaining strength, the goal of these agreements is to harmonize laws, policies, and standards of, or foster common policy positions among, the participating countries. (...) When the negotiating partners have unequal bargaining strength, such as in North-South FTAs and EPAs involving developed and less-developed countries, the goal of the agreements is to provide the needed »carrots and sticks« to induce less-powerful countries to change their laws, policies, and standards. Oftentimes, the agreements will lead to transplants from developed countries.[47]

Such asymmetry is visible in multiple ways.

First, as indicated above, the EU contingently and adaptively refines its trade agreements to the certain political, economic and social circumstances and the level intellectual property norms of its trading partner. Thus, the agreements might include (and require the implementation of) broader substantive norms or stronger law enforcement, but the exact contents of the agreements vary case-by-case.[48]

Second, the EU's agreements require the ratification of or accession to international treaties/agreements that the EU has long adhered to. Consequently, such requirements do not pose any extra obligation on the EU but only the other parties.

Third, the EU has only selectively transplanted its law enforcement provisions into its trade agreements. Namely, the strong enforcement measures are included almost verbatim in the texts, but the checks and balances are almost always left out from the agreements or only a conditional use of them is required. This is especially true with respect to the measures for preserving evidence, right of information and the provisional measures.[49] It is equally interesting how the EU-Korea FTA has eliminated[50] the optional rule of TRIPS Agreement that does not oblige member states to provide for an injunction against innocent or good-faith infringers.[51] Similarly, competition law related limitations are similarly missing from the

[46] Seuba (2014), p. 294; Matulionyte (2018), p. 3.

[47] Yu (2011a), pp. 963–964, 966.

[48] Roffe (2014), pp. 23–24; Jaeger (2014), p. 192; Drexl (2014), p. 267; Moerland (2017), p. 765.

[49] Jaeger (2014), pp. 194–198; Seuba (2014), pp. 299–302.

[50] EU-Korea FTA, Article 10.48.

[51] "Members are not obliged to accord such authority in respect of protected subject matter acquired or ordered by a person prior to knowing or having reasonable grounds to know that dealing in such

agreements.[52] All these instances represent a clear TRIPS+ or—as the EU's law enforcement regime is even broader than that of the TRIPS Agreement—*acquis communautaire+* logic. Occasionally the trade agreements miss to regulate unique European copyright norms. To use another example, although the EC-CARIFORUM EPA and the EU-Korea FTA included some rules on the copyright protection of databases,[53] the *sui generis* protection of database producers is missing from these (and all the four) agreements.[54] This might be explained by one of the two following arguments. It is possible that the contracting parties were reluctant to transplant such broad level of protection for the producers of databases. Alternatively, it is also possible that the EU was dread by the consequences of such regulation. Namely, the *sui generis* protection of database producers currently applies only to EU nationals. Should any trade agreement grant the *sui generis* protection to the nationals of the given contracting party (parties), the EU would be obliged to extend the protection *erga omnes*, that is, to nationals of all TRIPS signatories under the most-favoured-nation treatment principle. It is easy to imagine why the EU is not ready to do so. Such logic is similarly mirrored by the mere lack of regulating exhaustion by the agreements. In fact, the regional exhaustion doctrine, accepted by the EU in all fields of intellectual property law, will not be expanded to an international exhaustion regime, even though the fully free flow of goods (including copyrighted expressions or patents/trademarks etc.) could trigger more extensive global trade.

Finally, the limited (or no) transplantation of copyright limitations and exceptions (L&Es) similarly mirrors a TRIPS+ or *acquis communautaire+* logic. Thus, on the one hand, the partners of the EU are not required to provide for the same L&Es in their domestic regulations, but, on the other hand, all L&Es shall comply with the three-step test.[55] More precisely, such construction of the agreements mean that less-powerful countries are required to give up (some) flexibilities built into the international copyright norms.[56] This construction can lead to a situation where the nationals of the contracting parties have less L&Es, and so the European rights holders are protected stronger in the contracting states.[57] Indeed, in compliance with the most-favoured-nation treatment principle[58] EU's contracting partners are obliged

subject matter would entail the infringement of an intellectual property right." See: TRIPS Article 44(1) second sentence.

[52]Seuba (2014), p. 945.

[53]See EC-CARIFORUM EPA, Article 139(3); EU-Korea FTA, Article 10.2.2(a).

[54]Drexl (2014), p. 271.

[55]Such obligation exists under several multilateral treaties, and two of the bilateral trade agreements. See the EU-Korea FTA, Article 10.11 and EU-Japan EPA, Article 14.14.

[56]Yu (2011a), p. 982.

[57]Roffe (2014), p. 26; Moerland (2017), pp. 765–766.

[58]TRIPS Agreement, Article 4 first sentence. Indeed, the most-favoured-nation treatment is explicitly mentioned in the EU-Japan EPA, Article 14.5.

to automatically and unconditionally guarantee the broader protection to the nationals of all other parties to the TRIPS Agreement.[59]

4.4 Concluding Remarks

The above analysis introduced how widely—contingently, adaptively and asymmetric—the EU tries to transplant its norms into its trade agreements. Due to the dangers posed by this TRIPS+ or *acquis communautaire*+ logic the Max Planck Institute on Innovation and Competition has summarized the issues that third countries willing to negotiate with the EU shall cautiously take into consideration.[60]

Peter K. Yu has earlier introduced six fears related to the acceptance of ACTA.[61] Although the EU's new generation trade agreements and ACTA are quite different in their scope and purpose, they also share some similarities, especially the TRIPS+ treatment of law enforcement. At least two of these fears can have direct relevance with respect to the trade agreements of the EU as well. Namely, as ACTA, the FTAs will lock in some of the legal standards of the existing intellectual property regime. These lock-ins privilege existing business models and may "harm small and mid-sized enterprises and innovative start-ups".[62] Second, the lock-ins may also foreclose the European legislation to revise the copyright laws in the future. More precisely, legislation can always raise the level of protection, but in light of the trade agreements, and certainly only in the fields regulated by these agreements, it can not lower the level of copyright protection.[63] Such a notable example is the term of protection. The issue of limitations and exceptions is a much relevant example here. Although the currently negotiated copyright reform proposal under the Digital Single Market Strategy[64] includes some new L&Es, the EU cautiously refrained from discussing L&Es in details in the trade agreements.

Further, the new generation free trade agreements may also pose some implementation duties on the EU as well. Some provisions, like the criminal measures against wilful and commercial scale criminal infringements,[65] or the obligation to

---

[59]Roffe (2014), p. 26.

[60]Max Planck Institute on Innovation and Competition (2013) Principles for intellectual property provisions in bilateral and regional agreements 1–4, Part One, I.1. http://www.ip.mpg.de/fileadmin/ipmpg/content/forschung_aktuell/06_principles_for_intellectua/principles_for_ip_provisions_in_bilateral_and_regional_agreements_final1.pdf. Accessed 30 September 2018.

[61]Yu (2011b), pp. 975–1094.

[62]Yu (2011b), p. 1045.

[63]Yu (2011b), pp. 1066–1070.

[64]Amendments adopted by the European Parliament on 12 September 2018 on the proposal for a directive of the European Parliament and of the Council on copyright in the Digital Single Market [COM(2016)0593 – C8-0383/2016 – 2016/0280(COD)] (Ordinary legislative procedure: first reading).

[65]EU-Korea FTA, Article 10.57-61.

introduce criminal procedures and penalties for camcording[66] do not form a part of the harmonized EU law. Any failure to implement these rules by the EU may lead to a breach of the agreement. Some have argued that the inclusion of the above criminal law provisions were not accidental. Although many Member States have resisted against the direct harmonization of criminal law, the indirect unification through "backdoor lawmaking"[67] may be reached through the FTAs in Europe.[68]

What can we expect from the ongoing negotiations on the trade agreements with Australia, Mexico, New Zealand, Singapore and the Mercosur states? These agreements aim to contribute to the strengthening of trade between EU and the partner countries/regions. This can be reached through reducing existing barriers of trade in goods and services, growing competition of corporations, increasing investments, promoting sustainable development in trade. These purposes are generally unrelated to intellectual property law, with the exception of food and drink products and pharmaceuticals. In fact, we can expect that intellectual property, especially copyright law, will remain a part—and indeed a really small portion—of the package deal that the EU aims to reach with its negotiating partners. Further, the new negotiating partners have quite developed copyright regimes. The Australian, New Zealand and Singaporean copyright law have British roots. The copyright regime of Mexico and the Mercosur states (Argentina, Brazil, Paraguay and Uruguay) reflect the French or Spanish authors' rights systems. Based on this, there is a clear chance that the forthcoming trade agreements will mainly focus on law enforcement issues rather than substantive copyright norms.

References

Acquah D (2014) Extending the limits of protection of pharmaceutical patents and data outside the EU – is there a need to rebalance?. IIC Int Rev Intell Prop Compet Law 45(3):256–286

Aleman MM (2014) Impact of TRIPS-Plus obligations in economic partnership- and free trade agreements on international IP law. In: Drexl J, Ruse-Khan HG, Nadde-Phlix S (eds) EU bilateral trade agreements and intellectual property: for better or worse? MPI studies on intellectual property and competition law, vol 20. Springer, Berlin

Drexl J (2014) Intellectual property and implementation of recent bilateral trade agreements in the EU. In: Drexl J, Ruse-Khan HG, Nadde-Phlix S (eds) EU bilateral trade agreements and intellectual property: for better or worse? MPI studies on intellectual property and competition law, vol 20. Springer, Berlin

Eckes C (2018) Don't lead with your chin! If Member States continue with the ratification of CETA, they violate European Union law. European Law Blog. https://europeanlawblog.eu/2018/03/13/dont-lead-with-your-chin-if-member-states-continue-with-the-ratification-of-ceta-they-violate-european-union-law/. Accessed 30 Sept 2018

Geiger C (2012) Weakening multilateralism in intellectual property lawmaking: a European perspective on ACTA. WIPO J 3(2):166–177

[66]CETA, Article 20.10.

[67]Yu (2011a), p. 985.

[68]Drexl (2014), pp. 273–274.

Goodman PS, Kanter J (2016) With Europe-Canada deal near collapse, globalization's latest chapter is history. The New York Times. https://www.nytimes.com/2016/10/22/business/international/european-union-canada-trade-agreement-ceta.html. Accessed 30 Sept 2018
Jaeger T (2014) IP enforcement provisions in EU economic partnership agreements. In: Drexl J, Ruse-Khan HG, Nadde-Phlix, S (eds) EU bilateral trade agreements and intellectual property: for better or worse? MPI studies on intellectual property and competition law, vol 20. Springer, Berlin
Matulionyte R (2018) Future EU-Australia FTA and copyright: what could we expect in the IP chapter? Kluwer Copyright Blog. http://copyrightblog.kluweriplaw.com/2018/08/02/future-eu-australia-fta-copyrightexpect-ip-chapter/. Accessed 30 Sept 2018
Moerland A (2017) Do developing countries have a say? Bilateral and regional intellectual property negotiations with the EU. IIC Int Rev Intell Prop Compet Law 48(7):760–783
Nagy CI (2018) Free trade, public interest and reality: new generation free trade agreements and national regulatory sovereignty. In: Czech yearbook of international law, vol IX. Lex Lata BV, The Hague, pp 197–216
Okediji RL (2018) Creative markets and copyright in the fourth industrial era: reconfiguring the public benefit for a digital trade economy. ICTSD Issue Paper No. 43. Geneva
Rickeston S, Ginsburg J (2006) International copyright and neighbouring rights – the Berne convention and beyond, vol I. Oxford University Press, New York
Roffe P (2014) Intellectual property chapters in free trade agreements: their significance and systemic implications. In: Drexl J, Ruse-Khan HG, Nadde-Phlix S (eds) EU bilateral trade agreements and intellectual property: for better or worse? MPI studies on intellectual property and competition law, vol 20. Springer, Berlin
Seuba X (2013) The relevance of the principles for intellectual property provisions in bilateral and regional agreements vis-à-vis European preferential trade agreements. IIC Int Rev Intell Prop Compet Law 44(8):943–947
Seuba X (2014) Implementation issues arising from intellectual property chapters contained in trade agreements between the EU and developing countries. In: Drexl J, Ruse-Khan HG, Nadde-Phlix S (eds) EU bilateral trade agreements and intellectual property: for better or worse? MPI studies on intellectual property and competition law, vol 20. Springer, Berlin
Tabuchi H, Ewing J (2017) Europe and Japan near trade deal as U.S. takes protectionist path. The New York Times. https://www.nytimes.com/2017/06/23/business/europe-japan-trade-deal.html. Accessed 30 Sept 2018
Trebilcock MJ, Howse R (1999) The regulation of international trade, 2nd edn. Routledge, London
Upreti PN (2018) From TPP to CPTPP: why intellectual property matters. J Intell Prop Law Pract 13(2):100–101
Valdés R, McCann M (2014) Intellectual property provisions in regional trade agreements: Revision and update. WTO Staff Working Paper, No. ERSD-2014-14. https://www.econstor.eu/bitstream/10419/104752/1/797426418.pdf. Accessed 30 Sept 2018
Yu PK (2011a) Sinic trade agreements. U.C. Davis Law Rev 44(3):953–1028
Yu PK (2011b) Six secret (and now open) fears of ACTA. SMU Law Rev 64(3):975–1094

Part II

Chapter 5
Addressing Environmental Protection in the United States-Mexico-Canada Agreement (USMCA)

David A. Gantz

Abbreviations

BTD	Bipartisan Trade Deal
CAFTA-DR	Central American-United States-Dominican Republic Free Trade Agreement
CEC	Commission on Environmental Cooperation (NAFTA and USMCA)
CPTPP	Comprehensive and Progressive Trans-Pacific Partnership
FTA	Free Trade Agreement
JPAC	Joint Public Advisory Committee (NAFTA and USMCA)
MEAs	Multilateral Environmental Agreements
NAAEC	North American Agreement on Environmental Cooperation
NAALC	North American Agreement on Labor Cooperation
NAFTA	North American Free Trade Agreement
TPA	Trade Promotion Authority or Trade Promotion Agreement
TPP	Transpacific Partnership Agreement
USMCA	United States-Mexico-Canada Agreement (NAFTA 2.0)
WTO	World Trade Organization

D. A. Gantz (✉)
Rogers College of Law, The University of Arizona, Tucson, AZ, USA
e-mail: gantz@law.arizona.edu

C. I. Nagy (ed.), *World Trade and Local Public Interest*, Studies in European Economic Law and Regulation 19, https://doi.org/10.1007/978-3-030-41920-2_5

5.1 Introduction

The renegotiation of NAFTA,[1] was formally announced in May 2017[2] and completed with its signing as the United States-Mexico-Canada Agreement (USMCA) in its final version on December 10, 2019.[3] (The negotiations do not appear to have addressed environmental issues until relatively late in the process, probably because none of the three Parties were opposed to the environmental provisions agreed among the twelve original Parties to the Trans-Pacific Partnership).[4] Rather, the focus was on a series of proposals by the United States supposedly designed to reduce the United States' trade in goods deficits with Mexico (about $63 billion annually) and Canada (about $12 million) and to discourage the shifting of additional low-cost manufacturing to Mexico.[5] However, key U.S. proposals were significantly modified or eliminated in the course of the negotiations, as follows:

- United States rather than North American content rules for manufacturing of automobiles and perhaps other products, with 82.5% North American content (up from 62.5%), including 50% U.S. content (including steel and aluminum).[6] USMCA provides for 75% North American content (with no country-specific requirements), the use of 70% North American steel, and the production of 40% of auto content and 45% small truck content in factories paying their workers at least $16/hour[7];
- Limitation of the U.S. government procurement market to the same dollar value as U.S. procurement in the other two Parties, an impractical restriction given that

[1]North American Free Trade Agreement (15 Dec 1992) [Canada, United States, Mexico] (entered into force 1 Jan 1994).

[2]USTR: Trump Administration Announces Intent to Renegotiate the North American Free Trade Agreement (May 2017). https://ustr.gov/about-us/policy-offices/press-office/press-releases/2017/may/ustr-trump-administration-announces. Accessed 20 Dec 2017.

[3]30 Nov 2018, 10 December 2019 (not in force). https://ustr.gov/trade-agreements/free-trade-agreements/united-states-mexico-canada-agreement/agreement-between. Accessed 5 Mar 2020. While some have referred to USMCA as NAFTA 2.0 this article uses the official name.

[4]Trans-Pacific Partnership Agreement [Australia, Brunei, Canada, Chile, Japan, Malaysia, Mexico, New Zealand, Peru, Singapore, the United States and Vietnam], 4 Feb 2016 (effectively abandoned).

[5]See U.S.-Canada Trade Facts (2017). https://ustr.gov/countries-regions/americas/canada. Accessed 20 Dec 2017)(stating a trade deficit in goods of approximately $12 billion but a surplus in services trade of $24.6 billion); U.S. Mexico Trade Facts (2017). https://ustr.gov/countries-regions/americas/mexico. Accessed 20 Dec 2017. (showing a goods trade deficit of about $63 million and a services trade surplus of $7.6 billion).

[6]US Seeks to Include Steel, aluminum in NAFTA Autos: Sources. CNBC (13 Oct 2017). https://www.cnbc.com/2017/10/13/us-seeks-to-include-steel-aluminum-in-nafta-autos-rules-sources.html. Accessed 18 Oct 2017 (noting also the proposal for a 50% U.S. specific content and an increase in the total North American content to 85%).

[7]See Gantz (2018).

the U.S. economy is 18–20 times the size of the Mexican and of the Canadian economy, and one that was rejected by Canada and Mexico;

- A partial roll-back of US textile and clothing market access through greater restrictions on the use of non-North American fabrics and yarns, largely accepted by Canada and Mexico[8];
- Increases in so-called "unfair" trade remedy protection for U.S. growers against imports of labor intensive winter fruits and vegetables such as tomatoes and berries from Mexico (apparently designed to counteract Mexican comparative advantages in labor costs, lower humidity and a more favorable winter climate),[9] rejected by Mexico.[10]
- Elimination of Chapter 19 (AD/CVD binational panel) review of unfair trade law administrative actions imposed by the United States (and other Parties),[11] a "red-line" issue rejected by Canada[12];
- Conversion of state-to-state dispute settlement (Chapter 20) into a less legal and more diplomatic means for resolving disputes over the interpretation and application of NAFTA provisions, by allowing the United States (or other Parties) to ignore panel decisions that in the view of the United States are "clearly erroneous,"[13] rejected by Canada and Mexico[14];
- A provision that would allow a Party (e.g., the United States) to opt out of ISDS protection for inward investment.[15] The compromise eliminates ISDS between the United States and Canada after 3 years and reduces the scope of ISDS protection as between the United States and Mexico except for oil and gas, power, transportation, telecommunications and certain infrastructure projects[16];
- Strictly limiting the highly contentious provisions in NAFTA which permit Mexican and United States cross-border carriage of goods by motor freight on a reciprocal basis,[17] effectively accepted by Mexico[18];

---

[8]See USMCA, art 6.1.

[9]See Dewey (2017) (noting efforts of Florida tomato growers to increase their protection against Mexican competition).

[10]Gantz (2018), p. 4.

[11]Wingrove and Martin (2017).

[12]Gantz (2018), p. 7.

[13]Wingrove and Martin (2017).

[14]Gantz (2018), p. 7.

[15]Wingrove and Martin (2017).

[16]Gantz (2018), p. 5.

[17]USTR Considering a Carve out for Cross-Border Trucking Services in NAFTA, World Trade Online (6 Oct. 2017). https://insidetrade.com/daily-news/ustr-considering-carveout-cross-border-trucking-services-nafta; Cross-Border Trucking Services, USA-MEX-1998-2008-01 (6 Feb. 2001). https://www.nafta-sec-alena.org/Home/Dispute-Settlement/Decisions-and-Reports. Accessed 8 Oct 2017.

[18]See USMCA, Annex I-United States-9 (giving the Department of Transportation the right, inter alia, to impose regulatory restrictions on cross-border trucking services).

- A "sunset" provision under which a revised NAFTA could be reviewed and unilaterally terminated by the United States after 5 years based on yet undefined criteria, throwing the entire process into further uncertainty. USMCA incorporates a process whereby negotiations must begin after 6 years and if not successful result in the termination of USMCA only after 16 years.[19]

It is unlikely that the U.S. proposals, even if accepted by Mexico and Canada, would have significantly increased U.S. manufacturing employment because of disrupted supply chains and increased costs for parts and components in many sectors, including autos and auto parts and because any shift or production from Mexico to the United States would have been to highly automated factories in the United States or Canada. Thus, in most respects, even if the USMCA somewhat reduces the competitiveness of North American industry vis a vis Europe and Asia, the damage in my view is likely to be relatively minor.

USMCA, as noted above, includes environmental protection provisions, building on the evolution of such provisions in all U.S. free trade agreements starting with NAFTA and the accompanying North American Agreement on Environmental Cooperation (NAAEC)[20] and most recently with Chapter 20 of the Transpacific Partnership agreement (TPP).[21] While the Trump Administration withdrew from the TPP in January 2017,[22] the TPP language remains the most recent version of an FTA environmental chapter negotiated by the United States. Given that every U.S. FTA since NAFTA has included environmental protection provisions in its text and considering the requirement to negotiate environment provisions in the 2015 Trade Promotion Authority legislation,[23] the Trump Administration would not have considered submitted a revised NAFTA to Congress without addressing the environment in its text, as the Administration's negotiating objectives paper clearly states.[24]

It is therefore timely to analyze the USMCA environmental provisions, which are among the most far-reaching changes to NAFTA; these are addressed in Part 4 of this chapter. However, this chapter first discusses the NAFTA and NAAEC environmental provisions (Part 2), and then traces the evolution of environmental provisions in U.S. FTAs from NAFTA to the TPP (Part 3).

---

[19]Gantz (2018), p. 6.

[20]14 Sept 1993 [United States, Canada, Mexico], entered into force 1 Jan 1994. http://www.sice.oas.org/trade/nafta/Environ.asp. Accessed 20 Dec 2017.

[21]Transpacific Partnership Agreement (4 Feb 2016) (not in force) [Australia, Brunei, Canada, Chile, Japan, Malaysia, Mexico, New Zealand, Peru, Singapore and Vietnam]. https://ustr.gov/trade-agreements/free-trade-agreements/trans-pacific-partnership/tpp-full-text. Accessed 29 Jan 2019.

[22]Presidential Memorandum Regarding Withdrawal of the United States from the Trans-Pacific Partnership Negotiations and Agreement (23 Jan 2017). https://www.whitehouse.gov/the-press-office/2017/01/23/presidential-memorandum-regarding-withdrawal-united-states-trans-pacific. Accessed 4 October 2017.

[23]Title I-Trade Promotion Authority, P.L. 114-26, 129 Stat. 319 (29 June 2015). https://www.congress.gov/114/plaws/publ26/PLAW-114publ26.pdf. Accessed 20 Dec 2017.

[24]USTR, Summary of Objectives for the NAFTA Renegotiation (Nov 2017), 13. https://ustr.gov/sites/default/files/files/Press/Releases/Nov%20Objectives%20Update.pdf. Accessed 20 Dec 2017.

5.2 NAFTA and the Environment[25]

The environment provisions of NAFTA including but not limited to the NAAEC are unique in several respects. At the time NAFTA was negotiated by the George H.W. Bush Administration in 1991–1992 and modified by the Clinton Administration in 1993, these negotiations were among the first to address environment (and labor) issues in an FTA, both in the body of NAFTA itself and later with the separate NAAEC.[26] These first efforts represented an approach which, although modified, inter alia, to incorporate the environmental provisions in the body of the FTA rather than in a separate agreements, continue to affect all RTAs concluded by the United States.

Even though NAFTA itself contained initially only limited environmental provisions, it accomplished some of what the WTO Agreements did not achieve. For example, NAFTA established an order of precedence in relation to three major multilateral environmental agreements (MEAs), and two regional agreements.[27] Specifically, if NAFTA provisions conflict with the MEAs, or two regional agreements, the provisions of the MEAs prevail to the extent they are inconsistent with NAFTA.[28]

The NAAEC and an accompanying labor side agreement[29] were considered necessary when President Clinton succeeded President Bush in January 1993 after the NAFTA had been negotiated and signed, but before it had been submitted to

[25]Parts of this section II and section III draw extensively on an earlier article, Labor Rights and Environmental Protection under NAFTA and Other U.S. Free Trade Agreements (2011) U Miami Inter-Am L Rev 42:297.

[26]North American Agreement on Labor Cooperation (NAALC) (14 Sep 1993). https://www.dol.gov/ilab/reports/pdf/naalc.htm. Accessed 6 Dec 2017.

[27]Convention on International Trade in Endangered Species of Wild Flora and Fauna (3 Mar 1973) (amended 22 June 1979). http://www.cites.org/eng/disc/text.shtml. Accessed 6 Dec 2017; Montreal Protocol on Substances that Deplete the Ozone Layer (16 Sept 1987) (amended 29 June 1990). http://ozone.unep.org/en/treaties-and-decisions. Accessed 6 Dec 2017; Basel Convention on the Control of Transboundary Movements of Hazardous Wastes and their Disposal (22 Mar 1989). http://www.basel.int/Portals/4/Basel%20Convention/docs/text/BaselConventionText-e.pdf Accessed 6 Dec 2017; Agreement Between the United States of America and the United Mexican States on Cooperation for the Protection and Improvement of the Environment in the Border Area, La Paz (14 Aug 1983). http://www.presidency.ucsb.edu/ws/index.php?pid=41722. Accessed 6 Dec 2017;

Agreement Between the Government of Canada and the Government of the United States of America Concerning the Transboundary Movement of Hazardous Waste, Ottawa (28 Oct 1986). http://sedac.ciesin.org/entri/texts/bi-lateral/2.2X-CanXUS-Tby.Haz.html. Accessed 6 Dec 2017.

[28]Art. 104, Annex 104.1 NAFTA. The provision also specifies that "where a Party has a choice among equally effective and reasonably available means of complying with such obligations, the Party chooses the alternative that is the least inconsistent with the other provisions of this Agreement." It applies only to MEAs in force for all three NAFTA Parties; since the United States has not ratified the Basel Convention that convention is effectively excluded from the list.

[29]North Agreement on Labor Cooperation (NAALC) (14 Sept 1993). Entered into force 1 Jan 1994. https://www.dol.gov/ilab/reports/pdf/naalc.htm. Accessed 6 Dec 2017.

Congress for approval. As a presidential candidate in October 1993, Governor Clinton boldly endorsed NAFTA, but only on condition that NAFTA's environmental (and labor) provisions be strengthened.[30] Although those issues had been addressed earlier in an environmental impact assessment, candidate and then President Clinton's decision was driven in part by concerns of members of Congress and other elected officials on the U.S. side of the Mexican border that without attention to potential labor and environmental problems as part of the package working and living conditions on both sides of the border would deteriorate.[31]

Given the timing, and the reluctance of all Parties to reopen the text of an already concluded NAFTA, the most practical solution was to negotiate one or more parallel agreements to address NAFTA's perceived environmental and labor shortcomings. Thus, the decision to treat labor and environmental issues in separate agreements was driven by sequence and timing, and not by any nefarious plan to relegate such issues to an inferior status.

5.2.1 Environment-Related Provisions Within NAFTA Itself

In addition to NAFTA's preambular language and the hierarchy giving MEAs priority over inconsistent NAFTA provisions, NAFTA's chapters on sanitary and phytosanitary measures (relating primarily to foodstuffs) and standards, unlike their World Trade Organization counterparts, make explicit reference to "environmental conditions" and "the environment" as relevant factors in risk assessment and legal justification of standards, even where they affect international trade.[32] Probably for the first time in regional trade agreement, NAFTA contains provisions to protect human, animal and plant health and safety and facilitates the use of standards, including those designed for environmental purposes, although subject to certain constraints.[33] The NAFTA investment provisions preserve the Parties' right to apply environmental measures to firms operating within their territories and bar the relaxing of domestic safety, health or environmental (or labor) standards as a means of attracting foreign investment.[34] The NAFTA dispute settlement mechanism is in theory mandatory where environmental disputes under NAFTA's provisions are concerned, so that parallel World Trade Organization remedies are not

---

[30]Seib (2002), p. A14.

[31]See NAFTA: Report on Environmental Issues ES-1 (Nov. 1993) ("The Promotion of trade and investment throughout the continent under the NAFTA has potential effects on the physical environment and on environmental policies and programs.").

[32]Arts. 715(1)(f), 903-907 (NAFTA).

[33]Ibid ch 7, part B; Ch. 9.

[34]Ibid Art. 1114.

available.[35] Also, the General Exceptions in NAFTA, as noted earlier, make specific reference to permitting "environmental measures necessary to protect human, animal or plant life or health," as well as "conservation of exhaustible natural resources" and barring imports made with prison labor.[36]

5.2.2 *North American Agreement on Environmental Cooperation*

The NAAEC's objectives include protection and improvement of the environment; promoting sustainable development; increasing Party cooperation for conserving, protecting and enhancing the environment; supporting NAFTA's environmental goals; avoiding trade distortions or new trade barriers; strengthening cooperation to develop and improve environmental rules and regulations; enhancing compliance with environmental laws and regulations; promoting transparency and public participation in the development of environmental laws and regulations; promoting economically efficient environmental measures; and promoting pollution prevention policies and practices.[37] In the first instance, this is to be accomplished by each Party's obligation to enforce its environmental laws and regulations, provide private citizen access to legal remedies, and assure procedural due process for administrative and judicial proceedings.[38]

The NAAEC is also designed to provide a mechanism for requiring the NAFTA parties to enforce their own internal environmental laws and regulations. Each Party, while maintaining the right to establish its "own levels of environmental protection," is to "ensure that its laws and regulations provide for high levels of environmental protection and shall strive to continue to improve those laws and regulations."[39] The latter commitment is not realistically enforceable, because NAAEC sets no substantive environmental standards other than to call upon each Party to "ensure that its laws and regulations provide for high levels of environmental protection."[40] Thus, nothing prevents a Party from weakening its environmental laws, and then enforcing them at the weakened level.

[35]Ibid Art. 2005. But see United States — Measures Concerning the Importation, Marketing and Sale of Tuna and Tuna Products, DS381 (consultations requested 24 Oct 2008 (where the United States has insisted, unsuccessfully, that the action should have been brought under NAFTA rather than under the WTO's Dispute Settlement Understanding).

[36]Ibid Art. 2101(1), incorporating GATT, Arts. XX(b), (g) and (e); *see* Ludwiszewski and Seeley (1994), pp. 375–385.

[37]Art. 1 (NAAEC).

[38]Arts. 5–7 (NAAEC).

[39]Art. 3 (NAAEC).

[40]Ibid.

NAAEC creates a Commission for Environmental Cooperation ("CEC") consisting of a Council on Environmental Cooperation and a semi-autonomous Secretariat,[41] as well as a Joint Public Advisory Committee (JPAC) with four public members for each Party.[42] The Secretariat also performs a useful function in public outreach and conducts research on such matters as climate change, ecosystems and pollutants, with reports issued on each.[43]

Located in Montreal, Canada, the CEC is authorized to consider citizen complaints from private parties asserting failure to enforce environmental laws, with investigatory powers and authority to seek expert advice and issue reports.[44] The Secretariat has the authority to develop a "factual record" when the submission so warrants.[45] Where the investigation demonstrates a NAFTA Party's "persistent pattern of failure . . . to effectively enforce its environmental laws," a process of binding consultation and dispute resolution through an arbitral process is made available.[46] This arbitral process is open only to the government parties.[47] For the United States and Mexico, an adverse arbitral decision with which the Party does not comply could result in trade sanctions. For Canada, in lieu of trade benefit suspension, a fine may be assessed and enforced in the Canadian federal courts.[48] The process is clearly designed to encourage voluntary compliance; suspension of trade benefits is the last resort, occurring only after a complex and lengthy procedure that can be initiated only with the agreement of two of the three national representatives on the Commission (and never invoked after more than 25 years.

While there have been nearly 90 petitions filed with the CEC, no series of matters has been taken to arbitration or subjected to sanctions.[49] This reflects the requirement that two of the three governments must support the action and that only governments, not private parties, may initiate arbitration, as well as lack of enthusiasm on the part of all Parties for responding to citizen complaints. The principal value of the CEC/Secretariat mechanism is to expose a NAFTA government's failure to enforce its environmental laws in those cases in which the governments (acting through the CEC) permit the Secretariat to develop a factual record of the matter, rather than to compel compliance, which the Secretariat has absolutely no power to do. The

[41]Ibid Arts. 8–9.

[42]Ibid Art. 16.

[43]See Commission for Environment Cooperation. Our Work. http://www.cec.org/about-us/jpac/jpac-members. Accessed 6 Dec 2017.

[44]Arts. 14–15 (NAAEC).

[45]Ibid Art. 15.

[46]Ibid Art. 36.

[47]See ibid Art. 24 (providing that a panel may be convened by the Council 'on the written request of any consulting Party . . .').

[48]Annex 36A (NAAEC).

[49]See CEC. Registry of Citizen Submissions on Enforcement Matters. http://www.cec.org/Page.asp?PageID=751&SiteNodeID=250. Accessed 6 Dec 2017 (listing and discussing each of the enforcement matters under NAAEC); Arts. 24–36 (NAAEC).

Secretariat also has the authority to undertake reports on matters within the scope of its annual program, again with limitations that may be imposed by the CEC.[50]

The majority of cases brought and resolved before the CEC have been closed without the development of a factual record, usually on the grounds that the issues are already being dealt with by the national authorities or that the procedural requirements of the NAAEC have not been met. For example, in *Transgenic Maize in Chihuahua*, the Secretariat determined that the alleged violations of Mexican environmental law pertaining to risk assessment of growing transgenic maize were "indeed subject to a pending proceeding in Mexico," and as a result terminated the case.[51] Another matter, *Jetty Construction in Cancun*, was dismissed because the complainant's submission did not conform to procedural requirements.[52] Nevertheless, there have been more than 20 cases, or about 25% of the total, in which a factual record has been developed, often without the responding Party's full cooperation, and released to the public.[53]

While the factual records have provided the public with important information on the actions and omissions of the NAFTA governments, it is difficult to determine the extent to which such records have altered the behavior of the Parties. There are, however, a few success stories with the citizen submission process. For example, some observers believe that a citizen submission relating to the construction of a cruise ship pier at Cozumel, alleging Mexican government failure to enforce Mexican environmental law in the approval process, ultimately led to needed reforms in Mexican environmental law.[54]

The CEC process for responding to citizen submissions is subject to both procedural and substantive flaws. Jay Tuchton has suggested that in addition to the potential for significant delays, the process is deficient because the citizen complainant has little opportunity to participate in the review process once a submission has been made and has no access to the response of the NAFTA Party being challenged.[55] With regard to substance, even if the submitter of the complaint is successful in meeting the procedural requirements of the NAAEC causing the Council and Secretariat to create a factual record that is made public, there is still no guarantee that the Party will change its practices.[56]

---

[50]NAAEC, Art. 13.

[51]CEC decides not to recommend the development of a factual record on Transgenic Maize in Chihuahua submission. CEC ID: SEM-09-001 (Mexico) (28 Jan 2009). http://www.cec.org/Page.asp?PageID=122&ContentID=3155&SiteNodeID=532&AA_SiteLanguageID=1. Accessed 6 Dec 2017.

[52]CEC ID: SEM-08-003(Mexico) (17 Nov 2008). http://www.cec.org/sem-submissions/registry-of-submissions. Accessed 6 Dec 2017.

[53]See Chavez (2017).

[54]Wold (2008), pp. 201, 226, citing Ortega (2002), pp. 183, 184–185.

[55]Tuchton (2002), p. 10018.

[56]Ibid. See also Hunter et al. (2010), pp. 1275–1287.

However, there are also more fundamental problems with the manner in which the NAAEC process has been implemented by the NAFTA Parties. As Chris Wold has noted,

> The rigorous and professional manner in which the Secretariat has reviewed submissions has been instrumental in ensuring the integrity of the process. Nonetheless, actions and decisions of the Council have eroded public confidence in the process, leading the former director of the CEC's unit on Submissions on Enforcement Matters to declare that the submissions process—frequently referred to as the "teeth" of the NAAEC—suffers from "tooth Decay."[57]

In particular, "[t]he Council has sought to whittle away at the independence of the Secretariat by determining the scope of proposed factual records, a role designated to the Secretariat."[58] With regard to one submission, where the submitters requested the Secretariat to prepare a factual record regarding the failure of the United States to enforce the Migratory Bird Treaty Act against logging interests, and where the Secretariat agreed that preparation of the factual record was warranted based on the effectively barring review of any of the many other examples submitted by the applicants.[59]

The restrictive approach of the CEC continued during the Obama Administration. The environmental coalition Ecojustice recently withdrew a complaint against Canada. The complaint, filed in 2006, alleged that Canada had failed to protect some 197 species at risk under Canadian law.[60] In January 2011, the CEC decided to investigate this complaint, but limited the investigation to only 11 species and otherwise narrowed the issues. An Ecojustice representative protested that the CEC action "tells you that the citizen submissions process, touted by NAFTA promoters as the way to ensure the environment isn't trampled by free trade, is a sham."[61] In sort, the citizen complaint process is still being treated "as an adversarial, rather than a cooperative, process."[62]

The CEC and Secretariat, with officials who are well qualified to engage in technical analysis and research, have had significant accomplishments through cooperative work programs and data collection, as authorized by NAAEC.[63] The governments have used the CEC, albeit cautiously, to collaborate on various environmental issues, such as trade flows of used electronics for proper disposal, encouraging "green" buildings and "greening" the region's transportation

---

[57] Wold (2008), p. 228.

[58] Ibid.

[59] Ibid 228–229; see CEC Secretariat, Article 15(1) Notification to Council that Development of a Factual Record is Warranted, A14/SEM/99-002/11/ADV (15 Dec 2000). http://www.cec.org/sites/default/files/submissions/1995_2000/6466_acfa30.pdf. Accessed 21 Dec 2017.

[60] Ecojustice (2011) Species-at-risk defenders walk away from NAFTA Review Process. https://www.ecojustice.ca/pressrelease/species-at-risk-defenders-walk-away-from-nafta-review-process/. Accessed 21 Dec 2017.

[61] Ibid.

[62] Wold (2008), p. 232.

[63] See Arts. 10 (council functions), 13 (secretariat reports) (NAAEC).

corridors.[64] For example, the CEC has issued a number of important reports and "North American Regional Action Plans," particularly with regard to toxic chemicals.[65]

The CEC and Secretariat also produced "North American Environment Outlook to 2030," a report that summarizes CEC research concerning the major forces and underlying trends likely to shape the North American environment in 2030.[66] The CEC maintains a North American Environmental Atlas, which furnishes on-line information on environmental issues on a continent-wide basis.[67] This is only one feature of an excellent website that is well maintained despite CEC's chronic shortage of funds.

The original 1994 budget of $9 million annually must still support all CEC's activities including the processing of citizen complaints, compilation of factual records and production of reports, even though it has never been increased.[68] In real terms, $9 million in 2017 is worth far less and supports far fewer activities than it did in 1994, and the initial Trump Administration budget sought (unsuccessfully) to reduce or eliminate the current U.S. contribution of $3 million,[69] an action that would have strongly encouraged Canada and Mexico to do the same. More adequate funding would augment the ability of the CEC to fulfill its analysis and research functions as well as functions related to responding to citizen submissions, the latter of which do not appear to be popular with the three Parties.

More generally, the NAAEC has also been criticized for failing to provide any minimum standard of environmental protection in the Parties' laws and regulations and for near impossibility of reaching a meaningful level of enforcement of environmental violations. Regarding the former, it was probably impossible to consider specific standards without risking a "lowest common denominator" effect (a compromise among the Parties that would provide less environmental protection for some Parties than that afforded under then-effective domestic laws).

In Canada, NAAEC applies only to the federal government. NAAEC will not apply to the provinces' environmental laws and regulatory actions unless and until provinces representing more than 55% of the Canadian population have separately

---

[64]Joint Statement, Meeting of the NAFTA Free Trade Commission (10 Jan 2011) (Mexico City). http://www.international.gc.ca/trade-agreements-accords-commerciaux/agr-acc/nafta-alena/js-mexico-2011.aspx?lang=eng. Accessed 21 Dec 2017.

[65]Wold (2008), pp. 226–227.

[66]North American Environmental Outlook to 2030 (2010) 11. http://www3.cec.org/islandora/en/item/4066-north-american-environmental-outlook-2030-en.pdf. Accessed 21 Dec 2017.

[67]http://www.cec.org/Page.asp?PageID=924&SiteNodeID=495&AA_SiteLanguageID=1. Accessed 21 Dec 2017.

[68]1995 Annual Report 1995 Budget (showing $9 million in contributions); 2015 Secretariat Report 11 (showing Party contributions of $8.388 million). http://www.cec.org/about-us/annual-reports. Accessed 6 Dec 2017.

[69]See Pacheco (2017).

accepted an inter-governmental agreement concluded in 1995. Despite the passage the location of the CEC in Montreal, only a minority of provinces have signed on.[70]

It is thus evident that the NAAEC has had a mixed success record. The formal dispute settlement mechanism has been effectively useless, since the Parties are unwilling to subject each other to arbitration regardless of alleged violations. In contrast, the citizen submission mechanism could have worked well if the Parties had made a good faith effort to cooperate when they were respondents, and avoid unconscionable delays in responding to complaints. The Parties could also have benefitted if they had properly funded the secretariat so that it could have expanded its valuable research functions, and the JPAC, with its members from each of the three countries participating at their own expense, could have been more effective if supported properly. The fact that the citizen complaint function has not been successful is not primarily due to flows in the system but in the way the Parties have failed to support it.

5.3 Evolution of Environmental Provisions in Subsequent U.S. Free Trade Agreements

The significant post-NAFTA FTAs fall into several groups: the 2003–2004 agreements with Australia, Chile, Singapore CAFTA-DR and several others[71]; the 2006–2007 FTAs with Colombia, Panama, Peru and South Korea and the 2016 twelve-nation TPP. The first two groups were guided by the 2002 Trade Promotion Authority (TPA) while the finalization of the TPP negotiations in 2016 reflected the 2015 TPA, although it did not differ significantly from the earlier TPA version with respect to environmental negotiating objectives.

5.3.1 2002 TPA and Agreements with Chile, Singapore and CAFTA-DR

Because of the unusual approach to negotiation and enactment of trade agreements in the United States TPA (formerly "fast-track") as described below, the Congress plays and continues to play a significant role in determining the content of the trade agreements negotiated by any president, including but not limited to provisions relating to labor and the environment. This is not surprising given the existence of the Commerce Clause in the U.S. Constitution, which explicitly that Congress (not

[70]Kiy and Wirth (1998), p. 4.

[71]Bahrain, Morocco and Oman.

the President) shall have power "to regulate Commerce with foreign Nations, and among the several States, and with the Indian Tribes."[72]

As a practical matter the Bush Administration could not complete the negotiations with Chile and Singapore that were initiated in the final days of the Clinton Administration or pursue other subsequent FTAs without TPA. The negotiation and enactment of TPA resulted in further evolution of the U.S. approach to such addressing labor and environmental concerns. TPA as interpreted by the Bush Administration is reflected in the FTAs with Singapore, Chile, CAFTA-DR, Morocco, Bahrain, Australia and the initial versions of the agreements with Peru, Panama, Colombia and South Korea. While there are some variations in the labor and environmental provisions of the first six such agreements, most are quite similar. The focus of this section will be on relevant provisions in the CAFTA-DR, in part because it is the only such agreement outside of NAFTA with a functioning environmental secretariat and the ability to develop a factual record in response to citizen submissions.

While neither President Bush nor President Obama possessed Trade Promotion Authority between July 2007 and June 2015, the Obama Administration moved forward with the Trans-Pacific Partnership well before he sought TPA (waiting until 2015 to do so). The enactment of TPA in June 2015, noted earlier, made it possible to conclude the TPP negotiations a few months later. Unfortunately, the approximately one-year delay assured that TPP would become a key area of dispute in the 2016 Presidential election. Disagreements within Congress over the 2015 TPA did not extend to the environmental negotiating objectives but instead related primarily to investment protection and, more broadly, to growing domestic opposition to new trade agreements in general.[73] As a result, the 2015 TPA makes few material changes in the environmental negotiating objectives, although it does reflect those included in the 2007 Bipartisan Trade Deal (BTD).[74]

5.3.2 *General Considerations for "Fast-Track" and TPA*

For practical reasons, most foreign governments, including the other TPP Parties, have been unwilling to conclude substantive trade negotiations with the United States in the absence of TPA. Under the version of TPA in force through June 30, 2007 and similarly under the 2015 TPA,[75] once a trade agreement is formally submitted to Congress, Congress is authorized to cast only a "yes" or "no" vote;

---

[72]Art. I Sec. 8 (US Const).

[73]See Gantz (2017), pp. 249–251 (discussing broad U.S. opposition to TPA, TPP and new trade agreements in general).

[74]USTR Trade Facts: Bipartisan Trade Deal (May 2007) 2–3. https://ustr.gov/sites/default/files/uploads/factsheets/2007/asset_upload_file127_11319.pdf. Accessed 6 Dec 2017.

[75]19 U.S.C. § 4202 (2015) (Sec 103-Trade Agreements Authority).

Congress may neither amend any provisions. Nor may Congress unduly delay consideration of the agreement and the implementing legislation once the President submitted it to Congress, beyond 90 "legislative days" (about seven-eight calendar months).[76] In the absence of TPA, there would be nothing to prevent Congress from demanding amendment of a trade (or any other) pending international agreement, so as to make the agreement more attractive to Congress and inevitably less attractive to the foreign governments, or Congress may simply delay action indefinitely. Foreign governments want to avoid both of these negative effects.[77]

In return for the agreement by the House and Senate to these limitations, TPA legislation imposed detailed substantive criteria on the President for conducting trade negotiations. In addition, TPA (along with certain provisions of the House and Senate rules) required the President to obtain permission, in a process that effectively permits a congressional veto, before he may negotiate each specific agreement.[78] Also, consultations with Congress are required throughout the negotiating process.[79] An environmental impact assessment was required as were a series of trade advisory committee reports, including but not limited to labor and environmental issues.[80]

5.3.3 *Environmental Negotiating Objectives of the 2002 TPA*

The "Trade Negotiating Objectives" in the Trade Act of 2002 were designed to guide U.S. trade policy and represented a compromise between Congress (reflecting NGO and labor union misgivings) and President Bush (probably reflecting the

[76]19 U.S.C. § 3805(b)(2) (Supp. 2002).

[77]The Kennedy Round of GATT negotiations most clearly illustrated this problem, when Congress declined to vote on two of the major negotiated components (including a new Antidumping "Code"), prompting anger by the European Communities and a pledge that they would not negotiate again with the United States without assurances that such a result would not recur. Bergsten (2008).

[78]19 U.S.C. § 3803 (Supp. 2002).

[79]19 U.S.C. § 3805(a)(1)(A) (Supp. 2002). Also, the agreement had to be presented to Congress at least ninety days before either the President or his delegate may sign it. Congressional consideration would not begin until the President transmitted the final agreement to Congress. The completed agreement, when transmitted to Congress, was to be accompanied by a complete draft of the implementing legislation and a 'Statement of Administrative Action' explaining what changes in U.S. laws were required, and demonstrating the agreement's consistency with the negotiating objectives stated in the TPA legislation. 19 U.S.C. § 3805(a)(1)(C) (Supp. 2002). TPA also provided for a study by the U.S. International Trade Commission ('USITC') of the economic impact of each FTA on the United States. With regard to labor and environmental language in trade agreements, TPA directed the President to create consultative mechanisms (advisory committees) to promote respect for core ILO labor standards and for protection of the environment and human health. Consultations with prospective FTA partners were also required, with the provision of technical assistance if needed, and various review and reporting requirements. 19 U.S.C. § 3802 (c) (Supp. 2002).

[80]19 U.S.C. §§ 3802(c), 3804(e) (Supp. 2002).

predominant views of the business community). They were applicable to trade agreements negotiated beginning August 6, 2002, and signed by March 31, 2007.[81] That group included the then-ongoing Chile, Singapore, and WTO negotiations, the since-abandoned Free Trade Agreement of the Americas negotiations,[82] and subsequent FTAs concluded within ninety days before June 30, 2007, the day TPA expired.[83] The latter group included FTAs with Australia, Bahrain, CAFTA-DR, Colombia, Morocco, Oman, Panama and South Korea. This discussion is limited to the environment requirements, among the most controversial provisions in 2002 (such as investment protection) but less so in 2015.

The 2002 TPA "Overall trade negotiating objectives" included the following:

> * * *
>
> (5) to ensure that trade and environmental policies are mutually supportive and to seek to protect and preserve the environment and enhance the international means of doing so, while optimizing the use of the world's resources . . . and
>
> (7) to seek provisions in trade agreements under which parties to those agreements strive to ensure that they do not weaken or reduce the protections afforded in domestic environmental and labor laws as an encouragement for trade . . . .[84]

In addition, specific negotiating authority for environmental provisions was also incorporated. Congressional and public opinions on the subject had varied widely, from opposing such provisions entirely to seeking assurances that any violations of trade or environmental standards are punished in the same manner as any other violations of the FTAs and that strict labor and environmental standards are included in the FTA texts.[85] Many Republicans who found the language dictated in TPA overly strong likely supported the compromise because of the perceived need of the Bush administration to have the necessary trade agreement negotiating authority.

The adopted text favored the generally limited coverage of environment (and labor) espoused by the Republicans over the broader coverage preferred by some Democrats:

> The principal negotiating objectives of the United States with respect to labor and the environment are:
>
> (A) to ensure that a party to a trade agreement with the United States does not fail to effectively enforce its environmental or labor laws, through a sustained or recurring course of action or inaction, in a manner affecting trade between the United States and that party after entry into force of a trade agreement between those countries;
>
> (B) to recognize that parties to a trade agreement retain the right to exercise discretion with respect to investigatory, prosecutorial, regulatory, and compliance matters and to make decisions regarding the allocation of resources to enforcement with respect to other

---

[81] 19 U.S.C. §§ 3802–3803 (Supp. 2002).

[82] See Gantz (2009), pp. 263–272.

[83] 19 U.S.C. §§ 3805, 3806 (Supp. 2002).

[84] 19 U.S.C. § 3802(a) (Supp. 2002); see 2015 Trade Promotion Authority, 'overall trade negotiating objectives' with identical language in paragraphs (5) and (7).

[85] Bolle (2001), pp. 2–4.

labor or environmental matters determined to have higher priorities, and to recognize that a country is effectively enforcing its laws if a course of action or inaction reflects a reasonable exercise of such discretion, or results from a bona fide decision regarding the allocation of resources, and no retaliation may be authorized based on the exercise of these rights or the right to establish domestic labor standards and levels of environmental protection . . .

(C) to strengthen the capacity of United States trading partners to protect the environment through the promotion of sustainable development;

(D) to reduce or eliminate government practices or policies that unduly threaten sustainable development;

(E) to seek market access, through the elimination of tariffs and nontariff barriers, for United States environmental technologies, goods, and services; and

(F) to ensure that labor, environmental, health, or safety policies and practices of the parties to trade agreements with the United States do not arbitrarily or unjustifiably discriminate against United States exports or serve as disguised barriers to trade.[86]

The limiting provisions in paragraphs A and B reflect language like that in the NAALC.

5.3.4 Environmental Provisions in CAFTA-DR[87]

While CAFTA-DR followed the completion of the FTAs with Singapore and Chile by several years, the general approach to labor and the environment reflected only relatively minor changes from the earlier agreements, which were, as noted earlier, considered insufficient by many Democratic Members of Congress and their environmental NGO and labor union constituencies.

Chapter 17 of CAFTA-DR (environment) draws on the NAAEC, but with changes relating to enforcement. In Chapter 17, "[a] Party shall not fail to effectively enforce its environmental laws, through a *sustained or recurring course of action or inaction*, in a manner affecting trade between the Parties, after the date of entry into force of this Agreement."[88] Thus, as with the NAAEC, an isolated act of non-enforcement is not subject to mandatory state-to-state dispute settlement under CAFTA-DR Chapter 20. Enforcement is again subject to national discretion along the lines of the TPA language discussed earlier. Procedurally, "[e]ach Party shall ensure that interested persons may request the Party's competent authorities to investigate alleged violations of its environmental laws, and that each Party's competent authorities shall give such requests due consideration in accordance with its law."[89]

---

[86] 19 U.S.C. § 3802(b)(11) (Supp. 2002); 2015 TPA language, (10) Labor and the Environment, is substantially identical.

[87] See Gantz (2009), pp. 194–196.

[88] Art. 17.1 (CAFTA-DR); emphasis supplied.

[89] Ibid., Art. 17.3(2).

NAFTA specifically incorporated a list of MEAs, which prevail over NAFTA to the extent of any NAFTA inconsistency with them.[90] Under CAFTA-DR, there is no such list. CAFTA-DR contains only a vague recognition by the Parties of the fact that "multilateral environmental agreements . . . play an important role in protecting the environment globally and domestically and that their respective implementation of these agreements is critical to achieving the environmental obligations of these agreements" and a commitment to "seek means to enhance the mutual supportiveness" of MEAs and trade agreements.[91]

In CAFTA-DR, as in NAFTA, the Parties "recognize that it is inappropriate to encourage trade or investment by weakening or reducing the protections afforded in domestic environmental laws."[92]

With the environmental chapter in the body of the agreement, it is in principle subject to the same state-to-state dispute settlement mechanism as with trade disputes.[93] However, in lieu of trade sanctions, the most severe penalty for uncorrected environmental violations in this group of FTAs including CAFTA-DR is an "annual monetary assessment" to be determined by the arbitral panel. The panel is to take into account such factors as the trade effects of the non-enforcement; the pervasiveness and duration of the non-enforcement; the reasons for non-enforcement; the level of enforcement "that could be reasonably expected of the Party given its resource constraints."[94] Those assessments are not paid to other Parties or to groups that may have been injured by the violations, but rather into a fund established by the Commission to be used for appropriate labor or environmental initiatives in the territory of the Party complained against and consistent with its law.[95]

However, unlike the Singapore, Chile, Korea and most other post-NAFTA FTAs, in CAFTA-DR, "[a]ny person of a Party may file a submission asserting that a Party is failing to effectively enforce its environmental laws. Such submissions shall be filed with a secretariat or other appropriate body ("secretariat") that the Parties designate."[96] These procedures do *not* apply to U.S. persons challenging the United States' compliance with its own environmental laws; such complaints must be filed with the CEC pursuant to the provisions of the NAAEC, applied *mutatis mutandis*.[97] A person other than a person of the United States may avail herself of the CAFTA-DR environmental Secretariat.[98] As with the NAAEC, the Secretariat under CAFTA-DR is authorized to develop a factual record.[99] Under CAFTA-DR, there

[90]Art. 104, Annex 104.1 (NAFTA).

[91]Art 17.12.1 (CAFTA-DR).

[92]Art. 17.2.2 (CAFTA-DR;) Art 1114(2) (NAFTA).

[93]Ch. 20 (CAFTA-DR).

[94]Arts. 20.17.1 and 20.17.2 (CAFTA-DR).

[95]Art. 20.17.4 (CAFTA-DR).

[96]Art. 17.7(1) (CAFTA-DR).

[97]Ibid Art. 17.7(3).

[98]Ibid.

[99]Ibid Art. 17.8; Art. 15 (NAAEC).

is no requirement for a two-thirds vote of the Council in order for the Secretariat to amass a factual record; it is sufficient for one member of the Council to make the request,[100] again a potentially significant change although no state-to-state dispute has been brought to dispute settlement under CAFTA-DR.

Separate agreements among the CAFTA-DR Parties designate a new unit within the Secretariat for Central American Economic Integration ("SIECA") as the Secretariat for receiving citizen complaints against a Party and set out procedures for dealing with such submissions.[101]

As with the NAAEC, the scope of the environmental provisions goes beyond citizen submissions. CAFTA-DR and the other Latin American FTAs create an Environmental Affairs Council, composed of cabinet level officials and similar to the NAAEC's CEC in many respects.[102] The Council is to oversee "the implementation of and review progress under this Chapter and to consider the status of cooperation activities developed under the Dominican Republic – Central America – United States – Environmental Cooperation Agreement ("ECA").[103] An Environmental Cooperation Commission is charged under the ECA with developing cooperative work programs on environmental issues and fostering public participation.[104]

5.3.5 The Bipartisan Trade Deal (BTD) and the Peru TPA

The BTD was negotiated by U.S. Trade Representative Susan Schwab and the Congressional and Senate leadership in May 2007 for the principal purpose of obtaining the support of the Democratically controlled Congress and Senate for the four then-pending FTAs, particularly for the three with the Latin American nations of Peru, Colombia and Panama, although the results applied to the KORUS FTA as well.[105] With control of Congress passing to the Democrats in

[100]Ibid Art. 17.8.2.

[101]Understanding Regarding the Establishment of a Secretariat for Environmental Matters Under the Dominican Republic—Central America—United States Free Trade Agreement (18 Feb 2005). http://www.sice.oas.org/trade/cafta/caftadr_e/environment/environment_e.asp. Agreement Establishing a Secretariat for Environmental Matters under the Dominican Republic—Central America—United States Free Trade Agreement (27 Jul and 3 October 2006). https://www.state.gov/documents/organization/142890.pdf. Both accessed 9 Dec 2017.

[102]Art. 17.5 (CAFTA-DR).

[103]CAFTA-DR art 17.5.2; Agreement among the Governments of Costa Rica, the Dominican Republic, El Salvador, Guatemala, Honduras, and the United States of America on Environmental Cooperation (8 Feb 2005), arts IV, V. http://www.sice.oas.org/trade/cafta/caftadr_e/environment/envcoop_e.asp. Accessed 21 Dec 2017.

[104]Art. 17.9 (CAFTA-DR).

[105]Yerkey (2007), p. 373.

January 2007, it had become evident that the pending FTAs would require modifications to gain approval by Congress.[106]

The BTD, which effectively modifies the TPA requirement even though it is not legislation, covers six areas: labor, environment, intellectual property, investment, government procurement and port security, but the most significant elements relate to labor and the environment, with only the latter discussed herein. While the differences are not revolutionary several of them are notable. The BTD led directly to Congressional approval of the Peru TPA once the BTD language had been used to modify the earlier negotiated version, and several years later to the approval of the agreements with Colombia, Panama and South Korea, delayed for reasons unrelated to environmental issues.[107]

Under the BTD, a specific list of MEAs was to be incorporated into FTAs negotiated by the United States.[108] While such a list does not appear in the earlier Bush-era FTAs, the list approach represents an expansion of a NAFTA concept[109] rather than a totally new innovation. In the BTD, the incorporated MEAs include not only those listed in NAFTA, but also those related to endangered species, protection of the ozone layer, control of trans-boundary movement of hazardous waste, and certain bilateral agreements between Canada, the United States and Mexico.[110] The BTD also includes, *inter alia,* the Ramsar Convention on Wetlands, the International Whaling Convention, and the Convention on Conservation of Antarctic Marine Living Resources.[111] (The list does not include the Basel Convention on Hazardous Waste, presumably because it has never been ratified by the United States.[112])

As in NAFTA, the BTD language provides that "[i]n the event of any inconsistency between a Party's obligations under this Agreement and a covered

[106]Ibid (discussing the efforts by U.S. Trade Representative Susan Schwab to reach agreement with Democrats on standards in trade agreements "which would pave the way for the FTAs with Columbia, Peru, and Panama to move forward in Congress...").

[107]The Colombian FTA was delayed largely because of concerns regarding the widespread murder of labor leaders during the lengthy war between the Colombian government and Revolutionary Armed Forces of Colombia (FARC). See Santos (2017). The agreements with Panama and South Korea were also delayed despite any significant controversy surrounding them, until November 2011.

[108]"The list includes (with abbreviated titles) the Convention on International Trade in Endangered Species (CITES), Montreal Protocol on Ozone Depleting Substances, Convention on Marine Pollution, Inter-American Tropical Tuna Convention (IATTC), Ramsar Convention on Wetlands, International Whaling Convention (IWC), and Convention on Conservation of Antarctic Marine Living Resources (CCAMLR)." Bipartisan Trade Deal, n. 65 above, 2.

[109]Art 104 (NAFTA).

[110]Ibid.

[111]Bipartisan Trade Deal, Joint Statement, Meeting of the NAFTA Free Trade Commission (10 Jan 2011) (Mexico City). 2. http://www.international.gc.ca/trade-agreements-accords-commerciaux/agr-acc/nafta-alena/js-mexico-2011.aspx?lang=eng.

[112]The United States signed the Basel Convention on the Transboundary Movements of Hazardous Wastes and their Disposal (3 March 1990), but has not completed the ratification process. Parties to the Basel Convention. http://www.basel.int/ratif/convention.htm. Accessed 21 Dec 2017.

[environmental] agreement, the Party shall seek to balance its obligations under both agreements, but this shall not preclude the Party from taking a particular measure to comply with its obligations under the covered agreement, provided that the primary purpose of the measure is not to impose a disguised restriction on trade."[113] Also, the failure of an FTA Party to adhere to a listed MEA is a violation of the FTA that is subject to dispute settlement.[114]

The environmental non-derogation obligations are also somewhat tightened by substituting "shall enforce" for "strive to enforce" environmental laws, again through fines and trade sanctions, as with trade violations.[115] Further, government procurement contracts may include provisions that promote environmental protection.[116]

The Peru TPA environmental provisions, modified before the FTA was submitted to Congress for approval, generally track the BTD requirements. They incorporate the listed MEAs by reference and subject a sustained or recurring cause of action or inaction to the same government-to-government dispute settlement provisions applicable to other types of disputes.[117] Here, as in earlier FTAs, conflicts between the Agreement and MEAs are resolved in favor of the MEA language, assuming the conflict cannot otherwise be resolved. But the Peru TPA uses somewhat different language: "[i]n the event of any inconsistency between a Party's obligations under this Agreement and a covered agreement, the Party shall seek to balance its obligations under both agreements, but this shall not preclude the Party from taking a particular measure to comply with its obligations under the covered agreement, provided that the primary purpose of the measure is not to impose a disguised restriction on trade."[118]

Other aspects have not changed from NAFTA and earlier FTAs. For example,

> Recognizing the sovereign right of each Party to establish its own levels of domestic environmental protection and environmental development priorities, and to adopt or modify accordingly its environmental laws and policies, each Party shall strive to ensure that those laws and policies provide for and encourage high levels of environmental protection and shall strive to continue to improve its respective levels of environmental protection.[119]

As with other FTAs since 2002, the parties to the Peru TPA are required to provide opportunities for interested parties to request investigation by governmental authorities of alleged violations of national environmental laws and judicial,

[113] *See* Art 18.13.4 (Peru TPA); Art. 104(1)(d) (NAFTA).

[114] Ibid.

[115] Bipartisan Trade Deal, Joint Statement, Meeting of the NAFTA Free Trade Commission (10 Jan 2011) (Mexico City). 2–3. http://www.international.gc.ca/trade-agreements-accords-commerciaux/agr-acc/nafta-alena/js-mexico-2011.aspx?lang=eng.

[116] Ibid. 4.

[117] Art. 18.3, Ch. 21 (Peru TPA).

[118] Art. 18.13(4) (Peru TPA).

[119] Art. 18.1 (Peru TPA).

quasi-judicial or administrative remedies for the same.[120] As in CAFTA-DR, provision is made for designation of a secretariat to be established under separate agreement for the purpose of receiving citizen submissions. (The NAAEC Secretariat serves that function for complaints against the United States brought by U.S. persons; otherwise the mechanism under the FTA will be applicable.)[121] Where the Peru PTA diverges from some of the earlier agreements is with respect to efforts aimed at identifying and addressing Peru's legal, institutional and capacity building needs.[122]

Prior to the BTD, the United States and Peru had concluded an Environmental Cooperation Agreement.[123] Pursuant to that agreement and to the Peru TPA, the United States and Peru established an Environmental Cooperation Commission and agreed on a work program, which included the creation of a Secretariat within 18 months after the entry into force of the Peru TPA.[124] The secretariat was established administratively as part of the General Secretariat of the Organization of American States, although it is designed to function under the direction of the Environmental Council of the Peru TPA.[125] An executive director for the secretariat was appointed in November 2016, but it is unclear whether any submissions have been made.[126] A "United States-Peru Environmental Cooperation Work Plan (2015-2018)" makes no mention of the secretariat.[127]

While the environmental provisions of the other three FTAs of this period (Colombia, Panama and South Korea) are similar, one innovation was reserved for Peru alone. In the BTD, USTR "agreed to work with the Government of Peru on comprehensive steps to address illegal logging, including of endangered mahogany, and to restrict imports of products that are harvested and traded in violation of CITES."[128] The result, unique among U.S. FTAs up to that time and far-reaching

---

[120]TPA Art. 18.4(1), (2) (Peru TPA).

[121]TPA art. 18.8 (Peru TPA).

[122]Wold (2008), p. 246.

[123]Peru Environmental Cooperation Agreement (26 Jul 2006). https://ustr.gov/sites/default/files/Peru%20Environmental%20Cooperation%20Agreement.pdf. Accessed 21 Dec 2017.

[124]United States – Peru Environmental Cooperation (undated) 2009–2010 Work Program 10. http://www.state.gov/documents/organization/133528.pdf. Accessed 21 Dec 2017.

[125]Understanding for Implementing Article 18.8 of the United States-Peru Trade Promotion Agreement (5, 9 June 2016). https://ustr.gov/sites/default/files/Implementing-Article-18.8-US-Peru-Trade-Promotion-Agreement-English.pdf. Accessed 7 Dec 2017.

[126]See Joint Statement of the Meetings of the Peru-United States Environmental Affairs Council, Environmental Cooperation Commission and Sub-Committee on Forest Governance (4 Nov 2016). https://ustr.gov/about-us/policy-offices/press-office/press-releases/2016/november/joint-statement-meetings-peru-us Accessed 7 Dec 2017) (noting the appointment but providing no additional information on the functioning of the secretariat).

[127]https://ustr.gov/sites/default/files/US-Peru-ECA-Work-Program-2015-2018.pdf. Accessed 21 Dec 2017.

[128]Bipartisan Trade Deal, Joint Statement, Meeting of the NAFTA Free Trade Commission (10 Jan 2011) (Mexico City). 3. http://www.international.gc.ca/trade-agreements-accords-commerciaux/agr-acc/nafta-alena/js-mexico-2011.aspx?lang=eng. Accessed 21 Dec 2017.

with regard to the extent to which one FTA partner dictates the internal operations of another, is the incorporation of detailed obligations on the part of Peru to control illegal logging,[129] an area where compliance (or lack of it) remains controversial. At the same time, the Annex responds to concerns that were arguably unique to Peru among U.S. FTA partners, and thus represents an effort to depart from the more usual "one size fits all" U.S. approach, and approach which was later reflected in the TPP.

5.3.6 *Further Innovations: The Trans-Pacific Partnership Environmental Provisions*

As noted in the Introduction, TPP was signed in February 2016 after a long negotiation, with the United States withdrawing in January 2017. On March 8, 2018, the other eleven Parties signed a modified TPP—the "Comprehensive and Progressive TPP" incorporating the TPP. That agreement entered into force for Australia, Canada, Japan, Mexico, New Zealand, Singapore and Vietnam on December 30, 2018.[130] At this writing (February 2019) the CPTPP, incorporating chapter 20 of TPP without significant modifications, remains the most far-reaching environmental chapter in any regional trade agreement actually in force.

As noted earlier, the TPP provisions significantly influenced USMCA's environmental chapter. The TPP environmental chapter 20 also reflects many of environmental provisions in the post-BTD FTAs with Colombia, Panama, Peru and South Korea Group in such areas as objectives MEA obligations and the like.[131] Also similarly, disputes that cannot otherwise be resolved are subject to the same state-to-state dispute settlement mechanism as trade disputes, including consultations.[132] However, no independent CEC with a secretariat, or procedure for receipt of citizen complaints is contemplated in the TPP. Rather, citizen complaints are to be addressed by each Party according to national procedures.[133] TPP incorporates an environmental committee of high level representatives, in concept much the same as that found in other U.S. FTAs and in NAFTA's Committee on Environmental Cooperation or Peru's Environmental Affairs Council (but without the citizen

[129] Art. 18.3.4, Annex 18.3.4 (Peru TPA).

[130] See Government of Canada, Comprehensive and Progressive Agreement for Trans-Pacific Partnership (CPTPP).

[131] Arts. 20.2–20.4 (TPP). https://international.gc.ca/trade-commerce/trade-agreements-accords-commerciaux/agr-acc/cptpp-ptpgp/index.aspx?lang=eng. Accessed 2 Feb 2019. CPTPP text. https://www.mfat.govt.nz/en/trade/free-trade-agreements/free-trade-agreements-in-force/cptpp/comprehensive-and-progressive-agreement-for-trans-pacific-partnership-text. Accessed 2 Feb 2019. (Supplements the original TPP text.)

[132] Arts. 20.23, 28.5, 28.7 (TPP).

[133] Art. 20.9 (TPP).

complaint functions).[134] However, there is no mechanism similar to the JPAC (a unique NAFTA feature until the USMCA. Instead the Parties are to make use of existing or new consultative mechanisms such as national advisory committees.[135]

The innovations in TPP relate instead to greatly broadened coverage. The new coverage includes provisions addressing protection of the ozone layer; vessel pollution; corporate social responsibility; trade and biodiversity; invasive alien species; transition to a low emissions economy; marine capture fisheries (including subsidies); conservation and trade; and trade in environmental goods and services.[136] Among the most significant are these are those that relate to endangered species, which effectively include enforceable obligations to deal effectively with endangered species.[137] Taken together, they extend environmental provisions in trade agreements to a new level, and make what in my view is a serious attempt to deal with many of the most serious environmental challenges in the Pacific Rim nations. However, much of the language is hortatory, raising questions as to whether it will achieve the stated objectives with strong political will among the Parties.

5.4 USMCA's Treatment of Environmental Issues

The general negotiating guidelines for the USMCA's environmental chapter reflect much of the history discussed in Parts 1.2 and 1.3, above. These included inclusion of environmental provisions in the body of the agreement that are subject to the same dispute settlement as trade disputes; rules barring the use of weakening environmental laws to encourage trade and investment; incorporating MEA obligations; commitments to public advisory committees; a senior level environmental committee presumably similar to the Council or Environmental Cooperation; measures to combat illegal fishing, prohibit fisheries subsidies and promote sustainable fisheries management and conservation; protect and conserve flora and fauna and ecosystems (including measures to combat wildlife and timber tracking); and encouraging cooperative activities designed to facilitate implementation of environmental commitments.[138] As is obvious, many of these are borrowed from TPP and some from earlier U.S. FTAs.

The easiest way forward for the USMCA negotiators, as the U.S. Summary of Objectives suggests, was to incorporate much or most of TPP's Chapter 20. The many advantages of this approach included (1) relatively broad coverage of environmental issues such as fisheries and wildlife trafficking compared to NAFTA and

---

134 Art. 20.19 (TPP).

135 Art. 20.8.2 (TPP).

136 Arts. 20.5, 20.6,20.10, 20.13-18 (TPP).

137 Art. 20.17 (TPP).

138 USTR, Summary of Objectives, n. 15 above, 13–14.

subsequent U.S. FTAs; (2) making environmental violations subject to the state-to-state dispute settlement dispute settlement mechanism; (3) incorporation of the basic approach to environmental obligations found in earlier FTAs to which the U.S. is Party; and (4) a committee of high level representatives that if implemented could provide a useful oversight function for individual Member compliance with the obligations created by the environmental chapter.

The general satisfaction with the environment chapter in USMCA is reflected in the conclusion of the Trade and Environmental Policy Advisory Committee Report, which states that the September 30 draft of the Agreement:

> Largely meets the environmental objectives established by Congress in the Bipartisan Trade Act of 2015. It also includes several welcome new environmental initiatives e.g., to reduce marine litter, a prohibition on commercial whaling, enhanced language on IUU and sustainable fisheries management, and sustainable forest management, that will contribute to better environmental management in North America and beyond.[139]

Like many observers, the Advisory Committee strongly supported provisions of the chapter designed to eliminate fisheries subsidies that distort trade with transparency requirements for such programs; address illegal, unreported and unregulated fisheries as well as marine wild capture fisheries; support sustainable fisheries manage and conservation of marine species; and act on marine litter (an addition that goes beyond TPP).[140] As with many earlier post-NAFTA Agreements, provisions to restrict trade in wild flora and fauna, in illegally logged wood products (as with the U.S. agreement with Peru) and to address invasive species were also welcomed.[141] The area where the Advisory Committee reflected widely-shared disappointment was the failure of the environmental chapter to address climate change and global warming, particularly in the failure to include "provisions that incentivize trade and investment in areas like infrastructure investment and support for renewable energy supplies that promote constructive climate policies."[142]

Insofar as the actual text of USMCA chapter 24 is concerned, provisions include inter alia: respect for sustainable development; an obligation for each Party to effectively enforce its own environmental laws (but without any obligations as to the content of those laws); transparency requires including the provision of public information on environmental laws an opportunities for persons to ask questions or comment or request the investigation of alleged violations of environmental laws; provide fair, equitable and transparent judicial, quasi-judicial or administrative procedures for the enforcement of environmental laws; implement multilateral agreements to which it is Party; protect the Ozone Layer; and to address various marine

---

[139] Trade and Environmental Policy Advisory Committee Report, 27 Sep 2018, 2. https://ustr.gov/sites/default/files/files/agreements/FTA/AdvisoryCommitteeReports/Trade%20and%20Environment%20Policy%20Advisory%20Committee%20%28TEPAC%29.pdf. Accessed 30 Jan 2019.

[140] Advisory Committee Report 7–9.

[141] Ibid 9–10.

[142] Ibid 10–11.

pollution and air quality issues.[143] Other areas of particular interest addressed (in addition to those noted earlier) are corporate social responsibility, voluntary mechanisms to enhance environmental performance, protection of biodiversity and sustainable forest management, and trade in environmental goods and services (the latter long subject to unsuccessful multilateral efforts to reduce tariffs on trade in environmental goods). The chapter also potentially improves enforcement inter alia through establishing a presumption that any environmental violations affect trade under the agreement and establishing an interagency monitoring commission.[144]

While some observers, including the author, feared that the negotiators would fail to incorporate major structural features of the NAAEC, fortunately this did not happen. Rather, USMCA in a companion agreement preserves most of the best features, (1) a quasi-independent secretariat to receive citizen complaints and undertake valuable research and reports; (2) an internationalized citizen complaint procedure; and (3) a joint public advisory committee.[145] The "Agreement on Environmental Cooperation" explicitly continues the NAAEC Committee on Environmental Cooperation, including its Council, Secretariat and Joint Public Advisory Committee.[146] Also, as with NAFTA, "Any person of a Party may file a submission asserting that a Party is failing to effectively enforce its environmental laws. Such submissions shall be filed with the Secretariat of the Commission for Environmental Cooperation (CEC Secretariat)" with procedures like those in the NAAEC up to and including ministerial level consultations.[147] While as noted earlier environmental disputes are subject to the state-to-state mechanism in chapter 31,[148] one may question the practical significance of such jurisdiction. Under NAFTA, state-to-state dispute settlement has not worked well due to mechanisms which permitted Parties to delay the initiation of proceedings through chronic failure to appoint standing rosters of panelists.[149] Somewhat different treatment in USMCA in the author's view remains subject to potentially extensive delays for the same reasons despite improvements added under pressure from House Democrats.[150]

With respect to preservation of the CEC, USMCA is a significant improvement over the sparse use of secretariats in post-NAFTA agreements. The secretariats

---

[143]USMCA, arts 24.2 to 24.11.

[144]USMCA, arts. 24.12 to 24.24.

[145]2018 Agreement on Environmental cooperation among the Governments of the United States, of America, United Mexican States and Canada, Dec. 2018. https://www.epa.gov/international-cooperation/2018-agreement-environmental-cooperation-among-governments-united-states. Accessed 30 Jan 2019.

[146]Ibid art. 2.

[147]USMCA, art. 24.27–27.31.

[148]USMCA, art. 24.32.

[149]NAFTA, ch. 20, art. 2009. The most recent NAFTA Chapter 20 panel report was issued 6 February 2001. See In the Matter of Cross-Border Trucking Services, USA-MEX-98-2008-1, 6 Feb 2001. https://www.nafta-sec-alena.org/Home/Dispute-Settlement/Decisions-and-Reports. Accessed 2 Feb 2019.

[150]See USMCA, ch. 31, art. 31.8.

attached to the Central American Common Market secretariat or to the Organization of American States (Peru) lack even the limited independence of NAAEC's CEC. Probably of equal importance, they lack effective research and report preparation functions. Relegating citizen complaints to national government agencies is likely to reduce the effectiveness of the process, at least in Member countries that are not enthusiastic about the practice (which group in the author's view includes all three of the NAFTA Parties). Of course, these provisions will be useful only if the three USMCA Parties together make a good faith effort to support the USMCA secretariat financially or otherwise, a result that will be made more likely if interested members of Congress and environmental NGOs encourage such efforts through provisions in the USMCA implementing legislation (not available as of February 2019).

The preservation of the JPAC concept is in the author's view particularly important. For example, in November 2017, the JPAC recommended that the Council on Environmental Cooperation focus its limited resources on "environmental cooperation instead of punitive actions;" reaffirm the Parties' commitment to the secretariat; continue to encourage public participation in the CEC's activities; and continue to support the secretariat's research on trade and the environment.[151] The JPAC gently recommended continuation of the citizen complaint procedures:

> The CEC should continue to provide opportunities for the public to raise concerns about enforcement of environmental laws while providing a mechanism to ensure that issues and concerns are addressed by federal, state or provincial governments, as appropriate.[152]

The fact that the USMCA negotiators and the Advisory Committee appear to have paid attention to these recommendations gives cause for some optimism. It may be hoped that the USMCA environmental provisions and the provisions of the Agreement on Environmental Cooperation will be more successful than those of NAFTA and the NAAEC in meeting the objectives of Trade Promotion Authority and those in Congress and the public who are concerned with environmental protection. Moreover, the environmental provisions as revised by insistence of the Democratic Congress in December 2019 encouraged many members of Congress who otherwise would not have done so to support enactment of USMCA.

References

Bergsten CF (2008) Trade has saved America from Recession. Financial Times. http://www.ft.com/cms/s/0/d87f2158-46a4-11dd-876a-0000779fd2ac.html?nclick_check=1. Accessed 21 Dec 2017

[151]JPAC Expert Forum on the North American Agreement on Environmental Cooperation (NAAEC): Assessing the Past, Looking Towards the Future, Advice to Council No: 17-05 (Nov 2017). http://www.cec.org/sites/default/files/documents/jpac_advice_council/jpac-advice17-05.pdf. Accessed 7 Dec 2017.

[152]Ibid 5.

Bolle MJ (2001) Jordan-U.S. Free Trade Agreement: labor issues. Cong Research Serv. http://digital.library.unt.edu/govdocs/crs/permalink/meta-crs-2030:1. Accessed 21 Dec 2017
Chavez CR (2017) CEC at 23, a Certain Regard (PowerPoint presentation). http://www.cec.org/news-and-outreach/events/jpac-regular-session-17-03-nafta%E2%80%99s-environmental-side-agreement-assessing-past-looking-towards-future. Accessed 6 Dec 2017
Dewey C (2017) How a Group of Florida Growers Could Help Derail NAFTA. Washington Post. https://www.washingtonpost.com/business/economy/how-a-group-of-florida-tomato-growers-could-help-derail-nafta/2017/10/16/e1ec5438-b27c-11e7-a908-a3470754bbb9_story.html?utm_term=.92fc11aa67c7. Accessed 17 Oct 2017
Gantz DA (2009) Regional trade agreements: law, policy and practice. Carolina Academic Press, Durham
Gantz DA (2017) Increasing host state regulatory flexibility in defending investor-state disputes: the evolution of U.S. approaches from NAFTA to the TPP. Int Lawyer 50:231
Gantz DA (2018) The United States-Mexico-Canada agreement: overview and analysis. Baker Institute. https://wita.org/wp-content/uploads/2018/12/bi-report-121118-mex-gantz.pdf. Accessed 29 Jan 2019
Hunter D, Salzman J, Zaelke D (2010) International environmental law and policy, 4th edn. Foundation Press
Kiy R, Wirth JD (1998) Environmental management on North America's borders. Texas A&M Press
Ludwiszewski RB, Seeley PE (1994) "'Green" language in the NAFTA: reconciling free trade and environmental protection. In: Bello JH et al (eds) The North American free trade agreement: a new frontier in international trade and investment. ABA
Ortega GA (2002) Public participation within NAFTA's environmental agreement: the Mexican experience in linking trade, environment and social cohesion. In: Kirton JJ, MacLaren VW (eds) NAFTA experiences, global challenges. Routledge
Pacheco VF (2017) What the EPA budget cuts mean for North American environmental politics. http://duckofminerva.com/2017/04/what-the-epa-budget-cuts-mean-for-north-american-environmental-politics.html. Accessed 6 Dec 2017
Santos JM (2017) The promises of peace in Colombia. New York Times. https://www.nytimes.com/2017/05/18/opinion/colombia-peace-process.html. Accessed 9 Dec 2017
Seib GF (2002) Clinton backs the North American Trade pact, but candidates' stances on the issue aren't clear. Wall Street Journal
Tuchton J (2002) The citizen petition process under NAFTA's environmental side agreement: it's easy to use but does it work? Environ Law Rep 26:10018
Wingrove J, Martin E (2017) U.S. Proposes gutting NAFTA legal dispute tribunals. Bloomberg Markets. https://www.bloomberg.com/news/articles/2017-10-14/u-s-is-said-to-propose-gutting-nafta-legal-dispute-tribunals. Accessed 18 Oct 2017
Wold C (2008) Evaluating NAAEC and the commission for environmental cooperation: lessons for integrating trade and environment in free trade agreements. St Louis Pub Law Rev 28:201
Yerkey GG (2007) Veroneau "Confident" deal can be struck with congress on labor provisions of FTAs. Int Trade Rep (BNA) 24:373

Chapter 6
Member State Capitalism(s) and EU Law: Protecting Local Varieties in the Single Market

Marton Varju and Mónika Papp

6.1 Introduction

Governing a multi-layered marketplace, such as the EU Single Market involves foremost taking account of the differences among national varieties of capitalism. The different local models operated in the Member States are politically determined and may be constitutionally embedded, which represent crucial limitations to intervention from the EU challenging particular domestic institutional setups or aiming to homogenise them, potentially under centralising intentions. Despite the availability of a central economic policy agenda and the number of areas where near complete harmonisation has been achieved, the EU framework is not endowed with a general mandate to eliminate local institutional varieties; rather it is under pressure from the local level to accommodate and, if possible, reconcile them in policy-making. The limitations on EU intervention play out differently in the political domain of preparing and passing legislation and in the domain of the judicial application of the common obligations imposed in law. While in EU decision-making the comparative advantages and disadvantages of EU policies for national market economies are exposed and negotiated openly, before the EU Court of Justice the scrutiny of local institutional solutions holds the threat of subjecting them to transformation within the politically uncontrolled confines of the judicial application of the law.

This chapter is structured as follows. It commences with an overview of the academic discourse on varieties of capitalism in the EU and its impact on law and governance, in particular in the policy domain of market integration. This is followed by a detailed analysis of how EU legislative efforts promoting market

The research leading to this publication was supported by the Lendület-Programme of the Hungarian Academy of Sciences. This manuscript was finalised for publication in 2018.

M. Varju (✉) · M. Papp
ELRI, Centre for Social Sciences, Lendület-HPOPs Research Group, Budapest, Hungary
e-mail: varju.marton@tk.mta.hu

C. I. Nagy (ed.), *World Trade and Local Public Interest*, Studies in European Economic Law and Regulation 19, https://doi.org/10.1007/978-3-030-41920-2_6

integration have addressed the challenges arising from the varieties of local institutional setups, with special attention paid to legislation proposed under the recently established European Pillar of Social Rights (EPSR) which aims to reinforce the social dimension of the Single Market. This prepares the assessment of the EU Court of Justice's engagement with different national models of the market economy, the diversity of which may be accommodated under express provisions of EU legislation negotiated among the Member States. The focus here is on whether the Court's jurisprudence favours certain economic models and whether it—potentially illegitimately—'de-institutionalises' national capitalisms. In this part, the chapter examines the case law indicating the Court's understanding of the relationship of judicial power with political integration in the EU and its outputs, which is expected to enable drawing preliminary conclusions as to its approach towards the inter-State political compromises secured under the EPSR and the connected legislation in regards the different demands of national market economies.

6.2 Varieties of Capitalism and the Single Market

The Single Market, from the perspective of its governance, operates as a multilayered (federal) marketplace. Specific governance responses, usually which address an issue with a cross-border dimension, are produced at the European level; others are national, usually deeply embedded in local institutional and policy frameworks. The Single Market consists of national market economies, which in terms of their institutional models and the related policy priorities demonstrate a considerable degree of variety. The problems and dilemmas posed by the relevance of the local as well as by the diversity of national varieties of capitalism for the governance of EU market integration have been subject to extensive analysis, among others, in the domain that emerged as 'varieties of capitalism' (VoC) within the discipline of political economy. Even though its focus is rather specific,[1] its analysis and conclusions are of direct relevance for law and regulation in the Single Market. It highlighted in particular that the political and economic vision for market integration in the EU must take account of the diverse models of capitalism developed in the different Member States[2]; otherwise the most fundamental issues of its governance—European regulation, cross-border harmonisation and local deregulation—will remain unsettled (Leino 2017). As another fundamental proposition, it

[1]Such as industrial relations, corporate mergers, corporate governance, or corporate finance. See, inter alia, Hall and Soskice (2001), Amable (2003), Crouch (2005), Hancké et al. (2007), and Farkas (2016).

[2]See the analysis, following from the premise that 'neoliberalism's breadth and ambiguities' allow great flexibility in seeking to 'satisfy diverse internal and external preferences', that the EU neoliberal model 'is well equipped to accommodate (Member State) diversity' and that national varieties of capitalism can 'find their place and adapt to the EU's framework, while continuing to follow distinct paths of institutional development', Thatcher (2013), pp. 184–187.

was held that because the political mandate for determining the 'ultimate economic model' for the local polity is with the Member States, promoting a particular 'model of economic structures' and interference by the EU with national governance for that purpose face political and on that basis legal limitations (Leino 2017).[3]

The expectation that market integration in the EU accommodates the different institutional models in the Member States was raised particularly clearly under the 'clash of capitalisms' discourse in the VoC literature. Following the argument that EU integration reveals not only 'contending conceptions of the internal market' but also 'contending conceptions of capitalism' (Callaghan and Höpner 2005; Clift 2009; Copeland 2012), it was raised that legal harmonisation and the creation of a 'level playing field' among national economies in the Single Market will lead to undesirable institutional convergence among differently institutionalised markets, that is likely to impoverish competition based on the 'existing comparative (institutional) advantages' of national economies (Höpner and Schäfer 2010). Others claimed that the reduction of inter-State competition and the reduced possibilities to maintain national competitiveness will lead to systematic resistance to (constant political tensions within) market integration by national governments the political mandate of which demands the protection of the national economic interest (Clift 2009). Their main aim is to fulfil their political mandate and to be re-elected in the national political arena, which determines their actions in EU decision-making and their approach towards their earlier made commitments in the EU (Clift 2013). The governance of the Single Market thus has to contend with local opposition rooted in the political determination that the institutions of local capitalism must be protected so that local socio-economic needs can be addressed (Weaver 2015).[4]

By introducing the notion of 'economic patriotism', the VoC literature anchored even deeper the relevance of domestic interests and needs and domestic politics for the governance of market integration. Economic patriotism as a concept was used to emphasise that decisions about the national (market) economy are made within the confines of the domestic polity and on the basis of concerns which are those of 'one's homeland' (Clift and Woll 2012). Based on this premise, perhaps the most important dilemma of market integration was highlighted—that there are 'profound if not self-evident contradictions' between international market integration and the 'spatially limited political mandates' delimiting what national governments want to achieve (Clift and Woll 2012).[5] These contradictions are practically unavoidable in

[3]In other words, complete institutional convergence/full harmonisation is not a valid policy (political) objective for the EU.

[4]At the most general level, EU decision-making is confronted with a very real 'struggle' between the opposing ideological conceptions of a neoliberal and a regulated market economy, Hooghe and Marks (1997), Wincott (2003), Höpner and Schäfer (2010).

[5]It was also raised that under frameworks, such as the Single Market diversity in local varieties of capitalism is likely to increase as a result of the pressure on national governments to experiment creatively so as to find new means for satisfying local economic interests, which will then increase the necessity for the EU political and legal framework being able to accommodate and promote that variety as well as the necessity for local choices being spared from undemocratic and illegitimate

multi-layered marketplaces, such as the Single Market characterised by intensive cross-border interdependencies and 'an overlapping network of economic governance regimes' (Clift and Woll 2012). On the one hand, the political mandate and the political responsibility for shaping the national market economy are located with national governments, which, however, are constantly reminded of the territorial limitations of that mandate and also of the restrictions following for the use of the mandate from the transnational obligations undertaken.[6] On the other, law and governance in the Single Market are under constant pressure to secure its legitimacy, which demands that, despite the availability of common political objectives and the imperative of delivering effective trans-boundary solutions enabling intervention in national governance, the diversity of local needs arising in different socio-economic frameworks are accommodated and that the possibility of achieving the objectives set out in the Treaties under multiple local models is accepted.

The primary consequence for EU law—both legislation (and the Treaties) and the jurisprudence of the Court—of being positioned in such an environment is that its capacity to constrain, challenge and transform local institutions is not unlimited.[7] In particular, in case the premise is accepted that market economies within the Single Market are politically constructed within the confines of the national polity,[8] it cannot be utilised—without sufficient political authorisation—to dismantle the diversity of local capitalisms in Europe (Snell 2012).[9] In the domain of EU legislation (and EU Treaty rules), this means primarily, as raised earlier, that it has to accommodate and, potentially, reconcile different local economic models. It could

repression, in particular in the course of the enforcement of EU legal obligations, Clift and Woll (2012), pp. 309–312.

[6]National governments are no longer in exclusive control of 'large parts of economic governance', Clift and Woll (2012), pp. 311–312.

[7]EU law was said to threaten both neoliberal and regulated capitalisms: while liberal market economies are constrained by measures of positive harmonisation implementing common social objectives, coordinated market economies are threatened by 'neoliberal positive harmonisation', liberalisation through negative integration, and by the perceived consequences of cross-border regulatory competition, Snell (2012), pp. 428–429. See in regards EU State aid law, Clift (2013), p. 110.

[8]The arguments used by Snell against EU law being available to impose a single model of capitalism in the Member States were the following: the EU lacking democratic legitimacy to interfere with such local economic policy choices, in particular with redistributive policies, and the rule that the EU must not unnecessarily and unjustifiably eliminate national comparative advantages, Snell (2012), pp. 433–434.

[9]Overall, market integration in Europe has been more favourable to liberal market economies than to regulated capitalism. First, achieving regulated capitalism by legislation at EU level (positive integration) faces a politically nearly impossible decision-making process as affected by Member State heterogeneity. Second, the neoliberal project can proceed through (may even be facilitated by) judicially enforced market integration even under conditions of political-economic heterogeneity. See Höpner and Schäfer (2012), p. 3, 25.

entail, for example the inclusion of so-called 'autonomy-protecting solutions',[10] negotiated among the Member States in EU decision-making, which enable sustaining in national autonomy the heterogeneity of the institutions of the domestic market economy (Höpner and Schäfer 2012).[11] For the Court of Justice acting under its powers to interpret and apply the legal obligations undertaken by the Member States, the main limitation is that it cannot use judicial constructions, especially in an expansive manner, that are capable of imposing uniform conceptions of the market economy throughout the Union (Snell 2012).[12] In connection with the inter-State compromises secured in legislation so as to accommodated local variety, the jurisprudence is expected to avoid undermining them by enforcing the Member State obligations pertaining to the market integration agenda.[13]

The Court's involvement in the process of market integration and its perceived impact on the diversity of local capitalisms have received by far the strongest criticisms.[14] Some critiques went as far as accusing the Court of detaching democratic institutions (of market economies) from the (local) democratic units they were introduced to govern and of 'de-institutionalising' national capitalisms (Höpner and Schäfer 2010).[15] From the perspective of national governments, the core problem with such allegedly systematic challenges from supranational judicial power is, as already raised, that they interfere with the ability of the Member States to 'build on and foster their respective comparative advantage' in the integrated European market (Höpner and Schäfer 2010). The same analysis also pointed out that the judicial

---

[10]These are relied upon in particular when EU initiatives target 'highly sensitive institutions' that constitute the different political-economic regimes of the Member States. The importance of preserving national regulatory autonomy and defending national prerogatives has led to different Member State reactions in the EU decision-making process, such as the refusal to transfer competences, the Member States insisting on subsidiarity, or the Member States passing EU legislation which aims primarily at protecting national autonomy, Höpner and Schäfer (2012), pp. 15–16.

[11]Their ultimate aim is to shelter 'sensitive areas of national sovereignty from being transformed by European law', Höpner and Schäfer (2012), p. 23.

[12]This involves both the ignoring of the compromises secured in EU legislation and the pushing of the market integration agenda without regard to its impact on locally agreed and established models of capitalism.

[13]The examples identified (Höpner and Schäfer 2012, pp. 18–23): the jurisprudence enabling the abusive circumvention of applicable domestic regulatory burdens, the case law fuelling regulatory competition among the Member States, the judgments preventing the Member States from stepping up against races to the bottom in regulatory competition, the decisions expanding the legal effect of EU obligations to third parties, for instance to cover non-public law arrangements, such as trade union collective action.

[14]Even the balanced accounts of the Court's operation admit that there have been some adventurous judgments, for instance those in Viking and Laval (Case C-438/05, International Transport Workers' Federation and Finnish Seamen's Union EU:C:2007:772 and Case C-341/05, Laval un Partneri EU:C:2007:809) pushing liberalisation further than what was perhaps necessary, Snell (2012), pp. 428–429.

[15]The liberalisation attempts in question 'would not be possible either as outcomes of the political processes inside member states or as outcomes of negotiations between them', as they would not agree to them, Höpner and Schäfer (2010), pp. 355–356.

enforcement of the legal provisions (the fundamental freedoms), which promote liberalisation and the opening of national markets, target the 'institutions of organised capitalism asymmetrically'[16] favouring liberal market economies over regulated capitalist regimes (Höpner and Schäfer 2010; Höpner and Schäfer 2012).[17] It was claimed ultimately on this basis that the Court simply does not have the mandate and the legitimacy to demand the altering of the way in which organised capitalisms operate in Europe.[18] As a final criticism, the Court was found regularly overruling ('effectively nullifying') the solutions negotiated in EU legislation for the protection of Member State autonomy and thus for accommodating local diversity (Höpner and Schäfer 2012).

More balanced analyses denied, however, that diversity in varieties of capitalism would be in 'mortal danger' as a result of the operation of EU legislation or the Court's jurisprudence (Snell 2012).[19] In connection with the interferences by the Court, it was raised that most of the liberalisation achieved by means of the judicial enforcement of EU rules pursued specifically the interest of market integration and not a general economic liberalisation agenda, which must have been expected by the Member States as the market integration process inevitably entails the opening of national markets and the parallel removal of certain institutions and structures of the national economy. The intensity of changes in national market economies is also affected by the robust practice of the Court to defer, when scrutinising restrictive national measures introduced under local competences, the ultimate assessment of those measure to national courts, thereby enabling a contextually better positioned assessment of the obligations following from EU law.[20] As a further limitation on the EU judiciary undermining local capitalisms, it was pointed out that the Court proceeds on a 'fact-specific case-by-case basis' whereby its practice is open to the possibility of subsequent correction. In this regard, it was also indicated that the balancing exercise, which is central to the enforcement of the fundamental freedoms

[16]As a further problem, common political action to correct the asymmetry caused by the Court's jurisprudence is prevented by the diversity of Member State positions fuelled by the variety of local capitalisms, Höpner and Schäfer (2012), p. 23.

[17]They claimed that while political integration can serve both models of capitalism, judicial integration affects different capitalism in different ways, in particular it puts pressure on organised capitalisms to deregulate/de-institutionalise, Höpner and Schäfer (2012), p. 2.

[18]The Court was claimed to have assaulted local capitalisms and challenged 'institutional differences as such' in different capitalisms, especially the institutional frameworks of organised economies, Höpner and Schäfer (2010), p. 352.

[19]Snell, nevertheless, warned that cautiousness, modesty and sensitivity are needed in regards the potential negative, disruptive or destabilising impacts of EU legal developments, especially those coming from the Court, Snell (2012), p. 434. In regards EU legislation, both measures of positive harmonisation and 'neoliberal directives', he claimed that the political safeguards provided in the EU decision-making process can prevent that fundamental damages are inflicted by such measures upon national capitalisms, either liberal or regulated, Snell (2012), pp. 428–431.

[20]He also raised that the evidence about regulatory competition induced by the Court's jurisprudence and its impact on national capitalisms is rather uncertain, Snell (2012), pp. 428–431. See also the more general assessment of the review of national measures in Tridimas (2011).

against national policies and their implementing legal measures, can be carried out by the Court in a manner that the local deregulatory impact of its judgments is reduced.

6.3 EU Legislation and Member State Capitalism(s)

As discussed in the previous section, legislation adopted under the Single Market is expected—politically—to accommodate diversity in varieties of capitalism among the Member States. This does not apply to all aspects of the national economy; in specific domains (e.g., consumer protection, unfair commercial practices, or standards in certain product markets) EU law, not hindered (greatly) by comparative institutional advantages, is pushed towards complete harmonisation.[21] In other areas, the provisions of EU legislative measures bear the mark of the different institutional setups of national market economies and the compromises achieved among them,[22] as demonstrated foremost by the rules introduced to protect the autonomy of the Member States in policy-making (the so-called 'autonomy-protecting solutions').[23] The Member States, aiming to preserve their respective comparative advantages, usually eye the proposals of the Commission for the harmonisation and/or liberalisation of different sectors of the national economy with suspicion and are rather reluctant to release from their hands the controls exercised over those sectors in the national own territory. The latter is the consequence of the incompleteness of EU integration; it is neither a formalised federation, nor does it exclude competition between national economies, which drives national governments, limited in their sovereignty and in developing macro-economic policies, to compete 'fiercely' 'to defend their comparative institutional advantage' (Copeland 2014).

There are a number of well-documented examples of local institutional diversity having influenced legislative efforts introduced to deliver the Single Market.[24] These even include the instances of the Member States defeating initiatives on company law and corporate governance harmonisation[25] that were conceived as undermining core institutions of the domestic market economy and the continuing resistance of

[21]See, in this regard, Dawson and Durana (2017).

[22]The EU competences regime was also shaped with a view to ensuring that the market integration agenda does not interfere unduly with fundamental institutional arrangements at the local level, such as wages, social protection, or labour law.

[23]See, in addition to the earlier introduced literature, Menz (2005, 2010).

[24]See Deakin's analysis of a European model of regulatory competition, labelled as 'reflexive harmonisation', where in the context of harmonising corporate and labour law the preservation of national diversity had paramount importance and where there were conscious efforts to 'reconcile the conflicting demands of transnational economic integration and national legal diversity', Deakin (2006).

[25]See, in this regard, the analysis of the impact of varieties of capitalism on the Regulation on the statute of a European company (Regulation 2157/2001, [2001] OJ L294/251), Biermeyer (2011).

the Member States to harmonisation in capital taxation (Höpner and Schäfer 2012). The legislative history of the EU Takeover Directive[26] serves as a central example for Member State differences preventing that EU legislation regulates under a single common framework a crucial component of national economies on the basis of a model which favours a particular local institutional solution. As opposed to the solution promoted in the Commission's proposal, which fell victim of irreconcilable differences among Member State takeover regulations and their respective contexts, the directive as adopted made available in national law what was called 'hard law optionality' in terms of the takeover model followed in individual Member States (Clift 2009).[27] The regulation of optionality in the directive, because it enabled the application of multiple takeover models within national legal systems, was characterised as providing the potential 'for increased differentiation' between different models even within a single national market economy (Clift 2009).

The EU directives affecting employment and the labour market in the Member States faced similar political obstacles arising from fundamental differences among Member State capitalisms. The EU Working Time Directive,[28] in the course of its adoption and later during its revision, was suggested to have witnessed 'deep ideological divisions' and disagreement, which then directly influenced the formulation of some of its core rules, such as the reference period for the calculation of the average working week and the 'opt-out' allowed to 'pacify' the UK,[29] which Member State was left in minority in the negotiations because of its particular interests in the regulation of its employment market (Copeland 2012). The adoption of the Posted Workers Directive[30] was also influenced by irreconcilable differences among the Member States in terms of the applicable labour law standards, which led to the directive stopping short of full harmonisation and enabling through its rules the Member States to safeguard their autonomy in regulating national labour markets (Höpner and Schäfer 2012). Its follow-up measure, the 2014 Enforcement Directive, was adopted to anchor further national autonomy by enabling the Member States to

[26]Directive 2004/25 on takeover bids, [2004] OJ L142/12.

[27]The Commission's proposal was threatening to damage local interests (capitalisms) asymmetrically because it was to be implemented in very different takeover markets covering very different production regimes, Höpner and Schäfer (2010), pp. 359–361.

[28]Council Directive 93/104 concerning certain aspects of the organization of working time, [1993] OJ L307/18, now replaced by Council Directive 2003/88, [2003] OJ L299/9. See the national discrepancies in the implementation of the directive and the use of derogations by the Member States in Commission (2017c).

[29]The UK's legal challenge against the directive received a reserved response from the Court which argued in connection with the central claim that the principle of subsidiarity had been violated that once the need for harmonisation is established in the EU political process (by the Member States) there remains no doubt that EU action is necessary, para. 47, Case C.84/94, United Kingdom v Council EU:C:1996:431.

[30]Directive 96/71 concerning the posting of workers in the framework of the provision of services, [1997] OJ L18/1 (see Article 1(1)). In Article 1(2), it declares that's its provisions do not affect 'the exercise of fundamental rights' applicable to collective labour law 'in accordance with national law and/or practice'.

'prevent, avoid and combat' the abuse and circumvention of the applicable national rules.[31] The recent proposal for the amendment of the original directive[32] attracted serious opposition from the Member States, including national parliaments a group of which declared that the proposal runs counter to the principle of subsidiarity, in particular the provisions which enable the host Member State to enforce a range of requirements applicable in the national labour market, such as 'remuneration, including overtime rates' (Commission 2016).[33]

The EU Services Directive,[34] which was proposed originally to lay down the political and the legal foundation of across-the-board liberalisation in the entire integrated market for services, is the product of a genuine clash of capitalisms within the EU. It was claimed that its perceived impact before its adoption on local social models and public services, national labour law, and on the enforcement and supervision of the applicable local regulatory regimes in the home and the host Member States shed a clear light on 'different normative visions of what the EU's political economy should be about' (Copeland 2012). Its final version bore the mark of those divisions; its watered-down obligations reflected serious Member State resistance to the high risks of local de-institutionalisation as presented in the Commission's sweeping proposal (Höpner and Schäfer 2012). The Directive as adopted gave rise to analyses according to which the directive as an EU instrument, which traditionally had been used as a strict legal measure to induce institutional convergence (harmonisation) at the national level, now finds application as a policy tool, an instrument of political coordination capable of addressing and accommodating the economic, political and social tensions among the Member States (Wiberg 2014).[35]

The very recent proposal from the Commission, confirmed in a joint political proclamation at the Gothenburg Social Summit,[36] to develop a pillar for social rights in the EU (the EPSR), although it is far from clear what concrete obligations it will convey to the national level and in what form,[37] was developed with an acute understanding of the diversity of local varieties of capitalism and social models in

[31] Directive 2014/67 on the enforcement of Directive 96/71/EC concerning the posting of workers in the framework of the provision of services, [2014] OJ L159/11.

[32] Proposal for a Directive of the European Parliament and of the Council amending Directive 96/71/EC of the European Parliament and of the Council of 16 December 1996 concerning the posting of workers in the framework of the provision of services, COM (2016) 128 final.

[33] For a preliminary analysis, see Richard (2016).

[34] Directive 2006/123 on services in the internal market, [2006] OJ L376/36.

[35] The obligations of directives operate rather as binding incentives for the Member States to actively keep an eye on legal and regulatory frameworks, and thus their objectives are achieved by means of coordination instead of hard legal regulation or harmonisation, Wiberg (2014), p. 278. See, in connection with the Services Directive, Commission (2014).

[36] Proclamation of the European Pillar of Social Rights, Luxembourg: Publications Office of the EU (2017).

[37] See Commission (2017d).

the Member States.[38] The implementation of the 20 principles and rights listed, covering among others social protection, labour law standards, the protection of the unemployed, minimum pay and income, and access to essential services, which cut right to the heart of national economic and social policy, was declared to be subject to the division of competences between the Union and the Member States and to the express commitment that 'the diversity of the cultures and traditions of the peoples of Europe, as well as the national identities of the Member States and the organisation of their public authorities at national, regional and local levels' will be respected (Commission 2017a). The Commission made a further explicit commitment that the EPSR's implementation will not undermine the autonomy of the Member States to define the 'fundamental principles' of the national social security system and will avoid 'affecting' the financial equilibrium of those systems (Commission 2017a).

Although it has the potential to contradict national institutional arrangements and may damage the competitiveness of national economies, the EPSR does not give up at the outset the advancing of a common policy agenda and the introduction of common standards (Commission 2017a). It expresses a clear preference for constructing the Single Market as a highly competitive social market economy aiming at full employment and a high level of social protection, which model finds its origins in the objective-setting provision of Article 3(3) TEU. It talks about sustainable and further convergence in the social domain towards higher social standards, which objective was prioritised in the public consultation preceding the Commission proposal.[39] The Commission is also rather explicit about the EPSR, as a means of completing the Economic and Monetary Union, being driven not only by 'social necessity' but also by an 'economic imperative', which connects the EPSR to the visible agenda of institutional convergence ('deeper integration') under the EMU framework concerning national labour markets and systems of social protection pursuing the homogenising aim of establishing a 'fair and enforceable level-playing field'. The tying of the new framework to (mainstreaming it into) the European Semester framework, where its designated role is to counterbalance the now dominating growth-expectations, indicates that Member State performances will be regularly monitored on the basis of a common set of benchmarks.

Nevertheless, the EPSR readily admits that its expectations of institutional convergence in the social domain as necessitated by the long-term sustainability of EU economic governance need to be balanced against the earlier mentioned considerations of Member State autonomy and diversity. The Commission's explanations, addressing the question of how the diversity of local socio-economic arrangements may play out in its implementation, identify the EPSR as a mere 'reference framework' for locally initiated developments (Commission 2017b). It is also labelled as a 'dynamic instrument' which affords, having regard to local circumstances, a room for manoeuvring in its implementation. The constraints under this framework of

[38] See, in this regard, Esping-Andersen (1990), Scharpf (2002), Sapir (2006), Ter Haar and Copeland (2010), Copeland (2014).

[39] See Commission (2017d).

potential EU action, which in general was admitted to be rather limited in its scope, are openly discussed, which include in particular the 'specificies of national circumstances and institutional set-ups'.[40] The Commission also openly refuses to deliver the objectives of the EPSR by means of a '"one-size-fits all"' approach which would ignore the 'diversity of situations and the varying means available' in the Member States. With these, the EPSR reacted to the concerns revealed in the public consultations preceding its adoption.[41] These included demands that national must be fully respected, harmonisation of national social standards must be reduced to that absolutely necessary, and that local competitiveness and the sustainability of national public finances must not be jeopardised by unwarranted interventions driven by a common EU agenda.

The first legislative proposal produced under the new framework seems to have taken on board these limitations. The proposed directive on the 'work-life balance for parents and carers',[42] while it pursues an ambitious agenda of introducing common standards, contains several assurances that the autonomy and discretion of the Member States in the relevant domain will be respected. Its common standards, such as the laying down of common minimum requirements for leaves from work covered by its scope[43] and the regulation of common conditions for flexible working arrangements,[44] hold a clear potential for far-reaching intervention into domestic labour law imposing different burdens on different national regimes.[45] Nevertheless, the directive explicitly recognises that existing national arrangements for leaves from work and for flexible working arrangements for parents and carers will be respected and that the Member States may uphold provisions that are more favourable than those proposed or introduce higher domestic standards. This

[40]Further limitations include the presence of primary or exclusive Member State competences and national redistributive powers, as affected by financing capacities, which will be taken 'full account' of and will be fully respected in the course of the EPSR's implementation.

[41]See Commission (2017d).

[42]Proposal for a Directive on work-life balance for parents and carers and repealing Council Directive 2010/18/EU, COM (2017) 253 final.

[43]Article 4: a minimum of 10 working days paternity leave; Article 5: a minimum of 4 months of parental leave for each parent; Article 6: a minimum of 5 working days of carers' leave; Article 7: right to time off from work on grounds of force majeure. Article 8 poses the requirement of the Member States providing to workers on leave regulated in Articles 4, 5 or 6 a payment or an adequate allowance at least equivalent to what the worker concerned would receive in case of sick leave. Article 10 secures the employment rights of workers on leave under Articles 4, 5, or 6.

[44]Article 9: the right to request flexible working arrangements for parents and workers, the duration of which may be subject to a 'reasonable limitation'; the obligation of employers to consider and respond to such requests having regard to the needs of both employers and workers, and the obligation to justify refusals of such requests; the right to return to the original working pattern at the expiry of the flexible arrangement permitted and whenever 'a change of circumstances so justifies', and the corresponding obligation of employers to consider and respond to such request in light of the needs of both employers and workers.

[45]Variation within a single national regime may be a possibility as a result of the directive, as in case of the earlier mentioned Takeover Directive, on the basis of the opt-out offered to individuals and families from organising their lives according to the provisions of the directive.

provision—Article 16—in effect, contains an explicit prohibition on the deregulation of national standards so that they are levelled with those regulated in the directive. The proposal also contains a number of 'autonomy-protecting' clauses. Article 5 grants the Member States discretion to regulate in their own competences certain substantive and procedural conditions of parental leave. Article 7 makes it possible to delimit the right to time off from work on grounds of force majeure. Overall, it remains uncertain whether the Commission's proposal in its current form, which advocates considerable institutional convergence and recognises local discretion primarily when it serves objectives analogous to those of the directive, will be acceptable to national governments. They will be closely observing their political mandates, which demand maintaining the competitiveness of the national economy and securing policy leeway so that local interests and needs can be adequately addressed.

6.4 The Court and Member State Capitalism(s)

The Court of Justice's engagement in the construction of the Single Market, as indicated earlier, can be interpreted as involving a threat of 'de-institutionalising' national market economies. It may also be seen as capable of undermining the solutions secured in EU legislation for the accommodation of the diversity of local varieties of capitalism. For the implementation of the EPSR, it is an essential question whether the use of its mandate by the Court in fact destroys local institutional diversity, favours certain national models and jeopardises comparative advantages, or rather it entails targeted and adequately moderated interventions in the interest of achieving market integration. Under the EPSR, the Court's involvement will be framed by a number of parallel, potentially conflicting expectations. On the one hand, it will have to observe the explicit political intention that Member State competences, local institutional diversity and further local considerations pertaining to the financing and the operation of the national social system are respected. On the other, the Court must also have regard to the ambitious agenda, to be implemented in binding legal rules, of laying down common social standards for the Member States. Ultimately, both of these must be assessed in light of the imperatives formulated by the fundamental freedoms.

In order to have an understanding of the potential impact of the Court's involvement on local institutional diversity in such a complex political, policy and legal setting, it is necessary to revisit its previous jurisprudence where it laid down boundaries for its interventions capable of transforming institutions of Member State capitalism. The cases examined here concern the relationship of judicial power and the process and the outputs of political integration in the EU in the context of putting the Single Market into effect. In some instances, the matter was discussed candidly and directly in judicial reasoning indicating an understanding by the Court of the matters at stake. In a judgment closing an infringement procedure, the Court held that, as a matter of principle, the Treaty prohibitions enjoying enhanced normativity by means of direct effect 'are not sufficient in themselves to ensure the elimination of all obstacles' to the fundamental freedoms and the 'directives provided for by the Treaty in this matter preserve an important scope in the field of measures intended to make easier the effective exercise of the rights arising out of those provisions'.[46] On another occasion, it again confirmed that the implementation of the fundamental freedoms in the Member States through judicial enforcement must be assessed with reference to the political avenue regulated in the Treaties for their realisation[47] and held that the 'essential requirements' of the Single Market are supposed to be 'implemented' by means of EU directives.[48] In connection with freedom of establishment, the Court was prepared to recognise that the impact of deregulation in the Member States based on the enforcement of Treaty provisions may actually depend on the ability of the EU to regulate the particular domain, or to adopt rules that facilitate the exercise of Union rights.[49,50]

The Court's approach can look back on the original provisions of the EEC Treaty which accorded primary importance to implementing the fundamental freedoms by means of legislation adopted in the EU political process. Under ex Article 69 EEC, the freedom to provide services was regulated to be achieved through a progressive abolishment of restrictions during the transitional period and ex Article 63 EEC[51] tied that agenda to the Council producing a 'General Programme'[52] identifying the general conditions and stages under which liberalisation is achieved 'for each

---

[46]Para. 20, Case C-57/95 Commission v France EU:C:1997:164. This acceptance of the central relevance of the EU political process in the delivery of common policies led to the Court recognising a communication adopted pursuant a 'deadlock in the negotiations with Member States in the Council', which covered the subject-matter of a directive withdrawn by the Commission, as constituting an 'act intended to have legal effects of its own', paras. 21–25, ibid.

[47]Para. 12, Joined Cases 110 and 11/78, van Wesmael EU:C:1979:8.

[48]Para. 26, ibid.

[49]Paras. 10–13, Case C-340/89, Vlassopoulou EU:C:1991:193. The Court also accepted that in case EU directives 'provide for harmonization of the measure necessary to ensure the protection' of a ground for derogation, the derogation opportunity offered by the Treaty will no longer be available ('recourse to it is no longer justified') and 'the appropriate checks must be carried out and the measures of protection adopted within the framework outlined by the harmonising directive', para. 42, Case C-421/98, Commission v Spain EU:C:2000:646.

[50]In this connection, the Court confirmed that the EU institutions enjoy broad discretion as to the scheduling ('the stages') of legislative activity having regard to the difficulty of drawing up common rules when national rules are 'diverse' and 'complex' and having regard to the challenge of having those measures accepted by the Member States in the Council, paras10–11, Case C-63/89, Les Assurances EU:C.1991:152.

[51]The same rule provided that in case the 'General Programme' is not adopted, implementing directives are passed to 'complete one stage in the liberalisation of a specific service'. See also ex Article 54 EEC.

[52]General Programme for the abolition of restrictions on freedom to provide services, [1962] OJ 2/32. See also General Programme for the abolition of restrictions on the freedom of establishment, [1961] OJ 2/36.

category of services' by way of issuing directives.[53] Ex Article 64 EEC raised the possibility for the Member States to reach beyond the liberalisation obligations legislated in directives, but that possibility was made subject to the 'general economic situation' of the Member State concerned and the situation of the given sector. The EEC Treaty did, nevertheless, order in ex Article 65 that the central non-discrimination principle must be observed by the Member States even when the 'abolition of restrictions on the free supply of services has not been effected'. In regard capital movements, the Treaty regulated for a necessary and progressive abolishment of restrictions, which was to be achieved by the adoption of directives, first under unanimous vote, later by qualified majority (ex Articles 67–69).[54] Progression with liberalisation beyond what was required under the Treaty was permitted under ex Article 71 EEC depending on the condition of the national economy and the situation of the balance of payments in the Member State concerned.

The granting of direct effect to the relevant Treaty provisions, as the case of services and establishment shows, was directly exposed to the political intentions expressed in the Treaties.[55] The Court, following Treaty rules, recognised direct effect only after the expiry of the transitional period regulated in the Treaties for the adoption of the legislation required to implement the fundamental freedoms.[56] Its judgments can be interpreted as revealing the political intention that after that cut-off date the Treaty obligations will become 'unconditional'.[57] The different treatment accorded to the non-discrimination principle as a matter of its enforceability in the Member States, characterised as expressing a 'well-defined' obligation[58] which

[53]See also ex Articles 52, 54, 56 and 57 EEC concerning freedom of establishment. For workers, the categorically stated obligations of ex Article 48 EEC were followed by ex Article 49 holding that progressive liberalisation was to be achieved, especially in the specific regulatory areas identified by the Treaties, by way of adopting directives or regulations. Ex Article 51 EEC ordered the adoption of legislation under unanimity in the Council concerning the social protection of migrant workers.

[54]Ex Article 68 EEC ordered the application of the non-discrimination principle in respect of the Member States applying their domestic provisions on capital movements 'freed' in accordance with the Treaty in the capital market and credit system.

[55]See also the requirement that the provisions of EU legislation must be interpreted so as to achieve consistency with the relevant Treaty provisions rather than developing an interpretation 'which leads to it being incompatible with the Treaty', para. 15, Case 220/83, Commission v France EU:C:1986:461. See also paras. 69–70, Case 48/75, Royer EU:C:1976:57, concerning the discretion available to the Member States in the implementation of the particular directive and para. 15, Case 90/76, van Ameyde EU:C:1977:101, holding that specific harmonisation measures cannot be regarded as authorising national provisions or agreements which are incompatible with the Treaty provisions.

[56]Inter alia, para. 15, Case 81/87, Daily Mail EU:C:1988:456 and para. 19, Case 33/74, van Binsbergen EU:C:1974:131.

[57]Paras. 23–24, ibid. The applicability of the Treaty provisions was no longer 'conditional on the harmonization or the coordination of the laws of the Member States', para. 16, Case 220/83, Commission v France; para. 25, Case 205/84, Commission v Germany EU:C:1986:463.

[58]Para.26, Case 33/74, van Binsbergen, 'the fulfilment of which by the Member States cannot be delayed or jeopardised by the absence of provisions which were to be adopted in pursuance of powers conferred' under the Treaties. See also paras. 28–29, Case 2/74, Reyners EU:C:1974:68.

called for a sufficiently 'precise result',[59] can again be regarded as the Court following the intentions of the Treaty-makers, perhaps more closely than in the case of recognising direct effect for the full scope of the fundamental freedoms. The same consideration led to the Court declaring in this connection that apart from enforcing the requirement of non-discrimination it was still necessary for the Union to produce legislation enabling the exercise of the fundamental freedoms in the Member States.[60] In the case of capital movements, the same limitations were expressed even more categorically, when the jurisprudence established that the direct effect of what is now Article 63 TFEU depends on the Member States agreeing on the introduction of a general liberalisation obligation,[61] which took place first in the 1988 Capital Directive[62] and later in the Treaties.

In policy areas, in which implementation was reserved explicitly in the Treaties for the EU political process where national differences can be expressed and accommodated, the jurisprudence laid down largely similar limitations for judicial intervention. When the reservation was made in particularly clear terms, as in case of the common transport policy or the liberalisation of certain financial services involving capital movements, the Court, more or less consistently, refused to rely on direct effect to give effect to the Treaty's objectives. In regards transport services liberalisation, the Court acknowledged that Article 56 TFEU is subsidiary to the Treaty provisions on transport policy, which meant that the primary means of achieving the common objectives in the sector was the adoption of legislation as provided in the relevant Treaty rules.[63] As opposed to the general jurisprudence, the Court—on this basis—refused to acknowledge the direct effect of Article 56 TFEU.[64] When the relevant EU legislative measure had finally been adopted, the Court ruled, in harmony with its earlier mentioned case law determining the relationship between the fundamental freedoms and the legal measures adopted for their implementation, that economic operators are prevented from relying on the fundamental Treaty provisions and must resort to the rules of the relevant EU measure to secure their access to the transport market of another Member State.[65]

---

[59]Paras. 26–27, ibid. and para.12, Joined Cases 110 and 111/78, van Wesmael, the fulfilment of which was made easier by, 'but not made dependent on', the implementation of the Treaty's legislative programme.

[60]Paras. 30–31, Case 2/74, Reyners. See also para. 17, Case 11/77, Patrick EU:C:1977:113 in regard the delayed adoption of directives regulating the non-discrimination requirement.

[61]Contrast Case 203/80, Casati EU:C:1981:261 with para. 33, Case C-358/93, Bordessa EU:C:1995:54 and paras. 41–47, Joined Cases C-163, C-165 and C-250/95, Sanz de Lera EU:C:1995:451.

[62]Directive 88/361 for the implementation of Article 67 of the Treaty, [1988] OJ L178/5.

[63]Inter alia, para.62, Case 13/83, Parliament v Council EU:C:1985:220; paras. 8–9, Case 4/88, Lambregts EU:C:19898:320; para. 11, Case C-49/89, Corsica Ferries France EU:C:1989:649.

[64]Para. 63, Case 13/83, Parliament v Council; paras. 13–14, Case 4/88, Lambregts.

[65]Paras. 10–12, Case 4/88, Lambregts; paras. 13–14, Case C-49/89, Corsica Ferries France. This also meant that the Member States were allowed to maintain the restrictions on the freedom to

Article 58(3) TFEU provides that the liberalisation of banking and insurance services connected with movements of capital must be achieved according to the gradual, legislation-driven liberalisation agenda of the free movement of capital.[66] In this regard, the Court, paying close attention to the political intent thus expressed, insisted that where liberalisation had not been achieved by means of EU legislative activity the Member States may legitimately retain national measures designed to restrict capital movements without there being a possibility to contest those measures before courts under Article 56 TFEU.[67] It held, in particular that 'the only case in which the Treaty provisions on services do not apply to banking services is where there is a restriction on the free movement of capital relating to such transactions which is compatible' with EU law.[68] This conclusion is largely analogous to the general rule introduced by the Court under the free movement of capital that in policy areas governed in Member State competences the Treaty provisions are alone insufficient to require that the Member States adjust provisions of national regulation as such obligations may only arise from EU legislation adopted for the purpose of coordinating the relevant national rules.[69] In effect, the state of EU legislation in force at a given time governing the liberalisation of capital movements determines—as intended by the Treaties—whether a particular national restriction in the domains covered may need to be removed under EU law.[70]

As suggested earlier, the non-discrimination principle provided in various forms in the Treaties gave a robust empowerment to the Court of Justice to intervene at the national level even in instances when authorisation by EU legislation was

provide in services that were not covered by EU legislation, paras13–14, Corsica Ferries France (C-49/89).

[66]Generally, liberalisation under free movement of services cannot undermine the liberalisation programme under the free movement of capital and the liberalisation programme under the free movement of capital must not hinder the exercise of the freedom to provide services, paras. 19–20, Case 205/84, Commission v Germany.

[67]Para. 9, Case C-222/95, Parodi EU:C:1997:345.

[68]Paras. 8–10, ibid.

[69]Para. 11, Case 98/85, Bertini EU:C:1986:246. See also paras. 14–15, Case C-15/90, Middleburgh EU:C:1991:377 concerning the Member States' freedom to regulate social security entitlements in the context of freedom of movement in the absence of an EU measure to that effect. In Hervein, the advantageous or disadvantageous social security implications of exercising the right of establishment in the different Member States were held to be as not contravening Article 49 TFEU, paras. 50–51, Joined Cases C-393/99 and C-394/99, Hervein EU:C:2002:182. In contrast, when the matter regulated in national law has a direct basis in a generally applicable measure of EU law, the application of EU requirements faces no impediment, even when national laws diverge to a considerable degree, paras. 32–32, Case C-249/04, Allard EU:C:2005:329.

[70]Paras. 12–16, Case 98/85, Bertini. After the adoption of the 1988 Capital Directive, this meant that restrictions in these service domains were examined under the free movement of capital as well as under the freedom to provide services, para. 11, Case C-484/93, Svensson EU:C:1995:379.

absent.[71,72] The principle, indicating the availability of a clear and express intent by the Treaty-makers to achieve a fairly concrete outcome, enabled the Court to demand the transformation of local institutional setups without there being detailed instructions set out in legislation. For example, the Court felt licensed to rule in a transport policy setting that, from the perspective of the non-discrimination principle, the earlier noted agenda of progressive and gradual liberalisation through legislation fixed for the sector was 'without relevance'.[73] It also claimed that allowing the Member States, in the absence of the requisite legislative measures, to avoid their obligations made out clearly in Treaty 'would tantamount to rendering the extension of the freedom to provide services' to the transport sector 'to a substantial extent nugatory'.[74] In general, the jurisprudence has, however, accepted, in harmony with the general frame developed by the Court in this regard, that the non-discrimination requirement cannot alone ensure completely the achievement of the Treaty objectives and that the presence of restrictions, which may escape that requirement, necessitates EU legislative intervention facilitating the effective exercise of the fundamental freedoms.[75] The Court also raised that the availability of the non-discrimination principle does not allow the Member States to evade 'the obligation to implement a directive providing for specific measures to facilitate and secure the full application of that principle in the Member States.'[76]

The case law assessing the impact of EU legislation adopted to implement the fundamental freedoms on Member State derogations provides further indication as to how the Court interprets its mandate in areas where, apart from the core Treaty provisions, its intervention is subjected to further legal expressions of the relevant intent of the Member States. Consistent with the general approach, the poor state of (the lack of) EU measures regulating the area was regarded as securing greater freedom for the Member States to impose unilaterally, although subject to conditions, restrictions on free movement, without being required to take into account the availability of similar measures in the other Member States.[77] Such conclusions

[71]The interpretative formula that the fundamental freedoms and the measures adopted for the implementation of those provisions must be regarded as specific manifestations of that general principle (para. 6, Case 13/76, Donà EU:C:1976:115) allowed the Court to expand (clarify) the scope of application of the fundamental obligations arising from the non-discrimination requirement.

[72]See, in particular, paras. 29–31, Case C-164/94, Arantis EU:C:1996:23 discussing the applicability of the relevant EU directive and the non-discrimination principle in the circumstance when the particular economic activity was not subject to regulation at the national level.

[73]Para. 19, Case C-381/93, Commission v France EU:C:1994:370. Previous jurisprudence recognised the relevance of the central 'clearly defined' prohibition of discrimination in regards the implementation of the common transport policy, paras. 64–65, Case 13/83, Parliament v Council.

[74]Para. 20, Case C-381/93, Commission v France.

[75]Paras. 21–31, Case 2/74, Reyners.

[76]Para. 29, Case 29/84, Commission v Germany EU:C:1985:229.

[77]Para. 20, Case 220/83, Commission v France; para. 34, Case 205/84, Commission v Germany.

were, however, based on a careful analysis of the applicable legal rules. The Court evaluated in detail the relevant legislative provisions governing the application and the enforcement of EU obligations in the Member States and considered in particular whether common rules ('equivalent conditions and guarantees') were available in the EU and a sufficiently effective supervision of compliance with those rules was secured.[78] Its scrutiny focused essentially on the question of whether the state of EU legislation in the particular domain permitted that the Treaty provisions are used to transform the prevailing institutional framework in the affected national market.[79]

In contrast, in areas where EU legislative intervention was more robust and its substance governing matters, such as administrative cooperation among the Member States and the cross-border communication of administrative information, made the application of the relevance domestic rules unnecessary, the Court found much lesser limitations for it challenging local rules and institutions on the basis of Treaty provisions.[80] Its less constrained approach found support in the circumstance that the domestic regulatory and administrative frameworks threatened by 'de-institutionalisation' would be (should have been) replaced—at least in regards issues with a cross-border dimension—by that introduced by the applicable EU measure.[81] The rules of the applicable EU measure may also enable a closer scrutiny when they regulate the general interest ground raised to justify a derogation submitted by a Member State.[82] In such instances, the Court takes particular care to determine their actual impact, in particular in light of the level of harmonisation or coordination expected to be achieved at the national level. A similar approach is followed when the restrictive national measure was introduced to implement the provisions of the relevant EU legislative measure. The central issue examined in this regard is the

---

[78]Paras. 34–36, ibid.

[79]Para. 41, ibid. The Court recognised that an administrative regime (a licensing system), that is a genuine alternative in the EU of the Member States operating individually their own administrative and supervisory systems, may only be set up by means of legislative action at the EU level, and that until those common rules are introduced the Member States are entitled to retain local institutional frameworks governing national markets, with the condition that their operation does not entail the duplication of equivalent legal conditions and supervision in the different Member States, para.47, ibid.

[80]Paras. 61–62, 67–69, Joined Cases C-369/96 and C-376/96, Arblade EU:C:1999:575.

[81]Para. 79, ibid.

[82]Paras. 23–28, Case C-222/95, Parodi. The Court may determine the parameters that need to be taken into account by the national court when assessing the local impact of the relevant EU measure, in particular the issue of whether at the given time the Member State concerned may be permitted, despite the availability of common EU rules, to rely on general interest grounds of its own, paras. 26–27, ibid. In Essent, the Court set the interpretative scope for the general interest grounds on the basis of the relevant EU directive and was generally favourable to the grounds which coincided with the objective pursued by EU policy as defined that directive, which had been duly implemented in domestic law, paras. 58–65, Joined cases C-105/12–C-107/12 Essent EU:C:2013:677.

discretion guaranteed for the Member States in determining how (using what intensity of restrictions) to achieve the prescribed aims.[83]

6.5 Conclusions

Diversity among national varieties of capitalisms is a fundamental condition of EU market integration. It affects directly its implementation and imposes inescapable limitations on the conduct of the central actors of that process. Legislation adopted for the implementation of the Single Market is shaped by expectations that its provisions will be able to accommodate and, if possible, reconcile different local institutional setups. The application and the enforcement of Member State obligations by the Court of Justice are under pressure to avoid the unnecessary 'de-institutionalisation' of national market economies. For EU law, one of the central challenges is to draft legal provisions that satisfy these expectations and are, nevertheless, capable of realising the market integration objective, for instance by laying down common rules for the Member States. As the case of the EPSR shows, while this balancing between opposing imperatives may seem possible as a matter of political declarations, the balance manifested in the actual legal rules is in fact contestable. The main challenge for the jurisprudence of the Court in such environment is whether it is able to satisfy all relevant political expectations and determine the boundaries of its intervention accordingly. The robust practice developed in this regard indicates that even in such difficult setting as the EPSR the Court should be able to show due respect to different national models.

References

Amable B (2003) The diversity of modern capitalism. Oxford University Press

Biermeyer T (2011) EU company regulation between economic and social integration. In: Schiek D, Liebert U, Schneider H (eds) European economic and social constitutionalism after the treaty of Lisbon. Cambridge University Press, pp 148–173

Callaghan H, Höpner M (2005) European integration and the clash of capitalisms: political cleavages of takeover liberalization. Comp Eur Polit 3:307–332

Clift B (2009) The second time as farce? The EU takeover directive, the clash of capitalisms and the hamstrung harmonization of European (and French) corporate governance. J Common Mark Stud 47:55–77

Clift B (2013) Economic patriotism, the clash of capitalisms, and state aid in the European Union. J Ind Compet Trade 13:101–117

[83]Paras. 22–25, Case C-410/96, Ambry EU:C:1998:578. The usual benchmarks are applied: the national measure must be adequately targeted and there must not be less restrictive alternatives, paras. 32–34, 36–38, ibid.

Clift B, Woll C (2012) Economic patriotism: reinventing control over open markets. J Eur Publ Policy 19:307–323
Commission (2014) Staff Working Document: Work Plan for Reporting on National Reforms in Services Markets, SWD (2014) 131 final
Commission (2016) Proposal for a Directive Amending Directive 96/71/EC Concerning the Posting of Workers in the Framework of the Provision of Services, COM (2016) 128 final
Commission (2017a) Recommendation on the European Pillar of Social Rights, COM (2017) 2600 final
Commission (2017b) Communication Establishing a European Pillar of Social Rights, COM (2017) 250 final
Commission (2017c) Report on the Implementation by Member States of Directive 2003/88/EC Concerning Certain Aspects of the Organisation of Working Time, COM (2017) 254 final
Commission (2017d) Staff Working Document: Report of the Public Consultation Accompanying the Document Commission Communication Establishing a European Pillar of Social Rights, SWD (2017) 206 final
Copeland P (2012) EU enlargement, the clash of capitalisms and the European social model. Comp Eur Polit 10:476–504
Copeland P (2014) EU enlargement, the clash of capitalisms and the European social model. Manchester University Press
Crouch C (2005) Models of capitalism. New Polit Econ 10:439–456
Dawson M, Durana A (2017) Modes of flexibility: framework legislation v 'soft' law. In: de Witte B, Ott A, Vos E (eds) Between flexibility and disintegration: the trajectory of differentiation in EU law. Elgar Publishing, Cheltenham, pp 92–117
Deakin S (2006) Legal diversity and regulatory competition: which model for Europe? Eur Law J 12:440–454
Esping-Andersen G (1990) The three worlds of welfare capitalism. Polity Press, Cambridge
Farkas B (2016) Models of capitalism in the European Union: post-crisis perspectives. Palgrave, London
Hall PA, Soskice D (2001) An introduction to varieties of capitalism. In: Hall PA, Soskice D (eds) Varieties of capitalism: the institutional foundations of comparative advantage. Oxford University Press, pp 1–68
Hancké B, Rhodes M, Thatcher M (2007) Introduction: beyond varieties of capitalism. In: Hancké B, Rhodes M, Thatcher M (eds) Beyond varieties of capitalism: conflict, contradictions, and complementarities in the European economy. Oxford University Press, p 3–38
Hooghe L, Marks G (1997) The making of a polity: the struggle over European integration. EUI Robert Schumann Centre Working Paper No. 31
Höpner M, Schäfer A (2010) A new phase of European integration: organized capitalisms in post-Ricardian Europe. West Eur Polit 33:344–368
Höpner M, Schäfer A (2012) Integration among unequals: how the heterogeneity of European varieties of capitalism shapes the social and democratic potential of the EU. MPIfG Discussion Paper No. 12/5
Leino P (2017) Sovereignty and subordination: on the limits of EU economic policy coordination. Eur Law Rev 42:166–189
Menz G (2005) Varieties of capitalism and Europeanization: national response strategies to the single European market. Oxford University Press
Menz G (2010) Are you being served? Europeanizing and re-regulating the single market in services. J Eur Publ Policy 17:971–987
Richard S (2016) The reform of the Posted Workers Directive. Foundation Robert Schuman. European Issues No. 406
Sapir A (2006) Globalisation and the reform of the European social model. J Common Mark Stud 44:369–390
Scharpf F (2002) The European social model. J Common Mark Stud 40:645–670

Snell J (2012) Varieties of capitalism and the limits of European economic integration. Camb Yearb Eur Legal Stud 13:415–434
Ter Haar BP, Copeland P (2010) What are the future prospects for the European social model? An analysis of EU equal opportunities and employment policy. Eur Law J 16:273–291
Thatcher M (2013) Supranational neo-liberalization: the EU's regulatory model of economic markets. In: Schmidt VA, Thatcher M (eds) Resilient liberalism in Europe's political economy. Cambridge University Press, Cambridge, pp 171–200
Tridimas T (2011) Constitutional review of member state action: the virtues and vices of an incomplete jurisdiction. Int J Const Law 9:737–756
Weaver AM (2015) Convergence through the crisis: state aid modernization & West European varieties of capitalism. Columbia J Eur Law 21:587–614
Wiberg M (2014) The EU services directive: law or simply policy. TMC Asser Press, The Hague
Wincott D (2003) The idea of the European social model: limits and paradoxes of Europeanization. In: Featherstone K, Radaelli C (eds) The politics of Europeanization. Oxford University Press, pp 279–302

Chapter 7
South American Trade Policies Reconsidered: The "Convergence While Diversity" Mantra

Valentina Delich

7.1 Introduction

Although open regionalism in South America (SA) is still a legal base for trade and has been notably central in regional public political discourse, particular regional initiatives such the Andean Community of Nations and Mercosur had lost effectiveness since the beginning of the new century. This is quite astonishing since trade has expanded notably at least between 2003 and 2010.

Actually, it could be argued that South America has proceeded for at least 15 years according to two different projects: Pacific and Atlantic's. The Pacific project, led by Pacific Alliance's countries, would be more kind to sign FTAs and connect to Asian markets and the Atlantic one, pivoting on Mercosur, would be titled to a more European model of integration and therefore more reticent to include extra regional partners. Half a way, and broken apart as a result, the Andean Community of Nations.

Regional developments though, are framed within a global economy that still grieves and States striving for shaping new forms of global governance that take due care of the new scenario, namely the economic decline of the US, the European crisis (Brexit included), China's and India's emergence as important players, the loss of jobs out of the process of robotization, among others. From a South American perspective, it should be added the contraction of Chinese demand and the fall of commodities' prices and the Brazilian political and economic turnabouts.

Against this backdrop, Mercosur countries are reversing their trade policies to insert themselves more effectively in global value chains while Peru, Colombia and Chile are fine tuning them after the trade political turmoil caused by the United

V. Delich (✉)
University of Buenos Aires (UBA) and WTO Chair at FLACSO-Argentina, Buenos Aires, Argentina
e-mail: vdelich@flacso.org.ar

C. I. Nagy (ed.), *World Trade and Local Public Interest*, Studies in European Economic Law and Regulation 19, https://doi.org/10.1007/978-3-030-41920-2_7

States' retirement from the Trans Pacific Partnership (TPP). In addition, new trade talks, negotiations and debates exceed the quite simple tariff issue: they are about regulatory issues such as intellectual property rights, sanitary and phytosanitary standards, public procurement, data protection, among others. Since these areas traditionally pertain to States' discretionary power (they are considered to constitute States' policy space for implementing policies tackling down development or social needs) its negotiations at the international level questions fundamental notions on global governance, state sovereignty and regulatory autonomy.

In SA, trade issues are being addressed under the idea that is possible to converge throughout trade agreements or participation on common "institutional spaces" while keeping the regulatory margin of maneuver to implement different national policies. Also, that it is time for Mercosur to get flexible.

This piece discusses those ideas by first presenting the South American trade scenario; then, it moves to address the current situation of regional integration initiatives and negotiations underway; and, finally concludes with a reflection on such initiatives' prospects, highlighting its implications in terms of trade governance institutions.

7.2 South American Trade Scenario

South America had an extraordinary favorable cycle of growth between 2003 and 2010 due, grossly, to China's demand and commodities' high prices; then, it went smoothly through the global 2008 financial crisis. However, by 2014, deteriorated external conditions and domestic political turmoil shook Mercosur particularly: drove Argentina into international isolation and economic recession, submerged Brazil into an economic and political crisis and sunk Venezuela in a downward spiral of poverty and political violence. By now, and not without controversial domestic policies, Argentina and Brazil are expected to start recovering again while Venezuela constitutes a humanitarian catastrophe.[1]

As it can be seen in Fig. 7.1, SA exports had a very favorable cycle between 2003 and 2013 if measured by value which is consistent with having an

[1]For 2018, economic growth has been estimated at 1.2% in Latin America and the Caribbean, slightly down on the 1.3% achieved in 2017. Growth weakened both in South America (from 0.8% in 2017 to 0.6% in 2018) and in Central America, Cuba and Haiti (from 3.4% to 3.2%). Preliminary Overview of the Economies of Latin America and the Caribbean, Executive Summary, ECLAC, page 11, 2018, https://repositorio.cepal.org/bitstream/handle/11362/44327/122/S1801133_en.pdf.

In particular, Argentina's GDP has been positive from 2003 to 2011 (except 2009 due to the global financial crisis). After 2011, Argentina has been displaying interleaving positive and negative GDP: −1% in 2012, 2.4% in 2013, −2.5% in 2014, 2.7% in 2015, −1.8% in 2016, 2.9% 2007. Source: https://countryeconomy.com/gdp/argentin, visited on January 28 2019. Brazil, for its part, has had positive GDP rates while exceptionally negatives ones in 2015 and 2016. However, some years have exceptionally goods such as 2010 (7.5%) while others have been modest such as 2017 (1%). Source: https://countryeconomy.com/gdp/brazil visited on January 28, 2019.

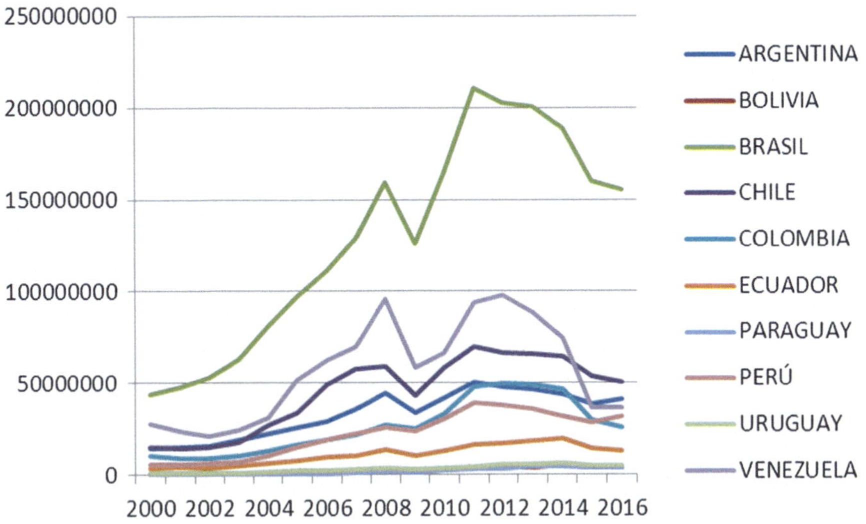

Fig. 7.1 Exports from SA to the World (including intra-trade) Value, U$S (thousands). Source: Own elaboration using IADB-INTAL database

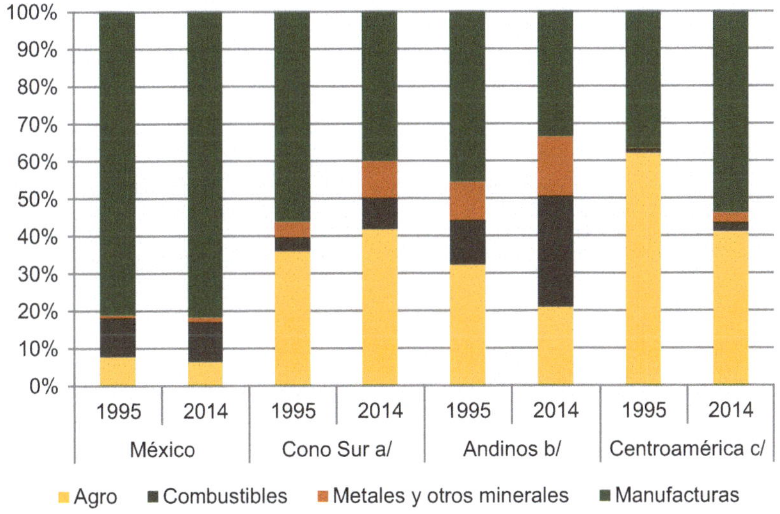

Fig. 7.2 SA Export Basket. Source: Carciofi and Gayá (2016). Venezuela and Dominican Republic not included

export basket dominated by commodities (Fig. 7.2) while enjoying high commodity prices (Fig. 7.3). Just to note, SA export basket is both grounded on commodities and concentrated in terms of proportion of exports covered by five products (Table 7.1).

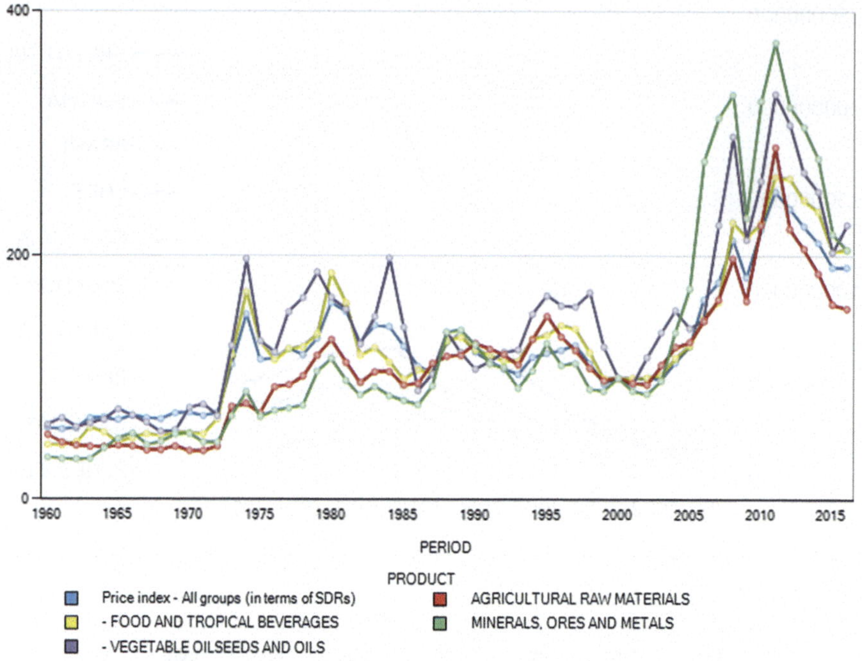

Fig. 7.3 MEASURE (PRICE INDICES 2000=100). Source UNCTAD http://unctadstat.unctad.org/wds/TableViewer/chartView.aspx

Table 7.1 Concentration of exports

Country	Proportion of exports covered by five main products in %	Herfindal-Hirschmann concentration Index for exports
Argentina	37.1%	0.05
Bolivia	75.4%	0.21
Brazil	32.9%	0.03
Chile	53.1%	0.1
Colombia	69.9%	0.15
Ecuador	74.3%	0.13
Paraguay	71.3%	0.13
Peru	46%	0.08
Uruguay	42.1%	0.05
Venezuela	97.7%	0.61

Source: IADB-Latinbarometro, visited on January 8, 2018

Furthermore, even with an expansion of exports during 2003–2010 measured by volume (Fig. 7.4), the expansion was more modest than other developing countries' (Figs. 7.5 and 7.6). As a result, SA trade expansion did not change its share of world trade (around 5%).

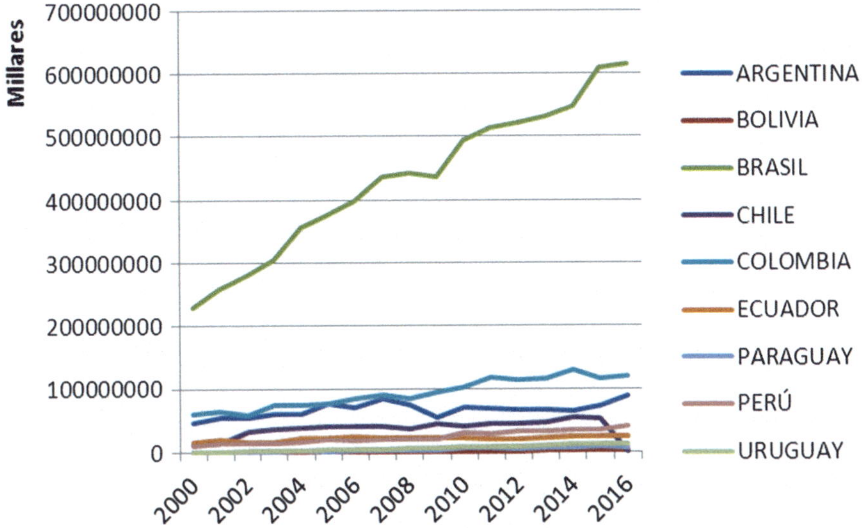

Fig. 7.4 Exports SA to World (including intra-trade) Volume (kg). Source: Own elaboration from IADB-Intal database. Venezuela excluded due to lack of data and Chile's value of year 2016 repeated for 2017 due to lack of data

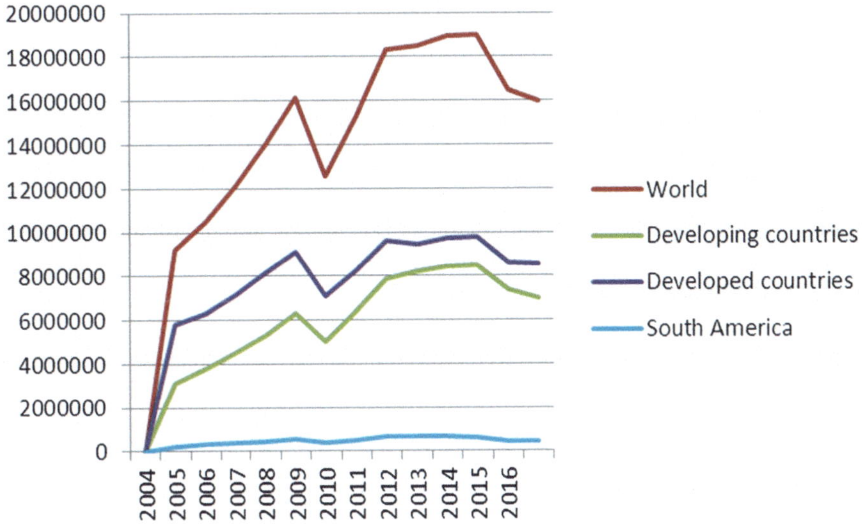

Fig. 7.5 Share of world trade. Exports. US Dollars at current price in millions. Source: own elaboration/data from UNCTAD

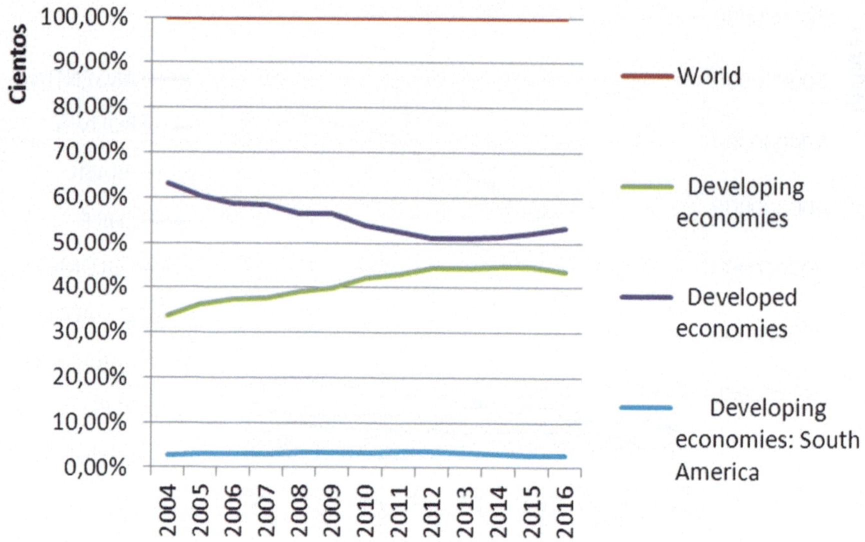

Fig. 7.6 Flow exports percentage of total world. Source: Own elaboration/data from UNCTAD

In addition, intraregional trade is poor (Fig. 7.9): it has the same level than in the 1990s, when has not declined in some cases.

7.3 Free Market Commodity Price Indices, Annual, 1960–2016

In Fig. 7.4 that follow it can be seen that SA exports grew also in volume, but since the rest of the world (and particularly developing countries) also grew, SA share in world trade did not change. Nor in volume (Fig. 7.4) neither in value (Fig. 7.5) or percentage (around 5%, Fig. 7.6).

Figure 7.6 shows clearly how developing countries did better than South America in terms of participation in world trade.

According to the most recent data, the total value of exports from Latin America and the Caribbean (LAC) grew at an estimated 9.9% in 2018 (compared to the 12.2% in 2017). Prices remained the main driving force in a context of low growth in export volumes. In 2018, the performance of LAC trade was relatively worse than that of global trade. The performance of LAC exports is mainly explained by lower growth in South America and, to a lesser extent, in Central America, partially offset by the vibrancy of exports from Mexico and the Caribbean. The slower growth in exports was essentially driven by a moderation, and in some cases a decline, of commodity prices (IADB 2019).

South America, particularly, recorded an estimated increase in exports value of 8.9% in 2018, after experiencing a 15.1% expansion in 2017. However, the value of exports is still 20% below the record high of 2011. The slowdown in the growth rate is explained by low export volumes and the reversal of price trends for some of the commodities exported. Exports to China played a major role in defining this scenario: although these grew at a lower rate than in 2017, they still outstripped the average growth rate by more than twofold and accounted for half of the total growth in the value of South American exports (IADB 2019).

Consistently, as it can be seen in Figs. 7.7 and 7.8, Andean countries exports in fuels and mineral declined to the world but recovered to China and also—although lesser—to the world (Fig. 7.7) while Mercosur data shows the importance of China's demand (Fig. 7.8).

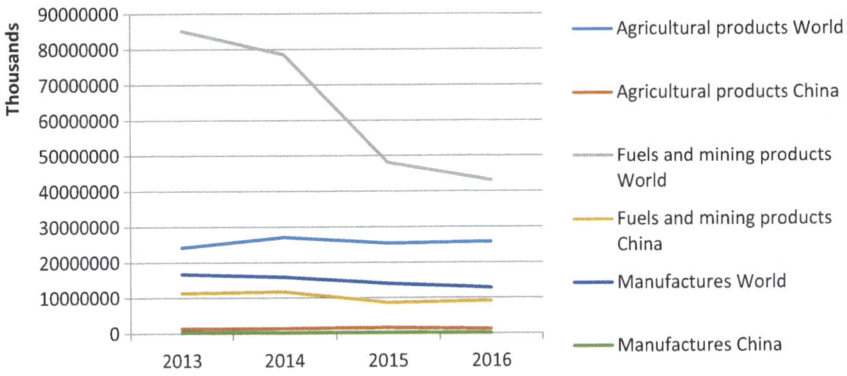

Fig. 7.7 Andean Community of Nations, Composition of Exports to the World and China. Source: World Trade Organization

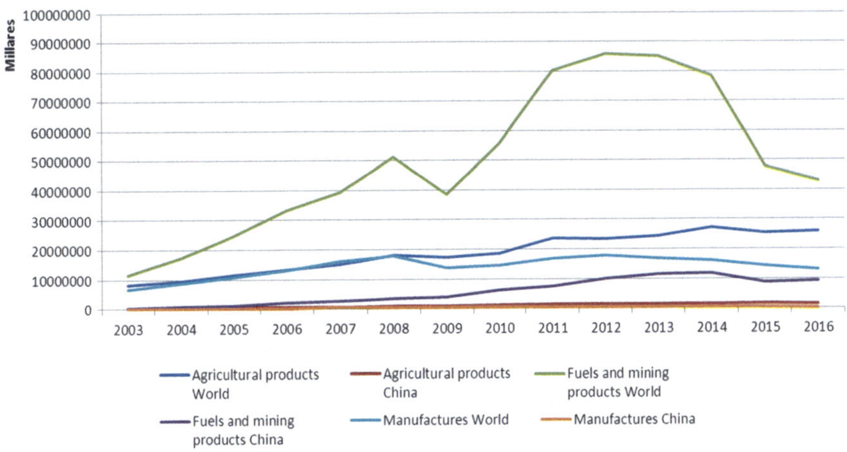

Fig. 7.8 Mercosur Composition exports/to the World and China. Source: World Trade Organisation

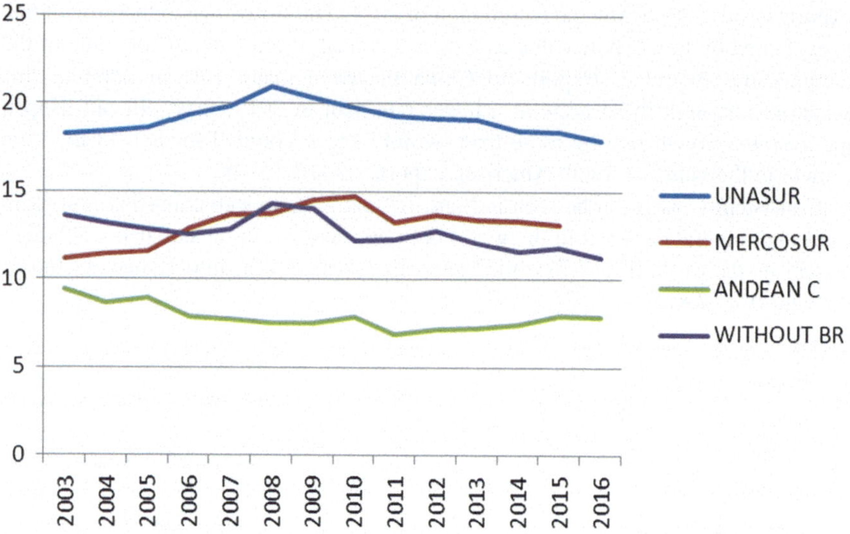

Fig. 7.9 Intra-Trade Exports %, per destination UNCTAD. Source: Own elaboration /data from UNCTAD Note: UNASUR include all South American countries

Last but not least, SA trade expansion was not caused by or ended in an increase in intraregional trade. As it can be seen in Fig. 7.9, intraregional trade kept at the same level of the 1990s when not declined. An explanation could be found in similar factor endowment, shocks recurrence, macroeconomic instability, high transportation costs and low investment in infrastructure (Carciofi and Gayá 2016).

7.4 Regional Trade Initiatives

South America has two well established regional trade integration initiatives: MERCOSUR (1991) formed by Argentina, Brazil, Paraguay and Uruguay (Venezuela's membership is suspended since 2016) and the Andean Community of Nations (ACN, 1969) constituted by Peru, Ecuador, Colombia and Bolivia. Chile, for its side, stands as the pioneer of a liberal trade policy in our region. Just to note, Chile was part of the ACN but abandoned it in the 1970s due to their regulations over multinational corporations (among other policy discrepancies). In addition, all South American countries are bound by ALADI (1980), a trade scheme including all Latin American countries that covers partial preferential agreements among them (i.e. trade liberalization agreements over a small number of products or just one sector). The very last initiative in the region is the Alliance of the Pacific (2011), uniting Chile, Colombia, Mexico and Peru.

Since the beginning of this century and even with trade expansion, neither Mercosur nor the ACN had deepened. Instead, Venezuela left the Andean

Community and entered Mercosur; then, the other Andean countries individually signed FTAS with the US (Peru and Colombia) and the European Union (Peru and Colombia on the one hand and Ecuador on the other); in addition, Mexico, Chile, Peru, and Colombia created the Pacific Alliance; furthermore, ALBA (Bolivarian Alliance for America) was created uniting Venezuela, Cuba, Bolivia, Ecuador and Nicaragua among others. In turn, Chile signed fourteen FTAs including those with Australia, China, the US and Vietnam. Mercosur froze all trade negotiations except for the inclusion of Venezuela. And last but not least, Chile, Peru and Mexico were part of the Trans Pacific Partnership Agreement (TPPA) negotiations between 2008 and 2015.

Hence, it has been argued that South America has become the land of at least two projects: the Pacific—more open to sign free trade agreements including notoriously Asian countries—and the Atlantic pivoting on Mercosur—reticent to a more open trade policy and focusing on its institutional, political or social agenda-. The very last development, of interest of this piece, is Mercosur reorientation of its trade policy to open to the world and, at the regional level, work towards the convergence with the Alliance of the Pacific (Fig. 7.10).

Some additional notes might shed light on the dynamics of regional trade agreements in South America.

First, in respect to Mercosur: since the graph shows agreements in force, those recently negotiated and signed are not reflected, notably Mercosur-European Union (2019) and Mercosur-EFTA (2019). Nor are included those agreements that are no RTAs but PTAs (Preferential Trade Agreements) and so they are notified under the Enabling Clause and do not cover substantial trade between Members. This is the case for Mercosur-Southern African Customs Union (SACU) from 2016, Mercosur-

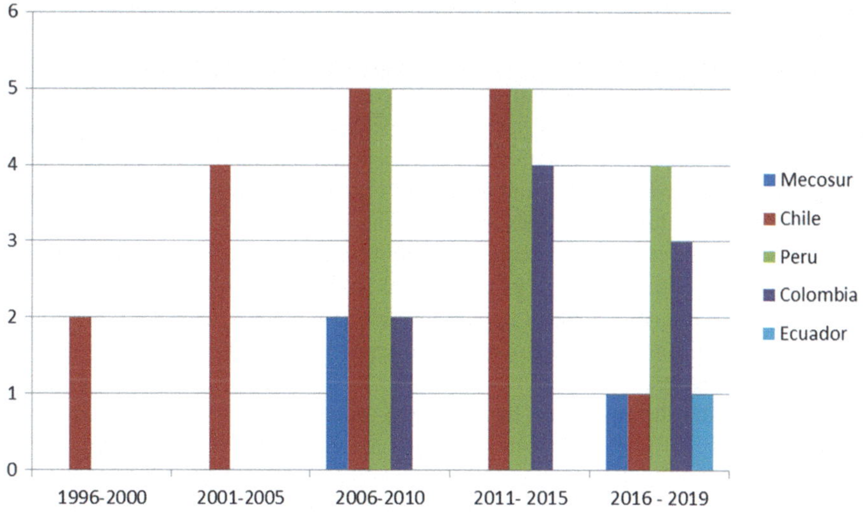

Fig. 7.10 South America, Regional Trade Agreements (Art. XXIV, in force). Source: Own elaboration out of WTO RTAs Database, http://rtais.wto.org/UI/PublicAllRTAList.aspx

Mexico, 2016, Mercosur-Chile 2017 and Mercosur-India, 2009. In addition, it must be noted that RTAs signed by Mercosur in the period 1990–2019 although already in force, they are not significant in terms of amount of trade involved: neither Israel (in force since 2009) or Egypt (in force since 2017) are significant trade partners.

Second, in the case of Ecuador, the only RTA in force is the one signed with the European Union, but it is still in provisional application while Ecuador has negotiated and signed with EFTA (2018) and with the United Kingdom (2019) but they are not in force.

Finally, it is important to remark that Bolivia is not in the graph because is a member of the Andean Community (1969) and associate member of MERCOSUR (and thus it does not benefit of Mercosur's RTAs). All the other trade agreements Bolivia has signed are not RTAs but PTAs, restricted to particular sectors or products.

7.4.1 The Atlantic project

The Atlantic project pivots around Mercosur, which dates back to 1991. Since then, South America has undergone profound makeovers of its economic, political and social profile and policies: from indebted to lenders countries (for some time at least), from negative to positive rates of growth, from the Washington consensus model to a more local model of development (including populism forms), among others. Mercosur has been part and parcel of these changes but has consolidated in the political discourse and social imaginary as a "strategic" regional project towards the creation of a common market. In fact, according to a public opinion survey performed by INTAL-Latinbarometro all over Latin America, to the question "Are you in favor or against integrating the countries of our region?, answers "Strongly in favor" and "very much in favour" receives more than 80% support.[2]

Mercosur is an "open regionalism" endeavor, meaning that is not intended to build up a trade fortress nor it is part of an import substitution policy. Accordingly, Mercosur trade liberalization among its members (Argentina, Brazil, Uruguay and Paraguay) proceeded very fast and with few exceptions: in 4 years (1991–1994) liberalization was almost complete among its members and by 1999 even tariffs of few items included in a list of exceptions were brought down to 0%. In addition, in 1994, Mercosur successfully negotiated—although never fully implemented—a common external tariff. Trade in agriculture was completely liberalized among its members with the only exception of sugar: no special calendars or safeguards nor list of excluded products.

However, after the successful liberalization process among members, Mercosur found extremely difficult to deepen its economic integration process: in part due to divergent economic policies with Brazil (Argentina kept fixed the convertibility of

[2]http://www19.iadb.org/intal/alianzalb/reporte.php. Accessed 5 March 2019.

its currency to US dollar while Brazil devaluated in January 1999) in part by the Argentinean crash of 2001–2002. All in all, after 2003 and for many years, Mercosur countries performed very well if considered individually but those results never translated into a deepening of Mercosur. In this sense, against a backdrop of economic growth and expansion of trade, and motivated by the airs of renovation of its political leaders, Mercosur was re-launched at the Asuncion Summit (2006) with the participation of Venezuela and Bolivia as guest countries. This re-launching stressed the need to deepen the political dimension of Mercosur and thus, its agenda was built upon issues such as the democratic compromise, protection of human rights, etc. Since then, the Mercosur agenda is often worked upon as "Political Mercosur", "Productive Mercosur" and "Social Mercosur".

In reviewing Mercosur developments between 2003 and 2015, it stands out that: intra-regional trade has followed the ups and downs of trade to the rest of world; in terms of regulations and disciplines the common agenda was frozen; the extra regional trade agenda did not advance[3]; in terms of Members' political relationship, Brazil's role and interests as a global player brought about discrepancies at regional and international fora[4]; furthermore, conflicts arouse as the financial crisis developed: Mercosur's countries did not coordinate in any way their response and also found very difficult to deal with their own provisional but protectionist measures; in terms of international trade policy, Members strongly disagreed: Paraguay did not want to accept Venezuela's incorporation to Mercosur, negotiations with the European Union were pushed by Brazil while cooled by Argentina, and Uruguay wanted to negotiate and eventually sign a FTA with the US or to be part of the Pacific Alliance (in fact Uruguay became observer in 2012). By 2015, as the economic situation deteriorated in Brazil and Argentina, conflicts were solved by Presidents, Ministers or brought to court, but none Mercosur's institutional instance proved either active or effective to solve conflicts. Even if true that Mercosur passed many norms regulating important social and institutional matters, most of them never operationalized.

While one part of the literature blamed Mercosur's lack of supranational character, the other alleged lack of flexibility. In fact, Mercosur institutional architecture is often characterized as "soft" or "flexible" since all organs are intergovernmental and decisions are made by unanimous consensus. What is not flexible is the possibility of negotiating Free Trade Agreements individually. In effect, Mercosur has three main decision instances and in all of them it is necessary the consensus of all members to take a binding decision, i.e. to create a norm. Although Mercosur institutional setting has been modified many times, the heart of the decision-making process has remained: all members' consensus for binding decisions and the need of all Members' "internalization or incorporation" of Mercosur norms at the domestic level in order to become operative.

---

[3]Except for a minor agreement with Israel.

[4]See for instance Brazilian and Argentinean positions at the WTO.

The need to strengthen Mercosur's institutional architecture, in particular its norm's creation and implementation mechanism, has been widely documented both by academics and official Mercosur's documents.[5] The main problem remains the gap between created norms and internalized norms (created and implemented commitments). Would it make the difference either voting in the norms making process or given them direct effect?

Finally, a trade policy shift begun both in Argentina and Brazil when President Macri took office in Argentina in December 2015 and Temer in Brazil in August 2016. In the case of President Macri, its foreign policy of "inserting Argentina into the world again" brought about Argentina's being host of the World Trade Organization Eleven Ministerial Conference in Buenos Aires in December 2017, getting the Presidency of the G20 during 2018, re-launching the Mercosur-European Union negotiations, starting the process of OECD membership, and powering negotiations with Mexico, Chile and Canada, among others. In Brazil, Temer is also pushing the process of Brazilian membership to the OECD, revamped Brazilian relationship with the US and the EU and supported the suspension of Venezuela from Mercosur. Last but not least, in relation to the object of this piece, both Temer and Macri promote Mercosur's rapprochement to the Pacific Alliance and by now, with President Bolsonario in Brasil since January 1st 2019, the flexibility of Mercosur.

7.4.2 The Pacific Project

The Pacific Project involves Chile, part of the Andean Community of Nations (Peru and Colombia) and Mexico. Their common vision is reflected in the Pacific Alliance initiative, although they converged from different trajectories.

In effect, when former US President Bush's Free Trade Area in the Americas (FTAA) initiative conceded and eventually collapsed,[6] Andean countries befell under US pressure to negotiate an FTA. While originally all three Colombia, Peru and Ecuador started conversations with the US in 2004, 2 years later, Ecuador step out.

US-Andean negotiations proceeded (and still do for Ecuador) under the influence of the Andean Trade Preferences Agreements (later on ATPDEA, Andean Trade Preferences for Drug Eradication Agreement), a law according to which some Andean products have US market access without tariffs. ATPA started in 1991 and was renewed until 2001 when it was converted into ATPDEA (and finally renewed until 2010).

[5]See, among many others, Bouzas and Fanelli (2001), Peña and Rozemberg (2005), pp. 45–62. Czar de Zalduendo (2003), p. 109. Dreyzin de Klor and Fernández Arroyo (undated), and FESUR (2004).

[6]By 2003, the FTAA, a former US President Bush initiative, was almost dead. Negotiations with the EU were set aside while China started a very active trade and investment policy in SA. In this context, the US pressed for FTA negotiations both to Central American and Andean countries.

As ATPDEA preferences were not consolidated but unilaterally given and renewed by the US, Andean countries were interested in locking in those preferences in an FTA. However, negotiating a FTA with the US would prove to have at least two main problems from the point of view of the Andean regional project: first, since there was no consensus among all ACP members to negotiate, the ACP would have to break down its common external trade policy and consent that some Members will have preferential trade with extra regional partners.

Second, the US proposed FTA included regulatory matters and standards, particularly some that the US had tried to advance at the multilateral level with no success. This is the case of intellectual property rights, where the US demanded for the extension for patents in case of administrative delays or/and granting exclusive rights for data protection. In these cases, Andean countries did have Andean community law and thus, had not only to modify national norms but Andean's.

In this line of thought, the preservation of the Andean legal base was quite difficult both because FTAs' tariff preferences affect the Common External Tariff and regulatory standards have in fact prevailed over Andean Community norms.[7] In a way, the ACN has "flexibilized" itself as far as its Members have individual and different FTAs and ACN norms had been modified to become compatible with FTAs standards. And this kind of flexibility is at the heart of the Pacific Alliance core idea: it is possible to add up or piling on initiatives, projects, preferences, and agreements.

Last but not least, in the Andean space to have the US in meant to have Venezuela out.[8]

In contrast to the Andean countries, Chile's itinerary to the Pacific Alliance is characterized by a continuing policy of openness. In effect, Chile started a process of unilateral liberalization by which tariffs decreased from 11% in 1991 to around 6% in 2003.

According to Alejandro Jara, Chile has used all means to open its economy: unilateral, bilateral, plurilateral and multilateral. Jara highlights some milestones: first, the Mexico-Chile Agreement in 1991 because it sent a strong signal to the private sector: as in Mercosur, liberalization did proceed in 4 years including almost all trade with few exceptions. Still, that first Chilean international agreement had minimal regulatory standards or disciplines. The second milestone was when negotiations to join NAFTA fell at almost its starting point: Chile responded negotiating an FTA with Canada, which became the first agreement that brought in services and

[7]The US Colombia Trade Promotion Agreement was signed in 2006 and it went into effect in 2012. It is worth mentioning that Colombia, as Ecuador, exports flowers and textiles to the US. Thus, as ATPDEA expired for Ecuador in 2013, Ecuador needed a FTA with the US to recover the preference and be on equal foot with Colombia. The Peruvian-US FTA was signed in 2006 and went into force in 2009.

[8]The ACN has a common Foreign Policy as set up in the Trujillo Protocol (1996). In the trade realm, Decision 322 restricted FTA negotiations by requiring full consensus. However, according to the new norm, Decision 598, countries may proceed with negotiations while preserving the ACN legal base and taking due account of other Members sensibilities. This flexibility of the ACN norm is what allow to have individual FTAs.

investment on board. And once the Free Trade of The Americas project collapsed, Chile was the first country in the region to sign an FTA with the US in 2003 including intellectual property rights, services and government procurement, among others issues. Also, by the end of the 1990s Chile started the first negotiation with an Asian partner, Korea, which was ready by 2002 (Jara 2005). Meanwhile and afterwards Chilean trade agreements flourished: Ecuador (1995), Peru (1998), Mercosur (1996), Bolivia (1993), EFTA (2004), China (2006), Hong Kong (2014), Turkey (2011), Vietnam (2014) and Thailand (2015) among others.

In turn, the Pacific Alliance (PA) itself was created in 2011 (formalized in 2012 through the so-called Framework Agreement). Rather than being a "traditional" FTA, it started and remains as a mechanism intended to build up economic and political initiatives. The objective would be to foster growth, trade and social inclusion. All Members share an active trade policy in terms of FTAs: Chile do have twenty-five, Colombia thirteen, and Peru and Mexico twenty each.

The PA is legally structured around the Framework Agreement that delineates its objectives and sets its institutional structure in 17 articles. In 2014, an Additional Protocol was signed that, in terms of matters covered, is much more comprehensive than former FTAs.

PA's institutional dynamics relies in Presidential Summits, a Ministers' Conseil (Trade Ministers) and high—level Groups (that in turn supervise Working Groups).[9] By now, it has more than fifty observer countries from all continents.

The PA main characteristic is that it is compatible with existing agreements or future trade agreements. In particular, the Framework Agreement recognizes that Peru and Colombia, because of its ACP Membership, do have ACP commitments to comply with. And so, firms may choose and use any available legal umbrella to trade: PA or ACP, whichever gives them more benefits.

As said, the Additional Protocol is where trade and trade related issues are elaborated. But it might be recalled that trade is already highly liberalized among its Members, particularly between Colombia and Peru due to the ACN existence. Just to note, 92% of goods have free access within the AP. In the case of Colombia, for instance, 100% of the Peruvian goods have free access because of the ACN and 95% of goods coming from Mexico as well. However, for Chile the AP makes a difference because only 2.4% of its exports to Colombia were free of tariffs.

Among the most praised feature of the PA is the rule of origin clause, according to which "origin" could be accumulated. As a result, it is possible to accumulate the percentage of origin among the four countries: in a given product, inputs from any PA country could be used to comply with the origin rule and be exported to any of its members. Interestingly enough, a recent study that compares rules of origin of different agreements, found that the PA rules of origin are not necessarily the most

[9]Institutional Issues, Trade and Integration, Experts Committee (deals with the private sector proposals), Public Procurement, Cooperation, Culture, Education, Communication Strategy, Gender, Innovation, Mining, Business Persons' mobility, Intellectual Property, SMEs, Services and Investments, International Fiscal Transparency, Tourism.

beneficial and that exporters should check for the specific product before making a decision (Concha et al. 2016).

Also, the PA chapter on government procurement has called the attention: when commitments among countries already existed, countries negotiated increasing the number of governmental agencies included or covered. In cases where a Member includes a new agency to favor a PA Member, this new advantage has to be given to the others (kind of most favored clause for government procurement).

The dominant official and public discourse around the PA is that it advances through soft law, thorough small but operative initiatives: for instance, the PA has created a platform for student mobility, a network of researchers on climate change, business rounds, etc.

Just to close this section, a geopolitical consideration: the Trans Pacific Partner Alliance put forward by the US (TPPA) excluded China; the RCEP put forward by China excluded the US; and, the Pacific Alliance, put forward by Mexico and others excluded Brazil.

7.5 Reflections Under Uncertainty

In a global context of incertitude, of trade governance reconfiguration and stress over trade institutions, trade negotiations are underway in South America. The dominant idea in leaders and institutions' discourses is "to converge" while keeping "diversity" in order to bridge the gap between the Atlantic and the Pacific project. Also, that Mercosur particularly requires flexibility in order to connect more efficiently to the world.

As we have seen, Latin America has a strong history of integration and regional initiatives, each one with its own theoretical premises and preferred policy actions. While the first wave, so called "old regionalism", proceeded under the idea of import substitution policies and supranational common institutions and norms, the second was marked by the idea of "open regionalism", open understood as compatible with multilateralism and intergovernmental institutions characterized by a consensus-based decision-making process.

Against this backdrop, while Mercosur was designed, thought and always considered soft or flexible, if compared to the European Union model or to previous Latin American experiences, nowadays is considered too restrictive of its partners' trade policy options, in particular, in terms of its external trade policy.

In effect and as said, Mercosur has a Common External Tariff (CET) in place since 1995 that takes away countries' power to set up or change unilaterally tariffs. While the multilateral commitment for most goods is at a 35% level, Mercosur CET is at around 16%. Therefore, and if Mercosur CET were not binding, there would be space to accommodate tariffs both to higher and lower tariffs as needed (although it must be said that there is a list of 300 products for each country that are CET-exempted).

Additionally, and also related to FTAs negotiations, there is a Mercosur norm (CMC 32/00) according to which Members commit themselves to negotiate together trade agreements in which tariffs preferences are given. Brazil seems to need flexibility to negotiate with the US and Uruguay with China.

Meanwhile, Mercosur has revived FTA negotiations with the European Union and initiated ones with EFTA, Canada and Korea. Mercosur's legal requirement to negotiate in bloc when harmonization of its Members' macroeconomic and trade policies as well as trade related disciplines are low produces a constant search, on the Mercosur side, of its minimum common ground. Accordingly, this common ground translates in or is expressed by very "defensive" positions due to Mercosur's different in productive structure and legal regulatory standards.

Without any doubt, negotiations between Mercosur and the European Union are the most comprehensive of all, if only because they have been undergoing for more than 15 years. Very sensitive issues at the negotiations constitute the European position on the automotive industry, geographical indications, intellectual property and maritime navigation. In turn, Mercosur focuses on market access for its food products. While some of these issues are only or mostly of European interest—IGs for instance—and therefore they do not arise in other negotiations, issues such as intellectual property have a wider impact.

In effect, since the Agreement on Trade Related aspects on Intellectual Property Rights (TRIPS Agreement) only foresees the exception to the Most Favored Clause to what was already in place by the time of its signature (1995), any extension given over TRIPs standards must be given to all WTO Members.

In this line, as Chile, Colombia and Peru (and Ecuador will join soon) do already have FTAs with the US and the European Union, they have regulations and standards that Mercosur has not yet (and might never have). And among the most conflictive standards are those related to intellectual property rights. Both the US and the EU have obtained, among others, the strengthening of IP enforcement, the extension of patents in case of administrative delays and exclusivity rights for test data protection, all TRIPs plus standards. While it could be argued that since those countries do not have a solid or significant domestic pharmaceutical industry these standards do not heavily impact on the configuration of their national market, it must be noted the impact of strengthening and extending exclusive rights over pharmaceutical and agrochemical products prices and State's health policies.

Hence convergence (keeping diversity) between Mercosur and the Pacific Alliance may advance using their common ground and piling up initiatives, with no great impact on trade and/or regulatory standards over its Member countries. In contrast, Mercosur flexibility, Mercosur negotiations with the European Union and the Pacific Alliance trade external policy, in particular the implementation of the Progressive TPP, might change Latin American trade landscape. Let's see.

First, the flexibility issue. As seen in the case of the Andean Community, "flexibility" meant to accept trade discrimination through its Members' bilateral negotiations of tariffs with their extra regional partners. Flexibility meant also that Andean norms were modified to make them compatible with the negotiated regulatory standards in the FTAs.

In the same vein, Mercosur flexibility could mean to reconfigure Mercosur as an FTA instead of a custom union. We do not find this trade reconfiguration too dramatic since the Common External Tariff in Mercosur even if existent, allowed for exceptions and it was never fully operationalized: imports cannot move freely in the Mercosur area. And some of the still praised and dynamic portion of intra trade, namely the automotive bargain between Brazil and Argentina, is a trade deal not only previous to Mercosur existence but, by now, industries are highly integrated. However, since Mercosur is so deeply anchored as a valuable common integration project in our societies, special care would be necessary not only to preserve its symbolic power but also to use it to fuel a new and more modern endeavor instead of destroying what has been built.

Second, the impact of Mercosur's ongoing negotiations. Mercosur negotiations with the European Union, or EFTA or Korea, just to illustrate, are not only or mostly about tariffs. Crucially, they are about regulatory standards (intellectual property, sanitary, government procurement, just to name a few). Standards do stress domestic public policies in Latin America: if proposed or negotiated regulatory standards are too high, they might exclude or consolidate the exclusion of lagged economic sectors; if they are too low, they might fail incentivizing technological up grading. The problem then is that in economies having both economic sectors and fields already globalized (where international standards are not a problem) and some not able to effectively compete regionally or globally, across the board high regulatory standards become very problematic.

Third, the effect of the Pacific Project trade policy. As said, the so-called Pacific Project's countries do have a very active trade policy in terms of signing trade agreements. One the consequences, seen from a Mercosur perspective, for instance, is that as those countries grant preferential treatment to extra regional partners, Mercosur can find itself losing regional markets. Therefore, in addition to the existent FTAs, once the PTPP is in place, other countries such as New Zealand and Australia will have better access conditions to many markets, competing directly with South American countries such as Argentina.

References

Bouzas R, Fanelli JM (2001) Mercosur: integración y crecimiento. Fundación OSDE, Buenos Aires

Carciofi R, Gayá R (2016) El comercio exterior de América Latina: Aspectos salientes de su desempeño desde la creación de la OMC. Paper, Cátedra OMC, FLACSO- Argentina

Concha V, Heilbron JRD, Suarez MA (2016) Análisis Comparativo de Reglas de Origen en la Alianza Pacífico y en los TLC de los Países Miembros. J Bus 8(1):2–34. Universidad del Pacifico, Colombia. http://revistas.up.edu.pe/index.php/business/article/view/74/75. Accessed 3 Mar 2019

Czar de Zalduendo S (2003) La institucionalización en los acuerdos regionales: el caso del MERCOSUR. In: Basevi G, Donato V, O'Connell A (eds) Efectos reales de la integración regional en la Unión Europea y el MERCOSUR. Ed. de la Universidad de Bologna, Buenos Aires

Dreyzin de Klor A, Fernández Arroyo D (undated) Avances y fracasos de los esquemas subregionales latinoamericanos. El caso del MERCOSUR. Suplemento mensual de Derecho Internacional Privado y de la Integración, Diario Jurídico elDial

FESUR (2004) Desafíos institucionales para el MERCOSUR: las relaciones entre estados, instituciones comunes y organizaciones de la sociedad. http://www.redmercosur.net/encuentro2004/ouro_preto_10_anos_despues/Desafios_institucionales_MERCOSUR.pdf. Accessed 3 Mar 2019

IADB (2019) Trade Trends Estimates, Latin America and the Caribbean, Edition 2019. Paolo Giordano (coordination), IADB. https://publications.iadb.org/publications/english/document/Trade-trends-estimates-latin-america-and-the-caribbean-2019-edition.pdf. Accessed 3 Mar 2019

Jara A (2005) Las virtudes de la promiscuidad: la apertura comercial de Chile. In: Estevadeordal A, Torrent Antoni R (eds) Regionalismo Global, Los dilemas para América Latina, Fundación CIDOB, Barcelona, Spain

Peña C, Rozemberg R (2005) MERCOSUR ¿una experiencia de desarrollo institucional sustentable?. Revista de Comercio Exterior e Integración, marzo. http://cei.mrecic.gov.ar/revista/02/parte%203-2.pdf. Accessed 3 Mar 2019

Part III

Chapter 8
The Supreme Court's Attempts Via Its Dormant Commerce Clause Jurisprudence to Navigate State Police Power and National Free Trade: Potential Lessons for International Trade

Lee J. Strang

8.1 Introduction

This Essay makes two modest moves. First, it identifies the circuitous path of the United States Supreme Court's Dormant Commerce Clause case law.[1] I describe the different legal doctrines and tests utilized by the U.S. Supreme Court since the beginning of the Republic to navigate the tension between, on the one hand, the reserved police power of individual states to regulate in their citizens' interests and, on the other hand, the Interstate Commerce Clause's grant of power to the federal government to make the United States free from interstate trade barriers.

Second, I suggest three potential lessons from the Supreme Court's experience for international free trade arrangements.[2] First, the Supreme Court's Dormant Commerce Clause case law shows that the line between legitimate state regulation in its citizens' interest and illegitimate state regulation of interstate commerce, is intractable. Second, the Supreme Court's Dormant Commerce Clause case law suggests that there is a relationship between institutional competence and the efficacy of different modes of analysis to ascertain whether a state regulation is legitimate or

Thank you to Professor Csongor Nagy for organizing this conference and inviting me to speak, for the conference participants' comments and suggestions, and for valuable research assistance by Jacob Williams.

[1]For an excellent comprehensive treatise on the Dormant Commerce Clause, see Denning (2017). For a thoughtful review on the history of the Supreme Court's Dormant Commerce Clause case law see Francis (2017), pp. 272–277.

[2]Let me sound a word of caution before proceeding. My expertise is in American constitutional law, so my goal is to contribute to the conversation on international trade agreements from that perspective.

L. J. Strang (✉)
University of Toledo College of Law, Toledo, OH, USA
e-mail: lee.strang@utoledo.edu

C. I. Nagy (ed.), *World Trade and Local Public Interest*, Studies in European Economic Law and Regulation 19, https://doi.org/10.1007/978-3-030-41920-2_8

illegitimate. Third, the Court's Dormant Commerce Clause case law shows the influence of different conceptions of sovereignty on the Court's analysis.

8.2 The U.S. Supreme Court's Dormant Commerce Clause Case Law Has Struggled to Identify Principled Mechanisms to Navigate the Tension Between Legitimate State Regulation in Its Citizens' Interest and Illegitimate Interference with Interstate Commerce

8.2.1 Introduction

In this Part, I describe the Supreme Court's numerous and different attempts to navigate the tensions between state police power and federal regulation of interstate commerce.[3]

First, however, let me briefly note how using the Dormant Commerce Clause as a model—both for good and for ill—for international trade makes sense, and for at least three reasons. First, the Dormant Commerce Clause regulates a large, diverse, federal system that possesses many of the same characteristics as international trade systems. Different American states value and prioritize goods differently.[4] For instance, California prioritizes environmental goods while Iowa prioritizes agricultural production. This intra-United States diversity is analogous to, though less robust than, the diversity faced in international trade regimes. Additionally, states within the United States retain a share of legal authority within the overall constitutional system separate from the federal government and protected by the Constitution.[5] This is comparable to, though lesser than, the legal authority and autonomy of parties to international trade agreements.

Second, the Supreme Court has employed the Dormant Commerce Clause for nearly two-hundred years,[6] giving it significant experience from which to draw, and providing a lengthy track record from which its various approaches may be evaluated. This is nearly four times longer than the relatively shorter experience of post-WW II international free trade agreements.

[3]For an overview of the Dormant Commerce Clause's history see Redish (1995), pp. 63–98.

[4]See McGinnis (2012), p. 115 (arguing that federalism allows states to experiment with different approaches to human flourishing); McGinnis and Somin (2004), pp. 106–107 (identifying federalism's capacity to cater to a diversity of preferences); see also Eskridge (2005), pp. 1293–1294 (describing the deep and increasing pluralism within the United States).

[5]See Texas v. White 74 U.S. 700, 725 (1868) ("The Constitution, in all its provisions, looks to an indestructible Union, composed of indestructible States.").

[6]The first clear Dormant Commerce Clause Case was Gibbons v. Ogden, 22 U.S. (9 Wheat.) 1 (1824).

Third, the Dormant Commerce Clause doctrine has evolved significantly over this time period so that different regulatory regimes are available for analysis.[7] Each of these different doctrinal analyses employed by the Supreme Court offer different costs and benefits.

8.2.2 *The Interstate Commerce Clause Was a Response to Problems Not Addressed by the Articles of Confederation*

The Articles of Confederation was the United States' first constitution, and it created a relatively weak central government.[8] For example, the Confederation Congress did not possess executive or judicial branches,[9] so it faced major challenges enforcing and applying its law.[10]

One of the key powers the Articles government did not possess was the ability to regulate interstate commerce.[11] This led to interstate squabbling over taxes and restrictions on goods traveling to and from other states,[12] which threatened the political stability of the fledgling United States and facilitated conflicts like Shay's Rebellion.[13]

Fearing the political disunity that the lack of national regulation of interstate commerce was creating, prominent Americans met in 1786 at the Annapolis Convention, in Maryland, called by James Madison.[14] Madison called the convention to propose and discuss amendments to the Articles.[15] In particular, Madison sought the powers to tax and to regulate interstate commerce.[16]

Unfortunately—or fortunately, for those of us who are fans of the U.S. Constitution!—only five of the thirteen states sent representatives,[17] so the

---

[7]I describe four different tests employed by the Supreme Court. Some scholars have characterized this history in slightly different ways. E.g., Francis (2017), pp. 272–302.

[8]See Freedman (1994), p. 786 ("The conventional view of the period between the Declaration of Independence and the Constitution, a view that has remained unchanged except in detail for nearly one hundred years, is that the country came to the very brink of dying in infancy.").

[9]Articles of Confederation (1778). In: Frohnen B (ed) The American Republic: Primary Sources 200.2002.

[10]See Freedman (1994), p. 786 (summarizing this conventional view).

[11]See Articles of Confederation IX (1778). In: Frohnen B (ed) The American Republic: Primary Sources 200.2002. (listing only the power of "regulating the trade and managing all affairs with the Indians").

[12]Clinton (1990), pp. 893–894, 896–897.

[13]Ibid 896–897; Johnson (1997), pp. 187–188.

[14]Clinton (1990), p. 897; Johnson (1997), p. 185.

[15]Clinton (1990), p. 897; Johnson (1997), p. 185.

[16]Johnson (1997), p. 185.

[17]Clinton (1990), p. 897; Johnson (1997), p. 185.

Convention was unable to conduct any meaningful business. The Convention, however, did produce a report, which it submitted to the Confederation Congress.[18] The Convention's report issued a call for "a general meeting[] of the States, in a future Convention, for the [purpose of interstate trade] and such other purposes, as the situation of public affairs may be found to require."[19]

The Framers of the current United States Constitution met in Philadelphia beginning in May, 1787,[20] and one of their key goals and changes they made from the Articles was empowering the new federal government to regulate interstate commerce. Located in Article I, Section 8, of the Constitution, where most of Congress' powers are located, the Interstate Commerce Clause grants to Congress the power to "regulate Commerce . . . among the several States."[21]

The Interstate Commerce Clause was part of a broader debate in the Constitutional Convention on the extent to which—it was not a question of whether—state regulation of interstate commerce should be limited.[22] There was a consensus among the Framers that the lack of such a power in the Confederation Congress had stifled commerce and resulted in unhealthy interstate rivalry. For example, in *Federalist 42*, James Madison noted that "[t]he defect of power in the existing confederacy to regulate the commerce between its several members [has] been clearly pointed out by experience. . . . . We may be assured by past experience that such a practise would be introduced by future contrivances [] and . . . that it would nourish unceasing animosities and not improbably terminate in serious interruptions of the public tranquility."[23] The Framers likewise argued that a federal power to regulate commerce would promote interstate trade and reduce interstate disunion. Alexander Hamilton, for instance, claimed in *Federalist 11* that "[a]n unrestrained intercourse between the states themselves will advance the trade of each by an interchange of their respective productions, not only for the supply of reciprocal wants at home, but for exportation to foreign markets."[24]

The history surrounding the drafting and ratification of the Commerce Clause also suggests that states would retain some regulatory authority over some of the same matters that Congress could regulate under its Interstate Commerce Clause authority, but no clear line was identified.[25] In James Madison's view, expressed during the Philadelphia Convention, the existence of the Commerce Clause itself would

[18]Proceedings of the Commissioners to Remedy Defects of the Federal Government (Sept. 14, 1786). Reprinted in: Commager HS (ed) Documents of American History 132. 1958.

[19]Ibid 133–134.

[20]Clinton (1990), p. 897; Johnson (1997), p. 186.

[21]U.S. Const., art. I, § 8, cl. 3.

[22]Clinton (1990), pp. 906–907.

[23]Madison (1788).

[24]Hamilton (1787).

[25]See Friedman and Deacon (2011), p. 1916 ("[N]o one at the Convention or thereafter has doubted that the states retained a wide range of powers and that they might exercise those powers in such a way that looked like a regulation of commerce.").

completely bar states from imposing a tax with extraterritorial effect.[26] Roger Sherman from Connecticut, and the progenitor of the express restrictions on states in what became Article I, Section 10, disagreed, stating that a concurrent jurisdiction of the federal and state governments on commerce will exist.[27] Sherman appeared to win the debate, and the Convention adopted Art. I, Section 10, Clause 1, which prohibits state taxation of imports and exports.[28] This prohibition assumes that states would have had the power to regulate commerce if Art. I, Section 10, did not exist.[29]

States that ratified the Constitution reduced and, in some cases, eliminated many facets of their authority over their citizens. State authority over trade with other states is an example of this. However, states retained all their authority not surrendered via the Constitution to the federal government.[30] For example, states retained their authority to protect their citizens' health. This retention of significant legal authority was made explicit textually in the Tenth Amendment[31] and is an implication of the constitutional principles of limited and enumerated powers,[32] and federalism.[33]

As I describe next, the U.S. Supreme Court used the textual grant of power to Congress, along with this historical background, to fashion its Dormant Commerce Clause doctrine as a restriction on states. However, the textual vagueness of the scope of the Commerce Clause's implied exclusion of state regulatory authority, coupled with the history and text of Article I, Section 10, and retained state powers, made it unclear how much state regulation was barred by the Constitution. Consequently, the Supreme Court continually struggled to identify a principled line.

8.2.3 The U.S. Supreme Court's Dormant Commerce Clause Jurisprudence Struggled to Identify Principled Mechanisms to Navigate the Tension Between Legitimate State Regulation in its Citizens' Interest and Illegitimate Interference with Interstate Commerce

The Supreme Court has utilized at least four different tests since 1824 to distinguish between constitutional and unconstitutional state regulation that affects interstate

[26]Madison (1787).

[27]Ibid.

[28]U.S. Const., art. I, § 10, cl. 1.

[29]Friedman and Deacon (2011), p. 1913.

[30]See Gibbons v. Ogden, 22 U.S. (9 Wheat.) 1, 81 (1824) ("[T]he States retain powers enabling them to pass the laws to which allusion has been made, not that those laws proceed from the particular power which has been delegated to Congress.").

[31]U.S. Const., amend. X.

[32]The Healthcare Cases, 567 U.S. 519, 531 (2012) ("In our federal system, the National Government possesses only limited powers; the States and the people retain the remainder.").

[33]United States v. Lopez, 514 U.S. 549, 552 (1995).

commerce. These four tests are: (1) the police power test; (2) local-national test; (3) the direct-effects test; and (4) the current doctrine. I discuss each in turn.

The first test, employed by the Court under Chief Justice John Marshall in the early nineteenth century, was the police power test.[34] But first, a short explanatory note on the concept of "police power."[35] In the American constitutional system, a state's police power is its inherent authority to regulate in the interests of its citizens' health, safety, and morals.[36] For example, American states prescribe speed limits on highways for their citizens' safety, and these laws are authorized by the states' police power. As a distinct concept in American constitutional law, it stretches back to the early nineteenth century,[37] and has its roots in English law,[38] and older roots in the Middle Ages concept of the common good,[39] and Roman law.[40]

Though *Gibbons v. Ogden* was primarily a case about the scope of Congress' *Interstate* Commerce Clause power, the Marshall Court also articulated the Dormant Commerce Clause for the first time.[41] In *Gibbons*' foundational description of the Dormant Commerce Clause, Chief Justice Marshall first argued that Congress' interstate commerce power was exclusive; that states could not regulate the subject of interstate commerce.[42] But, he went on to identify a category of state regulations that, though they affected interstate commerce, were still consistent with the Constitution, because these regulations were different—they were "police" power regulations.[43] Marshall summarized this relationship:

> That inspection laws may have a remote and considerable influence on commerce, will not be denied; but that a power to regulate commerce is the source from which the right to pass them is derived, cannot be admitted. . . They form a portion of that immense mass of legislation, which embraces every thing within the territory of a State, not surrendered to the general government: all which can be most advantageously exercised by the States themselves. Inspection laws, quarantine laws, health laws of every description, as well as laws for regulating the internal commerce of a State, and those which respect turnpike roads, ferries, &c., are component parts of this mass.[44]

Chief Justice Marshall concluded that the distinction between a (n unconstitutional) regulation of interstate commerce and a (constitutional) police power regulation was the state law's purpose.[45] For example, a state law's purpose to

[34]Francis (2017), pp. 273–275.

[35]See Barros (2004), pp. 473–498 (describing the history of the concept).

[36]New York v. Miln, 36 U.S. (11 Pet.) 102, 133 (1837).

[37]Brown v. Maryland, 25 U.S. (12 Wheat.) 419, 442–443 (1827).

[38]Blackstone Sir (1769b), p. 162.

[39]Legarre (2007), p. 763.

[40]Ibid 749.

[41]Gibbons, 22 U.S. (9 Wheat.), at 61.

[42]Ibid 201.

[43]Ibid 203.

[44]Ibid.

[45]Ibid 204–206.

restrict the import of or increase the price of out-of-state competitor goods was commerce, while a state law's purpose to protect its citizens' health, even if it hindered the importation of or increased the price of out-of-state competitor goods, was police.

This police power test possessed a number of virtues. It protected a free trade zone among the states by carving out a zone of interstate trade protected from direct and intentional state regulation. It preserved both federal and state power. The new national government's capacity to remedy the Articles of Confederation's key defect was maintained while, at the same time, states could continue to protect their citizens so long as they did not purposefully harm interstate commerce. Third, the police power test preserved a robust conception of federalism. Under the Marshall Court's dual federalism, the federal and state governments possessed analytically distinct and non-overlapping powers, and the police power test demarcated the line between federal and state power in the commerce context.

This virtue also opens the door to the police power test's corresponding vices. First, and most problematically, its line between federal and state power was vague. Whether a particular law was passed for a police power purpose is difficult to discern both because it is frequently difficult to discern legislative purposes and also because what counts as a police power purpose is imprecise. The police power test presumes that a state regulation that affects interstate commerce is—despite that negative effect—constitutional, which opens the question of "how much?" How much of a negative effect on interstate commerce must exist before it becomes reasonable to conclude that the ostensible police power purpose was a sham, and that the real purpose was to create the negative effect on interstate commerce? The test's vagueness also opened the door to the criticism that it was (capable of being) applied in an unprincipled manner. Judges could manipulate the police power test to further ends outside of the law, such as economic or ideological goals.[46]

The second Dormant Commerce Clause test, created by the Supreme Court under Chief Justice Taney in the mid-nineteenth century,[47] was the local-national test. The local-national test prescribed that states could regulate subjects that are "local" in nature—that is, subjects that do not need a uniform national rule—while states could not regulate "national" subjects—that is, subjects that need a one-size-fits-all rule. As stated by Justice Curtis in his majority opinion in the 1851 case of *Cooley v. Board of Wardens*: "whatever subjects are in their nature national, or admit only of one uniform system, or plan of regulation, may justly be said to be of such a nature

---

[46]See, e.g., Wilson v. The Black Bird Creek Marsh Co., 27 U.S. (2 Pet.) 245, 252 (1829) (stating, in one sentence, that a state-authorized bridge across a navigable water did not violate the Dormant Commerce Clause because "[w]e do not think that the act empowering the Black Bird Creek Marsh Company to place a dam across the creek, can, under all the circumstances of the case, be considered as repugnant to the power to regulate commerce in its dormant state, or as being in conflict with any law passed on the subject.").

[47]For an overview of the Taney Court, see Swisher (1974). For a biography of Chief Justice Taney, see Swisher (1935).

as to require exclusive legislation by Congress."[48] The Supreme Court in *Cooley* went on to hold that pilotage laws were inherently local because of the variety of local conditions at different ports across the nation.[49]

This local-national test abandoned the Marshall Court's focus on state purposes for the—to its mind—more reliable focus on the subjects of regulation. The Taney Court created the local-national test for two reasons. First, the local-national test was a response to the vagueness of the police power test. The Court in *Cooley* specifically identified some of the problems caused by this lack of clarity: "The diversities of opinion, therefore, which have existed on this subject, have arisen from the different views taken of the nature of this power."[50] Second, the Taney Court adopted the local-national test as part of its rejection of the Marshall Court's refusal to countenance any state regulatory authority over interstate commerce. Unlike *Gibbons*, where the Marshall Court stated (albeit in dicta) that states could not regulate interstate commerce in any way, in *Cooley*, the Court acknowledged that the Pennsylvania regulation—a "pilotage law" regulating by whom and how ships were brought into port—was a regulation of interstate commerce.[51]

The local-national test possessed a number of virtues. Like the police power test, it preserved both federal and state power. The national government had exclusive authority over subjects that needed uniform regulation, while states could regulate other subjects in their citizens' interest. Relatedly and, again, like the police power test, the local-national test continued the dual-federalism conception of federalism. The federal government had exclusive authority over subjects that necessitated uniformity, while states possessed presumptive authority over subjects that permitted a diversity of approaches.[52]

The local-national test also possessed a number of vices. First, it was relatively less protective of free trade because it allowed states to regulate activity that was

[48]Cooley v. Board of Wardens, 53 U.S. (12 How.) 299, 319 (1851).

[49]Ibid.

[50]Ibid.

[51]Ibid 319–320.

[52]However, the local-national test allowed for jurisdictional overlap between federal and state authority of interstate commerce that did not require a uniform rule. States could regulate such interstate commerce so long as and until the federal government permitted it. This made state authority over "local" subjects the default and presumptive, but rebuttable by congressional legislation. See Sinnot v. Davenport, 63 U.S. (22 How.) 227, 243–244 (1859) ("Beyond these limits the States have not surrendered their power over the subject, and may exercise it independently of any control or interference of the General Government; and there has been much controversy, and probably will continue to be, both by the bench and the bar, in fixing the true boundary line between the power of Congress under the commercial grant and the power reserved to the States. But in all these discussions, or nearly all of them, it has been admitted, that if the act of Congress fell clearly within the power conferred upon that body by the Constitution, there was an end of the controversy. The law of Congress was supreme.").

clearly interstate commerce.[53] This fit the Taney Court's broader jurisprudential perspective, which was relatively more state oriented and less nationalist than the Marshall Court. Second, and again like the police power test, the local-national test was vague and, consequently, subject to manipulation. Reasonable minds could and did disagree about whether a subject was local or national in nature and whether it required a uniform rule or permitted (or required) local variation. This vagueness opened the door to criticism of judicial misapplication or manipulation of the test to achieve ends desired for non-legal reasons.[54]

The third test, utilized by the Supreme Court with increasing clarity over the late-nineteenth and early twentieth centuries, was the direct-effects test.[55] Under this test, state regulation that directly affected interstate commerce violated the Constitution, while state regulation that indirectly affected interstate commerce was constitutional.[56] For example, in the 1927 case of *Di Santo v. Pennsylvania*, the Taft Court ruled that a state could not regulate the sale of tickets for ocean-going steamships because the tickets were directly related to interstate and international commerce.[57]

The direct-effects test retained the prior tests' virtues and vices. It protected free trade, guarded federal and state power, and preserved dual federalism. The direct-effects test also was vague and subject to misapplication and manipulation.[58]

---

[53]Doctrinally, this was clearly a change from the police power test; however, it is not clear in practice how much of a change it was because the police power test permitted laws to affect interstate commerce and still be upheld.

[54]For potential examples, see Conway v. Taylor's Executor, 66 U.S. (1 Black) 603 (1861) (ruling that Kentucky's regulation of ferries on the Ohio river from the Kentucky side of the river did not violate the Dormant Commerce Clause); Henderson v. New York, 92 U.S. (2 Otto) 259, 273 (1875) (concluding that nationwide uniformity was required regarding laws governing the landing of foreign passengers on U.S. soil).

[55]E.g., Mo. Pac. Ry. Co. v. Kansas, 216 U.S. 262, 276 (1910); Kidd v. Pearson, 128 U.S. 1, 11 (1888); Hall v. De Cuir, 95 U.S. (5 Otto) 485, 488 (1877).

[56]The direct-effects test in the Dormant Commerce Clause context was the analytical sibling of the same test in the Interstate Commerce Clause context. There, the Supreme Court ruled that Congress could regulate intrastate activity that directly affected interstate commerce, and that Congress could not regulate intrastate activity that indirectly affected interstate commerce. United States v. E.C. Knight Co., 156 U.S. 1, 12 (1895).

[57]Di Santo v. Pennsylvania, 273 U.S. 34, 37 (1927).

[58]See Hall, 95 U.S. (5 Otto) 488 ("The line which separates the powers of the States from this exclusive power of Congress is not always distinctly marked, and oftentimes it is not easy to determine on which side a particular case belongs. Judges not unfrequently differ in their reasons for a decision in which they concur. Under such circumstances it would be a useless task to undertake to fix an arbitrary rule by which the line must in all cases be located. It is far better to leave a matter of such delicacy to be settled in each case upon a view of the particular rights involved.").

As with many areas of American constitutional law,[59] the fourth Dormant Commerce Clause test developed during and since the New Deal.[60] Modern Dormant Commerce Clause doctrine has two key components.[61] First, for those state regulations that discriminate against out-of-state commercial interests, the state has the burden of establishing that the regulation directly advances an important state interest.[62] Second, for those state regulations that affect interstate commerce, but do so in a nondiscriminatory manner, the burden of persuasion is on the regulation's challenger to show that the regulation does not advance a legitimate state interest and that the regulation's harm to interstate commerce outweighs its benefit to the state.[63]

Under modern doctrine, therefore, the most important question is whether the state regulation favors in-state economic interests by discriminating against out-of-state interests. A state regulation that affects interstate commerce can be discriminatory if: (1) the text of the law discriminates against out-of-state interests; (2) the law's effect is to discriminate against out-of-state commercial interests; or (3) the law's purpose is to protect in-state interests at the expense of out-of-state interests.[64] In practice, if the state regulation is discriminatory, it is nearly always declared unconstitutional, unless the state has strong evidence supporting its reason for enacting it. In fact, the nearly unique example of the Supreme Court upholding a discriminatory state law is where Maine provided evidence that its law barring the importation of small fish into the state was necessary to preserve native fish species.[65]

If the state regulation is nondiscriminatory, it is usually held constitutional. For example, the Supreme Court upheld a state regulation identifying the maximum width of vehicles on its roads because, though the law affected interstate commerce, it applied neutrally and was passed for the purpose of highway safety.[66]

The current doctrine possesses a number of virtues. In practice, it has preserved both federal and state power, prevented the most egregious restrictions on interstate

[59]See Ackerman (1998), pp. 345–382 (describing the "amendments" to the Constitution that occurred during the New Deal).

[60]South Carolina St. Hwy. Dep't v. Barnwell Bros., 303 U.S. 177 (1938); Southern Pac. Co. v. Arizona, 325 U.S. 761 (1945).

[61]Hunt v. Washington State Apple Advert. Comm'n, 432 U.S. 333 (1977).

[62]Ibid 353.

[63]Pike v. Bruce Church, Inc., 397 U.S. 137, 142 (1970); Bibb v. Navajo Freight Lines, Inc., 359 U.S. 520, 524 (1959); Kassel v. Consolidated Freightways Corp. of Delaware, 450 U.S. 662, 670 (1981).

[64]Dean Milk Co. v. Madison, 340 U.S. 349, 354 (1951); Bacchus Imports, Ltd. v. Dias, 468 U.S. 263, 272 (1983).

[65]Maine v. Taylor, 477 U.S. 131, 146–151 (1986).

[66]South Carolina St. Hwy. Dep't v. Barnwell Bros., 303 U.S. 177 (1938); compare Bibb v. Navajo Freight Lines, Inc., 359 U.S. 520 (1959) (holding that an Illinois law requiring "contour" rear mud flaps on truck and trailers, though nondiscriminatory, violated the Dormant Commerce Clause because of its disproportionate burden on interstate commerce).

commerce, and preserved federalism. It also possessed a number of vices including ambiguity and a corresponding malleability.

8.2.4 *Conclusion*

In sum, the United States Supreme Court has employed four different analyses over the course of nearly two-hundred years to navigate the shoals of, on the one hand, protecting interstate commerce while, on the other hand, preserveing the capacity of both state and federal governments to legislate as they see fit in their respective spheres of authority. Next, I'll identify three lessons for international trade agreements drawn from the United States' Dormant Commerce Clause experiences.

8.3 Three Potential Lesson for International Trade Agreements Drawn from the United States Supreme Court's Dormant Commerce Clause Case Law

8.3.1 *Introduction*

The United States Supreme Court's more than two centuries of grappling with the problems posed by the relationship between states in a federal free trade zone provides possible lessons and resources for crafting international trade agreements. The three related lessons I identify below are: (1) the intractability of line-drawing; (2) the relationship between institutional competence and the appropriate modes of analysis of national regulations; and (3) the important role of (national) sovereignty.

8.3.2 *The Intractability of Line-Drawing*

First, and perhaps obviously, the Supreme Court's Dormant Commerce Clause case law shows that the line between legitimate state regulation in its citizens' interest, and illegitimate state regulation of interstate commerce, is intractable. All of the Court's various tests struggled with line-drawing.

First, looking historically, this is clear from the Court's repeated attempts at different doctrinal analyses to find a principled, judicially enforceable line. Each test articulated by the Court tried to distinguish legitimate from illegitimate state regulations, preserve an area of state regulatory authority, and simultaneously respect federal power over interstate commerce. None of the lines drawn by the Supreme Court—with one exception (the current prohibition on discriminatory state regulations) to which I will return to in a moment—have worked tolerably well. The

Supreme Court itself identified as one of its reasons for adopting new and different tests the inadequacy of the prior tests.[67]

Second, thinking of the subject theoretically, this intractability occurs because both legitimate and illegitimate state regulations have impacts beyond states' borders. Something as simple—something as obviously in a state's citizens' interest—and as neutral as a speed limit on its highways also impacts out-of-state economic interests by making it more (or less) time-consuming and costly to travel through the state. Therefore, the Supreme Court was left with the problem of drawing lines among regulations all-of-which affect interstate commerce. Almost any line drawn by the Court would involve contestable judgments.

Third, from the perspective of political theory, in-state interest groups that wish to protect themselves do not typically seek legislation that patently discriminates against out-of-state competitors. Instead, knowing that overtly-discriminatory laws would likely be found illegal by the Supreme Court, they seek competitive advantages through laws that ostensibly regulate for human health, safety, or morals. For example, in *Hunt v. Washington St. Apple Advert. Comm'n* (1977), North Carolina passed a regulation on the sale of apples that claimed a valid police power goal.[68] North Carolina apple growers secured legislation that precluded Washington state apple growers from utilizing their brand-name advantage.[69] The legislation was ostensibly done to prevent consumer confusion.[70] In-state groups will nearly always dress-up their protectionist goals under the guise of legitimate police power regulations, which has made it difficult for the Supreme Court to draw principled lines.

In fact, the intractability of this necessary line-drawing is exacerbated in the international trade context, and for at least two reasons. First, the scope of a nation-state's legitimate regulations in their citizens' interest is more capacious than the states in the United States. Nation states have responsibilities beyond American states, such as national defense, so there will be even more plausibility

[67]See, e.g., Southern Pac. Co. v. Arizona, 325 U.S. 761, 768–769 (1945) ("But between these extremes lies the infinite variety of cases in which regulation of local matters may also operate as a regulation of commerce, in which reconciliation of the conflicting claims of state and national power is to be attained only by some appraisal and accommodation of the competing demands of the state and national interests involved."); Kidd v. Pearson, 128 U.S. 1, 16 (1888) ("The line which separates the province of federal authority over the regulation of commerce from the powers reserved to the states, has engaged the attention of this court in a great number and variety of cases."); Hall v. De Cuir, 95 U.S. (5 Otto) 485, 487 (1877) ("There can be no doubt but that exclusive power has been conferred upon Congress in respect to the regulation of commerce among the several States. The difficulty has never been as to the existence of this power, but as to what is to be deemed an encroachment upon it."); Cooley v. Board of Wardens, 53 U.S. (12 How.) 299, 319 (1851) ("The diversities of opinion, therefore, which have existed on this subject, have arisen from the different views taken of the nature of this power."); see also Di Santo v. Pennsylvania, 273 U.S. 34, 44 (1927) (Stone, J., dissenting) (describing the direct-effects test as "too mechanical, too uncertain in its application, and too remote from actualities, to be of value").

[68]Hunt v. Washington St. Apple Advert. Comm'n, 432 U.S. 333, 349 (1977).

[69]Ibid 339.

[70]Ibid 349.

to a nation's proffered police powers justification. For instance, a nation state may more-plausibly justify a restriction on the importation or export of technology because of its impact on that nation's military capacity than could a U.S. state.

Second, nation states have more incentives to privilege their own economic interests over those of other nation states, as compared to states in the United States. For example, legislators in a national legislature have relatively stronger patriotic feelings for their nation over other nations than United States state legislators have for their states compared to other states.

Consequently, one should anticipate that adjudicatory bodies that evaluate disputes among nation states under international trade agreements will face difficult line-drawing problems and that their resolutions to those problems will be open to plausible criticism.

8.3.3 The Relationship Between Institutional Competence and the Appropriate Modes of Analysis of National Regulations

The United States Supreme Court's Dormant Commerce Clause case law suggests that there is a relationship between institutional competence and the efficacy of different modes of analysis to ascertain whether a state regulation is legitimate or illegitimate. This correlation suggests that judicial trade agreement enforcement mechanisms are most adept at identifying and prohibiting discriminatory trade barriers, and less well suited to other modes of enforcement, such as identifying and evaluating non-discriminatory regulations.

The United States Supreme Court has utilized a number of different analyses in its Dormant Commerce Clause case law. Nearly universally, the analysis that has received the *least* criticism is its discriminatory regulation analysis.[71] There are two reasons important to this Essay for this. First, scholars commonly agree that the Court does relatively well identifying discriminatory purposes, and this is partly because the Court, as an institution, has access to evidence of discrimination and can utilize it effectively. Moreover, the Supreme Court has significant experience across a wide variety of areas of constitutional law utilizing discrimination analyses. The Supreme Court easily identified discriminatory statutory text in *Granholm v. Heald.*[72] In *Dean Milk Co. v. Madison*, the Supreme Court ascertained that Madison's milk regulation that prohibited sale of milk bottled beyond five miles

[71] As a reminder, its discriminatory regulation analysis first ascertains whether a state regulation that affects out-of-state commerce discriminates against out-of-state commerce on its face, in its purpose, or in its effect. If so, then the state must justify the regulation by persuading the court that the regulation directly advances an important state interest.

[72] Granholm v. Heald, 544 U.S. 460, 473 (2005).

from the city did not embody a discriminatory protectionist purpose.[73] By contrast, the Supreme Court easily concluded that North Carolina's law caused a discriminatory effect against Washington state apples in *Hunt*.[74]

Second, scholars generally agree that the United States Supreme Court was generally effective maintaining a free-trade zone within the United States, despite the Court's lack of democratic pedigree.[75] In other words, Americans generally and Congress in particular have accepted this branch of the Court's Dormant Commerce Clause case law because it has maintained the national union's commitment to free trade.

On the international stage, the United States Supreme Court's relative facility with discriminatory regulation analysis suggests that international trade agreements that utilize judicial—as distinct from regulatory and administrative—enforcement mechanisms should at least authorize—and perhaps limit—them to utilizing a similar analysis.

Furthermore, the United States Supreme Court's use of a balancing analysis for nondiscriminatory state regulations has been strongly criticized by scholars and others[76] who argue that the Court cannot do so in a principled manner, either because such balancing of incommensurable goods is in principle impossible,[77] or because such balancing requires greater access to information about the relevant costs and benefits than courts can access.[78] For example, how can a court know whether the additional safety gained from state restrictions on the length of trains is more or less weighty than the harm to interstate commerce caused by such restrictions?[79]

This may suggest that, on the international stage, to lessen this same criticism, international judicial institutions should utilize burdens of proof. A burden of proof (also known as a burden of persuasion) is a standard tool of legal systems to address empirical uncertainty.[80] A burden of proof is allocating to one side in a litigation the burden of establishing the existence of factual or legal propositions.[81] For example, in American constitutional law, the plaintiff must establish by a preponderance of the evidence that the defendant government acted with discriminatory intent to establish an Equal Protection Clause violation.[82]

---

[73]Dean Milk Co. v. City of Madison, Wisconsin, 340 U.S. 349, 353 (1951).

[74]Hunt, 432 U.S., at 352–353.

[75]E.g., Holmes (1921), p. 328 ((quoting McLeod v. J. E. Dilworth Co., 322 U.S. 327, 330 (1944)); Dean Milk Co. v. Madison, 340 U.S. 349, 356 (1951).

[76]Heinzerling (1995), pp. 268–269; Sholley (1936), pp. 592–593; see also CTS Corp. v. Dynamics Corp. of Am., 481 U.S. 69, 95 (1987) (Scalia, J., concurring).

[77]Aleinikoff (1987), pp. 972–976.

[78]Ibid 984–986; Denning (2008), p. 454.

[79]S. Pac. Co. v. Arizona, 325 U.S. 761, 794 (1945) (Black, J., dissenting).

[80]See Lawson (2017), p. 25 (describing burdens of proof); Rogers v. Lodge, 458 U.S. 613, 623 (1982).

[81]Lawson (2017), p. 25; Siegel (1997), p. 1134.

[82]Kobick (2010), p. 532.

If, in a certain class of cases, it is typically not clear what the right answer is to a factual question, the legal system can allocate the risk of error on that question through its allocation the burden of proof to one of the parties. For example, the legal system may allocate the burden to the party with the best access to evidence, or the party who is most likely to "get it right," or the party whose judgment is more authoritative such as because of its democratic pedigree. In the international trade agreement context, this may suggest that agreements should allocate the burden of proof for claims of nondiscriminatory trade restrictions to the proponent of the claim, and the burden of proof for claims of discriminatory trade restrictions to the nation state.

This brings me to my third suggested lesson.

8.3.4 *The Important—Though Disputed—Role of Sovereignty Suggests that Enforcement of Trade Agreements Between Nation States Should be Relatively Deferential to the Nations' Judgments Embodied in Nondiscriminatory Regulations*

Sovereignty is a contested concept.[83] Though sovereignty is conventionally identified as the ultimate authority within a jurisdiction,[84] the United States Supreme Court's Dormant Commerce Clause case law shows the influence of different conceptions of sovereignty on the Court's analysis. Prior to the Court's major jurisprudential shift during the New Deal,[85] the Court's conception of dual sovereignty led it to try to draw lines that preserved significant areas of exclusive state regulatory control. For example, and as discussed above, the direct-effects test in the Dormant Commerce Clause context was the corollary to the same test in the Interstate Commerce Clause context. This coupling provided for limited federal authority and robust and independent state authority over wide swaths of American life, like workplace safety laws.[86] During the New Deal, the Supreme Court abandoned dual sovereignty, so that it had to identify another theoretical justification to identify and preserve state authority.

In the international context, nation states possess significantly more sovereignty than do states in the United States. They are, however, more analogous to United

[83]For the seminal discussion of this idea see Gallie (1956), p. 167.

[84]Blackstone Sir (1769a), Bodin (1576) ch. VIII.

[85]That is, prior to the Supreme Court's practical elimination of limits on Congress' enumerated powers, Wickard v. Filburn, 317 U.S. 111 (1942), and its elimination of legally enforceable federalism limits on Congress. United States v. Darby, 312 U.S. 100 (1941).

[86]See Hammer v. Dagenhart, 247 U.S. 251 (1918) (ruling that Congress could not regulate child labor under the Interstate Commerce Clause); Bailey v. Drexel Furniture Co., 259 U.S. 20 (1922) (ruling that Congress could not regulate child labor under its taxing power).

States states early in the Republic. This cuts in two related ways. First, it provides a reason for trade-dispute adjudicators to defer to nation-state determinations about the costs and benefits of neutral regulations. Nation states have relatively greater legitimacy to evaluate the costs and benefits of health, safety, and morals regulations than do international trade tribunals. Nation states possess relatively more of the quality that makes them nation states—including sovereignty—than do international tribunals. Second, it suggests that only strong reasons should justify limiting a nation's regulations, such as evidence that the regulation discriminated against other nations. This would restrict international trade tribunals to prohibiting discriminatory state regulations.

8.4 Conclusion

In conclusion, I made two moves in this Essay. First, I will described the different legal doctrines utilized by the U.S. Supreme Court since the beginning of the Republic to navigate the tension between, on the one hand, the reserved police power of individual states to regulate in their citizens' interests and, on the other hand, the Interstate Commerce Clause's commitment to making the United States free from interstate trade restrictions. Second, I will identified three lessons from the Supreme Court's experience applicable to international free trade agreements.

References

Ackerman B (1998) We the people: transformations II. Belknap Press

Aleinikoff TA (1987) Constitutional law in the age of balancing. Yale Law J 96:943

Barros DB (2004) The police power and the takings clause. Univ Miami Law Rev 58:471

Blackstone Sir W (1769a) Commentaries on the Laws of England I

Blackstone Sir W (1769b) Commentaries on the Laws of England 4

Bodin J (1576) Six books of the commonwealth bk. I. (trans: Tooley MJ). Macmillan 1955

Clinton RN (1990) A brief history of the adoption of the United States constitution. Iowa Law Rev 75:891

Denning BP (2008) Reconstructing the dormant commerce clause doctrine. William Mary Law Rev 50:417

Denning BP (2017) Bittker on regulation of interstate and foreign commerce, 2nd edn. Aspen Law & Business Publishers

Eskridge WN Jr (2005) Pluralism and distrust: how courts can support democracy by lowering the stakes of politics. Yale Law J 114:1279

Francis D (2017) The decline of the dormant commerce clause. Denv Law Rev 94:255

Freedman E (1994) Why constitutional lawyers and historians should take a fresh look at the emergence of the constitution from the confederation period: the case of the drafting of the articles of confederation. Tenn Law Rev 60:783

Friedman B, Deacon DT (2011) A course unbroken: the constitutional legitimacy of the dormant commerce clause. Va Law Rev 97:1877

Gallie WB (1956) Essentially contested concepts. Proc Aristot Soc New Ser 56:167

Hamilton A (1787) The Federalist No. 11
Heinzerling L (1995) The commercial constitution. Supreme Court Rev 1995:217
Holmes OW (1921) Collected Legal Papers
Johnson P (1997) A history of the American people. Harper Perennial
Kobick J (2010) Discriminatory intent reconsidered: folk concepts of intentionality and equal protection Jurisprudence. Harv Civil Rights Civil Libert Law Rev 45:517
Lawson G (2017) Evidence of the law. University of Chicago Press
Legarre S (2007) The historical background of the police power. Univ Pa J Const Law 9:745
Madison J (1787) Notes of Debates in the Federal Convention of 1787
Madison J (1788) The Federalist No. 42
McGinnis JO (2012) Federalism as a discovery process and a catalyst for humility. Harv J Law Pub Policy 35:115120
McGinnis JO, Somin I (2004) Federalism v. States' rights: a defense of judicial review in a federal system. Northwest Univ Law Rev 99:89
Redish MH (1995) The constitution as political structure. OUP
Sholley JB (1936) The negative implications of the commerce clause. Univ Chicago Law Rev 3:556
Siegel R (1997) Why equal protection no longer protects: the evolving forms of status-enforcing state action. Stanford Law Rev 49:1111
Swisher CB (1935) Roger B. Taney. The Macmillan Company
Swisher CB (1974) History of the Supreme Court of the United States: the Taney Period 1836-1864. MacMillan Publishing Co

Chapter 9
The Judicial History of the Federal Market of Australia: Free Trade Versus Free Enterprise

Gonzalo Villalta Puig

9.1 Introduction

Australia is a federal market. Section (s) 92 of the Australian Constitution (Commonwealth of Australia Constitution Act 1900) establishes freedom of trade, in such terms: 'trade . . . among the States . . . shall be absolutely free'. Freedom of trade is a constitutional norm that codifies the sale and purchase of goods and services among or within sovereign states and customs territories as an exchange without government discrimination. Constitutional courts interpret this norm either as a *right* to economic freedom or as a *principle* of free trade: in other words, the choice is between free enterprise or free trade; interstate traders or interstate trade. As a right, the freedom of trade is an individual right of merchant traders to engage in trade across State lines, a kind of laissez-faire economic freedom. As a principle, the freedom of trade is a principle of liberalisation of the market into a free trade area. This distinction has informed the interpretation of s 92 by the High Court and caused much judicial controversy.

The High Court maintained a free-trade-as-right interpretation for the early part of the history of Australia's federation in 1901 (Sharwood 1958) but for the last thirty years it has maintained a free-trade-as-principle interpretation. Throughout that century of judicial history, these theories of interpretation rose and fell, so much so that s 92 'has caused more differences of judicial opinion and greater conflict between decisions than any other provision of the Constitution' (Sawer 1952a, p. 71). The struggle of the High Court to give a clear and certain interpretation to the meaning of the phrase 'absolutely free' in s 92 has been the subject of much academic

This chapter relies and draws on Villalta Puig (2008); Villalta Puig (2018), pp. 287–304; and Villalta Puig (2017).

G. Villalta Puig (✉)
University of Navarra, Pamplona, Spain
e-mail: gvillalta@unav.es

C. I. Nagy (ed.), *World Trade and Local Public Interest*, Studies in European Economic Law and Regulation 19, https://doi.org/10.1007/978-3-030-41920-2_9

commentary and is more than notorious (Staker 1990, p. 322). Even then, it is not possible 'to appreciate the impact of the section or to argue what its future should be without referring to at least the highlights of the past and to the fundamental divergences that underlay some of the leading decisions' (Zines 1997, p. 108).

> Notwithstanding some one hundred and forty High Court and Privy Council cases and the spilling of over three million words of interpretation by the judges (not to mention the commentators' contribution of roughly three hundred and fifty articles, notes or comments of one kind or another), the true meaning of the section failed to emerge ... (Coper 1987, p. 258)

The judicial history of s 92 is indeed an incredible labyrinth, a Tennysonian *wilderness of single instances* (*Aylmer's Field*) 'in which contradictory decisions and obiter dicta jostle between the presumed intention of the "Founding Fathers" and the judicial concept of social welfare' (Davis 1950, p. 108). It is a labyrinth with no golden thread (*Commonwealth v Bank of New South Wales* 1949, p. 639):

> [J]udicially s 92 has been 'interpreted' from time to time to mean freedom from State ... law and action; freedom only from a law directed against ... or ... having the object of interference with interstate trade; freedom as at ... the point of entry into a State; freedom for a particular trader; not just for the general flow of interstate trade ... freedom by reference to the criterion of operation of a challenged law (that is, whether the law itself operates on interstate trade, or on an essential attribute of this trade, and so on), freedom by reference to the direct effect of the law ... freedom by reference to what the law does in the circumstances in which it is intended to operate or by reference to the practical effect of the law. (Lane 1988, p. 604)

9.2 Free Trade Versus Free Enterprise

Two theories rivalled for supremacy of interpretation in the attempt of the High Court to manage the *absolute* freedom of trade which the text, if not the purpose, of s 92 dictates (Carney 1991, p. 150). In other words, the duel was between 'a theory of free trade in the sense of the antithesis of state protectionism and a theory of freedom of trade in the simple laissez-faire sense of freedom from government interference' (Coper 1983, p. 58).

Followers of the free trade theory 'saw section 92 as concerned with protectionist discrimination, often according to a formalistic understanding' (Simpson 2005, p. 448). Even so, the free trade theory was not entirely monochromatic and presented a palette of shades, at least four in number. The first application of the theory interpreted s 92 as a prohibition of 'discriminatory burdens imposed upon interstate trade' (Coper 1983, p. 300). The second application interpreted the section as a prohibition of 'all forms of state protectionism whether resulting from the imposition of discriminatory or non-discriminatory burdens' (Coper 1983, p. 300). The third application interpreted the section as a mandate 'to protect the flow of interstate trade considered as a whole, in some sense beyond the prevention of regional economic advantage' (Coper 1983, p. 300). And the fourth application interpreted the section 'as a freedom from fiscal burdens in the nature of customs duties (or, in other words, from discriminatory fiscal burdens)' (Coper 1983, p. 297). In contrast, followers of the individual rights theory saw s 92 'principally as a guarantee of individuals' freedom to trade across State borders' (Simpson 2005, p. 448). In perhaps overly simplistic terms, the free trade theory was more about form whereas the individual rights theory was more about substance.

The case law over the course of the eight decades after Federation witnessed the struggle for supremacy between these two theories, their rise and fall.

9.2.1 Free Trade as Freedom from Discrimination

Initially, the free trade theory dominated. Indeed, the first five High Court cases on s 92 accorded with the free trade theory. In each case, the High Court struck down discriminatory laws and upheld non-discriminatory laws. These cases, collectively, presented the first of the three applications of the free trade theory. The first application of the theory interpreted s 92 as a non-discrimination norm. Indeed, the first case on s 92, *Fox v Robbins* (1909), involved 'a state law which infringed s 92 because it discriminated against interstate trade' (Coper 1983, pp. 11–12). In summation of the facts of the case, Chief Justice Samuel Griffith said:

> This provision (s 92) would be quite illusory if a State could impose disabilities upon the sale of the products of other States which are not imposed upon the sale of home products ... [T] he Act of Western Australia now in question, in so far as it makes a discrimination against wine the product of fruit grown in other States of the Commonwealth in favour of wine the product of fruit grown in Western Australia, is contrary to the Constitution ... The consequence is that no greater burden or restriction can now be laid upon the sale of other Australian wines in Western Australia than that laid upon the sale of Western Australian wine. (119–120)

In agreement, Justice Edmund Barton said:

> To impose one charge on the sale of the wines of other States, while allowing the sale of Western Australian wines at another and a lower fee, is discrimination of a kind which if lawful in this case is lawful in a thousand others – for this is a question of power. By burdens of this kind and that, whether under the name of licence fees or under any other name, the operation of inter-state free trade could be so hampered and restricted as to reduce the Constitution in that regard to mere futility ... There is no difference in substance or effect in its bearing on inter-state commerce between a burden such as this and a duty collected at the borders of the ports of one State on the products of another. In either case that commerce is restricted which the Constitution says shall be free; and in either case the disability may be made so great as to render the product unsaleable, and therefore virtually to prohibit its introduction. In a word, however the enactment may be phrased, it is inter-state protection, not inter-state free trade ... I must not for a moment be taken to cast any doubt on the capacity of a State to tax, together with its own products, goods produced in other States, when brought into it for sale or consumption. When the inter-state transit is over and they have become part of the mass of property within the State, any goods may be taxed, no matter whence they have come. But they must be taxed alike with all other such goods in the State. The tax must be general, and laid equally on all goods of the kind to be taxed, whether their State of origin be the taxing State or another. And what I say of taxes applies to other imposts and burdens. (123–124)

Justice Richard O'Connor similarly referred to the discriminatory operation of the tax against interstate trade, saying:

> It is clear that the Constitution does not permit a State by such discriminating charges to place at a disadvantage the goods of other States passing into it for sale. (126)

The other two justices on the bench also agreed. Justice Isaac Isaacs said:

> [I]f any of the provisions discriminate adversely to other States, it does impair that freedom, because it deters the residents of the State from selling or consuming, and therefore from purchasing and importing, the products of the other States ... Section 92 of the Constitution ... prevents adverse discrimination from being lawful. (129–130)

And Justice HB Higgins said:

> This involves a discrimination in favour of Western Australian products, and an infringement of the provisions of s 92 of the Constitution in favour of absolute freedom of trade among the States. (131)

Despite these confident judicial statements, the first application of the free trade theory was not to last.

9.2.2 *Free Trade as Freedom of Interstate Trade*

The free trade theory did continue to influence subsequent judgments albeit through a different application. A proponent of the last of the four possible applications of the free trade theory, Justice HV Evatt, considered that s 92 protected the freedom of interstate trade as a whole. The majority judgment in *R v Vizzard* (1933) presented his application of the theory:

> The predominant object of sec 92 was to secure free trade and free intercourse among what had formerly been self-governing colonies and what were then to become States which should still possess very large powers of internal self-government. To assert freedom of trade between such organized communities was to lay down in formal expression a well-known economic doctrine and ideal, which was one of the chief motive forces of Federation ... The declaration of sec 92 loses much of its significance if parts of it are analysed separately and the results of the analysis are subsequently put together again. The section, if read as a whole, postulates the free flow of goods inter-State, so that goods produced in any State may be freely marketed in every other State, and so that nothing can lawfully be done to obstruct or prevent such marketing. (86–87)

Justice Evatt considered that s 92 could not apply to a law or measure if did not have as its purpose or effect the decrease in volume of interstate trade (Zines 1973, p. 190).

9.2.3 Free Enterprise as Individual Rights

Justice Evatt's application of the free trade theory soon came under attack, as did the free trade theory more generally. Already a few months before the High Court handed down its judgment in *R v Vizzard*, Justice Evatt found himself in dissent in *Peanut Board v Rockhampton Harbour Board* (1933). This case was the first in which the individual rights theory and its most enthusiastic champion—Justice Owen Dixon—prevailed over the free trade theory. The individual rights theory was an attempt to strike a balance between the States and Commonwealth in the exercise of their respective competences (Zines 1964).

Within only two years, in *O Gilpin Ltd v Commissioner for Road Transport and Tramways (NSW)* (1935), Justice Dixon had developed the theory in full:

> Trade, commerce and intercourse among the States is an expression which describes the activities of individuals. The object of sec 92 is to enable individuals to conduct their commercial dealings and their personal intercourse with one another independently of State boundaries. The constitutional provision is not based on mere economic considerations. I am unable to agree with the view that trade, commerce and intercourse should, in applying sec 92, be regarded as a whole and not distributively. The Constitution is dealing with a governmental power. It is not easy to appreciate the meaning of a guarantee of freedom of trade and intercourse unless it gives protection to the individual against interference in his commercial relations and movements. Nor can I share the view that the protection is against none but direct interference with inter-State trade, commerce and intercourse. I do agree that it prevents only burdens or restrictions which apply to conduct or action as trade, commerce or intercourse, or because of its inter-State character. But such a burden or restriction may be indirect in its operation. However circuitous or disguised it may be, once it appears that such a burden or restriction is attempted, it is discovered to be an infringement upon the freedom preserved by sec 92. (211–212)

Justice Dixon saw s 92 as a guarantee of the individual right to interstate trade irrespective of whether the law or measure in question was likely to affect the volume of interstate trade or even its purpose (Zines 1973, p. 190). In other words, His Honour saw s 92 as a charter of economic rights for the exclusive exercise by members of the business community (O'Brien 1981, p. 203).

The Judicial Committee of the Privy Council—back then Australia's highest court of appeal—eventually came under Dixonian influence, gradually opening itself up to his laissez-faire idea of political economy. In *James v Commonwealth* (1936), Lord Robert Wright of the Privy Council said:

> ... 'free' means free from every sort of impediment or control by any organ of Government, legislature or executive to which s 92 is addressed with respect to trade, commerce or intercourse, considered as trade, commerce and intercourse ... It involves a conception of inter-State trade, commerce and intercourse commencing at whatever stage in the State of origin the operation can be said to begin, and continuing until the moment in the other State when the operation of inter-State trade can be said to end: the freedom is postulated as attaching to every step in the sequence of events from first to last. (56–57)

Some 15 years after this first acknowledgement of laissez-faire, the Privy Council finally vindicated the individual rights theory. In the *Bank Nationalisation Case*, Lord Samuel Porter said:

> The necessary implications of [*James v Commonwealth*] are important. First may be mentioned an argument strenuously maintained on this appeal that s 92 of the Constitution does not guarantee the freedom of individuals. Yet James was an individual and James vindicated his freedom in hard-won fights. Clearly there is here a misconception. It is true, as has been said more than once in the High Court, that s 92 does not create any new juristic rights, but it does give the citizen of State or Commonwealth, as the case may be, the right to ignore, and if necessary, to call upon the judicial power to help him to resist, legislative or executive action which offends against the section. And this is just what James successfully did. (635)

In this way, the Privy Council entrenched the individual rights theory into Australian constitutional law. Sir Owen, as Chief Justice of Australia, subsequently translated the individual rights theory into a criterion of operation in *Hospital Provident Fund Pty Ltd v Victoria* (1953). This criterion was an attempt to simplify and legitimate the application of the theory and, therefore, further entrench it into judicial doctrine:

> If a law takes a fact or an event or a thing itself forming part of trade commerce or intercourse, or forming an essential attribute of that conception, essential in the sense that without it you cannot bring into being that particular example of trade commerce or intercourse among the States, and the law proceeds, by reference thereto or in consequence thereof, to impose a restriction, a burden or a liability, then that appears to me to be direct or immediate in its operation or application to inter-State trade commerce and intercourse, and, if it creates a real prejudice or impediment to inter-State transactions, it will accordingly be a law impairing the freedom which s 92 says shall exist. (17)

9.2.4 Free Trade as Freedom from Fiscal Burdens

Despite the apparent supremacy of the individual rights theory throughout the Dixon Court years, several were the judicial acknowledgements of the free trade origins of s 92. Justice Lionel Murphy, for example, was an ardent proponent of the free trade theory and, albeit without any measure of judicial success, advocated for the fiscal burden application of the theory. This was the fourth of the four possible applications of the free trade theory of interpretation. It interpreted s 92 as a freedom from fiscal burdens in the form of customs duties.

In *Buck v Bavone* (1976), Justice Murphy rebelled against the individual rights regime:

> This case raises the question of the meaning and application of the first sentence of s 92 of the Constitution. Section 92 is in Ch IV of the Constitution, which is headed 'Finance and Trade'. This chapter deals with financial matters and the leit-motif of the sections surrounding s 92 (ss 88–90 and 93–95) is duties of customs . . .
>
> Section 92 is generally taken out of context and abbreviated, eliminating the reference to duties of customs and facilitating its misinterpretation. When s 92 is read in whole and in context, the command in the first sentence clearly concerns freedom from customs duties or similar taxes (often referred to as fiscal imposts) on trade, commerce and intercourse among

> the States. Section 92 does not guarantee economic anarchy. It is not a laissez-faire provision freeing trade, commerce and intercourse among the States from regulation.
>
> The judicial approach of injecting into s 92 the philosophy of laissez-faire has caused a substantial and serious inroad into the spheres of State and Federal legislatures. Many laws (mainly State) have been declared invalid and parliaments have consequently been inhibited from passing laws which might affect interstate trade and commerce. In this area, the Court has adopted a legislative role. It acts as an additional House but its role is necessarily negative. It can veto but not initiate. (132–133)

Often the rebel, Justice Murphy was dismissive of precedent and did not necessarily feel the obligation to follow the line of past judicial authority that had consistently vindicated the individual rights theory:

> Then there is the doctrine of precedent, one of my favourite doctrines. I have managed to apply it at least once a year since I've been on the Bench. The doctrine is that whenever you are faced with a decision, you always follow what the last person who was faced with the same decision did. It is a doctrine eminently suitable for a nation overwhelmingly populated by sheep. (Murphy 1980, pp. 2, 5)

With such unconventional declarations of principle, it is not at all a surprise to discover that Justice Murphy never quite had the support of his peers on the bench, who refused to even entertain his proposal of a fiscal burden application of the free trade theory. It is not without some irony that the fiscal burden application indeed never set precedent. The Privy Council had rejected it as early as 1950. In the *Bank Nationalisation Case*, Lord Porter resolved that the phrase 'absolutely free' in s 92 established a freedom that expands beyond the fiscal domain:

> Forty years of controversy on these words have left one thing at least clear. It is no longer arguable that freedom from customs or other monetary charges alone is secured by the section. (629)

Nonetheless, the fiscal burden application controversy 'contributed to the revival of the "free trade" idea in the interpretation of s 92 by expressly setting [its] face against the laissez-faire, individual right philosophy of the *Bank* case" (Coper 1983, p. 273).

9.2.5 Free Trade as Freedom from Protectionism

That revival inspired Justice Anthony Mason who, newly appointed to the High Court and only a couple of years after *Buck v Bavone*, voiced his wish for the return of the free trade theory to the doctrinal norm, this time as the second of its four possible applications. This second application interpreted s 92 as a prohibition against state trade protectionism. In other words, it interpreted the section as an anti-protectionist norm. In *Finemore's Transport Pty Ltd v New South Wales* (1978), Justice Mason said:

> To some it may seem surprising that s 92 confers an immunity on those engaged in interstate trade from liability to a tax which is imposed without distinction or discrimination on all those who register motor vehicles, whether the vehicles are engaged in or intended to be engaged in interstate trade or not. It is to carry the protection given by s 92 to the interstate trader very far indeed and to place him in a very privileged position. I have always doubted whether s 92 was intended to do more than protect interstate trade from burdens of a discriminatory kind of which *North Eastern Dairy Co Ltd v Dairy Industry Authority of NSW* (1975) 134 CLR 559 provides a convenient example. But I acknowledge that the cases have taken the section a good deal further and in conformity with the doctrine enunciated by the Court, the correctness of which has not been challenged in this case, I can only conclude that [the tax cannot validly apply to interstate vehicles]. (352)

Justice Kenneth Jacobs was equally supportive of this application of the free trade theory. That same year, in *Bartter's Farms Pty Ltd v Todd* (1978), His Honour argued for the doctrinal validity of an anti-protectionist norm:

> [I]n the process of decision it seems to me inevitable that the Court should bear in mind the purpose of the section, namely, that under the Constitution there was to be an economic union as well as a political union. The words 'common market', with which we are now so familiar, come instantly to mind. Attempts by one unit of a federation by legislative prohibition to give itself and its residents economic advantages over other units of a federation by way of prohibition of or burdens on trade and commerce with those other units can take a great variety of forms, as other economic federations have found, and are finding, out ... There is much in Ch IV to indicate that the framers of the Constitution had these possibilities very much in mind, and s 92 is an important part of the framework designed to prevent the attainment by one unit of such impermissible advantages. When the impugned legislation reveals no such purpose or effect, it seems to me that a challenge to the validity of legislation should have considerably less chance of success. (523)

Despite these jurisprudentially rigorous attempts to reinstate the free trade theory, individual rights was still the theory of reference, but not for long. A judicial revolution was near ...

9.3 Free Trade as Freedom from Discriminatory Protectionism

Indeed, by the 1980s, there was incremental consensus within the judiciary that the High Court had not made 'a good job of constitutional interpretation, on any standard of judgment, [of] Section 92' (Sawer 1952b, p. 228). The multitude of attempts to interpret the section had produced neither clarity of meaning nor certainty of operation, 'with past decisions difficult to reconcile and future decisions difficult to predict' (Coper 1989–1990, pp. 4–5). Many on the bench agreed on the need to resolve what, in *Miller v TCN Channel Nine Pty Ltd* (1986), Justice William Deane called 'the difficulties in the current state of authority about the nature and scope of s 92' (620). Thus, in that same case, Justice Mason complained that an almost centennial history of High Court cases had failed to establish the scope and effect of s 92:

> The judgments [on s 92] demonstrate in convincing fashion that there is now no interpretation of s 92 that commands the acceptance of a majority of the Court. There is much to be said for the view that in this situation the Court has a responsibility to undertake a fundamental re-examination of the section [that is, an examination of the judicial interpretations of s 92]. (571)

Justice Deane, again, was equal in his complaint (Heuzenroeder 2001, p. 29):

> This is another case about the operation and effect of s 92 of the Constitution. Both sides argued with apparent conviction on the basis of existing authority to support diametrically opposed conclusions. Perhaps that should not be seen as surprising since the more one becomes immersed in the decisions of the Privy Council and this Court on the subject of s 92, the plainer the impression becomes that one has entered an area where the ordinary processes of legal reasoning have had but a small part to play and where judicial exegesis has tended to confuse rather than elucidate. Indeed, it is as if many voices of authority have been speaking differently at the same time with the result that, putting to one side some basic propositions, it is all but impossible to comprehend precisely what it is that authority has said. (615–616)

His Honour further said:

> [F]ew would deny that, somewhere along the line, things have gone wrong. The simple words of s 92 have, in an unsuccessful search for certainty in the law, been overlaid by formulae which have given rise to many problems while solving almost none. (618)

The revival by Justice Murphy of the free trade theory in the 1980s had prompted a series of ever more confident judicial attacks on the individual rights theory. Proponents of the free trade theory had two objections. First, they took objection to the legal immunity that the individual rights theory purportedly conferred on interstate traders to the detriment of intrastate traders. In *Miller v TCN Channel Nine Pty Ltd*, Justice Deane explained the objection thus:

> The section was, plainly enough, intended to serve the essential function of reinforcing the economic and social unity of an emerging nation by removing the barriers to commerce, trade and intercourse which the frontiers between the federating colonies had previously represented. It has been converted into a form of constitutional guarantee of the economics of laissez-faire and the politics of "small government" ... In the result, interstate trade, commerce and intercourse has been placed in a position of significant and preferential immunity from non-discriminatory laws which the courts have, for reasons which still await currently authoritative identification, judged to be inconsistent with s 92. Where s 92 has been held to preclude the application of such non-discriminatory laws to interstate trade and commerce leaving them to apply to intrastate trade and commerce, the section, which was intended to preclude inequality between the treatment of the trade and commerce of the interstate trader and the treatment of the trade and commerce of the local trader, has become an actual source of such inequality of treatment to the detriment of the local trader. In cases where laws which were non-discriminatory as enacted have been made discriminatory by reason of the fact that s 92 has had the effect that intrastate trade and commerce alone remain subjected to them, a section which was adopted as a guarantee of unity and equality under the federation has been converted into a source of unfair and potentially divisive preference. (618–619)

The second objection was, Justice Mason said in *North Eastern Dairy Co Ltd v Dairy Industry Authority of New South Wales* (1975), that the operation of s 92 ought to 'fluctuate as the community develops and as the need for new and different modes of regulation of trade and commerce become apparent' (615). The individual rights theory had failed to manage the need—as a matter of public interest—for legislation to legitimately regulate intrastate and interstate trade (Kirk 1997, p. 14). For Justice Victor Windeyer in *SOS (Mowbray) Pty Ltd v Mead* (1972), the perception was that, as long as the individual rights theory continued to prevail, there was the 'danger of [the High Court] putting more and more matters outside the authority of all parliaments of Australia, Commonwealth and State' (574). The case law had reached such a state of judicial inconsistency, as well as doctrinal and practical inadequacy, that a revolution of and for the case law was not only inevitable but also desirable.

The revolution came with *Cole v Whitfield* (1988), under the leadership of Sir Anthony Mason as Chief Justice of Australia. In one unanimous strike, the High Court restored the free trade theory and dethroned the individual rights theory, but not without an attempt to legitimise its coup:

> No provision of the Constitution has been the source of greater judicial concern or the subject of greater judicial effort than s 92. That notwithstanding, judicial exegesis of the section has yielded neither clarity of meaning nor certainty of operation. (383–384)

The High Court prefaced its joint judgment with an acknowledgement of the judicial inconsistency that had continually contradicted the interpretation of s 92 until then:

> Over the years the Court has moved uneasily between one interpretation and another in its endeavours to solve the problems thrown up by the necessity to apply the very general language of the section to a wide variety of legislative and factual situations. Indeed, these shifts have been such as to make it difficult to speak of the section as having achieved a settled or accepted interpretation at any time since federation ... In these circumstances, it is not surprising that the Court is now pressed to reconsider the approximately 140 decisions of this Court and of the Privy Council which have attempted to illuminate the meaning and operation of the section. Nor is it surprising that the section should have defied judicial attempts to define enduring criteria of its application, for its enigmatic text does not state the area of immunity which it guarantees. (383–385)

9.3.1 Rationale Against the Individual Rights Theory of Interpretation

In continuation of the rationale that Justice Mason and Justice Deane had given in *Miller v TCN Channel Nine Pty Ltd*, the joint judgement of High Court in *Cole v Whitfield* advanced four reasons to explain its rejection of the individual rights theory of interpretation (Carney 1991, pp. 150–151).

9.3.1.1 Underdevelopment of the Trade and Commerce Power

First, the High Court explained that the individual rights theory did not allow the development of the economic constitution of Australia, specifically, the scope of the interstate trade and commerce power in s 51(i) of the Australian Constitution:

> It is ... necessary for present purposes that we make some general reference to the relationship between s 51(i) and s 92 for the reason that the guarantee of the absolute freedom of interstate trade and commerce contained in s 92 must be read in the context of the express conferral of legislative power with respect to such trade and commerce which is contained in s 51(i).
>
> We do not accept the explanation [favoured by history and context] ... that the key to the relationship between s 51(i) and s 92 is to be found in the presence of the words 'with respect to' in the opening words of s 51(i). The consequence of reconciling the two constitutional provisions in that way is to treat the legislative power conferred by s 51(i) as essentially peripheral in character. In our view, any acceptable appreciation of the interrelationship between the two sections must recognize that s 51(i) is a plenary power on a topic of fundamental importance. (398)

9.3.1.2 Artificial Criterion of Operation

Secondly, the High Court explained that the criterion of operation formula into which Chief Justice Dixon had translated the individual rights theory was without textual legitimacy:

> The interpretation which came closest to achieving [a significant] degree of acceptance was that embodying the criterion of operation formula ... That formula appeared to have the advantage of certainty, but that advantage proved to be illusory. Its disadvantage was that it was concerned only with the formal structure of an impugned law and ignored its real or substantive effect ...(384)
>
> [I]n the ultimate analysis the doctrine [embodying the criterion of operation formula] failed to command the acceptance of the Court for reasons which we shall state shortly ...
>
> The doctrine is highly artificial. It depends on the formal and obscure distinction between the essential attributes of trade and commerce and those facts, events or things which are inessential, incidental, or, indeed, antecedent or preparatory to that trade and commerce. This distinction mirrors another distinction, equally unsatisfactory, between burdens which are direct and immediate (proscribed) and those that are indirect, consequential and remote (not proscribed). What is more, the first limb of the doctrine ... looks to the legal operation of the law rather than to its practical operation or its economic consequences. The emphasis on the legal operation of the law gave rise to a concern that the way was open to circumvention by means of legislative device. To counter this possibility the doctrine was expressed to extend to circuitous devices but this extension of the doctrine seems itself to have turned on the legal operation of the law. At any rate, no law has been held not to apply to interstate trade on the ground that it burdened the trade by means of a circuitous device ...
>
> With the advantage of hindsight it is now obvious that such an artificial formula would create problems in the attempt to apply it to a variety of legislative situations ... [T]he doctrine was

seen as supporting a constitutional guarantee of the right of the individual to engage in interstate trade . . .

In truth the history of the doctrine is an indication of the hazards of seeking certainty of operation of a constitutional guarantee through the medium of an artificial formula. Either the formula is consistently applied and subverts the substance of the guarantee; or an attempt is made to achieve uniformly satisfactory outcomes and the formula becomes uncertain in its application. What we have said explains some of the reasons why the criterion of operation ceased to command the acceptance of members of the Court, with the consequence that we do not see ourselves as constrained by authority to accept it. (400–402)

9.3.1.3 Immunity of Interstate Traders

Thirdly, the High Court explained that the individual rights theory unfairly allowed interstate traders to avoid laws and measures for the legitimate regulation of intrastate trade:

> There are other features of the doctrine which compel its rejection as an acceptable interpretation of s 92. First, in some respects the protection which it offers to interstate trade is too wide. Instead of placing interstate trade on an equal footing with intrastate trade, the doctrine keeps interstate trade on a privileged or preferred footing, immune from burdens to which other trade is subject . . . The doctrine created protectionism in reverse. Both Mason J and Deane J have noted that s 92 had become in some circumstances a source of privileged and preferential treatment for that trade to the detriment of the local trade . . . (402–403)

9.3.1.4 No Legitimate Regulation of Intrastate and Interstate Trade

Fourthly and relatedly, the High Court explained that the individual rights theory did not permit the legitimate regulation of intrastate and interstate trade in the public interest:

> The . . . doctrine . . . fails to make any accommodation for the need for laws genuinely regulating intrastate and interstate trade. The history of the movement for abolition of colonial protection and for the achievement of intercolonial free trade does not indicate that it was intended to prohibit genuine non-protective regulation of intercolonial or interstate trade. The criterion of operation makes no concession to this aspect of the section's history. In the result there has been a continuing tension between the general application of the formula and the validity of laws which are purely regulatory in character. Judged by reference to the doctrine, the validity of a regulatory law hinged on whether it imposed a burden on an essential attribute or on a mere incident of trade or commerce. To say the least of it, this was not an appropriate criterion of validity of a regulatory law divorced, as it is, from considerations of the protectionist purpose or effect of the impugned law. It is not surprising that the Court found it necessary to develop a concept of a permissible 'burden' which was associated with a somewhat ill-defined notion of what is legitimate regulation in an ordered society . . . The problems which have arisen in this area . . . are the inevitable consequence of any interpretation of s 92 which offers protection to interstate trade going beyond immunity from discriminatory burdens having a protectionist purpose or effect. (403–404)

9.3.2 *Rationale for the Free Trade Theory of Interpretation*

With these four reasons for its rejection of the individual rights theory of interpretation, the history and context of s 92 became the two principal considerations for the acceptance by the High Court of the free trade theory.

9.3.2.1 Context of Section 92: Chapter IV of the Australian Constitution

First, the High Court referred to the location of s 92 in the Australian Constitution. Accordingly, it studied the provisions that accompany s 92:

> To complement the s 92 prohibition against discriminatory laws which prevented the free flow of trade, ss 99 and 102 were introduced to prohibit preferences . . . Sections 92, 99 and 102 were apt . . . to ensure that the Australian States should be a free trade area in which legislative or executive discrimination against interstate trade and commerce should be prohibited. (392–393)

The High Court also studied Chapter IV:

> There can be no doubt that s 92 guarantees absolute freedom of interstate trade and commerce from all interstate border duties and other discriminatory fiscal charges levied on transactions of interstate trade and commerce. Indeed, the reference in each paragraph of the section to uniform duties of customs creates the impression that the provision is directed to fiscal charges and burdens. This impression is reinforced by the context provided by the surrounding provisions, ss 89–91 and ss 93–95. All these provisions deal with fiscal charges and burdens, appearing, as they do, in Ch IV of the Constitution which is headed 'Finance and Trade'. (394–395)

The joint judgement found that, by reference to its context, s 92 could only require the abolition of border duties of customs, a finding which is consistent with a free trade interpretation of the section.

9.3.2.2 History of Section 92: Convention Debates

Secondly, the High Court referred to the drafting history of s 92—the Australasian Federal Conventions—in an attempt to discover the intention of the framers of the Australian Constitution for intercolonial freedom of trade (Lindsay 1999, p. 40):

> Reference to the history of s 92 may be made, not for the purpose of substituting for the meaning of the words used the scope and effect—if such could be established—which the founding fathers subjectively intended the section to have, but for the purpose of identifying the contemporary meaning of language used, the subject to which the language was directed and the nature and objectives of the movement towards federation from which the compact of the Constitution finally emerged. (385) . . . Attention to the history which we have outlined may help to reduce the confusion that has surrounded the interpretation of s 92. (392)

The High Court resolved that, in addition to the context of the section in Chapter IV of the Australian Constitution, the convention debates, drafts of the constitutional text (Villalta Puig 2011) as well as other primary sources on the movement towards Federation supported a free trade interpretation of s 92.

> As the 1891 Report of the South Australian Royal Commission on Intercolonial Free Trade shows ... , 'intercolonial free trade, on the basis of a uniform tariff', was a commonly accepted ideal. Subsequently, the first report of a Victorian Board of Inquiry in 1894 expressed the belief 'that the people of Victoria are practically unanimously in favour of free-trade between the colonies' ... Notwithstanding this popular support, concrete proposals for the implementation of free trade between the separate Australian colonies languished outside the growing movement towards federation. (386)
>
> ... In that [federation] movement, the problem of intercolonial free trade ... was, from the outset, a central question and problem: the 'lion in the path', as Mr James Service (a former Premier of Victoria) described it in 1890, which federalists must either slay or be slain by ... s 92 [was] the provision which was to slay the lion ... (386–387)
>
> That history [of the convention debates] demonstrates that the principal goals of the movement towards the federation of the Australian colonies included the elimination of intercolonial border duties and discriminatory burdens and preferences in intercolonial trade and the achievement of intercolonial free trade. As we have seen, apart from ss 99 and 102, that goal was enshrined in the various draft clauses which preceded s 92 and ultimately in the section itself. (392)

From its contextual and historical investigations, the High Court concluded that a free trade interpretation of s 92 was both legitimate and necessary:

> The purpose of the section is clear enough: to create a free trade area throughout the Commonwealth and to deny to Commonwealth and States alike a power to prevent or obstruct the free movement of people, goods and communications across State boundaries. (391)

This conclusion—that the section gives a guarantee of free trade nationally rather than an individual right to trade—did away with over four decades of unclear and uncertain interpretation. Without pomp and circumstance, the joint judgement made a simple, laconic even but, nevertheless, powerfully definitive statement of principle: 'Departing now from the [individual rights] doctrine which has failed to retain general acceptance, we adopt the [free trade] interpretation which, as we have shown, is favoured by history and context' (407).

The free trade theory now needed a test to apply s 92.

9.3.3 *From a Non-discrimination Norm to an Anti-protectionist Norm*

The High Court acknowledged that 'the records of the movement towards federation, to some of which we now refer, do not establish that the notion of absolutely free trade and commerce had any precise settled contemporary content' (389). And again, it affirmed that '[t]he delimitation of the precise scope and effect of the guarantee was left as an unresolved task for the future' (391).

The High Court considered that the delimitation of the scope and effect of s 92—'an unresolved task for the future' (391)—had indeed become an urgent task for the present:

> By refraining from defining any limitation on the freedom guaranteed by s 92, the Conventions and the Constitution which they framed passed to the courts the task of defining what aspects of interstate trade, commerce and intercourse were excluded from legislative or executive control or regulation. (392)

On that premise, the High Court resolved to develop a test for s 92—now an anti-protectionist norm—that would accord with the principle of free trade further to the context and history of the provision.

> The task which has confronted the Court is to construe the unexpressed; to formulate in legal propositions, so far as the text of s 92 admits, the criteria for distinguishing between the burdens (including restrictions, controls and standards) to which interstate trade and commerce may be subjected by the exercise of legislative or executive power and the burdens from which interstate trade and commerce is immune. (394)

The *Cole v Whitfield* test for s 92 recalled the earlier application of the free trade theory by Mason, as Chief Justice of Australia, now led his peers to the criterion of discriminatory protectionism. That criterion converted the section from an anti-discrimination norm to an anti-protectionist norm.

> The expression 'free trade' commonly signified in the nineteenth century, as it does today, an absence of protectionism, ie, the protection of domestic industries against foreign competition. Such protection may be achieved by a variety of different measures — eg, tariffs that increase the price of foreign goods, non-tariff barriers such as quotas on imports, differential railway rates, subsidies on goods produced and discriminatory burdens on dealings with imports - which, alone or in combination, make importing and dealings with imports difficult or impossible. (392–393)

For the High Court, then, section 92 is 'an intended guarantee of freedom from discriminatory protectionism' (317). Thus, among the four possible applications of the free trade theory of interpretation—namely, freedom from discrimination; freedom from protectionism; freedom for interstate trade; and, freedom from fiscal burdens—it selected and combined the first two. The High Court did so in opposition to the individual rights theory:

> As we have seen, the failure of the section to define expressly what interstate trade and commerce was to be immune from is to be explained by reference to the dictates of political expediency, not by reference to a purpose of prohibiting all legal burdens, restrictions, controls or standards. In that context, to construe s 92 as requiring that interstate trade and commerce be immune only from discriminatory burdens of a protectionist kind does not involve inconsistency with the words "absolutely free": it is simply to identify the kinds or classes of burdens, restrictions, controls and standards from which the section guarantees absolute freedom. (394)

The High Court did so too by reference to the history and context of the section:

> The history of s 92 points to the elimination of protection as the object of s 92 in its application to trade and commerce. The means by which that object is achieved is the prohibition of measures which burden interstate trade and commerce and which also have the effect of conferring protection on intrastate trade and commerce of the same kind. The

> general hallmark of measures which contravene s 92 in this way is their effect as discriminatory against interstate trade and commerce in that protectionist sense.

> In relation to both fiscal and non-fiscal measures, history and context alike favour the approach that the freedom guaranteed to interstate trade and commerce under s 92 is freedom from discriminatory burdens in the protectionist sense already mentioned. (395)

Since the case of *Cole v Whitfield*, the High Court has interpreted s 92 as a rule against discriminatory laws and measures of a protectionist kind, without qualification, without interruption. In a subsequent case, *Castlemaine Tooheys Ltd v South Australia* (1990), Chief Justice Mason together with Justices Gerard Brennan, Deane, Daryl Dawson and John Toohey confirmed the test:

> *Cole v Whitfield* established that a law which imposes a burden on interstate trade and commerce but does not give the domestic product or the intrastate trade in that product a competitive or market advantage over the imported product or the interstate trade in that product, is not a law which discriminates against interstate trade and commerce on protectionist grounds. (467)

The High Court continues to apply the *Cole v Whitfield* test for s 92. The judgments in *Betfair Pty Ltd v Racing New South Wales* (2012) and *Sportsbet Pty Ltd v New South Wales* (2012) which comprise the most recent interpretation of s 92 by the High Court, also rule against discriminatory burdens of a protectionist kind:

> It is the effects upon Betfair as an interstate trader, more particularly in its ability to compete with local traders, with which s 92 is concerned and to which the requirement of protectionism is directed. It is not enough, as Betfair's argument perhaps assumed, that it be an interstate trader. (289)

This chapter argues that an interpretation of s 92 as an anti-protectionist norm is not consistent with the federal purpose of the section to establish a national market for Australia because it can allow laws and measures that discriminate against interstate trade if they are not protectionist (Villalta Puig 2001, 2008, 2013, 2017, 2018; Villalta Puig and Kiefel 2014). Under the *Cole v Whitfield* test, the High Court can only invalidate a State law or measure if that law or measure places an unreasonable burden on interstate trade and, because of the burden, local trade gains a competitive advantage.

The problem, then, is that, under the *Cole v Whitfield* test for s 92, the High Court will not characterise a burden as protectionist, however unreasonable, if it affects intrastate and interstate trade equally. Thus, only a non-discrimination norm can translate the idea of free trade into a principle of market access, equal access to the national market for local and interstate traders alike. A non-discrimination norm is a more effective instrument of free trade than an anti-protectionist norm, quite simply, because a non-discrimination norm can more closely integrate a non-unitary market than an anti-protectionist norm (Villalta Puig 2001, 2008, 2013, 2017, 2018; Villalta Puig and Kiefel 2014).

9.4 Conclusion

This chapter has outlined the judicial history of the federal market of Australia through the role of the High Court in the constitutionalisation of free trade under s 92 of the Australian Constitution. The High Court first attempted to interpret the section in 1908, in the case of *Fox v Robbins*. Its last attempt to interpret the section was eight decades later, in 1988, in the case of *Cole v Whitfield*. In the period between these two cases, the High Court relied on one of two opposite theories of interpretation. One theory revolved around the idea of free enterprise. The other theory revolved around the idea of free trade. From 1908 to 1988, the two theories and their applications struggled for doctrinal supremacy. Each theory and each application commanded a period of judicial influence.

The initial dominance of the free trade theory was brief. Its interpretation of s 92 as either a prohibition of discrimination against interstate trade or as a protection of interstate trade flow was only ever influential in the period immediately after Federation. In comparison, the individual rights theory of interpretation dominated, almost without challenge, the latter part of the twentieth century. The free trade theory did timidly resurge in the 1970s, first through the fiscal burdens application of Justice Murphy and then through the still primitive discriminatory protectionism application of Justice Mason and Justice Jacobs. However, it was not until 1988, in *Cole v Whitfield*, that the High Court settled the interpretation of s 92, once and for all, as a rule against discriminatory burdens of a protectionist kind, an anti-protectionist norm rather than a non-discrimination norm.

References

Cases

Bartter's Farms Pty Ltd v Todd (1978) 139 CLR 499
Buck v Bavone (1976) 135 CLR 110
Cole v Whitfield (1988) 165 CLR 360
Commonwealth v Bank of New South Wales (*Bank Nationalisation Case*) (1949) 79 CLR 497
Finemore's Transport Pty Ltd v New South Wales (1978) 139 CLR 338
Fox v Robbins (1909) 8 CLR 115
Hospital Provident Fund Pty Ltd v Victoria (1953) 87 CLR 1
James v Commonwealth (1936) 55 CLR 1
Miller v TCN Channel Nine Pty Ltd (1986) 161 CLR 556
North Eastern Dairy Co Ltd v Dairy Industry Authority of New South Wales (1975) 134 CLR 559
O Gilpin Ltd v Commissioner for Road Transport and Tramways (NSW) (1935) 52 CLR 189
Peanut Board v Rockhampton Harbour Board (1933) 48 CLR 266
R v Vizzard (1933) 50 CLR 30
SOS (Mowbray) Pty Ltd v Mead (1972) 124 CLR 529

Books and Articles

Carney G (1991) The re-interpretation of Section 92: The Decline of Free Enterprise and the Rise of Free Trade. Bond Law Rev 3:149

Coper M (1983) Freedom of interstate trade under the Australian Constitution. Butterworths, Sydney

Coper M (1987) Encounters with the Australian Constitution. CCH, Sydney

Coper M (1989–1990) The curious case of the callow crayfish: the new law relating to Section 92 of the Australian Constitution. Commonwealth of Australia, Parliamentary Library Discussion Paper No 1

Davis SR (1950) The Australian Bank nationalisation case. Mod Law Rev 13:107

Heuzenroeder H (2001) Section 92: The Constitutional Project to Build a Federation (Part II). Law Soc S Aust Bull 23(2):28

Kirk J (1997) Constitutional guarantees, characterisation and the concept of proportionality. Melb Univ Law Rev 21:1

Lane PH (1988) The present test for invalidity under Section 92 of the constitution. Aust Law J 62:604

Lindsay K (1999) The Australian Constitution in context. LBC Information Services, Sydney

Murphy LK (1980) The responsibility of judges. In: Evans G (ed) Law, politics and the labor movement 2. Legal Service Bulletin, Melbourne

O'Brien B (1981) Inchoate rights to interstate communications under Section 92. Melb Univ Law Rev 13:198

Sawer G (1952a) Constitutional law. In: Paton GW (ed) The Commonwealth of Australia: the development of its laws and constitution. Stevens and Sons, London

Sawer G (1952b) The record of judicial review. In: Sawer G (ed) Federalism: an Australian jubilee study. F. W. Cheshire Pty Ltd, Melbourne

Sharwood RL (1958) Section 92 in the Federal Conventions: a fresh appraisal. Melb Univ Law Rev 1:331

Simpson A (2005) Grounding the High Court's Modern Section 92 jurisprudence: the case for improper purpose as the touchstone. Fed Law Rev 33:445

Staker C (1990) Section 92 of the Constitution and the European Court of Justice. Fed Law Rev 19:322

Villalta Puig G (2001) Free movement of goods: the European experience in the Australian context. Aust Law J 75(10):639–652

Villalta Puig G (2008) The High Court of Australia and Section 92 of the Australian Constitution. Thomson Lawbook Co, Sydney

Villalta Puig G (2011) Intercolonial free trade: the drafting history of Section 92 of the Australian Constitution. Univ Tasmania Law Rev 30(2):1–20

Villalta Puig G (2013) Betfair and Sportsbet: the remains of the federal purpose of s 92 of the Australian Constitution. Aust Law J 87(3):178–199

Villalta Puig G (2017) Freedom of trade and commerce. In: Grote R, Lachenmann F, Wolfrum R (eds) Max Planck encyclopedia of comparative constitutional law. OUP, Oxford

Villalta Puig G (2018) Free trade as an Australian constitutional value: a functionalist approach to the interpretation of the economic constitution of Australia. In: Dixon R (ed) Australian constitutional values. Hart Publishing, Oxford, pp 287–304

Villalta Puig G, Kiefel S (2014) The constitutionalisation of free trade by the High Court of Australia and the Court of Justice of the European Union. Glob J Comp Law 3(1):34–49

Zines L (1964) Sir Owen Dixon's theory of federalism. Fed Law Rev 1:221

Zines L (1973) The balancing of community and national interests by the European Court. Fed Law Rev 5:171

Zines L (1997) The High Court and the Constitution, 4th edn. Butterworths, Sydney, p 108

Chapter 10
India's Tryst with Free Trade: Overcoming the Inherent Challenges of Federalism

Wasiq Abass Dar

10.1 Introduction

Federalism as a system of governance is well acknowledged around the world. To put it lucidly, under a federal system there is a government for the entire country and there are separate governments at the subnational level for different states or regions. One of the significant features of federal system is that the federating units or the subnational units, generally, get to retain their financial autonomy to a great extent. Also, depending upon the federal structure, subnational units may get to play a role in country's multilateral trade relations. Although federal systems exists in many jurisdictions across the length and breadth of the globe, there is no one-size-fits-all kind of model of federalism.[1] A federal governance system that is well designed to cater the needs of its nation can significantly contribute to the prosperity and stability of that country.[2] Countries like Canada, Australia, Switzerland and the USA are the fitting ambassadors of federal form of government.

India, owing to its geographical, linguistic, cultural, and political diversity opted for a federal form of government. Though the seventh largest economy in the world, in terms of trade flow it is yet to reach a position where it can claim to be remarkable.[3] Despite the major economic reforms of 1991 that led to liberating its economy from the excessive trade barriers, India is still counted among the nations espousing significant tariff and non-tariff barriers.[4] Apart from the conventional tariff and

[1]Bagchi (2000), p. 3025.

[2]Bagchi (2001), p. 2.

[3]Sarkar and Patrick (2015), p. 2.

[4]Ibid.

W. A. Dar (✉)
Jindal Global Law School, O.P. Jindal Global University, Sonipat, India
e-mail: wadar@jgu.edu.in

C. I. Nagy (ed.), *World Trade and Local Public Interest*, Studies in European Economic Law and Regulation 19, https://doi.org/10.1007/978-3-030-41920-2_10

non-tariff barriers; extensive documentations, lengthy processing delays, corruption are also some of the significant non-tariff barriers that India has been criticized for.[5] Procurement policy of government, which varies among the State Governments, is another area of concern—as far as barriers to free trade in India are concerned.[6]

This predicament that is associated with India is basically a reflection of one of the major concerns international trade and commerce continues to face—i.e. the ever-growing protectionism, which has further amplified after the Global Financial Crisis of last decade.[7] Protectionism in international trade and commerce may not always be in the form of tariff barriers. Protectionism in the garb of legitimate discretion provided to States under multilateral agreements, through various non-tariff barriers, can also lead to restrictions and discrimination—obstructing free flow of trade.[8]

This chapter analyses the federal system of India from trade and commerce point of view, and examines how it responds to the demands of an international economic environment. Focus of the article remains on the inherent challenges to free trade and commerce that India has faced or continues to face due to its federal structure. The relevant fiscal autonomy guaranteed to the states under the Indian Constitution is discussed—followed by an analyses as to how such autonomy may be used or abused to interfere with or to obstruct the free flow of trade and commerce. The chapter also highlights the major reforms India has undergone to promote free trade and commerce, especially the introduction of Goods and Services Tax (GST) that aims at transforming India into a unified market—thereby mitigating the possible perils of provincialism and protectionism.

10.2 Indian Federal System: A Snapshot

One of the significant features under a federal system is distribution of competence between the federal and the subnational governments in terms of legislative, executive, judicial and financial responsibilities.[9] As far as India is concerned, it is established that India is a federal state—where federalism is considered as one of the basic structures of the Indian Constitution.[10]

However in case of India, the Central or the Union government enjoys a relatively more dominant character, because of which the form of government is sometimes referred to as 'quasi-federal' in nature.[11] The State governments do not get to operate in too much of free space, particularly in the context of economic policy. Issues

[5]Office of the United States Trade Representative (2017), p. 208.

[6]Ibid 209.

[7]Mikic and Wermelinger (2010), p. 8.

[8]Ibid.

[9]Singh (2016a), p. 451.

[10]Kuldeep Nayar v Union of India (2006) 7 SCC 1; Singh (2016a), p. 451.

[11]Bagchi (2000), p. 3033; Bagchi (2001), p. 2.

dealing with monetary policies, banking, macro-management of economics come under the domain of Union government, whereas States get to govern on local issues concerning public health, law and order, land and revenue matters etc.[12] Moreover, there are several escape clauses in the Constitution that basically give the national Parliament the ability to override the State's authority in special circumstances.[13]

But State governments in India do get to legislate in matters of taxes at the respective State level. The reason behind giving the States the power to impose local taxes falls back on the argument that States should also have their own revenue generating resources—so that they are not financially dependent upon the federal government, for everything.[14]

For the purposes of clarity and efficiency in governance, the Constitution of India provides in Schedule VII—the lists enumerating powers and functions of the Union government (Union List) and the State government (State List). There is a Concurrent list as well, which demarcates various areas where the Union government through the Union Parliament or the State government through the State legislature can legislate. It happens at times that certain issues that matter to a State may also be of interest to more than one State or the entire country; such matters are covered under the Concurrent list—where both Union and State governments have the authority to exercise powers.[15] It is important to note that, as far as Concurrent list is concerned, the Union gets primacy over State(s).[16]

In India, the power of the Parliament to legislate is clearly dominant—given the larger number of subjects on which it can legislate. Also, the preference given to the law made by the Parliament on subjects in the Concurrent List over the law made by State legislature(s) on the same subjects under the Concurrent List, confirms the position.[17]

International trade of India is primarily governed by The Foreign Trade (Development and Regulation) Act of 1992. Under Section 3 of the Act, the Union Government is authorized to make provisions with regard to development and regulation of foreign trade—which includes framing rules to prohibit, restrict, or otherwise regulate foreign trade. In case of imposing quantitative restrictions as well, it is the Union Government that is authorized under Section 9A of the Act, to take appropriate measures to protect domestic industry from serious injury.

The decisions with regard to international trade and commerce take place at the federal level, in India.[18] The major players that participate in the process are the representatives of the Union Ministry of Industries and Commerce, External Affairs, Agriculture, Consumer Affairs, Textiles, Public Distribution, Petroleum, Steel,

---

[12]Singh (2016b), p. 523; Bagchi (2001), p. 3.

[13]Singh (2016b), p. 523.

[14]Bagchi (2005), p. 1806.

[15]Singh (2016a), p. 453.

[16]Bagchi (2000), p. 3033.

[17]Singh (2016a), p. 454.

[18]Conceição-Heldt (2013), p. 437.

members from Confederation of Indian Industry (CII), members from the Federation of Indian Chamber of Commerce and Industry (FICCI), and representatives of the Reserve Bank of India.[19]

Though, on the face of it, India represents a federal system where Union and States share sovereignty; in reality the amount of authority that States can exercise in dealing with matters of international trade and commerce is almost negligible.[20]

Although, export and the import policy of India is driven by the domestic considerations; as a result of India's commitments towards the WTO, Union government has more or less overshadowed the State governments in deciding on the policy matters, even on the issues that were earlier under the domain of State governments.[21]

10.3 India and the World Trade: An Overview of Pre and Post 1991 Reforms

Immediately after independence, India decided to impose various kinds of restrictions on trade in the country by regulating 'production, supply, pricing, and distribution of commodities' that felt under the category of commodities 'essential for community'.[22] Restrictions entered a different level when in 1953, through a Constitutional amendment, the power of the Union government to regulate trade in various commodities was increased. As a result of this amendment the Parliament of India enacted the Essential Commodities Act of 1955 which empowered the Union government to regulate trade of some products that were regulated by State governments as well.[23]

First two decades, after independence, witnessed growing protectionism and restriction in trade and commerce within India and with partners from outside India. Following the policy of self-sufficiency, India evolved as a trade regime with a very high tariff and non-tariff barriers.[24] There was some amount of respite in this regard in 1970s and 1980s, though not enough to call it a major economic reform.[25]

The economic condition of the country, at the macro level, continued to deteriorate to a situation that there was a major Balance of Payment crisis by 1991.[26] The sudden surge in the oil prices, owing to the Gulf War in 1990, served as the final nail

[19]Secretariat WTO (2015) para 2.9; Conceição-Heldt (2013), p. 437.

[20]Jenkins (2003), p. 80.

[21]Secretariat WTO (2015) para 2.14–2.15; Jenkins (2003), p. 75.

[22]Bagchi (2002), p. 2303.

[23]Ibid.

[24]Topalova and Khandelwal (2011), p. 999.

[25]Bagchi (2008), p. 42.

[26]Ibid.

in the coffin. India was left with no choice but to approach the IMF to help managing the existing economic crisis. The IMF agreed to support, but with conditions that led to major economic reforms in India. India had to adopt the Structural Adjustment Policies allowing greater market access and less trade restrictive policies.[27]

As an obvious consequence, the only appropriate option left with India was to open up to the globalized and liberalized world market. The immediate outcome of opening up of the market was a great impetus in free trade in goods, services, and technology.[28] From 1991 onwards, India has been consistently working on reducing the tariff and non-tariff barriers by lessening trade hurdles like high taxes, licenses, cumbersome documentation—with an aim to promote eased trade and commerce at a multilateral level.[29]

However, this move of Indian government to open up to the global liberalized trade and commerce could not escape brickbats, particularly at the local level. One of the major criticisms made against this move was that economic globalization caused limiting the capacity of the subnational units, i.e. the State governments—in turn affecting the functioning of federalism.[30] Another criticism raised was that opening up to global market and acceding to international organizations has reduced the autonomy of the States to accomplish their own policy objectives, as it is the Union government that decides on matters of international trade—even on those areas, for example agriculture, that were otherwise Constitutionally under the domain of State government.[31]

Some of the examples, often cited, of how opening up to the international trade and international trade regulations has impacted interests of States are the adversities faced by local producers of raw silk in Karnataka due to reduced barriers to imports, tea growers in Tamil Nadu due to fluctuations in pricing, and coconut growers in Kerala due to strong competition from imports.[32]

10.4 Power of Indian States to Restrict Free Trade: Potential for Protectionism?

The Indian Trade Policy, which basically sets outs the foreign trade policy of India in detail, is released every five years by the Government of India. India's trade policy, in general, after liberalization has been to increase its contribution to global trade. However, it continues to maintain a protectionist approach when it comes to certain

[27]Topalova and Khandelwal (2011), p. 996.

[28]Goldar (2005), p. 2.

[29]Conceição-Heldt (2013), p. 436.

[30]Breton (2003); Bagchi (2008), p. 43.

[31]Jenkins (2003); Bagchi (2008), p. 46.

[32]Jenkins (2003), pp. 75–76.

sectors like agriculture.[33] India has imposed both tariff and non-tariff measures to protect domestic interests in such sectors.[34]

The major non-tariff measures exist under three heads; banned or prohibited products, restricted items for which importer requires license, and canalized products that can be imported by government trading monopolies only—with approval of the Union cabinet on timing and quantity of import.[35] Non-tariff measures like; labeling requirements, authorizations, licensing, sanitary and phytosanitary measures are regulated by the Union government.[36] The Union government is also empowered to impose non-tariff restrictions on the basis of security, self-sufficiency, balance-of-payments, health, and moral reasons.[37]

As far as tariffs are concerned, one of the problems that India's inland tax systems has been suffering from is the complex multiplicity of tax rates and their variation, not just in terms of commodities but States as well.[38]

Imports, in India, have been subject to various State level value added or sales taxes, in addition to several other local taxes and charges.[39] States on various occasions have restricted trade by resorting to various tax mechanisms such as imposition of taxes like state sales tax, octroi, and luxury tax. Fiscal autonomy at subnational level has its own vices, including varying tax rates and bases—that could go against the idea of unified market.[40] Such State level taxes such as sales tax, excise tax, entry tax are some of the fiscal barriers that have adversely affected trade and commerce in India.

For example, the State of West Bengal used to impose a luxury tax on all the items that were not manufactured in India—basically the imported products.[41] Owing to the pressure from local producers, States like Tamil Nadu and Maharashtra have in past resorted to entry tax on certain commodities.[42]

Art. 246 of the Indian Constitution, as a general rule, provides that both the Parliament and the State legislatures are authorized to legislate over imposition and collection of taxes, on relevant areas as provided under Schedule VII of the Constitution.[43] Tax laws, made in connection with trade and commerce within Indian territory, are expected to be drafted in a manner that such laws do not cast any impediment on the underlying objective of free trade—as enshrined under Article 301 of the Indian Constitution.[44]

[33]Conceição-Heldt (2013), p. 436.

[34]Pasha and Pasha (2012), pp. 13–14.

[35]Office of the United States Trade Representative (2017), p. 207.

[36]Pasha and Pasha (2012), p. 10.

[37]Secretariat WTO (2015) para 3.39.

[38]Bagchi (2005), p. 1806.

[39]Office of the United States Trade Representative (2017), p. 207.

[40]Das-Gupta (2006), p. 232.

[41]Bagchi (2002), p. 2305.

[42]Ibid.

[43]Singh (2016a), p. 456.

[44]Atiabari Tea Co. Ltd v State of Assam (1961) 232 SC AIR 9-11; Bagchi (2002), p. 2303.

Part XIII of the Indian Constitution comprises of Articles 301 to 307 which deals with 'Trade, Commerce, and Intercourse within the territory of India'. Founders of the Constitution while drafting Part XIII envisioned having a free flow of trade and commerce within India in the larger interest of the country—though not ignoring reasonable regional interests.[45] The India Supreme Court in *Atiabari Tea* case spelled out the underlying essence of the Part XIII of the Constitution of India, where it observed that elimination of trade barriers between different States of the independent India is quintessential for the economic unity of India.[46]

Though there is a constitutional mandate to ensure free flow of trade and commerce within India, it does not suggest that the Parliament or State legislatures cannot impose tax laws or other regulatory measures to restrict trade. However, such restrictions cannot stand the test of law unless the restrictions abide by the limitations provided under the Part XIII of the Constitution of India.

Where as Article 302 of the Constitution of India empowers the Parliament of India to impose restrictions on freedom of trade between one State and another, or in any part of the territory of India, to protect public interest; Article 304 authorizes the **State legislatures** to impose restrictions on freedom of trade and commerce. The Constitution of India, although, empowers Parliament and State legislatures to impose certain kinds of restrictions, the restrictions have to be in line with the underlying mandate of Article 301 of the Constitution of India, i.e. non-interference with the freedom of trade and commerce within the country.[47]

Here it is very crucial to appreciate that Article 304 implies two classes of restrictions. In clause (a) the State legislature is authorized to impose a non-discriminatory *tax* on goods imported into the State. And in clause (b) the State legislature is authorized to impose *other* reasonable restrictions, in public interest, that are not related to or levied as taxes. In effect, Article 304 (b) can be used by States to impose non-tariff barriers on imports to encourage protectionism, in the guise of public interest. However, it is important to note that Article 304 in its proviso states that; before the State legislature introduces a Bill or Amendment for the purposes of such restriction as provided in clause (b) of the Article, it is imperative to procure a prior sanction of the President of India—which in effect means the Central Government.[48] Therefore, not providing unqualified autonomy to the State government to impose any such measures, under the guise of public interest, that can obstruct free flow of trade and protect the vested interests of that State. Although, in theory there appears to be a safety value—in shape of the aforementioned proviso to Article 304 (b) that prohibits unqualified autonomy, in practice matters might not necessarily be so uncomplicated. State legislature, ignoring the pre-requisites, may misuse or abuse this provision of law to obstruct free flow of trade—even if it is only for a temporary period of time or unless resolved through lengthy or contentious litigations. A possibility that cannot be completely ruled out.

[45]Datar (2016), p. 488.

[46]Atiabari Tea Co. Ltd v State of Assam (1961) 232 SC AIR 9-11; Datar (2016), p. 487.

[47]Bagchi (2001), p. 13.

[48]Basu (2011), p. 1828; Jindal Stainless Steel Ltd. (2) v State of Haryana (2006) 241 SCC 33-34.

10.5 The GST Regime: Towards a Unified Indian Market

India has often been cited as an example of being a jurisdiction having a complex tax system owing to both structural and administrative problems.[49] India, in past, has on multiple occasions tried to cater to the demands of the market by reforming its tax structure. Its fiscal federal arrangements have been subject to a variety of modifications through Constitutional amendments.[50] One major reform was transforming from sales tax regime at State level and excise duty at Central level to Value Added Tax for both the taxes separately. The aim was to contain the cascading effect in indirect taxation, in order to make it more administration and competition friendly.

The latest reforms, introduced in India through the Constitutional Amendment in 2016, in the taxation sector led to a new regime for indirect taxation—called the Goods and Services Tax (GST), effective from 1st of July 2017. GST is basically a step towards getting rid of the convoluted and multilayered taxation anomalies that existed in Indian taxation system. GST simplifies the earlier complex tax structure by providing a national level comprehensive tax levy mechanism on manufacturing, sale and consumption of goods and services.[51] It has amalgamated various Central and State taxes, therefore significantly mitigating the long existing tribulations that were part of Indian indirect taxation system. Now the erstwhile indirect taxes like excise duty, service tax, value added tax, luxury tax, octroi and several other State taxes are incorporated into one GST across the country.[52] With the advent of GST, India aims at becoming more trade friendly, and emerge as a unified market economy.[53]

As far as imports are concerned, in addition to the taxes imposed by the Union government, there used to be considerable differences between the taxes imposed by various States of India, marring the trade flow and market integration within India.[54] For example, imports used to be subject to the following tariffs:

1. Basic Custom Duty under the Customs Act of 1962.
2. Additional Duty, also known as the Countervailing Duty.
3. Special Additional Duty (SAD), that was basically imposed on imports in order to provide a level playing field for domestic products there were subject to the State sales tax—that varied from State to State. In 2007, the Government of India provided an option to the importers to claim refund of SAD paid on products that

[49]Secretariat WTO (2015) para 1.7.

[50]Singh (2016b), p. 525.

[51]Dani (2016), p. 1.

[52]Banik and Singh (2017), p. 10.

[53]Notani (2017).

[54]Melchior (2010), p. 16.

were subsequently sold in Indian States and for which those States had charged sales tax.[55]

4. Education Cess on the aggregate of Custom duty on all imports.
5. Tariffs like Anti-Dumping duty, Ant-Subsidy duty, and Safeguard Duty, if applicable.
6. Other State level taxes, if applicable.

With the introduction of GST, the Additional Duty of Customs, the Special Additional Duty, and all other applicable State level tariffs are replaced with the levy of the Integrated Goods and Services Tax (IGST). Now import of Goods and Services is treated as inter-state supply for the purposes of levy of GST, or IGST in this case. The IGST on imports is levied at the time of imports along with the levy of the duties under the Customs Act.[56] This has not only simplified the otherwise complicated tax structure, but also removed the mess of varying tax rates and bureaucratic hurdles—therefore turning out to be a major step towards mitigating the challenges of protectionism that trade and commerce in India faced owing to the misuse of fiscal federalism.

10.6 Conclusion

General Agreement on Tariffs and Trade (GATT) that originated in 1947 has played a crucial role in harmonizing rules on international trade and commerce.[57] WTO, the successor of GATT, has further given impetus to the idea of a barrier free economic and commercial interaction between nations. Trade liberalization, in the last few decades, has become one of the most significant economic policies of nations across the globe. Despite that, one cannot discount the fact that countries do—at times—resort to policies that are otherwise allowed under the multilateral trade rules but used as disguised restrictions to protect vested domestic interests.[58] Subnational governments under federal system, depending upon the authority and autonomy they enjoy, can also impose such disguised trade restrictions—increasing challenges for the federal government to ensure free flow of trade and commerce.

The Constitution makers of India appreciated the significance of free trade within the country, therefore, advocated for it in Part XIII of the Constitution of India. However such freedom was not to be absolute, as the Constitution provides certain circumstances under which the Parliament and more importantly even the State legislatures may impose certain restrictions. In such a scenario, it is essential that the Union government gets the last say in matters of international trade and

[55]Secretariat WTO (2015) para 3.27; Office of the United States Trade Representative (2017), p. 207.

[56]Section 5, IGST Act 2017.

[57]Sharma (2012), p. 66.

[58]Mikic and Wermelinger (2010), p. 27.

commerce. Otherwise, State government(s) may resort to formulating restrictive regulations in garb of protecting their own domestic producers—affecting the greater underlying objective of free trade and commerce within the territory of India. Pertinent to mention, one cannot ignore the reality that in a federal form of government, trade offs between subnational fiscal autonomy and national economic efficiency are inevitable.[59]

References

Bagchi A (2000) 'Rethinking federalism' overview of current debates with some reflections in Indian context. Econ Polit Wkly 35(34):3025–3026

Bagchi A (2001) Fifty years of fiscal federalism in India: an appraisal. Paper presented at the Kale Memorial Lecture, Gokhale Institute of Politics & Economics, Pune, 8 December 2001

Bagchi A (2002) Enforcing the Constitution's common market mandate: time to invoke Article 307. Econ Polit Wkly 37(24):2303–2308

Bagchi A (2005) VAT and state autonomy. Econ Polit Wkly 40(18):1806–1807

Bagchi A (2008) Globalisation and federalism: uneasy partners? Econ Polit Wkly 43(38):41–48

Banik N, Singh S (2017) Demystifying the role of 'Barriers at and behind the Borders' in India: a case study of pharmaceutical products. http://www.cuts-citee.org/pdf/Discussion_Paper-Demystifying_the_Role_of_Barriers_at_and_behind_the_Borders_in_India.pdf. Accessed 05 Jan 2018

Basu DD (2011) Shorter constitution of India, vol 2, 14th edn. Lexis Nexis

Breton A (2003) Competitive federalism and incipient globalization. Paper presented at the National Institute of Public Finance and Policy, New Delhi

Conceição-Heldt E (2013) Emerging powers in WTO negotiations: the domestic sources of trade policy preferences. Int Trade J 27:431–449

Dani S (2016) A research paper on an impact of Goods and Service Tax (GST) on Indian economy. J Bus Econ 7(4):1–2

Das-Gupta A (2006) Internal trade barriers in India: fiscal check-posts. South Asia Econ J 7 (2):231–254

Datar A (2016) Inter-state trade, commerce, and intercourse. In: Sujit C, Madhav K, Pratab BM (eds) The Oxford handbook of the Indian Constitution. OUP, pp 487–501

Goldar B (2005) Impact on India of tariff and quantitative restrictions under WTO. Working Paper, Indian Council for Research in International Economic Relations, New Delhi. http://icrier.org/pdf/WP172.pdf. Accessed 03 Jan 2018

Jenkins R (2003) India's states and the making of foreign economic policy: the limits of the constituent diplomacy paradigm. J Federalism 33(4):663–681

Melchior A (2010) Globalization, domestic market integration, and the regional disparities of India. https://brage.bibsys.no/xmlui/bitstream/handle/11250/277887/WP-780-Melchior.pdf?sequence=3. Accessed 04 Jan 2018

Mikic M, Wermelinger M (eds) (2010) Rising non-tariff protectionism and crisis recovery: a study of Asia-Pacific Research and training network on trade. United Nations Publications

Notani S (2017) International trade in goods and services in India: overview. In International Trade and Commercial Transactions in Global Guide 2017. https://uk.practicallaw.thomsonreuters.com/w-009-2204?navId=062F0E851FA14CC566DB6CD93261DDB1&comp=pluk&transitionType=Default&contextData=(sc.Default). Accessed 10 Jan 2018

[59]Das-Gupta (2006), p. 232.

Office of the United States Trade Representative (2017) National trade estimate report on foreign trade barrier. https://ustr.gov/sites/default/files/files/reports/2017/NTE/2017%20NTE.pdf. Accessed 13 Jan 2018

Pasha HA, Pasha AG (2012) Non-tariff barriers of India and Pakistan and their impact, Institute of Public Policy. Beaconhouse National University, Pakistan. http://www.sjbipp.org/publications/PR/projectreport/PR-25-16.pdf. Accessed 11 Jan 2018

Sarkar P, Patrick M (2015) India's trade barriers: an analysis with reference to tariffs and customs. http://www.cppr.in/wp-content/uploads/2015/01/Trade-Report.pdf. Accessed 15 Jan 2018

Secretariat WTO (2015) Trade policy review report by the Secretariat. https://www.wto.org/english/tratop_e/tpr_e/s313_e.pdf. Accessed 07 Jan 2018

Sharma LM (2012) Vision 2020: transform, conform and perform. Paper presented at 40th National Convention of Company Secretaries, Pune, 4–6 October 2012

Singh MP (2016a) The federal scheme. In: Sujit C, Madhav K, Pratab BM (eds) The Oxford handbook of the Indian Constitution. OUP, pp 451–465

Singh N (2016b) Fiscal federalism. In: Chaudhary S, Khosla M, Mehta PB (eds) The Oxford handbook of the Indian Constitution. OUP, pp 521–539

Topalova P, Khandelwal A (2011) Trade liberalization and firm-productivity: the case of India. Rev Econ Stat 93(3):995–1009

Part IV

Chapter 11
Foreign Investors and Greater Transparency in Investor-State Dispute Settlement: Reevaluating Confidentiality Expectations in International Investment Arbitration

Rebecca E. Khan

11.1 The Paradigm Shift from Confidentiality to Transparency as a Parallel Movement with the Shift from Investor Protection to Balancing of Interests in Investor-State Dispute Settlement

The status of the investor in international law in general, and international investment law in particular, is an important starting point for the discussion on the treatment of investors, and the paradigm shift that has occurred alongside the transparency movement. The discussion in this section looks at the substantive aspects of international investment law in relation to the protection of investments, as the basis for the procedural shifts in investment arbitration towards increased transparency.

Before the development of the investor-State dispute settlement system through bilateral investment treaties and the International Centre for Settlement of Investment Disputes (ICSID) Convention, foreign investors did not have access to international methods of dispute settlement.[1] Investors had to rely on diplomatic protection by their home State.[2] When the ICSID Convention was being crafted, international arbitration was seen as "an attractive alternative to the settlement of investment disputes by national courts or through diplomatic protection."[3] Investment arbitration has allowed investors to take control of the arbitration process, liberating them from dependence on the politically-motivated decisions of their

[1]Schreuer et al. (2011), p. 6.

[2]Ibid.

[3]Ibid 7.

R. E. Khan (✉)
University of the Philippines, Diliman, Quezon City, Philippines
e-mail: rkhan@law.gwu.edu; rekhan4@up.edu.ph; rebecca.khan@dlsu.edu.ph

C. I. Nagy (ed.), *World Trade and Local Public Interest*, Studies in European Economic Law and Regulation 19, https://doi.org/10.1007/978-3-030-41920-2_11

home States on whether or not to espouse their claims.[4] Indeed, during the negotiations for the ICSID Convention, drafters rejected a suggested provision requiring authorization by the home State for the initiation of an investment claim.[5] That investors act independently from their home States is further underscored by the fact that investor-claimants bear the costs of the arbitration, not its home State,[6] and that any possible compensation is due to the investor-claimant only.[7]

One scholar proposes the dual interest that investors serve in contributing to the development of international investment law: “The investor makes a direct claim for the implementation of treaty standards in international law primarily out of self-interest; however, at the same time, the investor also indirectly serves the public interest in the effective application and enforcement of international law.”[8]

There are two types of investors: natural persons and legal persons.[9] While there have been a number of investor-claimants who are natural persons, the overwhelming majority of investment claims are brought by corporations,[10] and in several instances, multinational corporations. International investment law has developed rapidly in the past two decades, such that in the various spheres of international law where multinational corporations operate, “international investment law grants [multinational corporations] the most robust rights.”[11] Looking at the rights directly conferred upon foreign investors by the ICSID Convention and the international investment agreements that make up the investor-State dispute settlement system, a number of scholars have argued that investors have been elevated to the status of a partial subject of international law, and are regarded as more than mere holders of derivative rights vis-à-vis their home State.[12] Not an exclusive development in international investment law, this movement towards the recognition of the rights and interests of investors reflects the general trend in international law regarding the status of the individual.[13]

---

[4]Reinisch (2015), pp. 258–259.

[5]Tillmann (2014), p. 91.

[6]Reinisch (2015), p. 259.

[7]Tillmann (2014), p. 91.

[8]Ibid 76.

[9]OECD 10,17.

[10]Peters (2016), p. 282.

[11]Wouters and Chané (2015), p. 234.

[12]Peters (2016), pp. 306–308; Tillmann (2014), pp. 96–98; Reinisch (2015), p. 260. Peters examines the scholarship on the debate between direct and derivative rights and maintains that “the better arguments are in favor of acknowledging, as a matter of principle, the possibility of investors enjoying autonomous substantive rights, arising from investment protection treaties under international law.” Braun makes an affirmative argument for the status of investors as a partial subject of international law. Reinisch makes a survey of the arguments propounded in favor of and against considering investors as partial subjects of international law without proposing the adoption of one view over the other.

[13]Hindelang and Krajewski (2016), p. 379. Citing Peters (2014), p. 257 et seq.

The rights granted to investors in international investment agreements have led to the observation that the so-called "first-generation" bilateral investment treaties were exclusively oriented towards investment protection.[14] Up until the late 1990s, the objective of investment agreements "was only, or at least predominantly, to protect foreign investors and their investments against illegitimate actions of the host State, most notably expropriations without compensation."[15] Because these features are embodied in treaties, the "apparent bias in favor of claimants and against respondent States" is attributed to "structural features" of the investor-State dispute settlement system.[16]

Wälde discusses the "asymmetry" in investment arbitration, viewed both as a necessity and a criticism: in treaty-based arbitration in particular, "private investors can sue governments, but governments cannot sue private investors."[17] Wälde notes that this feature of investment treaty arbitration is "sometimes decried as indication of the one-sidedness (in favor of the investor) of investment treaties."[18] Another commentator echoes this thought, noting that "[s]cholars are in unison to consider the host States' consent to arbitrate incorporated in those treaties as a unilateral offer to arbitrate. [...] This power to accept the offer to arbitrate, vested solely in the figure of the foreign investor, has introduced an asymmetry between host States and investors that has become the hallmark of investment arbitration."[19] Similarly, Van Harten offers the following observations about the investor's consent:

> [...] in investment treaty arbitration, an investor decides whether to resort to arbitration only after a dispute with the state has arisen. The consent is thus retrospective: it is specific to a dispute arising from the regulatory relationship. Unlike the state, the investor does not agree to the compulsory arbitration of future disputes with the host state or with individuals affected by the investor's business activities. Tribunals do not have general jurisdiction to award damages against multinational firms for violations of treaty standards that regulate international investors. Generally speaking, only states are sanctioned and only investors are compensated.[20]

Wälde points out, however, that this perceived asymmetry was brought about by the rationale for investment protection in the first place: reverse mirroring the "inherent structural asymmetry" in which private investors are exposed to the regulatory and adjudicatory powers of the sovereign State.[21] The protection of foreign investments in international investment agreements was borne from the concern that unrestrained governmental power was a potential threat to the security of investments, and that national laws and procedures of the host State would be

[14]Muchlinski (2011a), p. 23; Sornarajah (2017), p. 540.

[15]Hindelang and Krajewski (2016), p. 379.

[16]Van Harten (2010), p. 433.

[17]Wälde (2006), p. 76.

[18]Ibid 77.

[19]Laborde (2010), p. 105.

[20]Van Harten (2007), pp. 68–69.

[21]Wälde (2006), pp. 77–78.

inadequate protection.[22] Van Harten also points out that investors, as private parties, are subject to the State's exercise of public authority, whereas "the reverse is never true."[23]

Looking towards current trends in international investment law, however, Sornarajah highlights a dramatic yet tentative shift in this treaty paradigm: "There has been an obvious movement away from the model of the investment treaty which emphasizes only protection of the foreign investment. The effect has been to bring about a balance in such a manner as to preserve the regulatory function of the state. Yet, in the tussle between these competing interests, primacy was still attached to investment protection."[24] Investment arbitrations filed pursuant to these first-generation investment treaties resulted in awards that demonstrated that investment treaty obligations could encroach on the regulatory power of the State to act in the public interest.[25] These developments ushered in the new era of "balanced treaties", which sought equilibrium between the State's protection of the public interest, and investment protection.[26]

The public interest sought to be better represented in the "balanced treaties" refer to the substantive defenses that States may raise against investment claims when governmental regulatory power is alleged to amount to a treaty violation.[27] The public interest involved as substantive issues is the same public interest that brings about demands for transparency in the arbitral process as a procedural issue.

Wälde's portrayal of the foreign investor being in an "unequal, hostage-like position subject to the domestic law and government control over the judicial process"[28] has fallen out of fashion with the paradigm shift away from an investment treaty regime focused on investment protection. The media has portrayed investor-State dispute settlement to the general public as a system skewed in favor of multinational corporations suing developing countries for billions of dollars.[29] This public perception of investment arbitration has given more leverage to the criticisms lodged against the investor-State dispute settlement system.

The concern about foreign investors suing States is not limited to developing countries, however. In a recent development, more than two hundred academics from universities in the United States penned an open letter to the U.S. President, urging the removal of investor-State dispute settlement from NAFTA and its exclusion from future international investment agreements in which the United States is a

---

[22]Muchlinski (2011b), p. 230.

[23]Van Harten (2007), p. 69.

[24]Sornarajah (2017), p. 262.

[25]Ibid 263.

[26]Ibid 263; Muchlinski (2011a), p. 23.

[27]Sornarajah (2017), p. 263.

[28]Wälde (2010a), p. 15.

[29]See e.g. Provost and Kennard (2015).

State party.[30] Citing the dissent of U.S. Supreme Court Chief Justice John Roberts in the case of *BG Group PLC v. Republic of Argentina*,[31] these academics oppose investment arbitration because tribunals "hold the alarming power to review a nation's laws and 'effectively annul the authoritative acts of its legislature, executive, and judiciary.'"[32] More than the issue of sovereignty, however, the academics see it as unjust that foreign investors can opt out of domestic courts. The "central problem" with investor-State dispute settlement, these academics argue, is that it establishes "a parallel and privileged set of legal rights and recourse for foreign economic actors."[33] They also decry a lack of non-disputing party participation, arguing that "[t]here are no mechanisms for domestic citizens or entities affected by ISDS cases to intervene or meaningfully participate in the disputes."[34]

Critics of investor-State dispute settlement hone in on the advantages granted to foreign investors, and portray the system as skewed in favor of the investor. The rationale of first-generation bilateral investment treaties wherein foreign investors were viewed as being at a disadvantage compared to the all-powerful State—and therefore in need of protection—has been neglected, at least by critics of investment arbitration.

Simultaneous with this shift away from bilateral investment treaties focused on the protection of investments is the movement reducing the confidentiality of proceedings, a holdover from the international commercial arbitration model upon which investment arbitration was initially based. With increased transparency comes non-disputing party participation. The next section will look at the impact of this development on investor-claimants.

11.2 Investor-Claimants and Third Parties: The New Relationships Brought About by the Transparency Movement

Arbitration is regarded as a consensual procedure. In investment treaty arbitration, the host State being sued gives its consent through the dispute resolution provisions of an international investment agreement. The foreign investor gives consent by

---

[30] 230 Law and Economics Professors Urge President Trump to Remove Investor-State Dispute Settlement from NAFTA and Other Pacts (2017). https://www.citizen.org/system/files/case_documents/isds-law-economics-professors-letter-oct-2017_2.pdf. Accessed 31 October 2017. [Hereinafter "US Academics Open Letter Against ISDS."]

[31] US Supreme Court Case No. 12-138, Writ of Certiorari to the United States Court Of Appeals for the District of Columbia Circuit, Decision and Dissenting Opinion dated 5 March 2014, 572 U.S. __, available at https://www.supremecourt.gov/opinions/13pdf/12-138_97be.pdf. Accessed 31 October 2017.

[32] US Academics Open Letter Against ISDS.

[33] Ibid.

[34] Ibid.

initiating the proceedings with a request for arbitration. In the commercial arbitration model upon which investment treaty arbitration was initially based, the only parties in the arbitration were the opposing parties who had consented to arbitration.

With the transparency movement in investment arbitration, non-disputing parties have joined the fray. The following section looks at the impact of third-party participation from the perspective of the investors that initiated the investment claim.

Non-disputing parties that seek to participate in investment arbitrations are typically non-governmental organizations that represent a particularized interest, sector, or concern. As Wälde has noted, *amicus* briefs filed by non-governmental organizations in investment arbitrations always oppose the Claimant.[35] This has likewise been a complaint by investors themselves.[36] This situation places an additional burden on Claimant, who effectively has two contrary positions to contend with in the arbitration: that of the sovereign respondent, and that of the *amicus curiae*—or *amici* if there are more than one.

There are additional burdens of delays and cost associated with allowing non-disputing party participation.[37] Merely granting access to *amici curiae* to some of the arbitral documents already imposes the practical burden on claimant of redacting documents to ensure the confidentiality of confidential business information.[38]

When allowing non-disputing parties to file written submissions, arbitral tribunals grant the disputing parties the opportunity to respond to these submissions. It would be very foolish for a disputing party to allow these third-party submissions to go without comment. Further complicating matters for the investor is that the alignment of an additional party with the position of the sovereign respondent might boost the State's arguments in the arbitration.[39] The investor then incurs additional costs for the review and rebuttal of these *amicus* briefs.[40]

11.3 Confidential Business Information as an Exception to Transparency

Article 7 of the United Nations Commission on International Trade Law (UNCITRAL) Rules on Transparency states that "confidential or protected information" is deemed an exception to transparency.[41] Article 7(2)(a) indicates that "confidential business information" falls under this broad exception, the only item in the

[35] Wälde (2010b), p. 178.
[36] Fach Gómez (2012), p. 551.
[37] Levine (2011), p. 219.
[38] Ibid 220.
[39] Fach Gómez (2012), p. 551.
[40] Wälde (2010b), p. 178.
[41] UNCITRAL Rules on Transparency, Art. 7.

list under Article 7(2) that appears to apply specifically to foreign investors. The other items in that provision[42] seem tailored for the sovereign respondent.

During the drafting of the UNCITRAL Rules on Transparency, the Working Group considered utilizing the phraseology "confidential and sensitive information".[43] Ultimately, however, the word "sensitive" was deleted,[44] and the final version "confidential or protected information" was adopted as the first sub-heading of Article 7.[45] With respect to "confidential business information", there were concerns within the Working Group as to whether this terminology was sufficiently broad:

> A concern was expressed that that phrase could be understood as not covering, for instance, industrial or financial information, or personal data. It was suggested that a list of situations where information would need to be protected could be elaborated that would include business, political, institutional sensitive information, personal data and legal impediments under a law. That list could be preceded by a general formulation which would define confidential and sensitive information in abstract terms, along the lines, for instance, of article 19 (2) of the Norwegian Model Bilateral Investment Treaty. It was suggested that subparagraph (a) should be deleted because the protection of "confidential business information" would fall under subparagraph (b) as being protected by applicable law. In response, it was said that some jurisdictions did not have laws protecting that information.[46]

Ultimately, no specific definition of "confidential business information" was provided in the UNCITRAL Rules on Transparency.[47] Under Article 3, the arbitral tribunal is given the prerogative to determine whether information is confidential or protected, after consulting the disputing parties.[48] Guidance from previous NAFTA jurisprudence indicates that the following have been deemed as "confidential business information":

- trade secrets;
- financial, commercial, scientific or technical information that is treated consistently in a confidential manner by the disputing party or third party which it relates, including pricing and costing information, marketing and strategic planning documents, market share data, or detailed accounting or financial records not otherwise disclosed in the public domain;

[42]I.e. Article 7(2), paragraphs (b), (c), and (d), respectively list the following sub-categories: Information that is protected against being made available to the public under the treaty; Information that is protected against being made available to the public, in the case of the information of the respondent State, under the law of the respondent State, and in the case of other information, under any law or rules determined by the arbitral tribunal to be applicable to the disclosure of such information; or Information the disclosure of which would impede law enforcement.

[43]Report of Working Group II (Arbitration and Conciliation) on the work of its fifty-fifth session (Vienna, 3–7 October 2011) A/CN.9/736, 110, 117 (2011).

[44]October 2012 UNCITRAL WG Report 83.

[45]February 2013 UNCITRAL WG Report 75.

[46]Ibid 118.

[47]Ausburger (2015), p. 265.

[48]UNCITRAL Rules on Transparency, Art. 3.

- information the disclosure of which could result in financial loss or gain to the disputing party or third party to which it relates;
- information the disclosure of which could interfere with contractual or other negotiations of the disputing party or third party to which it relates; and
- other communications treated as confidential in furtherance of settlement between the disputing parties.[49]

Because the tribunal has the discretion to decide whether information falls under the exceptions provided in Article 7 of the UNCITRAL Rules on Transparency, a claimant that seeks to retain the confidentiality of certain information must convince the tribunal regarding its position. This entails further legal costs for the claimant because written submissions will have to be made on the matter.

11.4 Criminal Proceedings and Foreign Investors: An Added Dimension to the Transparency Rhetoric

A notable item listed under the exceptions to transparency in Article 7 of the UNCITRAL Rules on Transparency is "information the disclosure of which would impede law enforcement."[50] Because the exception speaks of law *enforcement*, this provision clearly speaks to the concerns of the State involved in the dispute, as a foreign investor would not be involved in law enforcement. On the contrary, the foreign investor is the *subject* of law enforcement in the host State. A number of investment cases have involved arrests of foreign investors in the host State; this fact is known because investor-claimants have brought these matters to the attention of investment arbitration tribunals by way of requests for provisional measures.

In the case of ***Quiborax S.A., et al. v. Plurinational State of Bolivia***,[51] the three claimants (Quiborax, Allan Fosk, and Non Metallic Minerals S.A.) requested the ICSID tribunal for provisional measures to order Bolivia and its agencies to discontinue criminal proceedings relating to the arbitration, as well as to return the sequestered corporate administration of Non Metallic Minerals to the claimants.[52] The request for provisional measures related to criminal complaints filed by Bolivian authorities against a number of individuals that had participated in some of claimants' business transactions, after a corporate audit had revealed purported forged documents.[53] The ICSID Tribunal ordered the sovereign respondent to suspend the criminal proceedings until the completion of the arbitration, and to refrain from initiating any other criminal proceedings, stating that "[t]he Tribunal has been

[49]Ausburger (2015), pp. 265–266.

[5050] UNCITRAL Rules on Transparency, Art. 7.

[51]ICSID Case No. ARB/06/2. [Hereinafter Quiborax v.Bolivia]

[52]Quiborax v. Bolivia, Decision on Provisional Measures dated 26 February 2010, at 1–2.

[53]Ibid 23 et seq.

convinced that there is a very close link between the initiation of this arbitration and the launching of criminal cases in Bolivia."[54]

In the case of ***Churchill Mining PLC and Planet Mining Pty Ltd v. Republic of Indonesia***,[55] the claimants asked the ICSID Tribunal to recommend that Indonesia "refrain from threatening of commencing any criminal investigation or prosecution against the Claimants, their witnesses in [the ICSID arbitration], and any person associated with the Claimants' operations in Indonesia."[56] The tribunal in this case denied the Claimants' application for provisional measures, and distinguished the circumstances from those in the *Quiborax* case, stating that *Quiborax* had actual criminal investigations ongoing, whereas in the case of *Churchill Mining*, "the impairment of the Claimants' procedural rights is speculative and hypothetical."[57]

In the case of ***Hydro S.r.l. and others v. Republic of Albania***,[58] the Claimants alleged that Albanian authorities "sought to undermine its investments in Albania in a number of ways", including the launching of tax audit proceedings and money laundering investigations against the Claimants' Albanian entities and the individual claimants.[59] The Claimants requested the ICSID Tribunal to order Albania to suspend criminal proceedings and refrain from initiating any other proceedings, criminal or otherwise, directly or indirectly related to the ICSID arbitration.[60] The Tribunal recommended that the Republic of Albania suspend the criminal proceedings until the issuance of a Final Award in the ICSID arbitration, and to suspend extradition proceedings directed towards individual claimants.[61]

These cases are representative of a number of investment arbitration cases wherein the sovereign respondent has deployed law enforcement measures against claimants in investment disputes. Whereas the UNCITRAL Rules on Transparency exempt from disclosure any information which would "impede law enforcement",[62] no comparable protection is provided to the foreign investor to resist the production of documents that could be used against it by sovereign authorities in criminal proceedings or other types of cases. Considering that there has been at least one case (*Quiborax*, discussed above), where the Tribunal made a categorical observation about the correlation between the initiation of investment claim and the institution of criminal proceedings, it may be concluded that the situation wherein a sovereign respondent will use its governmental power against a foreign investor is a real possibility. Increased transparency should not be used to cause the investor to

---

[54]Ibid 164.

[55]ICSID Case No. ARB/12/14 and 12/40. [Hereinafter Churchill Mining v. Indonesia]

[56]Churchill Mining v. Indonesia, Procedural Order No. 9 (Provisional Measures) dated 8 July 2014, at 1.

[57]Ibid 99.

[58]ICSID Case No. ARB/15/28. [Hereinafter Hydro v. Albania]

[59]Hydro v. Albania, Order on Provisional Measures dated 3 March 2016, at 1.4.

[60]Ibid 1.5.

[61]Ibid 5.1.

[62]UNCITRAL Rules on Transparency Art. 7(2)(d).

produce documentary evidence that may, in turn, be used against it outside the arbitration proceeding. There is no provision in the UNCITRAL Rules on Transparency that specifically addresses this situation from the perspective of the foreign investor.

11.5 A Procedural Solution to a Substantive Law Problem: Looking at Corporate Nationality Planning as a Transparency Issue

The access of investors to investment treaty arbitration is conditioned on nationality. As observed by a noted commentator, "[t]he investor's nationality remains decisive for the jurisdiction of an arbitral tribunal, and it is also key to the application of substantial protection standards."[63]

While determining the nationality of a natural person is fairly straightforward, the nationality of a juridical entity is a more complicated matter. Determination of nationality is addressed in different ways in different investment treaties. The Investment Division of the Organisation for Economic Co-operation and Development (OECD) conducted a large sample survey of dispute settlement provisions in international investment agreements. With respect to corporate nationality, the study made the following findings:

> Some treaties' ISDS clauses contain delimitations of possible claimants which complement other language regarding ratione personae of the treaty protections. Two types of language were found in ISDS clauses in the treaty sample: One addresses the possible claimant status of companies that are established in the host state but are majority-owned or controlled by foreign investors; the other concerns the standing of foreign natural persons that have been residing in the host State at a given point in time.
>
> Close to 20% of the treaties address, in the ISDS clauses, the standing of foreign-controlled companies established in the host State. This is an issue because these companies' establishment in the host State may preclude their status as "foreign", which may in turn affect their standing under the ISDS mechanism. Article 25(2)(b) of the ICSID Convention, for instance, recognises this issue and, for the purpose of the ICSID Convention, makes the standing of such legal persons dependent on whether the host State has agreed to treat such legal person "as a national of another Contracting State for the purposes of the [ICSID] Convention". In the treaties addressing this issue, States consent to treat foreign-owned companies established in the host State as nationals of another contracting party entitled to bring their dispute to ISDS.
>
> One other ISDS provision in relation to claimants is found in the Argentina-United Kingdom BIT (1990): this treaty excludes access to ISDS under the BIT for foreign natural persons who were residents of a State party to the dispute; instead, it imposes an obligation to consult in order to settle disputes.[64]

[63]Dupuy (2009), pp. 48–49.
[64]Pohl et al. (2018).

Specific treaty provisions notwithstanding, the United Nations Conference on Trade and Development (UNCTAD) has observed that "complex corporate structures have become increasingly notorious in recent years."[65] UNCTAD illustrates the difficulty in pinning down corporate nationality:

> Firms, and especially affiliates of multinational enterprises (MNEs), are often controlled through hierarchical webs of ownership involving a multitude of entities. More than 40 per cent of foreign affiliates are owned through complex vertical chains with multiple cross-border links involving on average three jurisdictions. Corporate nationality, and with it the nationality of investors in and owners of foreign affiliates, is becoming increasingly blurred.[66]

The present section shall explore a topic that has received much attention in recent years: corporate restructuring to meet nationality requirements, i.e. corporate nationality planning. This is an issue that has been quite thoroughly examined in current academic literature, as well as in arbitral jurisprudence, in relation to the admissibility of claims and the jurisdiction of an investment tribunal hearing the claims.[67] However, it has not heretofore been analyzed from the perspective of transparency. The goal of the present section is to propose a possible procedural approach to address this substantive law issue.

11.5.1 Understanding the Substantive Issues Brought About by Corporate Nationality Planning

The practice that will be examined in the current section has been alternately called "treaty shopping", "treaty planning", "nationality planning" and "corporate maneuvering".[68] These terms refer to the act of corporate structuring (or in some cases, the alteration of the existing corporate structure) of a multinational enterprise, or the transfer of the investment to a corporate entity in another country, with the aim to qualify for more favorable investment protection under an international investment agreement by virtue of corporate nationality.[69] A corporation can acquire or change its nationality with relative speed and minimal cost by establishing itself, or setting up a corporate subsidiary, in a country of its choice.[70] An investor can also seek protection under a bilateral investment treaty by transferring its investment to a legal

---

[65] UNCTAD (ed) (2016), p. 124.

[66] Ibid.

[67] See e.g. Baumgartner (2016); Voon et al. (2014), pp. 41–68; Lee (2015), pp. 355–379; Schill (2010), pp. 59–86; Kirtley (2009), pp. 427–461; Borman (2011), pp. 359–389.

[68] Baumgartner (2016), pp. 7–8; Voon et al. (2014), pp. 42–43.

[69] Baumgartner (2016), pp. 10–12; Lee (2015), p. 355; De Brabandere (2012), p. 621; Ascensio (2014), p. 771.

[70] Schill (2010), pp. 73–74.

entity in another country.[71] By establishing corporate nationality in a country that has a preferential bilateral investment treaty with the country where the investment activity is to be carried out, corporations utilize corporate restructuring for enhanced investment protection.[72]

While corporate structuring of an investment for the purpose of investment protection is not an illegal act, there have been a number of investment treaty arbitration cases where the respondent State has argued that the investor-claimant has committed an abuse of process by doing so, positing that the investment claim should be deemed inadmissible.[73] Treaty shopping has been criticized by State parties, and is one of the practices that has threatened the legitimacy of the investor-State dispute settlement system.[74] In challenging the investment tribunal's jurisdiction or the admissibility of the investor's claims, sovereign respondents have argued that the corporate entity seeking to invoke the bilateral investment treaty has no real connection with the purported home State.[75] In these cases, sovereign respondents have portrayed claimants as shell corporations, "operating merely as a front for the real party in interest, an entity or natural persons with the nationality of a third State or sometimes the host State."[76]

Schill, who has written about the multilateralization of international investment law, notes that the practice of "treaty shopping" through corporate restructuring "undermines an understanding of [bilateral investment treaties] as expressions of bilateral bargains, because an investor can easily opt into almost any [bilateral investment treaty] regime it wishes."[77] As explained by another commentator, the practice "opens the doors to claims from multinational corporations substantially beyond what many State parties expected when they signed these investment agreements."[78]

Schill further notes that the practice "effectively allows investors to change their nationality for purposes of investment protection by hiding behind the corporate veil."[79] Other scholars have also noted that the term "piercing the corporate veil" has been utilized throughout the academic literature "to describe the possibility of a tribunal: (i) looking behind a company's State of incorporation to its shareholders and managers in identifying its nationality; (ii) involving in the dispute an entity that is not a party to the relevant treaty or proceedings; or (iii) investigating the ownership

[71]Kirtley (2009), p. 427; Voon et al. (2014), p. 42.

[72]Baumgartner (2016), p. 10; Schill (2010), p. 74.

[73]See De Brabandere (2012), p. 908; Ascensio (2014), p. 908; Gaffney (2010).

[74]Lee (2015), pp. 356–357.

[75]Thorn and Doucleff (2010), p. 4.

[76]Ibid 4.

[77]Schill (2010), p. 74.

[78]Lee (2015), p. 356.

[79]Schill (2010), p. 74.

or control behind a company's incorporation in order to prevent the benefits of a treaty from accruing to investors of non-parties."[80]

The scholarly instinct to use the terminology of "piercing the corporate veil" in the existing literature—language borrowed from corporation law referring to the liability of corporate shareholders for the actions of the corporate entity—points to the transparency dimension of corporate restructuring that has yet to be fully examined. A survey of the jurisprudence, which follows, will elucidate how corporate restructuring has been examined by tribunals in relation to jurisdiction and admissibility of claims. The trend in analysis will be used to suggest transparency-based procedural measures to address these substantive issues.

11.5.2 Jurisprudence on Corporate Nationality Planning

With respect to corporate nationality planning, a.k.a. "treaty shopping", the significant number of cases where investment tribunals have dealt with this issue means that "a constant jurisprudence has emerged, because of the coherence of the views expressed in a series of arbitral decisions, and has reached a high level of refinement."[81]

The most famous example of cases dealing with corporate nationality is ***Tokios Tokeles v. Ukraine***,[82] brought pursuant to the 1994 bilateral investment treaty between the Republic of Lithuania and Ukraine.[83] The claimant in this case was a corporation organized in 1989 under the laws of Lithuania.[84] However, the companies involved in the events giving rise to the ICSID arbitration were its two wholly-owned Ukrainian subsidiaries, which were under the control and management of two brothers who were Ukranian citizens, residing in Ukraine.[85] Ukraine raised objections to the jurisdiction of the ICSID Tribunal, arguing that the claimant is not a "genuine investor" from Lithuania,[86] and that allowing the case to proceed would "be tantamount to allowing Ukranian nationals to pursue international arbitration against their own government".[87] The sovereign respondent asked the ICSID Tribunal to "pierce the corporate veil" and to disregard the Claimant's state of

[80]Voon et al. (2014), pp. 43–44, citing the following sources: Lyons (2006), p. 523; Kryvoi (2010a, b), p. 169; Schill (2010), pp. 75–77; Thorn and Doucleff (2010), p. 3; Wisner and Gallus (2004), p. 941.

[81]Ascensio (2014), p. 771.

[82]ICSID Case No. ARB/02/18.

[83]Agreement Between the Government of Ukraine and the Government of the Republic of Lithuania for the Promotion and Reciprocal Protection of Investments dated 8 February 1994.

[84]Tokios Tokeles v. Ukraine, Award dated 26 July 2007, at 2.

[85]Ibid.

[86]Tokios Tokeles v. Ukraine, Decision on Jurisdiction dated 29 April 2004, at 21.

[87]Ibid 22.

incorporation.[88] Looking to the language of the Ukraine–Lithuania BIT,[89] the majority of the Tribunal concluded that the Claimant is an "investor" of Lithuania and therefore entitled to bring a case against Ukraine.[90]

A factual matter that led the majority to decide in favor of jurisdiction was the incorporation of the Claimant's enterprise in Lithuania six years before the bilateral investment treaty between Ukraine and Lithuania even existed.[91] Based on this, the majority concluded that the "Claimant manifestly did not create Tokios Tokeles for the purpose of gaining access to ICSID arbitration under the BIT against Ukraine."[92]

The case of ***Phoenix Action, Ltd. v. Czech Republic***[93] was initiated pursuant to the bilateral investment treaty between the Czech Republic and Israel.[94] This case marks the first time that an ICSID claim was dismissed for lack of jurisdiction because of an abuse of process.[95] The companies involved in the dispute were "two companies established under Czech law and owned by a Czech citizen."[96] The shares of the companies were transferred to an Israeli company created and controlled by the same Czech individual; the Tribunal in this case concluded that the sole purpose of the corporate restructuring was to utilize the bilateral investment treaty to sue the Czech Republic.[97]

Following the reasoning in these notable cases, subsequent tribunals have looked at: (1) timing, and (2) motivation for corporate structuring/restructuring as the essential elements to determine whether corporate nationality planning constitutes an abuse of process that merits a dismissal of the investment claim on the grounds of lack of jurisdiction.[98] The *Tokios Tokeles* case "illustrates the importance tribunals place on the express terms of the treaty. Where the contracting States have not chosen to define investor using such criteria as the origin of capital, the effective seat, ownership, control, or corporate structure, tribunals have, on the whole, refused to give these factors any dispositive weight. Rather, they have observed that the contracting States could have crafted the definition of investors more narrowly had that been their intent. In several cases, moreover, the tribunals have observed that the more recent treaties concluded by the host State use a more limited construction of investor."[99]

---

[88] Ibid.

[89] Specifically, Article 1(2)(b) of the Ukraine–Lithiania BIT.

[90] Tokios Tokeles v. Ukraine, Decision on Jurisdiction dated 29 April 2004, at 71.

[91] Ibid 56.

[92] Ibid.

[93] ICSID Case No. ARB/06/5.

[94] Agreement between the Government of the Czech Republic and the Government of the State of Israel for the Reciprocal Promotion and Protection of Investments of 16 March 1999.

[95] Ascensio (2014), p. 772.

[96] Ibid 772.

[97] Ibid 772–773.

[98] Ibid 773.

[99] Thorn and Doucleff (2010), p. 14.

It is important to note, however, that "[s]everal investor-State tribunals have rejected attempts by respondents to look beyond the text of the applicable investment treaty for limits on corporate nationality planning. In each instance, those tribunals emphasized that the express terms of the applicable treaty provided the necessary and sufficient criterion for determining corporate nationality: a company's place of incorporation."[100] In contrast, as some scholars have noted, "[w]here the investor's nationality hinges on control (usually because the investment is made through an entity incorporated in the host state), tribunals have used this as an opening to look beyond the corporate form and to evaluate more closely how the investment has been structured. In these cases, the treaty language has been interpreted to permit (and require) a more searching inquiry into the nationality of the entity with the ultimate control or ownership interest in the investment."[101]

11.5.3 *Transparency-Based Solutions to the Issue of Corporate Nationality Planning*

As can be seen by the above survey of jurisprudence, the language of the bilateral investment treaty is one of the determining factors on whether corporate nationality planning will bar the admissibility of an investment claim. Therefore, the principal means to prevent an abuse of process through corporate restructuring, is through carefully crafted treaty language. As one author points out, "States have the power to prevent treaty shopping by explicitly restricting it when negotiating the relevant treaty text, for example, through the use of the 'seat' or 'control' tests in defining what constitutes an eligible investor."[102] However, several treaties do not specifically address these issues through provisions defining protected investors and investments, thereby allowing investors "to qualify for protection through mere incorporation in a contracting State."[103]

Aside from treaty language, this paper proposes that disclosure of corporate structure can be a transparency obligation incorporated in the rules of arbitral institutions. The UNCITRAL Rules on Transparency are silent with respect to nationality, as the nationalities of the disputing parties are not among the information to be published at the commencement of the arbitral proceedings. However, "the treaty under which the claim is being made" is among such information to be published, and nationality can therefore be inferred.[104] The ICSID Rules of Procedure for the Institution of Conciliation and Arbitration Proceedings (the Institution

[100]Feldman (2012), p. 285.

[101]Thorn and Doucleff (2010), p. 15.

[102]Lee (2015), p. 356.

[103]Ibid 356.

[104]UNCITRAL Rules on Transparency, Art. 2.

Rules)[105] already requires that "if the party is a juridical person which on the date of consent had the nationality of the Contracting State party to the dispute," then the Request for Arbitration should indicate "the agreement of the parties that it should be treated as a national of another Contracting State for the purposes of the Convention."[106]

These existing provisions can be further refined to require additional information from the claimant with respect to nationality, such as the date of acquisition of the nationality relevant to the invocation of the bilateral investment treaty by virtue of which the investment claim is brought. Requiring this information at the very outset of the investment dispute can forestall lengthy exchanges between the parties on an abuse of process issue. Highlighting dates of the acquisition of nationality can immediately signal to an investment arbitration tribunal whether corporate restructuring was done exclusively to obtain access to a bilateral investment treaty.

11.6 Summary

This paper looked at the concerns of foreign investors in relation to a regime of increased transparency in investment treaty arbitration. To contextualize this analysis, this paper first presented a discussion regarding the paradigm shift in investor-State dispute settlement from confidentiality to transparency as a parallel movement with the shift from investor protection to balancing of interests in the investment treaty arbitration regime.

The new relationships brought about by the transparency movement were examined in this paper, specifically the added burden of non-disputing party participation on investors that bring investment treaty claims to arbitration.

Because the UNCITRAL Rules on Transparency contain a specific provision classifying confidential business information as an exception to transparency, this paper also dissected the development of this provision that is intended specifically for the investor-claimants in investment treaty arbitration.

The particular concerns of foreign investors as potential subjects of criminal proceedings in the host State was discussed in this paper by way of a survey of cases wherein the sovereign respondent deployed law enforcement measures against claimants in investment disputes. This paper presented the observation that the relevant provision in the UNCITRAL Rules on Transparency fails to address the concerns of the foreign investor in this regard.

This paper also presented corporate nationality planning as a transparency issue. Heretofore examined in academic literature and actual investment treaty arbitration cases as a jurisdictional issue, this paper proposes that transparency measures offer a

---

[105] Note: not to be confused with the ICSID Arbitration Rules.

[106] ICSID Rules of Procedure for the Institution of Conciliation and Arbitration Proceedings, Rule 2 (1)(iii).

procedural solution to this substantive law problem. Arbitration rules can be refined to require additional information from the claimant with respect to nationality.

References

Ascensio H (2014) Abuse of process in international investment arbitration. Chin J Int Law 13:763–785

Ausburger T (2015) Article 7. Exceptions to transparency. In: Euler D, Gehring MW, Scherer M (eds) Transparency in international investment arbitration: a guide to the UNICTRAL rules on transparency in treaty-based investor-state arbitration, pp 249–306

Baumgartner J (2016) Treaty shopping in international investment law. OUP

Borman YR (2011) Treaty shopping through corporate restructuring of investments: legitimate corporate planning or abuse of rights? Hague Yearb Int Law

De Brabandere E (2012) "Good faith", "abuse of process" and the initiation of investment treaty claims. J Int Dispute Settl 3:609–636

Dupuy P-M (2009) Unification rather than fragmentation of international law? The case of international investment law and human rights law. In: Petersmann E-U, Francioni F (eds) Human rights in international investment law and arbitration, pp 45–62

Fach Gómez K (2012) Rethinking the role of amicus curiae in international investment arbitration: how to draw the line favorably for the public interest. Fordham Int Law J 35:510–564

Feldman M (2012) Setting limits on corporate nationality planning in investment treaty arbitration. ICSID Rev 27:281–302

Gaffney JP (2010) Abuse of process in investment treaty arbitration. J World Invest Trade 11:515–538

Hindelang S, Krajewski M (2016) Conclusion and outlook: whither international investment law? In: Hindelang S, Krajewski M (eds) Shifting paradigms in international investment law: more balanced, less isolated, increasingly diversified

Kirtley WL (2009) The transfer of treaty claims and treaty-shopping in investor-state disputes. J World Invest Amp Trade 10:427–461

Kryvoi Y (2010a) Piercing the corporate veil in international arbitration. Global Bus Law Rev 1

Kryvoi S (2010b) The multilateralization of international investment law: emergence of a multilateral system of investment protection on bilateral grounds. Trade Law Dev 2(1):59

Laborde G (2010) The case for host state claims in investment arbitration. J Int Dispute Settl 1:97–122

Lee J (2015) Resolving concerns of treaty shopping in international investment arbitration. J Int Dispute Settl 6:355–379

Levine E (2011) Amicus curiae in international investment arbitration: the implications of an increase in third-party participation. Berkeley J Int Law 29:200–224

Lyons K (2006) Piercing the corporate veil in the international arena. Syracuse J Int Law Commerce 33

Muchlinski P (2011a) Corporations and the uses of law: international investment arbitration as a "multilateral legal order." Oñati Socio-Leg. Ser. 1. http://opo.iisj.net/index.php/osls/article/view/61. Accessed 30 Sep 2017

Muchlinski P (2011b) Social responsibility and international law. In: Weiler T, Baetens F (eds) New directions in international economic law: in memoriam Thomas Wälde, pp 233–244

Peters A (2014) Jenseits der Menschenrechte – Die Rechstellung des Individuums im Völkerrecht. Mohr Siebeck

Peters A (2016) Beyond human rights: the legal status of the individual in international law. Cambridge University Press

Pohl J, Mashigo K, Nohen A (2018) Dispute settlement provisions in international investment agreements: a large sample survey. OECD Work. Pap. Int. Invest. https://www.oecd-ilibrary.org/finance-and-investment/dispute-settlement-provisions-in-international-investment-agreements_5k8xb71nf628-en. Accessed 12 June 2018

Provost C, Kennard M (2015) The obscure legal system that lets corporations sue countries. The Guardian. http://www.theguardian.com/business/2015/jun/10/obscure-legal-system-lets-corportations-sue-states-ttip-icsid. Accessed 25 Oct 2017

Reinisch A (2015) Investors. In: Noortmann M, Reinisch A, Ryngaert C (eds) Non-state actors in international law, pp 253–271

Schill S (2010) The multilateralization of international investment law: emergence of a multilateral system of investment protection on bilateral grounds. Trade Law Dev II:59–86

Schreuer C et al (2011) The ICSID Convention: a commentary, 2nd edn. Cambridge University Press

Sornarajah M (2017) The international law on foreign investment. Cambridge University Press

Thorn R, Doucleff J (2010) Disregarding the corporate veil and denial of benefits clauses: testing treaty language and the concept of "investor." In: Waibel M et al (eds) The backlash against investment arbitration: perceptions and reality. Kluwer Law International, pp 3–28

Tillmann RB (2014) Globalization-driven innovation: the investor as a partial subject in public international law. J World Invest Amp Trade 15:73–116

UNCTAD (ed) (2016) Investor nationality: policy challenges

Van Harten G (2007) Investment treaty arbitration and public law. Oxford Scholarship Online

Van Harten G (2010) Perceived bias in investment treaty arbitration. In: Waibel M et al (eds) The backlash against investment arbitration: perceptions and reality, pp 433–453

Voon T, Mitchell A, Munro J (2014) Legal responses to corporate Manoeuvring in international investment arbitration. J Int Dispute Settl 5(1):41–68

Wälde TW (2006) The present state of research carried out by the english-speaking section of the Centre for studies and research. In: Les aspects nouveaux du droit des investissements internationaux: new aspects of international investment law. Centre for Studies and Research in International Law and International Relations, pp 63–154

Wälde TW (2010a) Procedural challenges in investment arbitration under the shadow of the dual role of the state: asymmetries and tribunals' duty to ensure, pro-actively, the equality of arms. Arbitr Int 26(1):3–42

Wälde TW (2010b) "Equality of arms" in investment arbitration: procedural challenges. In: Yannaca-Small K (ed) Arbitration under international investment agreements: a guide to the key issues. Oxford University Press, Oxford, pp 161–188

Wisner R, Gallus N (2004) Nationality requirements in investor-state arbitration. J World Invest Trade 5:927–945

Wouters J, Chané A (2015) Multinational corporations in international law. In: Noortmann M et al (eds) Non-state actors in international law. Hart Publishing, Oxford, pp 225–251

Chapter 12
Investment Protection and Sustainable Development in International Investment Agreements: Building Bridges Instead of Walls

Begaiym Esenkulova

12.1 Introduction

International investment agreements provide investors with various protection standards.[1] As justly observed by Pritchard, investment treaties have become such an important source of investment law that "[w]ithout a treaty, doubts about the investment climate cause investors. . .to think twice about investing in a particular country. . ." and, therefore, "[a]ccession to a relevant treaty . . .signals 'quality' to the global markets; non-membership signals 'danger'. . .".[2] It is, therefore, not surprising that the number of international investment agreements has increased exponentially over the last several decades. There are currently close to 3000 bilateral investment treaties (*hereinafter* BITs) and over 300 treaties with investment chapters or provisions in the world.[3]

This paper is concentrated on the analysis of the following major standards provided in most international investment agreements: (1) fair and equitable treatment, (2) national treatment, (3) most-favored-nation treatment, (4) full protection and security, and (5) observance of obligations or so-called "umbrella clause". While

[1]In this respect, as Gus Van Harten notes, ". . .investment treaties apply a range of standards of review designed to protect investors from regulation or interference by the state". See Van Harten (2008), pp. 80–81. These treaties also ". . .authorize arbitrators to scrutinize virtually any sovereign act of the states that may affect the assets of a foreign investor". See Ibid 93. For a comprehensive analysis of bilateral investment treaties see generally Vandevelde (2000), pp. 469–502; Salacuse and Sullivan (2005), pp. 67–129.

[2]Pritchard (2005), p. 85.

[3]UNCTAD (2019) International Investment Agreements. http://investmentpolicyhub.unctad.org/IIA. Accessed 3 March 2019.

B. Esenkulova (✉)
Law Division, American University of Central Asia, Bishkek, Kyrgyzstan
e-mail: esenkulova_b@auca.kg

C. I. Nagy (ed.), *World Trade and Local Public Interest*, Studies in European Economic Law and Regulation 19, https://doi.org/10.1007/978-3-030-41920-2_12

in general these standards are important for the protection of investors' rights, the broadly formulated, unbalanced or so-called 'old generation' versions of these standards are now being increasingly challenged for limiting host states' legislative and regulatory powers and for being "notoriously vague".[4] This has thus far resulted in a number of inconsistent arbitral awards, some of which have been criticized for imposing unjustifiably stringent obligations upon host states.[5]

At present, most of the international investment agreements can be considered 'old generation', as they are overprotective of investors and do not advance host states' sustainable development. In this regard, Wouters, Duquet and Hachez affirm that "...BITs have become so protective of investors that they sometimes prohibit host States from passing laws and regulations which were designed *bona fide* with a view to economic and social development...in the public interest...".[6] Therefore, one cannot but concur with Sornarajah who is of the view that "[u]nless investment treaties come to reflect a balance between the rights of the foreign investors and the regulatory concerns of the host state, their future viability will continue to be contested".[7] Sornarajah's point on the future of investment treaties in light of the present lack of balance is well taken, since some backlash against the existing investment treaty system is already possible to see. Internationally a number of states have started the process of reviewing their existing investment agreements in order to renegotiate them so that they could be better balanced in line with sustainable development goals.[8] Some countries have come up with new model BITs to reflect the new generation investment legal framework changes. For example, the United States of America revised its model BIT in 2004 and 2012.[9] India presented its new model BIT in 2015.[10] Europe has also made a policy shift to the advancement of new generation investment agreements,[11] with a focus on a new EU investment policy that is concentrated on "... finding a better balance between the right of states

[4]Maupin (2014), p. 382.

[5]See generally Hueckel (2012), Franck (2006), pp. 341–354; Cross (2012).

[6]Wouters et al. (2013), p. 48.

[7]Sornarajah (2012), p. 234; See also Wouters et al. (2013), p. 69 ("The emerging new generation of BITs, perhaps evidencing a convergence in the interests of the community of States as alternatively home and host States, and resulting in a rebalancing of respective rights and responsibilities, hopefully involves just such a development").

[8]A recent example is India, who has announced its decision to renegotiate more than 50 BITs. See Economic Times (2016) India to Renegotiate All Bilateral Investment Pacts. http://economictimes.indiatimes.com/news/economy/policy/india-to-renegotiate-all-bilateral-investment-pacts-nirmalasitharaman/articleshow/53385020.cms. Accessed 3 March 2019.

[9]U.S. Department of State. 2012 U.S. Model Bilateral Investment Treaty. https://www.state.gov/documents/organization/188371.pdf. Accessed 3 March 2019. Office of the United States Trade Representative. 2004 U.S. Model Bilateral Investment Treaty. https://ustr.gov/archive/assets/Trade_Sectors/Investment/Model_BIT/asset_upload_file847_6897.pdf. Accessed 3 March 2019.

[10]Patel (2016); India's Model Bilateral Investment Treaty. https://investmentpolicyhubold.unctad.org/Download/TreatyFile/3560. Accessed 3 March 2019.

[11]Titi (2015), pp. 639–661.

to regulate and the need to protect investors"[12] as well as on developing "clearer and better standards"[13] for the "[r]ebalancing [of] the system".[14] At the same time, there are also countries that have terminated their investment treaties or decided to let their treaties lapse without prolonging them as a reaction to this lack of balance in the treaties. For example, Ecuador terminated its BITs.[15] South Africa and Indonesia have officially declared that they will not extend any of their expiring BITs, as they realize that BITs impose significant limitations to their right to regulate in the public interest.[16]

All of these developments necessitate the analysis of the select core investment protection standards in international investment agreements and ways how they may be aligned with host states' sustainable development goals. In this regard, one cannot but agree with UNCTAD that the issue is no longer about whether to reform the legal framework of FDI for the advancement of sustainable development or not, "...but about the *what*, *how* and *extent* of such reform".[17] This paper is focused upon the issue of *how* to balance investment protection standards so that they can both protect foreign direct investors and at the same time not result in undermining legislative and regulatory powers of host states or not end up imposing unjustifiably stringent obligations on them. Accordingly, the paper analyzes investment protection standards via an examination of relevant arbitral awards and investment agreements and proposes ways how they can be better balanced so that both the interests of investors and states can be fully accommodated.

---

[12]European Commission (2013) Investment Protection and Investor-to-State Dispute Settlement in EU agreements 1. http://trade.ec.europa.eu/doclib/docs/2013/november/tradoc_151916.pdf. Accessed 3 March 2019.

[13]Ibid.

[14]Ibid 2.

[15]UNCTAD (2010) Denunciation of the ICSID Convention and BITs: Impact on Investor-State Claims. http://unctad.org/en/Docs/webdiaeia20106_en.pdf. Accessed 3 March 2019; IISD (2017) Ecuador denounces its remaining 16 BITs and publishes CAITISA audit report. https://www.iisd.org/itn/2017/06/12/ecuador-denounces-its-remaining-16-bits-and-publishes-caitisa-audit-report/. Accessed 3 March 2019.

[16]South Africa decided to let its BITs lapse without extending them after a group of investors filed an arbitral claim against it, arguing that the new mining legislation requiring each mining company to achieve 26% ownership by historically disadvantaged South Africans constitutes expropriation and unfair and inequitable treatment. See Piero Foresti et al. v The Republic of South Africa, International Centre for Settlement of Investment Disputes [ICSID], ARB (AF)/07/1, Aug. 4, 2010, https://icsid.worldbank.org/en/Pages/cases/casedetail.aspx?CaseNo=ARB(AF)%2f07%2f1. Accessed 3 March 2019; See also Tajti (2015), p. 196; Hamzah (2018), pp. 135–177.

[17]UNCTAD (2015) World Investment Report on "Reforming International Investment Governance." United Nations. xi. http://unctad.org/en/PublicationsLibrary/wir2015_en.pdf. Accessed 3 March 2019.

12.2 The Investment Protection Standard of Fair and Equitable Treatment

The right to a fair and equitable treatment (*hereinafter FET*) is an important right that is granted to investors in most international investment agreements.[18] This standard is aimed at protecting investors from unfair and inequitable treatment they may potentially face in FDI host states. Most BITs contain a broadly formulated provision on fair and equitable treatment. For example, Kyrgyzstan—UK BIT states that "[i] nvestments of nationals or companies of each Contracting Party shall at all times be accorded fair and equitable treatment...in the territory of the other Contracting Party".[19] What does FET mean? This is not an easy question to answer, since FET has been subject to various types of interpretation by international investment arbitral tribunals and, hence, does not have an exact definition.[20] This has been underscored by tribunals themselves. For example, the tribunal in *PSEG Global v. Turkey* case emphasized that "... [b]ecause the role of fair and equitable treatment changes from case to case, it is sometimes not as precise as would be desirable".[21] Below is the analysis of the various arbitral awards with respect to elements that constitute FET in order to provide a comprehensive explanation of the nature of this standard.

[18] As noted by Alvarez, "FET is not only the most frequently invoked claim by investors, it is also the most successful on their behalf". See Alvarez (2011), p. 177; See also Muchlinski et al. (2012) (FET "has emerged as the most relied upon and successful basis for IIA claims by investors"); Shan (2012), pp. 23–25 (discussing the nature of FET standard); Dolzer (2005a), pp. 87–106; Lester (2015), p. 78.

[19] Agreement for the Promotion and Protection of Investments, United Kingdom of Great Britain and Northern Ireland - the Kyrgyz Republic, Dec. 8, 1994, Art. 2 (2). https://investmentpolicyhubold.unctad.org/Download/TreatyFile/1863. Accessed 3 March 2019.

[20] See generally Schill (2009b), p. 263 ("[F]air and equitable treatment does not have a consolidated and conventional core meaning as such nor is there a definition of the standard that can be applied easily"); Sornarajah (2012), p. 204 (FET is "...vague and is open to different interpretations" and "...has caused much anxiety"); Muchlinski (2007), p. 635 ("[T]he fair and equitable treatment standard is shrouded with considerable uncertainty"); Muchlinski et al. (2012), p. 1 ("...[T]he vague and broad wording of the obligation carries a risk of an overreach in its application," since it "...may be applied in investor-State arbitration to restrict host-country administrative and governmental action to a degree that threatens the policymaking autonomy of that country"). For a comprehensive analysis of the FET standard see Kläger (2013).

[21] PSEG Global, Inc., Konya Ingin Electrik Üretim ve Ticaret Limited Sirketi v. Republic of Turkey. International Centre for Settlement of Investment Disputes [ICSID], ARB/02/5, Jan. 19, 2007, Sec. 239. http://www.italaw.com/sites/default/files/case-documents/ita0695.pdf. Accessed 3 March 2019.

12.2.1 The FET Standard as Prohibition of Denial of Justice

The FET standard has been understood to include the concept of denial of justice in a number of arbitral awards.[22] One of the recent arbitral awards finding the violation of the FET standard in the form of denial of justice is the ICSID case of *Dan Cake (Portugal) S.A. v. Hungary,* in which the investor is seeking more than 47 million Euro from Hungary under the Hungary—Portugal BIT.[23] According to the facts of the case, Danesita, a company seated and operating in Hungary, the majority of shares of which belonged to Dan Cake, a Portuguese company, could not repay its debts to creditors and, as a result, became subject to liquidation proceedings.[24] As the Hungarian bankruptcy legislation provides for the possibility of conducting a composition hearing, where a debtor company can reach an agreement with its creditors on its debt repayment obligations so as to avoid the forced sale of its assets by the court, Danesita requested the Metropolitan Court of Budapest to allow it to convene the composition hearing.[25] Although Danesita provided the Court with all three documents explicitly mandated by the Bankruptcy Act, the Court did not satisfy Danesita's request, since Danesita did not submit documents deemed to be necessary by the Court in addition to those stipulated in the Act.[26] The investment arbitration tribunal held Hungary liable for the violation of the FET standard under the Hungary—Portugal BIT, basing its decision on finding that liquidation proceedings of the Danesita company conducted by the Metropolitan Court of Budapest were "clearly improper and discreditable" and "seriously inadequate".[27] The tribunal considered the additional documents requested by the Court to be "absurd"[28] as well

[22]Jan de Nul N.V. Dredging International N.V. v. Arab Republic of Egypt. International Centre for Settlement of Investment Disputes [ICSID], ARB/04/13, Nov. 6, 2008, Sec. 188. http://www.italaw.com/sites/default/files/case-documents/ita0440.pdf. Accessed 3 March 2019. ("...the fair and equitable treatment standard encompasses the notion of denial of justice"); Compañía De Aguas Del Aconquija S.A., Vivendi Universal S.A. v. Argentine Republic. International Centre for Settlement of Investment Disputes [ICSID], ARB/97/3, Aug. 20, 2007, Sec. 7.4.11. http://www.italaw.com/sites/default/files/case-documents/ita0215.pdf. Accessed 3 March 2019. (noting that FET standard "... is commonly understood to include a prohibition on denial of justice"); Victor Pey Casado and others v. Republic of Chile. International Centre for Settlement of Investment Disputes [ICSID], ARB/98/2, May 8, 2008, http://www.italaw.com/sites/default/files/case-documents/ita0638.pdf. Accessed 3 March 2019; For a denial of justice claim see also Petrobart Limited v. The Kyrgyz Republic. Stockholm Chamber of Commerce [SCC], No. 126/2003, Mar. 29, 2005. http://www.italaw.com/sites/default/files/case-documents/ita0628.pdf. Accessed 3 March 2019.

[23]Dan Cake (Portugal) S.A. v. Hungary. International Centre for Settlement of Investment Disputes [ICSID], ARB/12/9, Aug. 24, 2015, Sec. 3. https://www.italaw.com/sites/default/files/case-documents/italaw4457.pdf. Accessed 25 March 2019.

[24]Ibid Sec. 2.

[25]Ibid.

[26]Ibid Sec. 94–102.

[27]Ibid Sec. 146.

[28]Ibid Sec. 29.

as "obviously unnecessary," and "impossible to satisfy".[29] According to the arbitral tribunal, as the Budapest court unjustifiably refused to satisfy Danesita's request to have a composition meeting among its creditors which may or may not have saved Danesita from liquidation before the commencement of liquidation procedures, the court's bankruptcy proceedings could be described as "...manifest injustice in the sense of a lack of due process leading to an outcome which offends a sense of judicial propriety".[30] As a result, Hungary has been found in violation of the FET standard in the form of a denial of justice.[31]

This case illustrates that FET violation may be found in cases, where investors are denied justice in host country courts. Although the Arbitral tribunal in *Dan Cake* notes that it is by no means a "court of appeal,"[32] in essence, it has reviewed the decision of the Budapest court as if it had been a court of appeal, stating that the Court imposed additional documents were "unnecessary," "unjustifiable obstacles," and constituted a "flagrant violation of the Bankruptcy Act".[33] In this regard, Zoltán Novák, a Hungarian lawyer, notes that the arbitral tribunal's decision is "disputable" and finds it astonishing that "a simple court order for supplementary filing" was found to be "...an act which shocks...a sense of judicial propriety".[34] Whether the decision reached by the Arbitral tribunal is disputable or not, this case clearly demonstrates that an FET provision in an investment agreement can have far-reaching consequences, reaching even to such new vistas not imagined herein-before.[35] Accordingly, host states' courts, be they of general jurisdiction or be they specialized, such as those handling bankruptcy disputes, be they courts of first instance or the highest courts (Supreme courts), are not immune from having their decisions found to be in violation of international agreement investment protection

[29]Ibid Sec. 30.

[30]Ibid Sec. 146.

[31]Ibid Sec. 162; For further analysis of the concept of denial of justice see Robert Azinian, Kenneth Davitian, & Ellen Baca v. The United Mexican States. International Centre for Settlement of Investment Disputes [ICSID], Additional Facility Rules, ARB (AF)/97/2, Nov. 1, 1999, Sec. 102. https://www.italaw.com/sites/default/files/case-documents/ita0057.pdf. Accessed 25 March 2019. ("A denial of justice could be pleaded if the relevant courts refuse to entertain a suit, if they subject it to undue delay, or if they administer justice in a seriously inadequate way"); See also Mondev International ltd. v. United States of America. International Centre for Settlement of Investment Disputes [ICSID], Additional Facility Rules, ARB (AF)/ 99/2, Oct. 11, 2002. http://www.italaw.com/sites/default/files/case-documents/ita1076.pdf. Accessed 25 March 2019; The Loewen Group, Inc. and Raymond L. Loewen v. United States of America. International Centre for Settlement of Investment Disputes [ICSID], Additional Facility Rules, ARB (AF)/ 98/3, June 26, 2003. http://www.italaw.com/sites/default/files/case-documents/ita0470.pdf. Accessed 25 March 2019.

[32]Dan Cake (Portugal) S.A. v. Hungary, Sec. 117.

[33]Ibid Sec. 142.

[34]Novák (2016).

[35]For the consequences regarding bankruptcy cases see Kökényesi (2016) ("The Dan Cake decision "...will not be without considerable affect on numerous domestic insolvency cases on a day-by-day basis...[and it]...will be subject to extensive legal debate among scholars and practitioners both at a domestic and international level in the upcoming years").

standards by arbitral tribunals. While this is intended to protect investors, it also means that developing countries, in particular, with malfunctioning bankruptcy systems, problems concerning the proper functioning of courts, and other similar problems, may be held liable to pay millions of USD to investors who are invited to come to these countries to contribute to their development. Therefore, one cannot but agree with Matos and Leitão, Portuguese lawyers, who affirm that the Dan Cake decision "...inevitably establishes a higher threshold for national judges and legislation when dealing with the liquidation of investments made by international investors".[36] Although the decision does not have a precedential effect, it, nevertheless, sets the bar high for the conduct of court proceedings in general in countries that have international investment agreements with broad FET provisions.

12.2.2 FET and Investors' Legitimate Expectations

Apart from the denial of justice being found to be an element of the FET standard as evidenced by the Dan Cake and other cases, a number of arbitral tribunals have held host states liable for the breach of the FET standard for violating investors' legitimate expectations.[37] For example, in *Occidental v. Ecuador* the tribunal found Ecuador liable for the violation of the FET standard.[38] According to the facts of the case, Ecuador used to reimburse Occidental the Value-Added-Tax (*hereinafter* VAT) paid by it on various purchases required for its operation, but in 2001 Ecuador issued resolutions stopping the practice of VAT reimbursement to Occidental and other companies operating in the country's oil sector.[39] The tribunal noted that "...[t]he tax law was changed without providing any clarity about its meaning and extent and the practice and regulations were also inconsistent with such changes".[40] Affirming the importance of upholding investors' legitimate expectations regarding the stability of the legal regime, the tribunal stated that "...there is certainly an obligation not to alter the legal and business environment in which the investment has been made" and, accordingly, the change in tax regulation was "...not fair and equitable".[41] While stability is indeed important for the security of investors' operations, it is hard to agree with the tribunal on that there is an obligation not to change the legal environment. As countries develop, they do amend their laws and

[36]de Matos and Leitão (2016).

[37]For further analysis of the notion of investors' legitimate expectations see Téllez (2012), pp. 432–442.

[38]Occidental Exploration and Production Company v. The Republic Of Ecuador (I), London Court of International Arbitration [LCIA], No. UN 3467, July 1, 2004. http://www.italaw.com/sites/default/files/case-documents/ita0571.pdf. Accessed 25 March 2019.

[39]Occidental Exploration and Production Company v. The Republic Of Ecuador (I), Sec. 2–3.

[40]Ibid Sec. 184.

[41]Ibid Sec. 191.

regulations. Yet, *Occidental v. Ecuador* is not a single case equating changes in the regulatory regime to the breach of the FET standard due to the violation of investors' legitimate expectations. A number of other awards, recognizing investors' expectations regarding the stability of the legal framework as an element of FET, have been rendered by various tribunals.[42]

While it is difficult to agree with the reasoning of the awards in *Occidental v. Ecuador* and other similar cases with respect to host states' obligation not to change the legal regime and business environment for investors, one must mention that some tribunals have displayed a more nuanced approach to this issue by contextualizing investors' expectations. For example, even though the tribunal in *Parkerings v. Lithuania* has noted that legitimate expectations must be considered when determining the FET standard violation, it has emphasized that the legitimacy of expectations depends on whether a host state has made any promises to the investor, and in the absence of such representations, whether "…the circumstances surrounding the conclusion of the agreement" as well as "…the conduct of the State at the time of the investment" justify such expectations.[43] In this case, the tribunal did not find investors' expectations to be legitimate, since, according to the tribunal, at the time the investment was made, investors understood that Lithuania was transitioning from its Soviet past to EU membership and, hence, changes in the legal regime were to be expected with the investors simply taking the "…business risk to be faced with changes of laws possibly or even likely to be detrimental to its investment".[44] This decision is a clear departure from the line of cases that have

---

[42]CMS Gas Transmission Company v. The Argentine Republic. International Centre for Settlement of Investment Disputes [ICSID], ARB/01/8, May 12, 2005, Sec. 274. https://www.italaw.com/sites/default/files/case-documents/ita0184.pdf. Accessed 25 March 2019 (noting that "…a stable legal and business environment is an essential element of fair and equitable treatment"); LG&E Energy Corp., LG&E Capital Corp., LG&E International Inc. v. Argentine Republic. International Centre for Settlement of Investment Disputes [ICSID], ARB/02/1, Oct. 3, 2006, Sec. 124. https://www.italaw.com/sites/default/files/case-documents/ita0460.pdf. Accessed 25 March 2019 (noting that "…stability of the legal and business framework is an essential element of fair and equitable treatment in this case"); Enron Corporation, Ponderosa Assets, L.P v. Argentine Republic. International Centre for Settlement of Investment Disputes [ICSID], ARB/01/3, May 22, 2007. http://www.italaw.com/sites/default/files/case-documents/ita0293.pdf. Accessed 25 March 2019; Sempra Energy International v. Argentine Republic. International Centre for Settlement of Investment Disputes [ICSID], ARB/02/16, Sep.28, 2007. https://www.italaw.com/sites/default/files/case-documents/ita0770.pdf. Accessed 25 March 2019; Marvin Feldman v. Mexico. International Centre for Settlement of Investment Disputes [ICSID], Additional Facility Rules, ARB (AF)/ 99/1, Dec. 16, 2002. https://www.italaw.com/sites/default/files/case-documents/ita0319.pdf. Accessed 25 March 2019.

[43]Parkerings-Compagniet AS v. Republic of Lithuania. International Centre for Settlement of Investment Disputes [ICSID], ARB/05/8, Sep.11, 2007, Sec. 330-331. https://www.italaw.com/sites/default/files/case-documents/ita0619.pdf. Accessed 25 March 2019. In this case investors reached an agreement with Vilnius Municipality, whereby they were to build car parks in the city. As investors proposed to have the car parks in the inner part of the Old Town, a UNESCO heritage site, the proposal was declined.

[44]Ibid Sec. 335–336. In this regard, it is interesting to note the findings of the AES v. Hungary tribunal, which stated that "…legitimate expectations can only be created at the moment of the

established very stringent standards upon host states.[45] The paper argues that such contextualization of circumstances is vital if the interests of both investors and host states are to be respected.

Another interesting case in this regard is *Genin v. Estonia*. In this case the claimants argued that Estonia breached a number of investment protections standards, including FET, under the U.S.—Estonia BIT by revoking the license and forcing the liquidation of Estonian Innovation Bank controlled by Mr. Genin, a U.S. citizen.[46] However, the tribunal dismissed this claim. The tribunal found the FET standard to "...require an "international minimum standard" that is separate from domestic law, but that is, indeed, a *minimum* standard".[47] The tribunal, thereby, established a high threshold for the FET violation claim. In addition, the tribunal also considered the context of the country in which the investment was made and in which "...Claimants knowingly chose to invest in an Estonian financial institution, EIB".[48] The tribunal found it to be "...imperative to recall the particular context in which the dispute arose, namely, that of a renascent independent state [Estonia], coming rapidly to grips with the reality of modern financial, commercial and banking practices and the emergence of state institutions responsible for overseeing and regulating areas of activity perhaps previously unknown".[49] Hence, the arbitral tribunal in this case also underscored the importance of the context in which the investment was made to determine the legitimacy of investors' expectations.

Apart from this, in *International Thunderbird Gaming Corporation v. Mexico* the tribunal explicitly affirmed that legitimate expectations refer to a "...situation where a Contracting Party's conduct creates reasonable and justifiable expectations on the part of an investor (or investment) to act in reliance on said conduct, such that a failure by the NAFTA Party to honour those expectations could cause the investor

---

investment". See AES Summit Generation Limited and AES-Tisza Erömü Kft. v. Republic of Hungary. International Centre for Settlement of Investment Disputes [ICSID], ARB/07/22, Sep. 23, 2010, Sec. 9.3.8. https://www.italaw.com/sites/default/files/case-documents/ita0014_0.pdf. Accessed 25 March 2019.

[45]It is important to underscore that awards taking into account the special context of developing states or states in transition are in minority. See Alexander (2008), p. 823 ("...[I]international investment law tribunals generally do not consider the context of a country's individual capabilities or needs in judging the country's compliance with investment obligations").

[46]Alex Genin, Eastern Credit Limited, Inc. and A.S. Baltoil v. The Republic of Estonia. International Centre for Settlement of Investment Disputes [ICSID], ARB/99/2, June 25, 2001. http://www.italaw.com/sites/default/files/case-documents/ita0359.pdf. Accessed 25 March 2019.

[47]Id. at Sec. 367. But see Total S.A. v. Argentine Republic. International Centre for Settlement of Investment Disputes [ICSID], ARB/04/1, Dec. 27, 2010, Sec. 125, http://www.italaw.com/sites/default/files/case-documents/ita0868.pdf. Accessed 25 March 2019 (The tribunal in this case did not equate FET with the international minimum standard of treatment, noting that "...the phrase "fair and equitable in conformity with the principles of international law" cannot be read as "treatment required by the minimum standard of treatment of aliens/investors under international law").

[48]Alex Genin, Eastern Credit Limited, Inc. and A.S. Baltoil v. The Republic of Estonia, Sec. 348.

[49]Ibid.

(or investment) to suffer damages".[50] As it can be seen, this tribunal also highlighted the importance of reasonableness and justifiability of expectations. Several other tribunals adopted the same approach, emphasizing the need to examine various factors, including political, social and others, when making the final determination on the breach of the FET standard.[51] The contextualization of investors' legitimate expectations is a good practice, since it allows rendering balanced arbitral awards with consideration of all the relevant interests and circumstances. Yet, as arbitral awards, such as *Occidental v. Ecuador* demonstrate, there are also cases that deem investors' expectations taken as such to be the ultimate factor when deciding whether to find the FET standard's violation.

[50]International Thunderbird Gaming Corporation v. the United Mexican States. International Centre for Settlement of Investment Disputes [ICSID], Jan.26, 2006, Sec. 147. https://www.italaw.com/sites/default/files/case-documents/ita0431.pdf. Accessed 25 March 2019. The tribunal decided this case in favor of Mexico, as it did not find that the investor had legitimate expectations. For a case, where the FET standard breach was determined based on the violation of investors' expectations arising out of specific representations made by the Government see MTD Equity Sdn. Bhd. and MTD Chile S.A. v. Republic of Chile. International Centre for Settlement of Investment Disputes [ICSID], ARB/01/7, May 25, 2004. http://www.italaw.com/documents/MTD-Award_000.pdf. Accessed 25 March 2019.

[51]Suez, Sociedad General de Aguas de Barcelona S.A., and Vivendi Universal S.A. v. Argentine Republic. International Centre for Settlement of Investment Disputes [ICSID], ARB/03/19, July 30, 2010, Sec. 228. https://www.italaw.com/sites/default/files/case-documents/ita0826.pdf. Accessed 25 March 2019 (The tribunal noted the need to examine whether violation of FET took place or not by analyzing the case "...from an objective and reasonable point of view" via consideration of "... the concession's legal framework and bearing in mind...[the] country's history and its political, economic, and social circumstances..."); Duke Energy Electroquil Partners & Electroquil S.A. v. Republic of Ecuador. International Centre for Settlement of Investment Disputes [ICSID], ARB/04/19, Aug. 18, 2008, Sec. 340. https://www.italaw.com/sites/default/files/case-documents/ita0256.pdf. Accessed 25 March 2019 ("To be protected, the investor's expectations must be legitimate and reasonable at the time when the investor makes the investment. The assessment of the reasonableness or legitimacy must take into account all circumstances, including not only the facts surrounding the investment, but also the political, socioeconomic, cultural and historical conditions prevailing in the host State"); Edf (Services) Limited v. Romania. International Centre for Settlement of Investment Disputes [ICSID], ARB/05/13, Oct. 8, 2009, Sec. 217. http://www.italaw.com/sites/default/files/case-documents/ita0267.pdf. Accessed 25 March 2019 ("The idea that legitimate expectations, and therefore FET, imply the stability of the legal and business framework, may not be correct if stated in an overly-broad and unqualified formulation. The FET might then mean the virtual freezing of the legal regulation of economic activities, in contrast with the State's normal regulatory power and the evolutionary character of economic life. Except where specific promises or representations are made by the State to the investor, the latter may not rely on a bilateral investment treaty as a kind of insurance policy against the risk of any changes in the host State's legal and economic framework. Such expectation would be neither legitimate nor reasonable").

12.2.3 FET as Obligation to Act Transparently and Not to Engage in Manifest Arbitrariness, Discrimination, and Abusive Treatment

A number of arbitral tribunals have found that manifest arbitrariness, discrimination, and abusive treatment amount to the violation of the FET standard.[52] Apart from this, some arbitral tribunals have also decided that this standard includes the obligation of host states to be transparent.[53] In particular, in *TECMED v. Mexico* Técnicas Medioambientales or TECMED S.A., a Spanish company, filed a claim against Mexico, alleging that the country violated various investment protection

---

[52]Eureko B.V. v. Republic of Poland. Ad Hoc Arbitration, Aug. 19, 2005, at Sec. 233, http://www.italaw.com/sites/default/files/case-documents/ita0308_0.pdf (last visited Mar. 25, 2019) (finding that Poland "...acted not for cause but for purely arbitrary reasons linked to the interplay of Polish politics and nationalistic reasons of a discriminatory character); Waste Management, Inc. v. United Mexican States. International Centre for Settlement of Investment Disputes [ICSID], Additional Facility Rules, ARB(AF)/00/3, Apr. 30, 2004 Sec. 98. https://www.italaw.com/sites/default/files/case-documents/ita0900.pdf. Accessed 25 March 2019 (noting that "...fair and equitable treatment is infringed by conduct attributable to the State and harmful to the claimant if the conduct is arbitrary, grossly unfair, unjust or idiosyncratic, is discriminatory and exposes the claimant to sectional or racial prejudice..."); Biwater Gauff ltd. v. United Republic Of Tanzania. International Centre for Settlement of Investment Disputes [ICSID], ARB/05/22, July 24, 2008, Sec. 602. https://www.italaw.com/sites/default/files/case-documents/ita0095.pdf. Accessed 25 March 2019 (noting that FET "...implies that the conduct of the State must be...consistent and non-discriminatory, that is, not based on unjustifiable distinctions or arbitrary"); S.D. Myers, Inc. v. Canada. Ad Hoc Arbitration, Nov. 13, 2000, Sec. 263, 266. http://www.italaw.com/sites/default/files/case-documents/ita0747.pdf. Accessed 25 March 2019; Continental Casualty Company v. Argentine Republic. International Centre for Settlement of Investment Disputes [ICSID], ARB/03/9, Sep. 5, 2008, Sec. 261. http://www.italaw.com/documents/ContinentalCasualtyAward.pdf. Accessed 25 March 2019; Bayindir Insaat Turizm Ticaret Ve Sanayi A.Ş. v. Islamic Republic of Pakistan. International Centre for Settlement of Investment Disputes [ICSID], ARB/03/29, Aug. 27, 2009, Sec.178, https://www.italaw.com/sites/default/files/case-documents/ita0075.pdf. Accessed 25 March 2019 (holding that the obligation to refrain from taking arbitrary or discriminatory measures is a constitutive element of FET); Desert Line Projects LLC v. The Republic of Yemen. International Centre for Settlement of Investment Disputes [ICSID], ARB/05/17, Feb. 6, 2008. https://icsid.worldbank.org/ICSID/FrontServlet?requestType=CasesRH&actionVal=showDoc&docId=DC791_En&caseId=C62. Accessed 25 March 2019; Tokios Tokelės v. Ukraine. International Centre for Settlement of Investment Disputes [ICSID], ARB/02/18, July 26, 2007. http://www.italaw.com/documents/TokiosAward.pdf. Accessed 25 March 2019.

[53]Rumeli Telekom A.S. And Telsim Mobil Telekomikasyon Hizmetleri A.S. v. Republic of Kazakhstan. International Centre for Settlement of Investment Disputes [ICSID], ARB/12/9, July 29, 2008, at Sec. 609, http://www.italaw.com/documents/Telsimaward.pdf (last visited Mar. 25, 2019) (noting that the FET standard includes the State's obligation to "...act in a transparent manner"); Metalclad Corporation v. United Mexican States. International Centre for Settlement of Investment Disputes [ICSID], Additional Facility Rules, ARB (AF)/ 97/1, Aug. 30, 2000, at Sec. 99, http://www.italaw.com/sites/default/files/casedocuments/ita0510.pdf (last visited Mar. 25, 2019) (finding Mexico to be in violation of the FET standard under NAFTA, as it "...failed to ensure a transparent and predictable framework for Metalclad's business planning and investment").

standards, including the FET, under the Mexico—Spain BIT.[54] TECMED claimed that Mexico's failure to renew the permit for landfill operation to Cytrar, a company established by TECMED for this purpose, amounted to the breach of the FET standard, since it "…frustrate[d] its justified expectation of the continuity and duration of the investment made and…impair[ed] recovery of the invested amounts and the expected rate of return".[55] TECMED emphasized that the decision not to renew the permit was arbitrary, unjustified and had political motives.[56] The tribunal upheld TECMED's claim and ordered Mexico to pay 5.5 mln. USD in compensation.[57] According to the Tribunal, compliance with the FET standard means that that the state should "…act in a consistent manner, free from ambiguity and totally transparently in its relations with the foreign investor, so that… [the investor] may know beforehand any and all rules and regulations that will govern its investments, as well as the goals of the relevant policies and administrative practices or directives, to be able to plan its investment and comply with such regulations".[58] This decision has sparked much controversy, as the requirement of total transparency and consistency is very demanding and can hardly be fulfilled even by most developed countries. It is not surprising that Douglas, a well-known international investment law scholar, characterized the award in the following way: "… Tecmed 'standard' is actually not a standard at all; it is rather a description of perfect public regulation in a perfect world, to which all states should aspire but very few (if any) will ever attain…".[59] Indeed, it is very difficult, if not impossible, to attain absolute transparency. Therefore, if the FET standard is interpreted in line with the TECMED decision, the standard can become too burdensome, especially to developing states.

12.2.4 FET and the Problem of Conflicting Arbitral Awards

As the language of the FET standard is broad and rather vague in most international investment agreements, the FET liability threshold varies in awards of tribunals. While some tribunals set a low threshold, thereby interpreting the standard more in favor of investors, others provide more balanced considerations in their awards. *TECMED v. Mexico* is the award that clearly represents the former, since the tribunal noted the importance of total transparency and consistency on the part of host states.

---

[54]Tecnicas Medioambientales TECMED S.A. v. The United Mexican States. International Centre for Settlement of Investment Disputes [ICSID], Additional Facility Rules, ARB (AF)/ 00/2, May 29, 2003. https://www.italaw.com/sites/default/files/case-documents/ita0854.pdf. Accessed 25 March 2019.

[55]Ibid Sec. 41.

[56]Ibid Sec. 43.

[57]Ibid Sec. 201.

[58]Ibid Sec. 154.

[59]Douglas (2006), p. 28.

If FET is to be interpreted in line with the TECMED award, it may be relatively easy for investors to claim the FET violation which can then jeopardize host states' legitimate regulatory interests. At the same time, there are other awards that are more balanced in their consideration of interests of both investors and host states. Three arbitral awards are important to mention in this regard. In *Eastern Sugar v. Czech Republic* the investment tribunal noted the importance of qualifying the FET. The tribunal stated the following in this regard:

> A BIT may... not be invoked each time the law is flawed or not fully and properly implemented by a state. Some attempt to balance the interests of the various constituents within a country, some measure of inefficiency, a degree of trial and error, a modicum of human imperfection must be overstepped before a party may complain of a violation of a BIT. Otherwise, every aspect of any legislation of a host state or its implementation could be brought before an international arbitral tribunal under the guise of a violation of the BIT. This is obviously not what BITs are for.[60]

Similarly, in *Saluka v. Czech Republic* the arbitral tribunal underscored the importance of balancing the interests of investors and host states. The tribunal held that "[n]o investor may reasonably expect that the circumstances prevailing at the time the investment is made remain totally unchanged" and that when deciding on whether the FET standard was violated "...the host State's legitimate right subsequently to regulate domestic matters in the public interest must be taken into consideration as well".[61] These arbitral awards' reasoning is indeed justified, since it accords protection to investors' rights in consideration of the context in which the investments were made and in light of host state's legitimate regulatory interests. Yet, as it may be seen from the above case analysis, different arbitral tribunals render different decisions, with some tribunals setting the threshold for violation of the FET standard high, some of them setting it low and some of them reaching decisions somewhere in the middle between the two approaches. Therefore, there is still a disparity of outcomes.

It is also important to note that the FET standard has been interpreted differently even in cases that have had the same factual circumstances. In this respect, it is important to analyze two cases—*CME v. Czech Republic* and *Lauder v. Czech Republic* decided by two different tribunals (one in Stockholm, the other in London) on the same facts, but with diametrically opposing outcomes (with the former finding the Czech Republic in violation of the FET standard and awarding damages and the latter determining no violation by the Czech Republic and denying claims for compensation).[62] In *Lauder v. Czech Republic* Ronald Lauder, an

[60]Eastern Sugar B.V. (Netherlands) v. The Czech Republic. Stockholm Chamber of Commerce [SCC], No. 126/2003, Mar. 27, 2007, Sec. 272. https://www.italaw.com/sites/default/files/case-documents/ita0259_0.pdf. Accessed 25 March 2019.

[61]Saluka Investments BV (The Netherlands) v. The Czech Republic. Permanent Court of Arbitration [PCA], Mar.17, 2006, Sec. 305. http://www.italaw.com/sites/default/files/case-documents/ita0740.pdf. Accessed 25 March 2019.

[62]Ronald Lauder v. Czech Republic. Ad Hoc Arbitration. Sep. 3, 2001. https://www.italaw.com/sites/default/files/case-documents/ita0451.pdf. Accessed 25 March 2019; CME Czech Republic

American citizen, who ultimately controlled CNTS broadcasting company in the Czech Republic via his company CME Media Enterprises B.V., initiated arbitration proceedings against the Republic, claiming that the country violated a number of investment protection standards, including the FET.[63] He noted that the Czech Republic's Media Council "…demonstrated hostile conduct towards CNTS, by the totality of its…actions and inactions that undermined the rights which had been provided to CNTS".[64] However, the tribunal rejected this argument and denied all claims for damages brought by Lauder.[65]

In *CME v. Czech Republic* CME, a company established under the Dutch laws, that held a 99% equity interest in CNTS, brought a claim against the Czech Republic, alleging that the country violated investment standards, including the FET, under the 1991 BIT between the Netherlands and Czech and Slovak Federal Republic.[66] CME claimed that CNTS "…has been commercially destroyed by the actions and omissions attributed to the Media Council, an organ of the Czech Republic".[67] The tribunal upheld CME claims, ordering the Czech Republic to pay CME 269.814.000 mln. USD.[68] The different outcomes in these two arbitration proceedings have fueled debate in the international investment academic literature, with Reinisch, a renowned investment law scholar, calling these cases "…[t]he ultimate fiasco in investment arbitration…".[69] Whether fiasco or not, they demonstrate the reality of interpretation and application of FET standards in investment arbitration, where such results may take place.

Two more interesting cases that illustrate the problem of conflicting interpretation of the FET standard are *Glamis Gold v. USA* (2009) and *Bilcon v. Canada* (2015). In *Glamis Gold v. USA* the tribunal interpreted FET in the NAFTA Agreement as a standard requiring an "egregious," "shocking," and "gross" denial of justice,[70] whilst in *Bilcon v. Canada* the tribunal interpreted the same standard in the same treaty as requiring that the conduct of the host state be merely "arbitrary" and

---

B.V. (Netherlands) v. The Czech Republic. Ad Hoc Arbitration, Mar. 14, 2003. http://www.italaw.com/sites/default/files/case-documents/ita0180.pdf. Accessed 25 March 2019. For a comprehensive analysis of these two cases see Dimsey (2008), pp. 93–96.

[63]Ibid Sec. 42. The claim was brought under the BIT between the United States of America and the Czech and Slovak Federal Republic.

[64]Ibid Sec. 289.

[65]Ibid page 74.

[66]CME Czech Republic B.V. (Netherlands) v. The Czech Republic. The claimant in this case—CME Czech Republic B.V., a Dutch company—was the wholly owned subsidiary of CME Media Enterprises B.V., a Dutch company controlled by Ronald Lauder.

[67]CME Czech Republic B.V. (Netherlands) v. The Czech Republic, Sec. 19.

[68]Ibid Sec. IX.

[69]Reinisch (2008), p. 116.

[70]Glamis Gold, Ltd. v. United States of America. International Centre for Settlement of Investment Disputes [ICSID], June 8, 2009, at paras. 612, 616, 828–829. https://www.italaw.com/sites/default/files/casedocuments/ita0378.pdf. Accessed 25 March 2019.

"unjust",[71] noting that "...there is no requirement in all cases that the challenged conduct reaches the level of shocking or outrageous behaviour".[72] Hence, as these and other cases show, the broad and vague language of FET standards in most international investment agreements give way to various, often conflicting ways of interpreting their meaning.

12.2.5 *Balancing FET Clauses with Host States' Sustainable Development Goals in International Investment Agreements*

As FET standards are generally broad, their exact meaning is thus left to arbitral tribunals to be interpreted on a case-by-case basis. However, such latitude does not provide legal certainty to host states and often produces conflicting arbitral awards. States' obligations under this protection standard may be rather heavy, especially if these states are developing ones. A number of tribunals' interpretation of the FET standard, such as that of *TECMED v. Mexico*, may even go beyond what the states agreed to when signing relevant BITs. As is importantly underscored by UNCTAD, "[t]he vagueness of the FET standard is at the core of the problem,"[73] making it "...particularly prone to expansive interpretation"[74] which in turn "...increases the chances that a wide range of State regulations or measures can be found to infringe the FET standard including those that have a legitimate public purpose".[75] Similarly, Kläger notes that it is "...astonishing that fair and equitable treatment has developed from an almost vacant expression into an obligation of such potential breadth within a few years".[76]

What may be done to address the problem of vague and broadly formulated FET clauses in international investment agreements? One solution may be to remove FET clauses from investment agreements. For instance, there is no FET provision in Australia–Singapore FTA.[77] This move may be justified in the case of such developed countries, as Singapore and Australia. However, such a move may be

[71]William Ralph Clayton, William Richard Clayton, Douglas Clayton, Daniel Clayton and BILCON of Delaware, Inc v. Government of Canada. Permanent Court of Arbitration [PCA], Case No. 2009-04, March 17, 2005, at paras. 442–444, 591–592. https://www.italaw.com/sites/default/files/case-documents/italaw4212.pdf. Accessed 25 March 2019.

[72]BILCON v. Canada, para 444.

[73]Muchlinski et al. (2012), p. 2.

[74]Ibid 11.

[75]Ibid 2; See also Cordonier Segger et al. (2011), p. 779 ("...[A]n overly broad interpretation of this standard may not favour host State attempt to enact effective measures to achieve sustainable development objectives").

[76]Kläger (2010), p. 443.

[77]Singapore—Australia Free Trade Agreement, Feb. 17, 2003. https://investmentpolicyhubold.unctad.org/Download/TreatyFile/2649. Accessed 25 March 2019.

unjustified in the case of poor developing states with a weak rule of law. While the absence of the FET guarantee can provide more legal certainty to such host states, it will deprive investors of an important investment protection standard. Investors do need to be protected from unfair and unequal treatment. However, this protection should not be accorded at the expense of states' right to regulate in the public interest, and it should not be unlimited in scope. Accordingly, the paper argues for the need to qualify the FET standard. How may this be done? Below is the analysis of possible legal mechanisms proposed by this work.

12.2.5.1 Tying the FET Standard to the Customary International Law Minimum Standard of Treatment of Aliens

One way of qualifying the FET standard could be to tie it to the customary international law minimum standard of treatment of aliens instead of treating FET as a separate and more demanding standard by either revising existing investment treaties or when negotiating new ones.[78] This can also be made via host states issuing an interpretative statement linking FET to the minimum treatment standard together with its investment treaty Contracting parties or, if this is not possible, at least via issuing a unilateral interpretative statement to that effect.[79] While issuing notes of interpretation may not be as effective as revising the treaties, it does offer a mechanism of allowing states to voice their views on the meaning of the standards listed in their investment protection treaties. Such notes of interpretation may or may not be received well by tribunals, but at least they provide for a possibility to address the broad scope of FET clauses. For example, the North American Free Trade Agreement (NAFTA) parties issued the following note of interpretation with respect to the FET standard in NAFTA agreement: "The concept... of "fair and equitable treatment" ....[does] not require treatment in addition to or beyond that which is required by the customary international law minimum standard of treatment of aliens".[80] While there are debates as to the exact meaning of the international law

[78]An instructive example in this regard is the USA—Rwanda BIT which provides that the fair and equitable treatment concept does "...not require treatment in addition to or beyond that which is required by that standard and do[es] not create additional substantive rights". See United States of America—Rwanda Treaty concerning the Encouragement and Reciprocal Protection of Investment, Feb. 19, 2008, Art. 5. https://investmentpolicyhubold.unctad.org/Download/TreatyFile/2241. Accessed 25 March 2019.

[79]For a comprehensive analysis on the use of interpretative statements for the purpose of qualifying investment protection standards see Lise Johnson and Merim Razbaeva, State Control over Interpretation of Investment Treaties, 2014. http://ccsi.columbia.edu/files/2014/04/State_control_over_treaty_interpretation_FINAL-April-5_2014.pdf. Accessed 25 March 2019; Roberts (2013), pp. 59–61; Roberts (2010), pp. 179–225.

[80]NAFTA Free Trade Commission, North American Free Trade Agreement Notes of Interpretation of Certain Chapter 11 Provisions, July 31, 2001. http://www.sice.oas.org/tpd/nafta/Commission/CH11understanding_e.asp. Accessed 25 March 2019. A number of international investment agreements currently tie the FET standard to the customary international law minimum standard of

minimum standard, Mexico, USA, and Canada have argued that the threshold for finding violation of the international minimum standard is high, with the standard being subject to violation only in case of egregious or outrageous conduct of States.[81] In this regard, the *Neer* case has often been used as the case illustrating what the level of violation should be to amount to the breach of an international minimum standard.[82] In fact, a number of NAFTA arbitral awards have confirmed the relevance of the Neer standard following the NAFTA party note of interpretation of the FET standard. For instance, in *Cargill v. Mexico* the tribunal stated that "...the current customary international law standard of "fair and equitable treatment" at least reflects the adaptation of the agreed Neer standard to current conditions," further noting that "[i]f the conduct of the government toward the investment amounts to gross misconduct, manifest injustice or, in the classic words of the Neer claim, bad faith or the willful neglect of duty, whatever the particular context the actions take in regard to the investment, then such conduct will be a violation of the customary obligation of fair and equitable treatment".[83]

---

treatment of aliens. See Agreement for the Promotion and Protection of Investments, Canada—Republic of Latvia, May 5, 2009, Art. 2. http://investmentpolicyhubold.unctad.org/Download/TreatyFile/618. Accessed 25 March 2019 ("Each Contracting Party shall accord investments or returns of investors of the other Contracting Party treatment in accordance with the customary international law minimum standard of treatment of aliens, including fair and equitable treatment..."). For similar clauses see also Agreement for the Promotion and Reciprocal Protection of Investments, Canada—Romania, May 8, 2009, Art. 2. http://investmentpolicyhubold.unctad.org/Download/TreatyFile/3503. Accessed 25 March 2019; Free Trade Agreement, Republic of Korea—Socialist Republic of Viet Nam, May 5, 2015, Art. 9.5. http://investmentpolicyhubold.unctad.org/Download/TreatyFile/3584. Accessed 25 March 2019; Agreement on Investment under the Framework Agreement Establishing a Free Trade Area, the Republic of Korea—the Republic of Turkey, Feb. 26, 2015, Art. 1.6. http://investmentpolicyhubold.unctad.org/Download/TreatyFile/4729. Accessed 25 March 2019; Agreement on the Reciprocal Promotion and Protection of Investments, The Belgium-Luxembourg Economic Union—The Republic of Colombia, Feb. 4, 2009, Art. 3. https://investmentpolicyhubold.unctad.org/Download/TreatyFile/342. Accessed 25 March 2019; Free Trade Agreement, Canada—The Republic of Korea, Sep. 23, 2014, Art. 8.5. http://investmentpolicyhubold.unctad.org/Download/TreatyFile/3076. Accessed 25 March 2019.

[81]Magraw et al. (2011), p. 46.

[82]Ibid. For the full text of the Neer case see L. F. H. Neer and Pauline Neer (U.S.A.) v. United Mexican States. Oct. 15, 1926, Sec. 4. http://legal.un.org/riaa/cases/vol_IV/60-66.pdf. Accessed 25 March 2019 (The Commission in this case held that an international minimum standard of treatment means the following: "...[T]he treatment of an alien, in order to constitute an international delinquency, should amount to an outrage, to bad faith, to wilful neglect of duty, or to an insufficiency of governmental action so far short of international standards that every reasonable and impartial man would readily recognize its insufficiency").

[83]Cargill, Incorporated v. United Mexican States. International Centre for Settlement of Investment Disputes [ICSID], Additional Facility Rules, ARB (AF)/05/2, Sep. 18, 2009, Sec. 286. http://www.italaw.com/sites/default/files/case-documents/ita0133_0.pdf. Accessed 25 March 2019; See also International Thunderbird Gaming Corporation v. the United Mexican States, Sec. 194 ("Notwithstanding the evolution of customary law since decisions such as Neer Claim in 1926, the threshold for finding a violation of the minimum standard of treatment still remains high...For the purposes of the present case, the Tribunal views acts that would give rise to a breach of the minimum standard of treatment prescribed by the NAFTA and customary international law as those that, weighed against

Nevertheless, there are also a number of tribunals that have found that the international minimum standard goes beyond the Neer standard. In particular, in *Mondev v. USA* the arbitral tribunal found it "...unconvincing to confine" the interpretation of FET to the Neer standard, noting that "[t]o the modern eye, what is unfair or inequitable need not equate with the outrageous or the egregious" with a state being able to "treat foreign investment unfairly and inequitably without necessarily acting in bad faith".[84] Similarly, in *ADF v. USA* the tribunal held that the international minimum standard is a constantly evolving standard and not "...a static photograph of the minimum standard of treatment of aliens as it stood in 1927 when the Award in the Neer case was rendered".[85] The presence of awards that do not recognize that the international minimum standard amounts to the violation of rights as described in the Neer decision may, thus, leave no difference between an investment treaty with a broad, unqualified FET standard and the one which ties FET to the international minimum standard. Therefore, while the example of NAFTA countries' and other states' attempts at limiting the scope of FET is interesting to note, their solution may not necessarily work in practice as the *ADF* and *Mondev* cases demonstrate. Nevertheless, host states may still try adopting this solution, especially if it is not possible to renegotiate the text of their international investment agreements.

12.2.5.2 Qualifying the Scope of the FET Standard by Concretizing Its Content

In light of the above problem of conflicting awards regarding the meaning of the international minimum standard of treatment, the paper proposes that a better solution for host states would be to qualify the FET standard by listing what they mean by this standard. This will help to both protect investors' rights and provide enough room for states to exercise their regulatory functions. One instructive example in this regard is Malaysia—Australia Free Trade Agreement. According

the given factual context, amount to a gross denial of justice or manifest arbitrariness falling below acceptable international standards.").

[84]Mondev International ltd. v. United States of America, Sec. 116. See also Pope & Talbot Inc. v. Canada. Ad Hoc Arbitration, Apr. 10, 2001, at Sec. 108, 111. http://www.italaw.com/sites/default/files/case-documents/ita0678.pdf. Accessed 25 March 2019 (The tribunal held that "...compliance with the fairness elements [FET] must be ascertained free of any threshold that might be applicable to the evaluation of measures under the minimum standard of international law" despite Canada's argument in this case that FET can be found to be breached in case the state's conduct toward the investor is egregious.).

[85]ADF Group Inc. v. United States of America. International Centre for Settlement of Investment Disputes [ICSID], Additional Facility Rules, ARB (AF)/00/1, Jan. 9, 2003, Sec. 179. https://www.italaw.com/sites/default/files/case-documents/ita0009.pdf. Accessed 25 March 2019 (The tribunal further noted that "[t]here appears no logical necessity and no concordant state practice to support the view that the Neer formulation is automatically extendible to the contemporary context of treatment of foreign investors and their investments by a host or recipient State". See Ibid Sec. 181).

to Art. 12.7 of the Agreement, investors are accorded with the FET standard.[86] However, the FET standard is qualified in two ways. First, the parties state that "[f]or greater certainty... "fair and equitable treatment" requires each Party not to deny justice in any legal or administrative proceedings" and that the FET standard does not "require treatment in addition to or beyond that which is required under customary international law, and do[es] not create additional substantive rights".[87] Other useful examples include investment treaty provisions on FET between EU and other countries. In particular, in EU—Canada agreement the Parties stipulate the following:

> A Party breaches the obligation of fair and equitable treatment...if a measure or series of measures constitutes:
>
> (a) denial of justice in criminal, civil or administrative proceedings;
> (b) fundamental breach of due process, including a fundamental breach of transparency, in judicial and administrative proceedings;
> (c) manifest arbitrariness;
> (d) targeted discrimination on manifestly wrongful grounds, such as gender, race or religious belief;
> (e) abusive treatment of investors, such as coercion, duress and harassment....[88]

The qualification of FET in this Agreement makes it possible to define FET more specifically. Although there is no reference to the Neer standard, the use of the words "fundamental" and "manifest" suggest that the standard has influenced the meaning of FET in this Agreement. Similar examples may be found in EU—Viet Nam and EU—Singapore agreements.[89]

Another instructive example is the South African Community Model BIT which fully adopts the language of the Neer Standard. It provides investors with the FET protection, but limits the scope of FET by stating that the violation of the standard requires "...the demonstration of an act or actions by the government that are an outrage, in bad faith, a wilful neglect of duty or an insufficiency so far short of international standards that every reasonable and impartial person would readily recognize its insufficiency".[90] This qualification of FET establishes a rather high

---

[86]Free Trade Agreement, Malaysia-Australia, May 22, 2012. https://investmentpolicyhubold.unctad.org/Download/TreatyFile/2634. Accessed 25 March 2019.

[87]Ibid Art. 12.7.

[88]European Union—Canada Comprehensive Trade and Economic Agreement, Art. 8.10. https://investmentpolicyhubold.unctad.org/Download/TreatyFile/3593. Accessed 25 March 2019.

[89]European Union—Singapore Comprehensive Free Trade Agreement, Art. 2.4. https://investmentpolicyhubold.unctad.org/Download/TreatyFile/5714. Accessed 25 March 2019 ("To comply with the obligation to provide fair and equitable treatment ...neither Party shall adopt measures that constitute: (a) Denial of justice in criminal, civil and administrative proceedings; (b) A fundamental breach of due process; (c) Manifestly arbitrary conduct; (d) Harassment, coercion, abuse of power or similar bad faith conduct..."); European Union—Viet Nam Free Trade Agreement (Draft Version), Art. 14. https://investmentpolicyhubold.unctad.org/Download/TreatyFile/3563 Accessed 25 March 2019.

[90]Southern African Development Community, July 2012, Art. 5. https://investmentpolicyhubold.unctad.org/Download/TreatyFile/2875. Accessed 25 March 2019.

threshold for the violation of the standard, but at the same time it does accord investors with adequate protection against unfair and inequitable treatment.

It is also interesting to note that a number of countries have specifically noted that the FET standard should not prevent them from exercising their regulatory powers in good faith. For instance, Colombia—Turkey BIT provides investors with the "...international law minimum standard of treatment, including the fair and equitable treatment...".[91] At the same time, the BIT specifies that the FET standard "...includes the prohibition against denial of justice...in accordance with the principle of due process of law" and that this standard "...shall not be construed as to prevent a Contracting Party from exercising its regulatory powers in a transparent and non-discriminatory manner and in accordance with the principle of due process of law".[92] Similarly, Japan—Colombia BIT specifies the content of the minimum standard of treatment provided to investors by noting that "[f]or greater certainty, a change of the regulation of a Contracting Party does not constitute by itself a violation of ... [the international minimum standard of treatment]".[93] A number of other countries have also signed agreements specifying the meaning of the FET standard.[94] As it may be seen from the analysis of these agreements, the qualification of the FET standard allows balancing the interests of investors and host

[91] Agreement concerning the Reciprocal Promotion and Protection of Investment, Republic of Colombia—Republic of Turkey, July 28, 2014, Art. 4. https://investmentpolicyhubold.unctad.org/Download/TreatyFile/3249. Accessed 25 March 2019.

[92] Agreement concerning the Reciprocal Promotion and Protection of Investment, Republic of Colombia—Republic of Turkey, July 28, 2014, Art. 4. https://investmentpolicyhubold.unctad.org/Download/TreatyFile/3249 (last visited Mar. 25, 2019).

[93] Agreement for the Liberalization, Promotion and Protection of Investment, Japan—The Republic of Colombia, Sep. 12, 2011, Art. 4, https://investmentpolicyhubold.unctad.org/Download/TreatyFile/797. Accessed 25 March 2019.

[94] Agreement on Investment under the Framework Agreement on Comprehensive Economic Cooperation, the Association of Southeast Asian Nations—the Republic of India, Nov. 12, 2014, Art. 7. https://investmentpolicyhubold.unctad.org/Download/TreatyFile/3337. Accessed 25 March 2019; Bilateral Agreement for the Promotion and Protection of Investments, The Republic of Colombia—The People's Republic of China, Nov. 22, 2008, Art. 2. http://investmentpolicyhubold.unctad.org/Download/TreatyFile/720. Accessed 25 March 2019; Agreement for an Economic Partnership, Japan—Mongolia, Feb. 10, 2015, Art. 10.5. http://investmentpolicyhubold.unctad.org/Download/TreatyFile/3372. Accessed 25 March 2019; Agreement for the Promotion, Protection and Liberalisation of Investment, Japan—the Republic of Peru, Nov. 22, 2008, Art.5. http://investmentpolicyhubold.unctad.org/Download/TreatyFile/1733. Accessed 25 March 2019; Bilateral Agreement for the Promotion and Protection of Investments, United Kingdom of Great Britain and Northern Ireland—Republic of Colombia, Mar. 17, 2010, Art. 2. http://investmentpolicyhubold.unctad.org/Download/TreatyFile/3253- Accessed 25 March 2019. Free Trade Agreement, The People's Republic of China - Republic of Korea, June 1, 2015, Art. 12.5. http://investmentpolicyhubold.unctad.org/Download/TreatyFile/3461. Accessed 25 March 2019; Agreement for the Promotion and Protection of Investments, The Republic of Colombia—The Republic of India, Nov. 10, 2009, Art.3. http://investmentpolicyhubold.unctad.org/Download/TreatyFile/796. Accessed 25 March 2019; Free Trade Agreement, Australia—the Republic of Korea, Apr. 8, 2014, Ch.11, Art. 11.5. http://investmentpolicyhubold.unctad.org/Download/TreatyFile/2971. Accessed 25 March 2019.

states. Therefore, in light of conflicting arbitral awards on the FET standard, the paper recommends that host states qualify the scope of FET in their investment agreements.

12.3 The Investment Protection Standard of National Treatment

The national treatment standard is another important investment protection standard. It may generally be defined as "...the obligation to provide foreign investors with treatment not-less-favourable to that provided by a State to its own nationals under like circumstances".[95] This standard involves "...a comparative test – whereby the claimant is required to identify a comparator... in receipt of better treatment than it has received from the respondent state".[96] Although providing the national treatment standard in IIAs is an important legal tool for the protection of investors' rights, an unqualified inclusion of such a clause may result in consequences detrimental to host states' sustainable development. First, as the standard involves the comparison of domestic companies and foreign investors in like circumstances, it is important to focus on the meaning of the phrase "like circumstances". There is currently conflicting arbitral practice when it comes to the interpretation of the term "like". For example, the tribunal in *Feldman v. Mexico* found foreign and domestic companies to be 'like,' since they engaged in the same business—the business of reselling cigarettes for the purpose of exporting them.[97] In *Occidental v. Ecuador* the tribunal adopted a different, more expansive approach. It held that the phrase "in like circumstances" was not limited to companies in one particular sector of business activity, noting that such interpretation would be too narrow and found that in this case the term "like" referred to all companies engaged in the export business.[98] Consequently, the tribunal found Ecuador liable for discriminating between oil exporters and companies involved in the business of exporting flowers as well as mining and seafood products, since it denied VAT reimbursement to the former, while still reimbursing VAT payments to the latter.[99] A different approach was taken by the tribunal in *S.D. Myers v. Canada* case. In its award the tribunal affirmed that the "...assessment of "like circumstances" must...take into account circumstances that would justify governmental regulations that treat them differently in order to

[95]Cordonier Segger et al. (2011), p. 778. For a comprehensive analysis of the national treatment standard see also Dolzer (2005b); UNCTAD (1999) National Treatment. United Nations. http://unctad.org/en/Docs/psiteiitd11v4.en.pdf. Accessed 25 March 2019; Kurtz (2010), pp. 243–278.

[96]Grierson-Weiler and Laird (2008), p. 262.

[97]Marvin Feldman v. Mexico, Sec. 172.

[98]Occidental Exploration and Production Company v. The Republic Of Ecuador (I), Sec. 173.

[99]Ibid Sec. 167–179.

protect the public interest".[100] As the tribunal treated Canada's ban as a move to protect its own market of waste disposal operators concealed in the form of environmental regulation, it found Canada liable for the violation of the national treatment obligation.[101]

As it may be seen, there is no uniform and consistent interpretation of "like circumstances" in international investment arbitral jurisprudence. In this regard, one cannot but concur with Miles who writes that the national treatment standard's "...wide scope allows arbitrators in investor-State disputes to apply an overly expansive interpretation of the standard, and, in so doing, to categorize public welfare regulation of general application as a violation of the national treatment standard".[102] As there is currently a divergent arbitral practice in interpreting 'like circumstances', the paper proposes for host states to clarify which criteria are to be used when determining likeness. One instructive example in this regard is the Agreement on Economic Cooperation between ASEAN and India. Article 3 of the Agreement does not only provide investors with the national treatment standard, but also specifies that the term "like circumstance" should be interpreted "...based upon an objective assessment of all circumstances on a case-by-case basis, including, inter alia: (a) the sector the investor is in; (b) the location of the investment; (c) the aim of the measure concerned; and (d) the regulatory process generally applied in relation to the measure concerned".[103] Furthermore, the Article specifies that "...[e]xtension of financial assistance or measures taken by a Party in favour of its investors and their investments in pursuit of legitimate public purpose including the protection of health, safety, the environment shall not be considered as a violation of [the national treatment standard]".[104] This detailed provision on the national treatment standard is better able to balance between the protection of investors' rights and protection of host states' legitimate regulatory interests.[105]

Another issue regarding the national treatment standard which may be problematic for host states is that by its nature it requires equal treatment of domestic and foreign companies. Although ideal, the equal treatment is not always possible due to

---

[100]S.D. Myers, Inc. v. Canada, Sec. 250.

[101]Ibid Sec. 162, 168–195.

[102]Miles (2011), p. 268; See also Cordonier Segger et al. (2011), p. 778 ("When it comes to the examination of 'like circumstances', it is clear that focusing on commercial similarity alone without taking into consideration the potential environmental and social impacts of otherwise 'like' investments, could result in the exclusion of sustainable development goals").

[103]Agreement on Investment under the Framework Agreement on Comprehensive Economic Cooperation, the Association of Southeast Asian Nations—the Republic of India, Nov. 12, 2014, Art. 3. http://investmentpolicyhubold.unctad.org/Download/TreatyFile/3337. Accessed 25 March 2019.

[104]Ibid.

[105]For analysis on the importance of finding a proper balance in drafting the national treatment clause see Wouters et al. (2013), p. 65 ("The balance to be found in respect of the national treatment standard is to protect foreign investors from discrimination by host States without overly constraining the latter's sovereign right to regulate").

various considerations, including certain policy objectives. Therefore, the paper proposes to limit the scope of the national treatment by specifying exceptions to this standard. For example, Turkey–Bangladesh BIT notes that the national treatment standard "...shall not oblige Contracting Parties to accord investments of investors of the other Contracting Party the same treatment that it accords to investments of its own investors with regard to acquisition of land, real estates, and real rights upon them".[106] Such a qualification of the national treatment standard is important, if this is in line with the state policy. The failure of the country to specify exceptions to the national treatment standard in investment treaties may result in costly arbitral proceedings and liability.

12.4 The Investment Protection Standard of Most-Favored-Nation Treatment

The most-favored-nation treatment (*hereinafter* MFN) is one of the most widely used investment standards that is aimed at prohibiting discrimination among foreign investors.[107] Most IIAs have the MFN standard. For example, according to Art. 4 (2) of Switzerland—Kyrgyzstan BIT, "[e]ach Contracting Party shall ensure...treatment [which] shall not be less favourable than that granted by each Contracting Party...to the investments made within its territory by investors of the most favoured nation, if the latter is more favourable".[108] This standard, hence, provides for the equal treatment of foreign investors.

The MFN standard is one of the most controversial investment standards,[109] since it has been subject to both narrow and expansive interpretation by arbitral tribunals.[110] Some tribunals have interpreted the MFN standard rather widely. For

---

[106] Agreement concerning the Reciprocal Promotion and Protection of Investments, The Republic of Turkey—The People's Republic of Bangladesh, April 12, 2012, Art. 3. http://investmentpolicyhubold.unctad.org/Download/TreatyFile/274. Accessed 25 March 2019.

[107] For the definition of MFN see Shan (2012), p. 21 (The MFN standard is meant to "...create a level playing field among different foreign states by prohibiting discrimination based on the basis of different foreign nationalities"); See also UNCTAD (2015) United Nations Conference on Trade and Development, Investment Policy Framework for Sustainable Development 96. https://unctad.org/en/PublicationsLibrary/diaepcb2015d5_en.pdf. Accessed 25 March 2019 (MFN "is designed to prevent nationality-based discrimination and to ensure a level-playing field between investors from the IIA home country and comparable investors from any third country"); For analysis of the MFN clauses see Tawil (2009), pp. 9–30; Hober (2009), pp. 31–41; Dolzer and Schreuer (2012), pp. 206–212; Schill (2009a), pp. 496–569.

[108] Kyrgyzstan—Swiss Federal Council Agreement on the Promotion and Reciprocal Protection of Investments, Jan. 29, 1999. http://investmentpolicyhubold.unctad.org/Download/TreatyFile/3261. Accessed 25 March 2019.

[109] Acconci (2008), p. 366.

[110] As noted by UNCTAD, "[a] number of arbitral decisions have read the MFN obligation as allowing investors to invoke more investor-friendly provisions from third treaties, e.g. to

example, in *Bayindir v. Pakistan* the tribunal extended the MFN clause of Turkey—Pakistan BIT to the fair and equitable treatment standard contained in Switzerland—Pakistan BIT, as a result of which the investor could rely on a standard which was absent in Turkey—Pakistan BIT.[111] Another noteworthy example of the extension of the MFN clause is the case of *Maffezini v. Spain.* In this case Mr. Maffezini initiated arbitration against Spain based on Chile-Spain BIT which he invoked in reliance on the MFN clause of the Argentina-Spain BIT.[112] Mr. Maffezini did this, since while the BIT of Spain with Argentina made the initiation of the arbitration claim conditional on investors' litigation of their cases in courts of Spain for a period of eighteen months, Spain's BIT with Chile did not impose any of such conditions except for the lapsing of a six month period given for negotiation.[113] Despite Spain's objections with respect to the reliance on Chile-Spain BIT, the arbitral tribunal agreed to apply Chile-Spain BIT, noting that "...if a third party treaty contains provisions for the settlement of disputes that are more favorable to the protection of the investor's rights and interests than those in the basic treaty, such provisions may be extended to the beneficiary of the most favored nation clause...".[114] At the same time, the tribunal underscored that the MFN clause "...should not be able to override public policy considerations that the contracting parties might have envisaged as fundamental conditions for their acceptance of the agreement in question...".[115] In this case the tribunal did not find any public policy considerations against applying the MFN clause.[116]

Following the *Maffezini v. Spain* decision a number of arbitral tribunals extended the MFN clause to dispute resolution provisions of investment treaties.[117] However,

---

incorporate standards not included in the base treaty, to benefit from higher protection standards compared to the ones found in the base treaty or to circumvent procedural (ISDS-related) requirements in the base treaty". See UNCTAD (2015) United Nations Conference on Trade and Development, Investment Policy Framework for Sustainable Development 96. https://unctad.org/en/PublicationsLibrary/diaepcb2015d5_en.pdf. Accessed 25 March 2019.

[111]Bayindir Insaat Turizm Ticaret Ve Sanayi A.Ş. v. Islamic Republic of Pakistan. International Centre for Settlement of Investment Disputes [ICSID], ARB/03/29, Aug. 27, 2009, Sec. 167. https://www.italaw.com/sites/default/files/case-documents/ita0075.pdf. Accessed 25 March 2019.

[112]Emilio Agustín Maffezini v. The Kingdom of Spain. International Centre for Settlement of Investment Disputes [ICSID], ARB/97/7, Jan. 25, 2000, Sec. 1. http://www.italaw.com/sites/default/files/case-documents/ita0479.pdf. Accessed 25 March 2019.

[113]Ibid Sec. 39.

[114]Ibid Sec. 56.

[115]Ibid Sec. 62.

[116]Ibid Sec. 64. When analyzing the public policy considerations, the tribunal examined Spain's other BITs and found out that many of Spain's BITs imposed no litigation related conditions prior to the submission of arbitration claims. See Ibid 58.

[117]Gas Natural SDG, S.A. v. The Argentine Republic. International Centre for Settlement of Investment Disputes [ICSID], ARB/03/10, June 17, 2005, Sec. 31. http://www.italaw.com/sites/default/files/case-documents/ita0354.pdf. Accessed 25 March 2019; ROSINVESTCO UK LTD. v. The Russian Federation. Stockholm Chamber of Commerce [SCC], No. 079/2005, Sep. 12, 2010, Sec. 137. https://www.italaw.com/sites/default/files/case-documents/ita0720.pdf.

some tribunals did not do it.[118] For example, in *Telenor v. Hungary* the investor Telenor Mobile Communications AS, a Norwegian company, filed an arbitration claim against Hungary, alleging that Hungary violated the standards of expropriation as well as fair and equitable treatment and protection.[119] Hungary contested the investor's claim of violation of the fair and equitable treatment and protection, arguing that the Norway—Hungary BIT limits arbitration only to expropriation claims.[120] The Claimant rejected Hungary's position by arguing that the MFN clause in Norway—Hungary BIT allows it to "...invoke the widest of the dispute resolution clauses under other BITs entered into by Hungary with other States".[121] The tribunal in this case did not extend the MFN clause, noting that "...the effect of the wide interpretation of the MFN clause is to expose the host State to treaty-shopping by the investor among an indeterminate number of treaties to find a dispute resolution clause wide enough to cover a dispute that would fall outside the dispute resolution clause in the base treaty".[122] The tribunal also underscored that the wide application of the MFN clause "...generates both uncertainty and instability in that at one moment the limitation in the basic BIT is operative and at the next

Accessed 25 March 2019; Siemens A.G. v. The Argentine Republic. International Centre for Settlement of Investment Disputes [ICSID], ARB/02/8, Aug. 3, 2004, Sec. 108-110. http://www.italaw.com/sites/default/files/case-documents/ita0788.pdf. Accessed 25 March 2019; Telefónica S.A. v. The Argentine Republic. International Centre for Settlement of Investment Disputes [ICSID], ARB/03/20, May 25, 2006, Sec. 100–108. http://www.italaw.com/sites/default/files/case-documents/ita0856.pdf. Accessed 25 March 2019; See also Camuzzi International S. A. v. The Argentine Republic. International Centre for Settlement of Investment Disputes [ICSID], ARB/03/2, May 11, 2005, Sec. 120, 121. http://www.italaw.com/sites/default/files/case-documents/ita0108.pdf. Accessed 25 March 2019. (In this case the investor also brought up the argument on the MFN clause similar to the Maffezini claim. However, as the Respondent state did not object to the claim, the tribunal did not examine it).

[118]Renta 4 S.V.S.A., Ahorro Corporacionemergentes F.I., Ahorro Corporacion Eurofondo F.I., Rovime Inversiones Sica V S.A., Quasar De V Alors Sica V S.A., Orgor De V Alores Sica V S.A., Gbi 9000 Sica V S.A. v. The Russian Federation. Stockholm Chamber of Commerce [SCC], Award on Preliminary Objections, Mar. 20, 2009, Sec. 119, http://www.italaw.com/sites/default/files/case-documents/ita0714.pdf. Accessed 25 March 2019; Wintershall Aktiengesellschaft v. Argentine Republic. International Centre for Settlement of Investment Disputes [ICSID], ARB/04/14, Dec. 8, 2008, Sec. 160, 197. https://www.italaw.com/sites/default/files/case-documents/ita0907.pdf. Accessed 25 March 2019; Plama Consortium Limited v. Republic Of Bulgaria. International Centre for Settlement of Investment Disputes [ICSID], ARB/03/24, Feb. 8, 2005, Sec. 240. http://www.italaw.com/sites/default/files/case-documents/ita0669.pdf. Accessed 25 March 2019; Vladimir Berschader and Moïse Berschader v. The Russian Federation. Stockholm Chamber of Commerce [SCC], No. 080/2004, Apr. 21, 2006, Sec. 208. http://www.italaw.com/sites/default/files/case-documents/ita0079_0.pdf. Accessed 25 March 2019.

[119]Telenor Mobile Communications A.S. v. The Republic of Hungary. International Centre for Settlement of Investment Disputes [ICSID], ARB/04/15, Sep. 13, 2006, Sec. 17. https://www.italaw.com/sites/default/files/case-documents/ita0858.pdf. Accessed 25 March 2019; For further analysis of this case see Di Pietro (2012), pp. 798–814.

[120]Ibid Sec. 19.

[121]Ibid Sec. 20.

[122]Ibid Sec. 93.

moment it is overridden by a wider dispute resolution clause in a new BIT entered into by the host State".[123] Hence, as the above cases illustrate, various arbitral tribunals have rendered different arbitral awards on the extension of the MFN clause. The existence of such a conflicting arbitral jurisprudence does not promote legal certainty. As rightfully observed by Faya-Rodríguez and Joubit-Bret, "[some view]. . .the countless possible combinations and rather unforeseeable consequences as seriously damaging the predictability, certainty and even legitimacy of the system".[124]

As MFN clauses may be used to reach out for the various provisions in different investment treaties,[125] it is important that a host country takes concrete measures to address this issue. One possibility could be to omit the MFN clause altogether from its investment agreements. However, this option is not efficient in the case of developing states with a weak rule of law, since it will significantly lessen the protection of investors and their investments. Another way could be to specify what the MFN clause does not apply to.[126] An instructive example in this regard is the MFN provision of Israel—Myanmar BIT, according to which "[f]or the sake of avoiding any misunderstanding, it is further clarified that the [MFN] treatment. . .shall not apply to definitions, nor to mechanisms for dispute settlement between one Contracting Party and an Investor of the other Contracting Party. . .".[127] Host states could follow the example of countries that limit the scope of the MFN treatment, as such limitation is justified in order to promote greater legal certainty and stability in light of various conflicting arbitration awards regarding the scope of MFN clauses. The decision regarding what to exclude from the scope of MFN should be made by host states based on their countries' policy objectives.

As the MFN clause may render useless any new generation investment law changes made to existing investment treaties or new investment treaties entered

[123]Ibid Sec. 94.

[124]Faya-Rodríguez and Joubin-Bret (2010), p. 100.

[125]In this regard, Wouters, Duquet, and Hachez write that "[m]ost-favoured-nation clauses in bilateral agreements have significant effects, as they may be used to endow the network of BITs with the multilateral role and non-discriminatory fashion a multilateral treaty was never able to provide". See Wouters et al. (2013), p. 60.

[126]For examples of such agreements see generally Agreement on the Promotion and the Reciprocal Protection of Investments, Republic of Albania—The Republic of Cyprus, Aug. 5, 2010, Art. 4 (3). http://investmentpolicyhubold.unctad.org/Download/TreatyFile/3145. Accessed 25 March 2019; Agreement on the Promotion and Protection of Investments, Republic of Turkey - Republic of Slovenia, Mar. 23, 2004, Art. 3. http://investmentpolicyhubold.unctad.org/Download/TreatyFile/2274. Accessed 25 March 2019; Agreement for the Promotion and Reciprocal Protection of Investments, Republic of Albania—Republic of Azerbaijan, Feb. 9, 2012, Art. 4. http://investmentpolicyhubold.unctad.org/Download/TreatyFile/4. Accessed 25 March 2019.

[127]Agreement for the Reciprocal Promotion and Protection of Investments, State of Israel—Republic of the Union of Myanmar, Oct. 5, 2014, Art. 3. http://investmentpolicyhubold.unctad.org/Download/TreatyFile/3161. Accessed 25 March 2019.

into,[128] the paper also proposes to limit the scope of MFN by stating that it is not applicable to international investment agreements concluded prior to the one, where the MFN clause is provided for. This is especially important for host states that would like to reform their 'old generation' investment agreements. This will also bring the much-needed legal certainty for investors.[129] Therefore, the paper proposes for host states to qualify MFN provisions in new investment treaties ratified or when renegotiating the old ones.

12.5 Investment Protection Standard of Full Protection and Security

The full protection and security standard (*hereinafter* FPS) is also one of the most frequently provided investment standards. In general, FPS "...requires, as a minimum, the abstention of the host state from interference with the rights of the investor, in particular violations of his or her property".[130] It also "...requires positive action by the host state to protect foreign investment through preventive and repressive action, and also against harm caused by private actors".[131] At the same time, it is commonly understood not to provide absolute protection.[132]

Although the FPS standard may in general be understood to mean protection against physical harm, the arbitral jurisprudence demonstrates that the exact scope of this standard is far from settled. In a number of cases arbitral tribunals found host states liable for the breach of the FPS standard, where such states failed to provide the physical security to investors.[133] In several cases the tribunals specifically noted

[128]Faya-Rodríguez and Joubin-Bret (2010), p. 106 ("A broad MFN obligation...makes it difficult to update, refine or improve new IIAs, as the new treaties may be modified by reason of past treaties.").

[129]Ibid 96 ("[T]he uncertainty and ongoing discussions and debates [regarding the scope and effect of the MFN clause]...affect investors who are left unclear about the way to use or invoke MFN treatment commitments made by their host State.").

[130]Zeitler (2010), p. 183. For a comprehensive analysis of the FPS standard see also De Brabandere (2015), pp. 332–346; Salacuse (2013), p. 388.

[131]Zeitler (2010), p. 183.

[132]Dolzer and Schreuer (2012), p. 161. See also Asian Agricultural Products LTD. (AAPL) v. Republic of Sri Lanka. International Centre for Settlement of Investment Disputes [ICSID], ARB/87/3, June 27, 1990, Sec. 48, http://www.italaw.com/sites/default/files/case-documents/ita1034.pdf. Accessed 25 March 2019.

[133]Wena Hotels Limited v. Arab Republic of Egypt. International Centre for Settlement of Investment Disputes [ICSID], ARB/98/4, Dec. 8, 2000, Sec. 77, 84–95. http://www.italaw.com/sites/default/files/case-documents/ita0902.pdf. Accessed 25 March 2019; American Manufacturing & Trading, Inc. v. Republic of Zaire. International Centre for Settlement of Investment Disputes [ICSID], ARB/93/1, Feb. 21, 1997, Sec. 6.11. http://www.italaw.com/sites/default/files/case-documents/ita0028.pdf. Accessed 25 March 2019.

that the FPS standard refers to the obligation of provision of physical security.[134] Nevertheless, there are also a number of tribunals that have understood the FPS standard to mean more than the physical security.[135] For example, in *Azurix v. Argentina* the tribunal held that the FPS standard should be understood "…to go beyond protection and security ensured by the police" and that "[i]t is not only a matter of physical security," but also about "…the stability afforded by a secure investment environment…".[136] Similarly, the tribunal in *National Grid v. Argentina,* despite objections by Argentina, held that "protection and constant security" standard "…does not carry with it the implication that this protection is inherently limited to protection and security of physical assets".[137] Although tribunals in these awards have held that FPS should be interpreted to mean more than physical security, other tribunals have in turn held the opposite, voicing criticisms at awards that found FPS to mean more than the protection against physical harm. The tribunal in *Suez v. Argentina* noted that "…the stability of the business environment and legal security are more characteristic of the standard of fair and equitable

[134]Saluka Investments BV (The Netherlands) v. The Czech Republic. Permanent Court of Arbitration [PCA], Mar.17, 2006, Sec. 484. http://www.italaw.com/sites/default/files/case-documents/ita0740.pdf. Accessed 25 March 2019 ("…[The FPS] standard obliges the host State to adopt all reasonable measures to protect assets and property from threats or attacks which may target particularly foreigners or certain groups of foreigners. The practice of arbitral tribunals seems to indicate, however, that the "full security and protection" clause is not meant to cover just any kind of impairment of an investor's investment, but to protect more specifically the physical integrity of an investment against interference by use of force."); Noble Ventures, Inc. v. Romania. International Centre for Settlement of Investment Disputes [ICSID], ARB/01/11, Oct. 12, 2005, Sec. 167. http://www.italaw.com/sites/default/files/case-documents/ita0565.pdf. Accessed 25 March 2019 (In this case the tribunal dismissed the Claimant's argument that Romania violated the FPS standard, noting that "[t]he Claimant has failed to prove that its alleged injuries and losses could have been prevented had the Respondent exercised due diligence in this regard, nor has it established any specific value of the losses." See Ibid Sec. 166).

[135]As Sornarajah writes, "…there has been a tendency to expand the scope of the provision well beyond its moorings in customary law to include a wider notion that the clause mandates the maintenance of conditions of stability for the investment". See Sornarajah (2012), p. 205. See also Schefer (2013), p. 312.

[136]Azurix Corp. v. The Argentine Republic. International Centre for Settlement of Investment Disputes [ICSID], ARB/01/12, July 14, 2006, Sec. 408. http://www.italaw.com/sites/default/files/case-documents/ita0061.pdf. Accessed 25 March 2019; For another tribunal applying the same position as the Azurix tribunal see Biwater Gauff ltd. v. United Republic of Tanzania. International Centre for Settlement of Investment Disputes [ICSID], ARB/05/22, July 24, 2008, Sec. 729. http://www.italaw.com/sites/default/files/case-documents/ita0095.pdf. Accessed 25 March 2019 ("The Arbitral Tribunal adheres to the Azurix holding that when the terms "protection" and "security" are qualified by "full", the content of the standard may extend to matters other than physical security. It implies a State's guarantee of stability in a secure environment, both physical, commercial and legal. It would in the Arbitral Tribunal's view be unduly artificial to confine the notion of "full security" only to one aspect of security, particularly in light of the use of this term in a BIT, directed at the protection of commercial and financial investments.").

[137]National Grid PLC v. The Argentine Republic. International Centre for Settlement of Investment Disputes [ICSID], Nov. 3, 2008, Sec. 189. http://www.italaw.com/sites/default/files/case-documents/ita0555.pdf. Accessed 25 March 2019.

treatment, while the full protection and security standard primarily seeks to protect investment from physical harm".[138] In *BG v. Argentina* the tribunal also emphasized that FPS has "...traditionally been associated with situations where the physical security of the investor or its investment is compromised,"[139] explicitly denouncing awards that have interpreted FPS to mean more than physical security.[140] As it may be seen, arbitral awards on the scope of the FPS clause are conflicting. This makes the standard ambiguous, as it is difficult to understand how future arbitral tribunals will interpret it. Apart from this, one cannot but agree with UNCTAD that "...if FPS is understood to include economic, legal and other protection and security, it can constrain government regulatory prerogatives, including for sustainable development objectives".[141] Indeed, the understanding of FPS as a standard providing for all types of security would be too demanding upon host states.

In light of the above vagueness of the FPS standard, the paper argues that host states should take concrete measures to counter this problem. One way of dealing with this issue may be to omit FPS clauses from investment agreements. Yet, this solution will threaten investors' physical security. Therefore, it is not rational to exclude FPS altogether. Another possible legal mechanism is to limit FPS to physical security and to customary international law treatment when negotiating new BITs or renegotiating the old ones. A BIT that can serve as an example is the USA—Uruguay treaty. The treaty provides investors with the FPS standard. However, it qualifies it by noting that the obligation of full protection and security "...requires each Party to provide the level of police protection required under customary international law".[142] Another instructive example is the draft EU—Viet Nam FTA which stipulates that "...[f]or greater certainty, 'full protection and security' refers to the Party's obligations to act as may be reasonably necessary to

138Suez, Sociedad General de Aguas de Barcelona S.A., and InterAgua Servicios Integrales del Agua S.A. v. The Argentine Republic. International Centre for Settlement of Investment Disputes [ICSID], ARB/03/17, Dec. on Liability, July 30, 2010, Sec. 167. http://www.italaw.com/sites/default/files/case-documents/ita0813.pdf. Accessed 25 March 2019 (The tribunal also added that the FDS standard may "...may also include an obligation to provide adequate mechanisms and legal remedies for prosecuting the State organs or private parties responsible for the injury caused to the investor." See Ibid.)

139BG Group PLC v. the Argentine Republic. Ad Hoc Arbitration, Dec. 24, 2007, Sec. 324. http://www.italaw.com/sites/default/files/case-documents/ita0081.pdf. Accessed 25 March 2019.

140Ibid Sec. 326 (in particular, criticizing Azurix v. Argentina and Siemens v. Argentina cases which have provided broad interpretation of the FPS standard).

141UNCTAD (2015) United Nations Conference on Trade and Development, Investment Policy Framework for Sustainable Development 98. https://unctad.org/en/PublicationsLibrary/diaepcb2015d5en.pdf. Accessed 25 March 2019.

142Treaty concerning the Encouragement and Reciprocal Protection of Investment, The United States of America—The Oriental Republic of Uruguay, Nov. 4, 2005, Art. 5 (2). http://investmentpolicyhubold.unctad.org/Download/TreatyFile/2380. Accessed 25 March 2019.

protect physical security of investors and covered investments".[143] Such a qualification of FPS clauses allows meeting both the needs of the state for regulatory space and those of investors for physical security. Legal stability, on the other hand, may be provided via the FET standard or stabilization obligations. Therefore, the paper argues that host states should limit the scope of the FET standard to physical security.

12.6 Observance of Obligations or So-Called "Umbrella Clause"

An umbrella clause is a provision that appears in some international investment treaties.[144] It brings "...obligations a host state assumed vis-à-vis a foreign investor....under the protective umbrella of an investment treaty by creating an international law obligation for the host state to observe its undertakings vis-à-vis the investor".[145] These undertakings may be provided orally, in investment contracts, or in investment legislation. Consequently, as noted by UNCTAD, "[t]he clause thus brings contractual and other individual obligations under the "umbrella" of the IIA, making them potentially enforceable through ISDS [investment treaty-based arbitration]".[146]

An umbrella clause is effective in protection of investors' rights, since in general it allows investors to bring contractual and other issues to international forum. However, there have been many debates regarding the meaning and scope of the umbrella clause in international investment arbitration.[147] In general, one line of arbitral cases upholds the idea that an umbrella clause does not transform private obligations into obligations under public international law. *SGS v. Pakistan* is the

---

[143]European Union—Viet Nam Free Trade Agreement(Draft Version), Art. 14(4). http://investmentpolicyhub.unctad.org/Download/TreatyFile/3563. Accessed 25 March 2019; For a similar provision see also India's Model Bilateral Investment Treaty, Art. 3 (3.2). http://investmentpolicyhubold.unctad.org/Download/TreatyFile/3560. Accessed 25 March 2019.

[144]See generally Dumberry (2012), p. 236 ("While some States (Switzerland, Netherlands, United Kingdom, Germany) often include umbrella clauses in their BITs, other States rarely do (France, Australia) and others never do (Canada)."); Vandevelde (2010), p. 257 (An umbrella clause is "...not as common as the fair and equitable treatment or full protection and security standards or the expropriation, transfers, or war and civil disturbance provisions.").

[145]Schill (2010), p. 317; For comprehensive analysis of umbrella clauses see also Wong (2006), pp. 135–177; Schill (2009c), pp. 1–97; Yannaca-Small (2006), Newcombe and Paradell (2009), pp. 437–480; Wälde (2005), pp. 183–236; Miles (2008), pp. 3–23; Subedi (2012), pp. 102–104; Schokkaert and Heckscher (2009), pp. 480–489.

[146]UNCTAD (2015) United Nations Conference on Trade and Development, Investment Policy Framework for Sustainable Development 102. https://unctad.org/en/PublicationsLibrary/diaepcb2015d5_en.pdf. Accessed 25 March 2019.

[147]As Salias notes, "[t]heir interpretation has led to controversy and to conflicting decisions." See Salias (2009), p. 490; See also Jamieson (2012), pp. 621–625.

first case like this.[148] According to the facts of the case, in 1994 a Swiss company Société Générale de Surveillance S.A. (*hereinafter* SGS) and the Government of Pakistan concluded a contract on the provision by SGS of pre-shipment inspection of goods exported to Pakistan.[149] In 1996 Pakistan sent a notice to SGS that it terminated the agreement.[150] SGS viewed this termination as wrongful and unlawful and, subsequently, applied for ICSID arbitration, claiming the violation of the umbrella clause (Article 11) of Switzerland—Pakistan BIT by Pakistan.[151] Article 11 of the BIT provides that "[e]ither Contracting Party shall constantly guarantee the observance of the commitments it has entered into with respect to the investments of the investors of the other Contracting Party".[152] Pakistan objected to SGS claim, noting that this claim was based on a contractual breach and, hence, could not be reviewed by an international investment arbitral tribunal.[153] SGS disagreed, arguing that Article 11 "...has the effect of elevating a simple breach of contract claim to a treaty claim under international law".[154]

The key issue in this regard was whether an umbrella clause of the BIT transformed purely contractual claims into BIT claims. The tribunal held that it did not.[155] The tribunal noted that an umbrella clause was "...not meant to project a substantive obligation..." similar to such obligations, as FET and others,[156] stating the following in this regard:

> A violation of a contract entered into by a State with an investor of another State, is not, by itself, a violation of international law... [A contrary decision would be] far-reaching in

---

[148]SGS Société Générale de Surveillance S.A. v. Islamic Republic of Pakistan. International Centre for Settlement of Investment Disputes [ICSID], ARB/01/13, Aug. 6, 2003, Sec. 164. https://www.italaw.com/sites/default/files/case-documents/ita0779.pdf. Accessed 25 March 2019.

[149]Ibid Sec. 2, 11.

[150]Ibid Sec. 16.

[151]Ibid Sec. 17.

[152]Ibid Sec. 53.

[153]Ibid Sec. 43.

[154]Ibid Sec. 98. The counsel for SGS called this a 'mirror effect'—"You have a violation of the contract, and the Treaty says, as if you had a mirror, that this violation will also be susceptible to being characterized as a violation of the Treaty". See Ibid Sec. 99.

[155]Ibid Sec. 166 ("...Article 11 does not purport to state that breaches of contract alleged by an investor in relation to a contract it has concluded with a State (widely considered to be a matter of municipal rather than international law) are automatically "elevated" to the level of breaches of international treaty law"). The tribunal also noted that if one were to accept the position of SGS, then it would result in undesirable consequences. In particular, the tribunal stated that it would mean that any allegation of breach of "...an unlimited number of State contracts, as well as other municipal law instruments setting out State commitments including unilateral commitments to an investor of the other Contracting Party" could be "...treated as a breach of the BIT". See Ibid Sec. 168.

[156]Ibid Sec. 170.

> scope,...unqualified and sweeping in...operation,...burdensome in...potential impact upon a Contracting Party.[157]

According to the tribunal, a wide interpretation of umbrella clause would render many of the BIT articles "substantially superfluous": "There would be no real need to demonstrate a violation of those substantive treaty standards if a simple breach of contract, or of municipal statute or regulations, by itself, would suffice to constitute a treaty violation on the part of a Contracting Party and engage the international responsibility of the Party".[158] Hence, the tribunal concluded that it did not have the jurisdiction to consider this case, since the claim was based on the contract, not the treaty.

Nevertheless, there is also a diametrically opposing arbitral award on the interpretation of the meaning of an umbrella clause in the case of *SGS v. Philippines.* According to the facts of the case, the same Swiss company SGS concluded an agreement on import supervision related services with the Government of the Philippines in 1991.[159] Due to some disputes with Philippines, SGS filed an arbitration claim against the country, arguing that it violated Switzerland-Philippines BIT by failing to pay money owed to it under the contract.[160] One of the key issues before the tribunal was whether the umbrella clause[161] of the BIT "...gives the

[157]Ibid Sec. 167; A similar stance toward an umbrella clause was taken up by the Pan American v. Argentina tribunal. The tribunal noted the following: "...[An] umbrella clause cannot transform any contract claims into a treaty claim, as this would necessarily imply that any commitments of the State in respect to investments, even the most minor ones, would be transformed into treaty claims. These far reaching consequences of a broad interpretation of the so-called umbrella clauses...[are] quite destructive of the distinction between the national legal orders and the international legal order...". See Pan American Energy LLC, BP Argentina Exploration Company v. The Argentine Republic. International Centre for Settlement of Investment Disputes [ICSID], ARB/03/13, July 27, 2006, Sec. 110. http://www.italaw.com/sites/default/files/case-documents/ita0616.pdf. Accessed 25 March 2019.

[158]SGS Société Générale de Surveillance S.A. v. Islamic Republic of Pakistan, Sec. 168. It is interesting to note that following this Award Switzerland issued a note, where it stated that "...Swiss authorities are alarmed about the very narrow interpretation given to the meaning of Article 11 by the [SGS v. Pakistan] Tribunal which not only runs counter to the intention of Switzerland when concluding the Treaty but is quite evidently neither supported by the meaning of similar articles in BITs concluded by other countries..." and concluded that an investor should be allowed to bring a BIT claim for violation of the umbrella clause. See Swiss Authorities' Note on the Interpretation of Article 11 of the BIT of Switzerland and Pakistan cited in Gaillard (2005), pp. 341, 342.

[159]SGS Société Générale de Surveillance S.A. v. Republic of the Philippines. International Centre for Settlement of Investment Disputes [ICSID], ARB/02/6, Jan. 29, 2004, Sec. 1. http://www.italaw.com/sites/default/files/case-documents/ita0782.pdf. Accessed 25 March 2019. For a comprehensive analysis of this case see Wendlandt (2008), pp. 523–559.

[160]Ibid Sec. 15, 16.

[161]The clause reads as follows: "Each Contracting Party shall observe any obligation it has assumed with regard to specific investments in its territory by investors of the other Contracting Party". See Ibid Sec.115.

Tribunal jurisdiction over essentially contractual claims against the Respondent".[162] The tribunal held that it had jurisdiction over these claims based on the BIT umbrella clause. In particular, it noted that the umbrella clause "...makes it a breach of the BIT for the host state to fail to observe binding commitments, including contractual commitments, which it has assumed with regard to specific investments".[163] The tribunal also criticized the decision in *SGS v. Pakistan,* stating that "[n]ot only are the reasons given by the Tribunal in *SGS v. Pakistan* unconvincing: the Tribunal failed to give any clear meaning to the "umbrella clause"".[164] Hence, as it may be seen, the tribunals in *SGS v. Pakistan* and *SGS v. Philippines* interpreted the meaning of an umbrella clause differently.

The non-uniform interpretation of umbrella clauses generates much legal uncertainty.[165] While some tribunals provide a very narrow interpretation of such a clause by not allowing investors to elevate contractual claims into BIT claims, others provide an expansive interpretation, treating an umbrella clause as a standard on the same level as full protection and security, fair and equitable treatment, expropriation, and other standards. In this regard, UNCTAD notes that a key challenge related to umbrella clauses is that they ".... effectively expand the scope of the IIA by incorporating non-treaty obligations of the host State into the treaty, which may increase the risk of being faced with costly legal proceedings".[166] How can host states address this situation? One option could be not to include umbrella clauses in investment agreements. This is in line with the treaty making practice of a number of countries. For example, Canada has never included an umbrella clause in any of its BITs.[167] However, this approach may lessen the protection of investors' rights, tilting the balance too much in favor of states.

Therefore, the paper proposes that host states consider making umbrella clauses in their investment treaties applicable exclusively to contractual written commitments with regard to specific investments. Although this formulation may still be broad, at least, it will allow qualifying the scope of an umbrella clause to (1) written commitments in the form of contracts as opposed to oral commitments and (2) to concrete obligations undertaken with respect to specific investments. One instructive example in this respect is the 2015 Japan—Uruguay BIT which provides the following umbrella clause:

---

[162]Ibid Sec. 92.

[163]SGS Société Générale de Surveillance S.A. v. Republic of the Philippines, Sec. 128.

[164]Ibid Sec. 125.

[165]In this respect, one cannot but agree with Potts who notes that "[w]ithin the field of international investment law, the legal status of umbrella clauses is in a state of disarray" and that "[t]he current jurisprudence provides little predictive power for current and future investors concerning the redress of contractual breaches". See Potts (2011), p. 1045.

[166]UNCTAD (2015) United Nations Conference on Trade and Development. Investment Policy Framework for Sustainable Development. 102, https://unctad.org/en/PublicationsLibrary/diaepcb2015d5_en.pdf. Accessed 25 March 2019.

[167]Dumberry (2012), p. 236.

Each Contracting Party, subject to its laws, shall do all in its power to ensure that a written agreement with regard to a specific investment, between a national authority of that Contracting Party and an investor of the other Contracting Party or its investment that is an enterprise in the Area of the former Contracting Party, is respected, provided that the written agreement is with respect to:

(a) natural resources that a national authority controls;
(b) supply of services to the public on behalf of the former Contracting Party; or
(c) infrastructure projects, that are not for the exclusive or predominant use and benefit of the government".[168]

The BIT further specifies the meaning of a written agreement by noting that "(a) a unilateral act of an administrative or judicial authority, such as a permit, license or authorization issued by a Contracting Party solely in its regulatory capacity, or a decree, order, or judgment, standing alone; and (b) an administrative or judicial consent decree or order, shall not be considered a written agreement".[169] Another relevant example is the EU—Singapore Agreement which limits an umbrella clause to a contractual written agreement and provides that the "...Party shall not frustrate or undermine the said commitment through the exercise of its governmental authority either: (a) deliberately; or (b) in a way which substantially alters the balance of rights and obligation in the contractual written obligation unless the Party provides reasonable compensation to restore the investor or investment to a position which it would have been in had the frustration or undermining not occurred".[170] Thus, the more concrete formulation of umbrella clauses is recommended in order to avoid the threat of elevating all kinds of breaches of obligations to investors to the level of international investment treaty breaches.

12.7 Conclusions

As discussed in this paper, while in general the investment protection standards are important for the protection of investors' rights, the broadly formulated and unbalanced versions of these standards are now being increasingly challenged for limiting host states' legislative and regulatory powers and for being unclear which has thus far resulted in a number of inconsistent arbitral awards. Accordingly, one of the most pressing challenges facing the international community in the twenty-first century is advancing a new generation international investment agreement regime, which unlike the previous generations that have prioritized investor protection, will be able to balance the protection of investors' rights and promotion of host states'

[168]Agreement for the Liberalization, Promotion and Protection of Investment, Japan—The Oriental Republic of Uruguay, Jan. 26, 2015, Art. 6. http://investmentpolicyhubold.unctad.org/Download/TreatyFile/3284. Accessed 25 March 2019.

[169]Ibid.

[170]European Union—Singapore Comprehensive Free Trade Agreement, Art. Art. 9.4. (5). https://investmentpolicyhubold.unctad.org/Download/TreatyFile/5714. Accessed 25 March 2019.

sustainable development. It is the hope of the author that the investment agreement reform proposals advanced in this paper will be applied in practice so that both the interests of investors and host states can be fully accommodated.

References

Acconci P (2008) Most-favoured-nation treatment. In: Schreuer C et al (eds) The Oxford handbook of international investment law. Oxford University Press

Alexander E (2008) Taking account of reality: adopting contextual standards for developing countries in international investment law. Va J Int Law 48:817

Alvarez J (2011) The public international law regime governing international investment. Pocketbooks of The Hague Academy of International Law

Cordonier Segger M-C et al (2011) Promoting sustainable development through international law. In: Cordonier Segger M-C et al (eds) Sustainable development in world investment law. Kluwer Law International

Cross KH (2012) Converging trends in investment treaty practice. N C J Int Law Commer Regul 38:151–231

De Brabandere E (2015) Host states' due diligence obligations in international investment law. Syracuse J Int Law Commer 42:320

de Matos AA, Leitão JB (2016) When international investment arbitration meets insolvency. https://www.insol-europe.org/download/documents/776. Accessed 25 Mar 2019

Di Pietro D (2012) Observations on Telenor Mobile Communications A.S. v. The Republic of Hungary. In: Rubins N (ed) Investment arbitration decisions. JurisNet, LLC

Dimsey M (2008) The resolution of international investment disputes: the challenges and solutions. Eleven International Publishing

Dolzer R (2005a) Fair and equitable treatment: a key standard in investment treaties. Int Lawyer 39:87

Dolzer R (2005b) National treatment: new developments. https://www.oecd.org/investment/internationalinvestmentagreements/36055356.pdf. Accessed 25 Mar 2019

Dolzer R, Schreuer C (2012) Principles of international investment law. Oxford University Press

Douglas Z (2006) Nothing if not critical for investment treaty arbitration: occidental, Eureko and Methanex. Arbitr Int 22:27

Dumberry P (2012) International investment contracts. In: De Brabandere E et al (eds) International investment law: the sources of rights and obligations. Martinus Nijhoff

Faya-Rodríguez A, Joubin-Bret A (2010) Most-favoured-nation treatment: UNCTAD series on issues in international investment agreements II. United Nations Conference on Trade and Development. http://unctad.org/en/Docs/diaeia20101_en.pdf. Accessed 25 Mar 2019

Franck S (2006) Foreign direct investment, investment treaty arbitration, and the rule of law. Pac McGeorge Glob Bus Dev Law J 19:337

Gaillard E (2005) Investment treaty arbitration and jurisdiction over contract claims – the SGS cases considered. In: Todd W (ed) International investment law and arbitration: leading cases from the ICSID, NAFTA, bilateral treaties and customary international law. Cameron May

Grierson-Weiler T, Laird I (2008) Standards of treatment. In: Schreuer C et al (eds) The Oxford handbook of international investment law. Oxford University Press

Hamzah H (2018) Bilateral investment treaties (BITs) in Indonesia: a paradigm shift, issues and challenges. J Leg Ethical Regul Issues 21:1

Hober K (2009) MFN clauses and dispute resolution in investment treaties: have we reached the end of the road? In: Binder C et al (eds) The international investment law for the 21st century: essays in Honour of Christoph Schreuer. Oxford University Press

Hueckel J (2012) Rebalancing legitimacy and sovereignty in international investment agreements. Emory Law J 61:601–640

Jamieson S (2012) A model future: the future of foreign direct investment and bilateral investment treaties. South Tex Law Rev 53:605

Johnson L, Razbaeva M (2014) State control over interpretation of investment treaties. http://ccsi.columbia.edu/files/2014/04/State_control_over_treaty_interpretation_FINAL-April-5_2014.pdf. Accessed 25 Mar 2019

Kläger R (2010) Fair and equitable treatment: a look at the theoretical underpinnings of legitimacy and fairness. J World Invest Trade 11:435

Kläger R (2013) 'Fair and equitable treatment' in international investment law. Cambridge University Press

Kökényesi G (2016) 'Denial of Justice' as a basis for the ICSID ruling against hungary. http://kluwerarbitrationblog.com/2016/03/01/denial-of-justice-as-a-basis-for-the-icsid-ruling-against-hungary/. Accessed 25 Mar 2019

Kurtz J (2010) The merits and limits of comparativism: national treatment in international investment law and the WTO. In: Schill S (ed) International investment law and comparative public law. Oxford University Press

Lester S (2015) Reforming the international investment law system. Md J Int Law 30:70

Magraw K et al (2011) Standards under the North American free trade agreement: fair and equitable/minimum standard of treatment, expropriation of rights and contracts, and the standard of compensation and the determination of damages for violations of the fair and equitable/minimum standard of treatment. http://graduateinstitute.ch/files/live/sites/iheid/files/sites/ctei/shared/CTEI/Law%20Clinic/Memoranda%202011/Standerds_NAFTA.pdf. Accessed 25 Mar 2019

Maupin J (2014) Public and private in international investment law: an integrated systems approach. Va J Int Law 54:367

Miles C (2008) Where's my umbrella? An "ordinary meaning" approach to answering three key questions that have emerged from the "umbrella clause" debate. In: Weiler T (ed) Investment treaty arbitration and international law. JurisNet 3–23

Miles K (2011) Sustainable development, national treatment and like circumstances in investment law. In: Cordonier Segger M-C et al (eds) Sustainable development in world investment law. Kluwer Law International

Muchlinski P (2007) Multinational enterprises and the law. Oxford University Press

Muchlinski P et al (2012) Fair and equitable treatment: UNCTAD series on issues in international investment agreements II. United Nations Conference on Trade and Development. http://unctad.org/en/Docs/unctaddiaeia2011d5_en.pdf. Accessed 3 Mar 2019

Newcombe A, Paradell L (2009) Law and practice of investment treaties: standards of treatment. Kluwer Law International

Novák Z (2016) ICSID Complaint as alternative to supplemental filing. https://efilablog.org/2016/04/26/icsid-complaint-as-alternative-to-supplemental-filing/. Accessed 25 Mar 2019

Patel N (2016) India's new model BIT: a shift towards protecting host state sovereignty. http://minnjil.org/indias-new-model-bit-a-shift-towards-protecting-host-state-sovereignty/. Accessed 25 Mar 2019

Potts J (2011) Stabilizing the role of umbrella clauses in bilateral investment treaties: intent, reliance, and internationalization. Va J Int Law 51:1005

Pritchard R (2005) Safeguards for foreign investment in mining. In: Thomas Wälde et al (eds) International and comparative mineral law and policy: trends and prospects. Kluwer Law International

Reinisch A (2008) The proliferation of international dispute settlement mechanisms: the threat of fragmentation vs. the promise of a more effective system? Some reflections from the perspective of investment arbitration. In: Crawford J et al (eds) International law between universalism and fragmentation (In Honour of Gerhard Hafner). Brill

Roberts A (2010) Power and persuasion in investment treaty interpretation: the dual role of states. Am J Int Law 104:179

Roberts A (2013) Clash of paradigms: actors and analogies shaping the investment treaty system. Am J Int Law 107:45–94
Salacuse J (2013) The three laws of international investment: national, contractual, and international frameworks for foreign capital. Oxford University Press
Salacuse J, Sullivan N (2005) Do BITs really work? An evaluation of bilateral investment treaties and their grand bargain. Harv Int Law J 46:67
Salias MCG (2009) Do umbrella clauses apply to unilateral undertakings? In: Binder C et al (eds) the International investment law for the 21st century: essays in Honour of Christoph Schreuer. Oxford University Press
Schefer KN (2013) International investment law: text, cases and materials. Edward Elgar
Schill S (2009a) Multilateralizing investment treaties through most-favored-nation clauses. Berkeley J Int Law 27:496
Schill S (2009b) The multilateralization of international investment law. Cambridge University Press
Schill S (2009c) Enabling private ordering: function, scope and effect of umbrella clauses in international investment treaties. Minn J Int Law 18:1
Schill S (2010) Umbrella clauses as public law concepts in comparative perspective. In: Schill S (ed) International investment law and comparative public law. Oxford University Press
Schokkaert J, Heckscher Y (2009) International investments protection: comparative law analysis of bilateral and multilateral interstate conventions, doctrinal texts and arbitral jurisprudence concerning foreign investments. Editions juridiques Bruylant
Shan W (2012) General standards of treatment. In: Shan W (ed) The legal protection of foreign investment: a comparative study. Hart Publishing
Sornarajah M (2012) The international law on foreign investment. Cambridge University Press
Subedi S (2012) International investment law: reconciling policy and principle. Hart Publishing
Tajti T (2015) The dynamic conception of alternative dispute resolution. In: Burda R et al (eds) Alternative means of conflict resolution in business. Kazimiero Simonavičiaus University, Vilnius, Lithuania
Tawil G (2009) Most favoured nation clauses and jurisdictional clauses in investment treaty arbitration. In: Binder C et al (eds) The international investment law for the 21st century: essays in Honour of Christoph Schreuer. Oxford University Press
Téllez FM (2012) Conditions and criteria for the protection of legitimate expectations under international investment law. ICSID Rev 27:432
Titi C (2015) International investment law and the European Union: towards a new generation of international investment agreements. Eur J Int Law 26:639
Van Harten G (2008) Investment treaty arbitration and public law. Oxford University Press
Vandevelde K (2000) The economics of bilateral investment treaties. Harv Int Law J 41:469
Vandevelde K (2010) Bilateral investment treaties: history, policy and interpretation. Oxford University Press
Wälde T (2005) The "umbrella" clause in investment arbitration: a comment on original intentions and recent cases. J World Invest Trade 6:183
Wendlandt M (2008) SGS v. Philippines and the role of ICSID tribunals in investor-state contract disputes. Texas Int Law J 43:523
Wong J (2006) Umbrella clauses in bilateral investment treaties: of breaches of contract, treaty violations, and the divide between developing and developed countries in foreign investment disputes. George Mason Law Rev 14:135
Wouters J et al (2013) International investment law: the perpetual search for consensus. In: De Schutter O et al (eds) Foreign direct investment and human development: the law and economics of international investment agreements. Routledge
Yannaca-Small K (2006) Interpretation of the umbrella clause in investment agreements. OECD Working Papers on International Investment. https://doi.org/10.1787/415453814578. 25 March 2019
Zeitler HE (2010) Full protection and security. In: Schill S (ed) International investment law and comparative public law. Oxford University Press

Chapter 13
New Model of Investment Protection Under CETA

Zoltán Víg and Gábor Hajdu

13.1 Introduction

Disputes between foreign investors and their host countries have been omnipresent, ever since the emergence of transnational economic activity. This has become increasingly prominent with the emergence of a global world economy, where capital frequently crosses borders and foreign financing has become the norm for considerable new projects. Foreign investments represent a peculiar kind of business, one that often (but not always) stands outside the country's traditional framework of domestic businesses and investments. Furthermore, as foreign-originating ventures, they have long attracted the ire of the overly nationalist and those in need of funds. Unlike the seizure of domestic-owned property and businesses, many developing countries saw foreign investments as easy victims, assets that their local powerbases would not be sad to see expropriated or nationalized. There might be several reasons for this, eliminating competition or desire to "get even", if they had a history of being victims to colonialism. After all, the world of foreign investments only took off significantly after the advent of decolonization, when many new countries appeared, rich in resources and manpower, but poor in capital.

Regarding foreign investors, it is easy to see why such investments were desirable. These developing countries with natural and human resources represented great opportunities for their capital, and they were eager to invest for the promise of future profit. However, the primary concern of these investors was political and economic

Z. Víg (✉)
University of Szeged, Faculty of Law and Political Sciences, Szeged, Hungary

G. Hajdu (✉)
University of Szeged, Faculty of Law and Political Sciences Doctoral School, Szeged, Hungary

C. I. Nagy (ed.), *World Trade and Local Public Interest*, Studies in European Economic Law and Regulation 19, https://doi.org/10.1007/978-3-030-41920-2_13

stability.[1] Foreign investors quickly became all too aware in the post-World War II world, that the initially welcoming developing countries, could turn bellicose at any moment, friendly regimes getting replaced by more hostile ones, or simply the existing rulers deciding to reap the benefits of short-term profit through the expropriation of foreign assets. Under such circumstances, some kind of special investment protection system was necessary.

There are several ways to handle a dispute arising from the treatment of a foreign investment. The simplest way is for the foreign investor to use the domestic court system of the host country, and try to remedy the situation through the laws of this country. However, the feasibility of such a solution is questionable at best. Not only are the domestic laws subject to the caprices of the very entity that caused harm to the foreign investor, but domestic courts can have a tendency towards favoring their own state, especially in developing countries, where the separation of powers is typically not as advanced as in more developed countries. To compound this issue, there is also the lack of the rule of law to consider. In many developing countries, the rule of law is still something that is not fully implemented, or in the process of implementation.

All this has resulted in the fact that foreign investors try to avoid domestic courts of host countries, and search for other solutions. One of these is diplomatic solution, a popular method in the nineteenth century, but less relevant in an age not defined by protectionism and gunboat diplomacy. A foreign investor could entreat its own country of origin to negotiate with the host country regarding the maltreatment or damages suffered by the foreign investment there. Obviously, this diplomatic solution requires significant clout on the part of the foreign investor. That is to say, a foreign investor without sufficient pull and influence in its own nation would likely not be able to convince its own government that it needs political assistance. And even so, success is far from guaranteed, as diplomatic negotiations can easily break down or end up in an unsatisfying compromise for the foreign investor.

Therefore, some foreign investors undertake to make their own agreements with the host country, before the dispute could even arise. Such agreements outline the obligations of both parties, including the conditions the host country must maintain. Even more significantly, these agreements deal with disputes. They typically provide for international arbitration as the accepted method for resolving potential future differences. Arbitration is a seemingly impartial method, that assuages the concerns of the foreign investors. However, not every foreign investor is influential enough to procure such a special agreement.

Therefore, the foreign investor's home country comes in once again. Countries frequently sign with each other bilateral investment treaties (BITs), as well as multilateral investment treaties. These agreements also contain alternative dispute

[1]Beside the specific elements of an investment protection system, investors are more and more interested in the general qualification of the legal system of different countries. On this quantitative approach and on international indices, see Jakab and Lőrincz (2017) and especially on Doing Business Index: Jakab and Lőrincz (2016), pp. 878–882.

resolution methods, especially, international arbitration, due to its perceived impartiality and its well-supported existing infrastructure through such institutions as ICSID.

Finally, in recent times, it has become typical that instead of separate investment treaties, comprehensive free trade agreements (FTAs) contain investment related provisions, both substantial and procedural. Typical dispute resolution method in these treaties is arbitration. However, international investment arbitration has recently received criticism, with some arguing that due to the specifics of the mechanism (such as that only foreign investors are entitled to launch arbitration, and that arbitrators are basically interested in having such cases) arbitrators might not be fully impartial. As indicated by the title, the subject of this article concerns CETA, which attempted to create another method of dispute resolution as a result of these concerns about traditional arbitration.

13.2 Creation of the CETA

The famous European Union-Canada Comprehensive Economic and Trade Agreement (CETA) is one of these aforementioned FTAs. It came about as the result of a long negotiation process between the European Union and Canada. To be specific, even back in 2002, there were plans on developing a comprehensive trade agreement between the parties.[2] Preliminary to the negotiation, the Commission submitted to the Council of the European Union a proposal, which would entitle the Commission to start formal negotiations on an economic integration agreement with Canada. This was granted in 2009. This entitlement was later amended in 2011, when the Commission got mandate to negotiate on detailed investment protection issues and investment related dispute settlement procedure. Both directives became partially public on December 15, 2015, due to the decision of the Council.[3] The amendment of 2011, mentioned above, is of critical importance for this work, as this made it possible for the CETA to contain comprehensive investment protection rules. However, we know from leaked information that the CETA draft has already contained a chapter on investment protection back in 2010. This chapter showed the influence of NAFTA, as it equated "fair and equal treatment" with the "minimum standard" of treatment of foreigners in international customary law. The term "like circumstances" used by NAFTA was also taken over in the provisions on national treatment and most favored nation treatment.[4] NAFTA's evident influence might have been the result of Canada's outlook and the Commissions' limited authority.

[2]Víg and Hajdu (2018), p. 45.

[3]http://www.consilium.europa.eu/en/press/press-releases/2015/12/15-eu-canada-trade-negotiating-mandate-made-public/. Accessed 15 September 2018.

[4]Fontanelli and Bianco (2014), p. 231.

Thus, the draft of the CETA got significant criticism from European Union based interest groups because of the application of NAFTA's solutions, as they were unwilling to accept such a system of protection due to the many controversies surrounding it. As a result of this criticism, the Commission has partly changed its standpoint regarding the investment protection chapter in 2013, and tried to guarantee better protection for European investors' foreign investment abroad, however, these were only minor changes. Nevertheless, according to some opinions, the investment protection chapter of the CETA still shows the influence of the NAFTA.[5] The change of the Commission's position can be explained by the 2011 amendment, which gave free hand to the Commission to negotiate investment protection issues related to the CETA. Furthermore, the 2008 financial crisis might have affected its position, as the European Union needed capital, and the easiest way was to get it from North American investors. However, these investors likely wanted to have an investment protection system familiar to them, which would be something similar to the protection system of NAFTA.

CETA reached the next step of its development on October 18, 2013, when the President of the European Commission José Manuel Barroso and Stephen Harper Prime Minister of Canada reached a consensus regarding the most significant parts of the CETA. However, the details still had to be worked out.[6] The Committee on International Trade of the European Parliament, the INTA, received the text of the agreement as a classified document in August 2014.[7] The negotiations on the content of the agreement were closed in the same month. The next important step happened only two years later in July 2016 when the Commission made a formal proposal to the Council for signing the CETA. Here we should mention the case of Belgium, where the Vallon Regional Parliament was in the position to force Belgium to block the ratification of the CETA. This would have frustrated the conclusion of the agreement. In the end, Belgium and the European Union managed to handle the issue.[8] Thus, each member state gave consent on October 28, 2016, and the agreement was signed on October 30, 2016.[9]

13.3 The New Model

The dispute settlement system established by the CETA is called Investment Court System (ICS), contrary to the earlier Investor State Dispute Settlement (ISDS) system used for similar disputes.[10] In this section, we are going to discuss the

[5]Fontanelli and Bianco (2014), p. 232.

[6]Ibid.

[7]Delimatsis (2016), p. 12.

[8]Horváthy and Szép (2016).

[9]http://www.bbc.com/news/world-europe-37814884. Accessed 17 September 2018.

[10]Deli (2016), p. 2; Horváthy (2016).

competence and organization of the two tribunals, and the procedure established by CETA. However, before starting to discuss these issues, we would like to mention that the CETA contains two alternative disputes settlement methods as well: one is consultation, provided for in article 8.19, and the other is mediation, discussed in article 8.20. The parties to the dispute can resort to any of these any time during the dispute, even in line with arbitral proceedings.[11] Presumably, these articles aim to help the parties to find a solution to their dispute effectively and in the least costly manner, and to reduce the load of the tribunals set up under the CETA.

According to article 8.18, an investor of a party may submit to the tribunal constituted under the CETA a claim only in cases where an obligation under section C or D of chapter 8 has been breached and where the investor has suffered loss or damage as a result of the alleged breach.[12] This excludes claims based on the breach of other provisions of the CETA, in which cases typically the contracting parties should act instead of the investors in the dispute settlement.

The set-up of the first instance tribunal (the so-called "Tribunal") is regulated in article 8.27. Section 2 states that the CETA Joint Committee shall, upon the entry into force of the Agreement, appoint fifteen members of the Tribunal, from which five are nationals of a member state of the European Union, five nationals of Canada, and five nationals of third countries.[13] According to section 3 the Joint Committee may increase or decrease this number, however, only with numbers divisible with three and on the same basis as provided for in paragraph 2.[14] Pursuant to these two sections, the Tribunal should have the same number of EU, Canadian and third country members, with which solution the drafters tried to guarantee the neutrality and impartiality of the Tribunal. According to section 5 of the Agreement seven arbitrators appointed immediately after the entry into force of the CETA will serve for 6 years. Otherwise, arbitrators are chosen for 5 years term and this term can be renewed once. Vacancies are filled as they arise. A person appointed to replace an arbitrator of the Tribunal whose term of office has not expired holds office for the remainder of the predecessor's term. A member of the Tribunal serving on a division of the Tribunal when his term expires may continue to serve on the division until a final award is issued.[15] This latter element was inserted to the Agreement supposedly to prevent needless continuance of the procedures because of the expiry of the term of an arbitrator.

Here we would also like to discuss service requirements for the members of the Tribunal. According to section 4 of article 8.27 the arbitrators have to possess the qualifications required in their respective countries for appointment to judicial office, or be jurists of recognized competence. They shall have demonstrated expertise in public international law. It is desirable that they have expertise in particular, in

[11]CETA art. 8.19, art. 8.20.

[12]CETA art. 8.18.

[13]CETA sec. 2, art. 8.27.

[14]CETA sec. 3, art. 8.27.

[15]CETA sec. 5, art. 8.27.

international investment law, in international trade law and the resolution of disputes arising under international investment or international trade agreements.[16] Article 8.30 imposes additional requirements: they have to be independent and not affiliated with any government, they shall not take instructions from any organization, or government with regard to matters related to the dispute. They shall not participate in the consideration of any disputes that would create a direct or indirect conflict of interest. In addition, upon appointment, they shall refrain from acting as counsel or as party-appointed expert or witness in any pending or new investment dispute, irrespective from the fact if it is under the CETA or other international treaty.[17] Conflict of interest rules are laid down in detail in article 8.30.

The President and Vice-President of the Tribunal shall be responsible for organizational issues and will be appointed for a two-year term and shall be drawn by lot from among the Members of the Tribunal who are nationals of third countries. They shall serve on the basis of a rotation drawn by lot by the Chair of the CETA Joint Committee. The Vice-President shall replace the President when the President is unavailable. The Tribunal may draw up its own working procedures.[18] The reason for the selection of these office holders from third countries can be that the Agreement tries to strengthen with this the impartiality of the Tribunal, as these arbitrators are responsible for operational tasks.

The other tribunal established by the CETA is the second instance, the so-called Appellate Tribunal. The CETA itself does not provide for the number of its members, composition, and similar issues, instead section 3 of article 8.28 states that these issues are, as well as the appointment of its members, is decided by the CETA Joint Committee.[19]

At the same time, the CETA stipulates some basic organizational issues, like conditions of appointment mentioned in article 8.27 and ethical and conflict of interest rules from 8.30 also apply to Appellate Tribunal's arbitrators as well.[20] We suppose that the parties did not find that important the issue of the organization of the Appellate Tribunal as that of the first instance tribunal, and this is the reason that they referred the majority of these issues into the competence of the Joint Committee (instead of regulating these issues in the Agreement).

Another provision that should be highlighted, related to the Appellate Tribunal, is that the earlier mentioned Committee on Services and Investment periodically reviews its functioning according to the Agreement. It can make recommendations to the Joint Committee, which can revise its decisions related to the functioning, composition, etc. of the Appellate Tribunal.[21] Thus, two committees can be linked to the functioning of the Appellate Tribunal.

---

[16]CETA sec. 4, art. 8.27.

[17]CETA sec. 1, art. 8.30.

[18]CETA sec. 8 and 10, art. 8.27.

[19]CETA sec. 7, art. 8.28.

[20]CETA sec. 4, art. 8.28.

[21]CETA sec. 8, art. 8.28.

It should also be discussed that after organizational issues is the procedure of these two tribunals. First of all, the course of the procedure in front of the Tribunal should be examined, with highlighting the most relevant elements. One of these is that the foreign investor can submit the claim not only on its own behalf, but also on behalf of a locally established enterprise which it owns or controls directly or indirectly.[22]

The next issue that should be discussed are (f) and (g) items of section 1, article 8.22, according to which the investor cannot have an ongoing proceeding before a national or international tribunal or a court related to the same claim, and waives its right to initiate a proceeding related to the same issue in the future if he wants to submit his claim to the ICS system.[23] This provision is aimed to eliminate concurrent procedures.

Another important provision of CETA is the one which explicitly prohibits an investor from submitting a claim if the investment has been made through fraudulent misrepresentation, concealment, corruption.[24] This might have dissuasive power against proceeding in bad faith during the course of investment.

The CETA provides the possibility for Tribunal to dismiss the claim if the respondent files an objection about how a claim is manifestly without legal merit. Furthermore, the Tribunal may address and decide as a preliminary question any objection by the respondent that, as a matter of law, a claim, or any part thereof, is not a claim for which an award in favor of the claimant may be made under CETA, even if the facts alleged were assumed to be true.[25] These two articles are aimed to make the Tribunal's work more efficient and speedy.

Going back to the main elements of the procedure, it should be stated that the Tribunal hears cases in divisions consisting of three members, one of whom is a national of a Member State of the European Union, one a national of Canada and one a national of a third country. The national of the third country chairs the tribunal. At the same time, the parties may agree that a case be heard by a sole arbitrator appointed at random from the third country nationals. Such a request shall be made before the constitution of the division of the Tribunal.[26] This strengthens CETA's idea to ensure impartiality of the tribunals through third country members, and makes the procedure more cost efficient as well.

Tribunals cannot oblige states to amend or to revoke their legislative acts. Instead, they can be obliged to pay monetary compensation. Such compensation cannot exceed the damage suffered by the investor. The Agreement explicitly forbids

[22]CETA sec. 1, art. 8.23.

[23]CETA items (f) and (g), sec. 1, art. 8.22.

[24]CETA sec. 3, art. 8.18.

[25]CETA art. 8.32 and 8.33.

[26]CETA sec. 6 and 9, art. 8.27. The same article furthermore states that "The respondent shall give sympathetic consideration to a request from the claimant to have the case heard by a sole Member of the Tribunal, in particular where the claimant is a small or medium-sized enterprise or the compensation or damages claimed are relatively low."

punitive damages used in the United States. The CETA also states that costs related to the proceedings shall be borne by the unsuccessful disputing party.[27] The before-mentioned provisions are primarily in the interest of states: preserving their right to legislate, and putting the burden of paying for the costs on the losing party.

We would also like to mention special procedural rules related to the Appellate Tribunal. Similarly to organizational issues, the Joint Committee decides on procedural issues as well.[28] The most important provisions related to the Appellate Tribunal is that it may uphold, modify or reverse a Tribunal's award based on: (a) errors in the application or interpretation of applicable law; (b) manifest errors in the appreciation of the facts, including the appreciation of relevant domestic law; (c) the grounds set out in Article 52(1) (a) through (e) of the ICSID Convention, in so far as they are not covered by paragraphs (a) and (b).[29] Thus, as we can see, the Appellate Tribunal can examine not only legal issues, but factual issues as well.

The Appellate Tribunal is also constituted of three members, who are elected randomly. Regarding the award, the same rules apply as to the first instance tribunal.[30] The issue of transparency is also very important. The CETA essentially took over the UNCITRAL rules on transparency with certain digressions. For example, section 5 of article 8.36 states that hearings are open to the public. The reason for this might be that potential compensations are paid from public funds. At the same time, the CETA makes it possible to have a private hearing if the Tribunal determines that there is a need to protect confidential or protected information.[31]

On the future of ICS, article 8.29 should be mentioned, according to which Canada and the European Union will aspire to establish a multilateral investment tribunal and appellate mechanism for the resolution of investment disputes with their other trading partners. Once it is set up, the CETA Joint Committee will decide how to fit in the "current" rules into that system.[32] This definitely represents the goals of the European Union in establishing a single international tribunal for investment dispute issues, based on the ICS in the CETA.

In conclusion, it can be said that the CETA has introduced a new form of investment dispute settlement procedure. Instead of the earlier ad hoc ISDS, it has introduced the new ICS system, which could be more stable and predictable.[33]

[27] CETA art. 8.39.

[28] CETA sec. 7, art. 8.28.

[29] CETA sec. 2, art. 8.28.

[30] CETA sec. 5 and 6, art. 8.28.

[31] CETA art. 8.36.

[32] CETA art. 8.29.

[33] http://europa.eu/rapid/press-release_IP-15-5651_en.htm. Accessed 15 September 2018.

13.4 Conclusions

As we have seen, the CETA introduced an entirely new model of investment protection. However, this is not necessarily solution for the problems of the old system, there is still the possibility that these arbitration panels favor multinational companies (they have the incentive: more cases, more fees), and thus make governments reluctant to adopt appropriate policies. This stillness in legislation due to such fear is called regulatory chill. In a wider sense, "regulatory chill" means that the given state's lawmaker will avoid regulation which might have generally negative effect on foreign investors, and in a narrower sense it means that they will avoid special legislation having negative effect on certain investments.[34]

Regarding CETA and regulatory chill, two kinds of issues might arise. The first relates to the fact that when the ICS becomes operational, there will be no cohesive body of precedents for the Tribunal to rely on. For the first cases, the Tribunal will have to establish its own interpretation of the CETA, perhaps cherry pick earlier investment arbitrational decisions from other treaties as a frame of reference. Under, such circumstances, decision-making will necessarily be inconsistent for a time. Though alleviated by the continuity of the Tribunal, there will still be period of fluidity, only after which will the court's practice solidify. Generally, this would not be an issue. However, we are talking about investment disputes here that often concern sizeable sums. Thus, the risk is incredible, especially for host countries, being only passive defendants in such cases with uncertain outcomes. This could potentially create a situation reminiscent of quasi-regulatory chill; at least until the Tribunal's practice successfully stabilizes enough that its decisions will become predictable to an extent.

The second aspect comes from the definition of investor found in the CETA. To be specific, as defined in article 8.1, the term is too broad. Although CETA excludes the possibility of establishing shell companies, the text is not precise enough to exclude companies from non-contracting states having a detached subsidiary in a contracting state, in our view. This not only applies to investors from third countries, but also investors that would usually be classified as domestic ones. If a detached subsidiary is created, and the investment is made through it, it allows both domestic and third country investors to indirectly benefit from CETA and its dispute resolution method. This is particularly a concern in Canada, thanks to the various US subsidiaries operating in the country.[35] At the same time, smaller domestic enterprises are in disadvantageous position because of this, in the sense that they do not have the means to establish subsidiaries in other contracting states.

Despite these potential problems, the authors believe that the ICS still provides a potentially better solution to investment disputes than the traditional arbitrational route. However, it is questionable how well the EU will be able to advance the use of this ICS in its other treaties.

---

[34]For more information on this issue, see: Van Harten (2016), pp. 1–3.

[35]For more information on this phenomenon, see: Kanyuk (2016).

While Canada has a reputation of being amenable to such solutions, other trade partners can prove more resistant to change, and would likely prefer sticking to the old, tried-and-true system of dispute resolution. The coming years will tell if this new model has a future, but even if it doesn't, it is still noteworthy as a potential alternative to arbitration in the resolution of investment disputes.

References

Deli Z (2016) New ways of dispute resolution in investment protection cases. https://ssrn.com/abstract=3102277. Accessed 30 Sep 2018

Delimatsis P (2016) TTIP, CETA, TiSA behind closed doors: transparency in the EU trade policy. Tilburg Law and Economics Center

Fontanelli F, Bianco G (2014) Converging towards NAFTA: an analysis of FTA investment chapters in the European Union and the United States. Stanford J Int Law 50(2)

Horváthy B (2016) A CETA új vitarendezési mechanizmusa. https://jog.tk.mta.hu/blog/2016/04/a-ceta-uj-vitarendezesi-mechanizmusa. Accessed 30 Sep 2018

Horváthy B, Szép V (2016) International trade agreements captured by domestic politics? Lessons learnt from the CETA case. https://hpops.tk.mta.hu/en/blog/2016/11/international-trade-agreements-eu-ceta. Accessed 30 Sep 2018

Jakab A, Lőrincz VO (2016) A jogrendszerek mérése indexek segítségével. In: Jakab A, Gajduschek G (eds) A magyar jogrendszer állapota. MTA Társadalomtudományi Kutatóközpont, Jogtudományi Intézet

Jakab A, Lőrincz VO (2017) International indices as models for the rule of law scoreboard of the European Union: methodological issues. Max Planck Institute for Comparative Public Law & International Law (MPIL) Research Paper No. 2017-21

Kanyuk PÁ (2016) CETA – "Trójai egyezmény" a kapuink előtt? http://kozjavak.hu/ceta-trojai-egyezmeny-kapuink-elott. Accessed 30 Sep 2018

Van Harten G (2016) The EU-Canada Joint Interpretive Declaration/Instrument on the CETA. https://ssrn.com/abstract=2850281. Accessed 30 Sep 2018

Víg Z, Hajdu G (2018) CETA and regulatory chill. In: Görög M, Mezei P (eds) A szellemi tulajdonvédelem és a szabadkereskedelem aktuális kérdései. Pólay Elemér Alapítvány

Chapter 14
Screening of Foreign Investments: Promises and Perils of Technological Sovereignty

Marcin J. Menkes

14.1 Introduction

In March 2019 the European Union established a framework for the screening of foreign direct investments into the Union (Regulation).[1] The EU thus hesitantly follows in footsteps of all the G7 countries and—the catalyst for this emerging normative trend—China. International economic law scholars aptly identified reasons behind this trend. Given the changing nature of economy growth, increasingly based on intellectual capital, and resulting business and public security challenges, ever more depending on information, technologies and respective infrastructures, screening mechanisms are both needed and justified.[2] Some authors rightly acknowledge the risks of misusing such security measures for economic purposes,[3] or blurring the distinction between economics and politics.[4]

This most recent normative cautiousness in respect of foreign investments coalesces with broader criticism of investor-state arbitration and the ongoing investment arbitration efforts. The anomalies identified in respect of international investment

[1](2019) Regulation (EU) 2019/452 of the European Parliament and of the Council of 19 March 2019 establishing a framework for the screening of foreign direct investments into the Union.

[2]Hindelang S, Moberg A Debate: A Common European Law on Investment Screening? In: Verfassungsblog. https://bit.ly/2Inohhh. Accessed 8 April 2019.

[3]Wang E et al. (2019) Told U.S. security at risk, Chinese firm seeks to sell Grindr dating app. In: Reuters. https://reut.rs/2YxaiuO. Accessed 5 April 2019.

[4]Bakker A The Political Economy of Capital Controls and Liberalization. In: Verfassungsblog. https://bit.ly/2UptBrN. Accessed 8 April 2019.

M. J. Menkes (✉)
Warsaw School of Economics, Warszawa, Poland
e-mail: marcin.menkes@sgh.waw.pl

C. I. Nagy (ed.), *World Trade and Local Public Interest*, Studies in European Economic Law and Regulation 19, https://doi.org/10.1007/978-3-030-41920-2_14

law,[5] and the resulting legitimacy crisis,[6,7] have led to more[8] or less[9] revolutionary, responses invariably based upon premise of Westphalian nation-state legal order[10]; some more ambitious strategies advocate crossing the private-public law divide.[11] However, this time it is not the international investment regime that is in transition,[12] but the entire socio-economic environment.

Unlike mentioned above most prominent scholars, I believe that the social unease we are experiencing has much deeper roots. It is a socio-economic change driven by the technological progress. Proper acknowledgment of this factor dramatically changes functions of international law. On the one hand, technologies created unprecedented economies of scale and open space for further, supra-national integration. On the other hand, new technologies also create new cyber-risks. As I explain in greater detail below, both tapping economic benefits and providing security require huge investments and coordination beyond capacity of any individual state. Although socio-economic changes could occur without states (emancipation of companies) or they could be artificially delayed, the adequate function for international economic law in the transition period is to create normative conditions fostering technological development and allowing to capture part of returns in order to provide public goods (safety and justice) and to distribute profits.

Unlike the most prominent adherents to the materialist conception of history, whether prophesying ultimate reign of socialism[13] or capitalism,[14] I neither claim that human nature depends upon economic forces exclusively, nor that any particular path of socio-political evolution is inevitable. Sufficient to acknowledge different development trajectories of free-market democratic states compared to others. If development was inevitable, it would have occurred everywhere. As I argued in respect of relationship between economic growth theories, international financial & monetary law and the rule of law,[15] if there was a single economic formula for growth, everyone would have replicated it.

My claims are more limited. First, inadequate international law framework entails social costs and limits benefits. Second, would there be a socio-political momentum for a change, international investment law can lower transformation costs. Third, it is the law that should frame economic activity and not the economic activity dictate normative framework.

---

[5]Waibel et al. (2010).

[6]Brower and Schill (2008).

[7]Franck (2005).

[8]Cheng (2005).

[9]Brower (2003).

[10]Chung (2007).

[11]Maupin (2013).

[12]Sauvant and Alvarez (2011), pp. 1–12.

[13]Marx and Engels (1932).

[14]Fukuyama (2006).

[15]Menkes (2019).

It is not an idealistic call for supranational integration, but a pragmatic approach to managing the ongoing change. Accordingly, I don't asses desirability of further integration and I certainly do not advocate such integration because of its desirability. Yet, I also differ from realist heralds of a *nascent global state.* Not only do they argue that this new social order has already been established, even though it is hardly visible,[16] but crucially that the new centers of power already enjoy normative and enforcement capacities.[17] On the contrary, I believe that while conditions may already be ripe for change, a new normative paradigm will emerge in a painful adaptation process, which can, however, be mitigated by international law.

I start by analyzing significance of new technologies for the stability of international stage (Sect. 14.2). Against this background I highlight the most important elements of the EU-wide, one EU Member-State and the US investments screening frameworks (Sects. 14.3–14.5). Finally, I consider possible application of such mechanisms and consequences thereof for the development of international economic law (Sect. 14.6).

14.2 Technology Development and Technology Trap

While no one can authoritatively declare a twilight of an era, until they are already a history, the predominant mood in the democratic world is that we are experiencing profound changes of the socio-economic structure. Some believe that it is the free market model that has run out. Others argue that it is the democracy that has lost its resonance. Whichever is true, if any, international economic order without anyone to defend makes an easy prey for populist politicians. These "surface eruptions" are analysed through various scientific lenses, including the following examples.

As Yale's historian Timothy Snyder argues, disruptions Western democracies are everything but haphazard or exogenous. He shows, how Russia's failure of politics focused on growth (politics of *inevitability*) resulted in replacement thereof of with one focused on mythical past and the consolidating effect of struggle against ultimate evil (*politics of eternity*).[18] As Russia was unable to advance on the development path and meet expectations of its own society, it shifted its energy to undermine such efforts elsewhere. Accordingly, aggression of Ukraine and Georgia, but also Russian interference in the US presidential election of Donald Trump, UK's Brexit vote and the on-going expansion of European far right make part of a larger picture.

---

[16]Slaughter (2005).

[17]Chimni (2004).

[18]Snyder (2018).

From the sociological perspective, we can see further standing on shoulders of Sigmund Freud[19] and Zygmunt Bauman.[20] The former explained in the 1930s that the modernity brought a newly emancipated individual a devilish choice. One gained "beauty, hygiene and control" at the expense of suppressing "individual instincts". In other words, modern man traded liberty for security. As the neoliberal agenda dominated the post-Cold War order, the latter argued that while the original Freudian equation remained valid, postmodern civilisation gave up part of security for an unrestrained liberty to fight for happiness. From this perspective, current backlash against (economic) liberalism and caving for comforting populist promises of security is history coming full circle.

These dynamics appear coherent with the psychological and sociological insight into emergence of authoritarian and totalitarian regimes. First, how come freedom, and resulting accountability, become unbearable.[21] Second, how even the good intentioned populist quick-fixes based on grant of extraordinary powers to overcome problems that are inherently build-in the democratic model, ultimately lead to authoritarian, if not totalitarian, state.[22]

One could multiply examples of various analytical lenses that allow to trace correlation between instability in various regions, yet each time coming across alternative causation theory. Alternatively, all these specific anomalies may suggest a deeper, "tectonic change". If that is the case, then acknowledgment of this additional factor would allow to move from a merely descriptive to a proscriptive approach.

The "tectonic move" in question are technological advancements that increase economic pressure on moving towards the next stage of *supra* national integration.

At the international economic stage designed by and for Westphalian states, there were no reasons to change the nation-state premise, even though states, or even public inter-state organizations, have long lost their monopoly over international relations.[23] Idea-driven integration projects, notably by conquest, proved unstable, as they anticipated economic development. As a result, Westphalian international law was mostly concerned with harnessing individual ambitions.[24]

However, the above does not mean that the nation-state will remain the point of equilibrium between centralization and decentralization pressures forever. Once equilibrium shifts towards integration (or the other way), normative premises of international law would have to adapt. It can be a post-factual, reactive, change, as results from first academic commentaries on investment screening mechanisms. But law could also become an enabling factor during the transition period, thus lowering transition costs.

---

[19]Freud et al. (2010).

[20]Bauman (2000).

[21]Fromm (1994).

[22]Hayek and Caldwell (2007).

[23]Menkes (2017a).

[24]Cassese (2006), pp. 29–56.

Now the emergence of contemporary nation-state and rapid economic growth were possible thanks to a particular set of circumstances. Core functions of a state consist of providing publicly funded public goods: safety and justice. In the High Middle Ages these functions were performed by manors. Until population remained scarce and trade limited, benefits of providing security over hardly populated continent did not exceed the costs.[25] Similarly, defense and justice were most efficiently provided within a fortified domain. Beneficiaries of the manorialism/ feudalism were keen on preserving their preferential institutional status. Even the economically rational "theft strategy" (as an alternative to production) employed "marauding bands" like Vikings, Moslems, or Magyars did not change the total utility.[26]

In time, both costs and benefits of the manorial organization changed. Growth of population entailed pushing the frontier, until the land supply has been exhausted, thus expanding market space and allowing to develop trade (further strengthened by the expansion across various climate zones and resulting production specialization). As the scarcely populated areas have gradually been colonized and the trade intensified, benefits of enlarging the safety zone and securing justice increased. At the costs side, development of offensive weapons entailed growth of necessary military units, which required additional revenues.[27] To this extent, economic expansion played a mutually-reinforcing role with the demand for and supply of justice and security. Crucially, the pressure to change normative framework—and overcome transformation frictions—emerged only as resources became increasingly scarce relative to society's needs.[28]

Current development of new technologies and the shift towards knowledge economy produces strikingly similar dynamics. On the one hand, the mentioned above multifaced research captures, how new technologies increase risks, both directly (e.g. cyberwarfare) and indirectly (cyberterrorism, mass-scale manipulation).[29] Due to global technological, environmental and economic interconnectedness of the world, regional (or even global) safety often hinges upon *the weakest-link*. Hence, safety requires both unprecedented coordination and ever larger investments. On the other hand, knowledge economy offers unprecedented economies of scale.[30] Yet again, development of new technologies require unprecedented level R&D investments.

[25]North and Thomas (1973).

[26]Ibid 19–20.

[27]Ibid 17.

[28]Ibid 19.

[29]Dugain and Labbé (2016).

[30]Ip (2018) The Antitrust Case Against Facebook, Google and Amazon. Wall Street Journal.

14.3 The EU Screening Mechanism

14.3.1 Regulatory Context

The EU decision to establish a screening mechanism of foreign direct investments (i.e. excluding portfolio investments, Regulation preamble par. 9 and art. 2(1)) constituted a response to concerns about predominantly Chinese abuses of the access to the European market. It was, France, Germany and Italy to originally request the European Commission to take steps necessary to safeguard reciprocity of treatment (including public procurements) and prevent "a possible sell-out of European expertise".[31] Yet, as only 13 out of 28 EU states have an investment screening mechanism in place, the proposal for a EU-wide mechanism received mixed reactions.[32]

So far the EU established merely a cooperation framework and overarching principles i.e. each Member State remains free to decide whether or not to screen, and allow, a particular foreign direct investment (Regulation art. 1(3)). In doing so, States shall ensure efficiency of such measures, i.e. prevent circumvention thereof (Regulation art. 3(6)). This normative approach stems from the competence overlap between the FDI regulation, belonging to the EU trade policy exclusive powers, and the Member States responsibility for their own national security.[33]

14.3.2 Screening Purpose, Scope, Factors and Procedures

The screening mechanism is understood as a normative instrument of general application (e.g. a law or regulation) and accompanying administrative requirements, implementing rules or guidelines, setting out the terms, conditions and procedures to assess, investigate, authorise, condition, prohibit or unwind foreign direct investments on grounds of security or public order (Regulation art. 2(4)).

The mechanisms are to allow assessment, whether the FDI in question is likely to affect security or public order notably in respect of (Regulation art. 4(1)):

- critical infrastructure, whether physical or virtual, including energy, transport, water, health, communications, media, data processing or storage, aerospace,

[31](2017) Joint statement of ministers of France, Germany and Italy calling for FDI screening mechanism.

[32]For a comparison between various EU member state models (including a comparative table) see: European Parliament EU framework for FDI screening.

[33]On the problematic issue of legal basis of the EU screening mechanism, whether conceived as a part of Common Commercial Policy (as suggested in Regulation, Preamble par. 7) or freedom of capital movement (as could results from Regulation, Preamble par. 4), see: Korte S In Search of a Role for the Member States and the EU to Establish an Investment Screening Mechanism. In: Verfassungsblog. https://bit.ly/2U3tzRs. Accessed 8 April 2019.

defence, electoral or financial infrastructure, and sensitive facilities, as well as land and real estate crucial for the use of such infrastructure;
- critical technologies and dual use items, including artificial intelligence, robotics, semiconductors, cybersecurity, aerospace, defence, energy storage, quantum and nuclear technologies as well as nanotechnologies and biotechnologies;
- supply of critical inputs, including energy or raw materials, as well as food security;
- access to sensitive information, including personal data, or the ability to control such information; or
- the freedom and pluralism of the media.

The EC will be particularly concerned with projects likely to affect projects or critical technologies of Union interest, which includes programs involving a substantial amount or a significant share of Union funding, or which are covered by Union law regarding critical infrastructure, critical technologies or critical inputs which are essential for security or public order (Regulation art. 8(1, 3)).

In course of the assessment, Member States and/or the European Commission should take into account direct or indirect control by a foreign government, previous record of affecting security or public order in a Member State, as well as serious risk of engaging in illegal or criminal activities.

Powers of the European Commission mainly consist of issuing legally non-binding opinions in respect of foreign direct investments likely to affect security or public order (Regulation arts. 1(1), 6(3), 7(2)). Specific coordination procedure depends on whether the investment in question is subject to screening by the jurisdiction directly concerned or not. The Member State in question is only obliged to give due consideration to comments received from the EC and/or other members (Regulation art. 6(9)). The Commission will maintain a publicly available list of national screening mechanisms (Regulation art. 3(8)).

14.3.3 Investor Legal Status

As for the foreign investor rights, the stated purpose of the EU rules on screening mechanisms is to create legal certainty, while upholding, *inter alia*, EU values (Regulation, Preamble par. 7, 2).

In a legally non-binding manner Regulation stipulates that "[i]t is appropriate" for the States to "lay down the essential elements of the framework for the screening" to allow investors to understands its nature, including timeframes, appeal relevant procedures and possible recourse against unfavorable decision (Regulation, Preamble par. 15). Rules and procedures relating to the screening mechanism should be transparent and non-discriminatory between third states (Regulation art. 3(2)). States remain free to decide, whether they establish screening mechanisms or screen specific investments (Regulation, Preamble par. 8). In particular, grounds for triggering the screening and detailed procedural norms should be "set out by Member States" (Regulation art. 3(2)).

Opinions and comments expressing views about possible threat to security or public order shall be duly justified (Regulation arts. 6(5), 7(4)).

Confidentiality of information submitted for the screening purposes (Regulation art. 3(4), 10), as well as personal data (Regulation art. 14), should be protected.

Most importantly, foreign investors and the undertakings concerned "shall have the possibility to seek recourse against screening decisions of the national authorities" (Regulation art. 3(5)). Designated contact points with screening mechanisms should be established (Regulation art. 11). The Regulation is directly applicable (as confirmed by virtue of art. 17).

On the downside, the Member States and the EC may respectively issue comments and opinions regarding completed new investments that had **not** undergone screening in the state directly concerned for up to 15 months after the completion of the foreign direct investment (Regulation preamble par. 21, art. 7(8)). In terms of regulatory burdens foreign investors and investments are obliged to provide information necessary for the screening, concerning, *inter alia*, the ownership structure and the ultimate investor and participation in the capital, other completed or planned business activities, as well as the funding of the investment and its source (Regulation art. 9(2, 4)).

14.3.4 International Coordination

From the perspective of systemic coherence of international economic law, one should note that Regulation allows for the EU and its Member States to coordinate their screening efforts with relevant bodies from third states, where security or public order can be affected (Regulation art. 13). Also, an expert group has been established, which, aside assisting the Commission in screening efforts, is tasked with exchanging information on best practices and trends and issues of common concern.

As a result, investors interested in sensitive sector not only are now obliged to take into account national position and/or European Commission's DG Competition in respect of antitrust law, but also DG Trade and, possibly, other DGs and states concerned about policy or security concerns.

14.4 Germany

14.4.1 Regulatory Context

In December 2018 Germany amended the Foreign Trade and Payments Act ("AWG") and Foreign Trade and Payment Ordinance ("AWV"). As a result the

Federal Ministry of Economics acquired an extensive ex-post examination competence regarding the acquisition of shares of German companies by third-country nationals.[34] It is yet another tightening of the regulatory regime, following the 2017 review.

14.4.2 Screening Purpose, Scope, Factors and Procedures

In 2018 Bundestag introduced a list of civil areas (i.e., non-military products or areas) with special security relevance including "critical infrastructures" (sector of energy, information technology, telecommunications, transport, traffic, healthcare, water, food, finance and insurance where a failure could endanger public security), manufacturing of software for such infrastructures, telecommunications surveillance, cloud computing, data transmission.[35] Now the civil areas with special security relevance also encompasses "companies in the media industry which contribute to the formation of public opinion", which in light of the ensuing Snyder's theory seems of particular relevance.

In case of military and encryption sector (military areas), as well as in the field of critical infrastructure (listed civil area), the threshold for FDI screening is as low as 10% of voting rights. To this extent some expressed doubts, whether such a limitation of free flow of investments does not violate the EU free movement of capital.[36] Although in accordance with art. 65(1)(b) TFEU, Member States are entitled to adopt measures justified on grounds of public policy or public security, in accordance with the ECJ *Scientology* judgment, that "public policy and public security may be relied on only if there is a genuine and sufficiently serious threat to a fundamental interest of society. Moreover, those derogations must not be misapplied so as, in fact, to serve purely economic ends". Restrictions must also clear the threshold of proportionality, legal certainty and predictability. AWG and AWV mentioned, however, merely a risk for public policy or public security, without clear procedure for its assessments or circumstances under a transaction will not be allowed.

For the acquisitions involving companies in non-listed civil areas, the threshold remains at 25%.

The review, prompted by an obligatory notification, can last up to 4 months.

Similarly to the US approach, German mechanism covers both direct and indirect acquisitions.

---

[34] van den Broek N et al. (2018) EU and Germany Move to Further Tighten FDI Screening Process. In: WilmerHale News & Insights. https://bit.ly/2UKJQPx. Accessed 9 April 2019.

[35] Kaman H-G, Seyfarth M German Government Amends German Foreign Trade and Payments Ordinance to Widen Control of Foreign Takeovers of Critical German Companies. In: WilmerHale News & Insights. https://bit.ly/2VAbUlF. Accessed 9 April 2019.

[36] Stompfe P Rebuilding the Berlin Wall? In: Verfassungsblog. https://bit.ly/2KjYcm5. Accessed 8 April 2019.

By comparison, the UK white paper of July 2018[37] expands so-called trigger events, which can undermine national security, encompassing any investment or activity that involves the acquisition of more than 25% of an entity's shares or votes by a 'hostile actor', acquisition of significant influence or control over an entity, or finally further acquisitions of significant influence or control over an entity beyond the above thresholds (par. 25).

In accordance with French *Code monétaire et financie* (art. L. 151-3 et seq.), there are 12 business sectors for which foreign investments are subject to prior authorization by the state. These concern public order, public authority, public security and interests of national defense. In case of acquisition, as a result of which one passes the threshold of 33.33% shares or voting rights in a French company or business, the transaction qualifies as an investment for the purposes of Investissements étrangers en France (IEF) control.[38] In such case, it is within the Minister for the Economy prerogative to authorize the investment. On January 1, 2019 governmental screening powers have been broadened by virtue of Décret n° 2018-1057. New changes include substantive broadening of the authorization procedure to include, *inter alia*, spatial operations, electronic and computer-specific systems for public security purposes, data-hosting activities, as well as R&D in cybersecurity, AI or robotics.[39]

In France an investor himself can request to government to declare, whether the investment requires an authorization (*rescrit*).

14.5 The United States

14.5.1 Regulatory Context

In 2018 the US adopted the John S. McCain National Defense Authorization Act for Fiscal Year 2019 (NDAA), which repeals and replaces the Export Administration Act of 1979. NDAA Title XVII on Review of Foreign Investments and Export Controls, *inter alia*, modernized the Committee on Foreign Investment in the United States (CFIUS),[40] which is the principal body responsible for the oversight of

[37] Clark G National Security and Investment. A consultation on proposed legislative reforms (White Paper).

[38] Brice N et al. Investissements étrangers en France (IEF): Renforcement du contrôle et extension des secteurs stratégiques. In: Jones Day. https://bit.ly/2GwpkZM. Accessed 25 April 2019.

[39] (2019) Renforcement du dispositif de contrôle des investissements étrangers dans les entreprises sensibles. In: Direction générale du Trésor. https://www.tresor.economie.gouv.fr/Articles/2019/01/04/renforcement-du-dispositif-de-controle-des-investissements-etrangers-dans-les-entreprises-sensibles. Accessed 25 April 2019.

[40] Originally provisions were introduced as a separate bill, Foreign Investment Risk Review Modernization Act (FIRRMA), and only later incorporated to NDAA.

foreign "covered transactions"[41] in the US. Similarly to the (subsequent) EU regulation, the US bill is, first and foremost, about China.[42]

The principal effects of NDAA include expanding CFIUS jurisdiction—broader range of covered transactions including non-passive minority shareholders in critical technology or infrastructure, joint ventures involving technology transfers to a foreign entity or sensitive real estates. It also introduces the notion of states of special concern and expands screening factors. Aside substantive developments, NDAA contributes towards incremental institutionalization of screening activities.[43]

14.5.2 Screening Purpose, Scope, Factors and Procedures

The covered transactions include mergers, acquisitions, and takeovers by or with any foreign entity that could result in foreign "control" of a U.S. business relevant to domestic national security.

While the national security *per se* is not defined, NDAA provides factors to be considered as a part of security assessment of "covered transactions" such as real estate sensitive location, critical nature of infrastructures or technologies, but also any transaction that leads to a foreign control of a domestic company (sec. 1703(4)(B)). Screening can cover both direct and indirect investments (sec. 1703(4)(D)(i)).

CFIUS may consider in particular (NDAA sec. 1702(c)): whether a covered transaction involves a country of special concern, the potential national security-related effects of the cumulative control of the entity in question, pattern of recent transactions, history of complying with US laws and regulations, impact on domestic sector in terms of national security, personal data and sensitive information, cybersecurity.

Particular significance is attached to

- critical infrastructures,
- energy assets,
- critical materials,
- critical technologies.

Investments screening starts with a voluntary notice. However, CFIUS can also compel such a filing, if it determines that a transaction poses a potential risk to national security (CFIUS will be partly funded by fees for filing notices). While the screening can take up to 2 months (NDAA sec. 1706, 1714), the ultimate decision on allowing the investment belongs to the President. One interesting NDAA procedural

[41] 50 U.S. Code § 4565 - Authority to review certain mergers, acquisitions, and takeovers.

[42] Williams R (2017) CFIUS Reform and U.S. Government Concerns over Chinese Investment: A Primer. In: Lawfare. https://bit.ly/2GAqMJC. Accessed 10 April 2019.

[43] Zable S (2018) The Foreign Investment Risk Review Modernization Act of 2018. In: Lawfare. https://bit.ly/2UkLJOV. Accessed 12 April 2019.

development is the introduction of an expedited procedure, whereby a party can submit declaration with "basic information" instead of a notice, and CFIUS could take decision based on this submission (although it can refer the matter to the regular procedure).

Depending on circumstances, CFIUS may impose certain conditions or suspend transaction pending review or require a mitigation agreement to address security risks (NDAA sec. 1718, 50 USC 4565(1)). CFIUS control powers cover transactions performed by joint ventures, which is a clear attempt to curtail circumvention of investment screening mechanism.

Unlike German "quantitive approach", based on a numeric screening threshold, NDAA stipulates for screening of "covered transactions" that could result in foreign "control" of a U.S. business. Control is broadly yet flexibly defined as the power, direct or indirect, whether exercised or not exercised, to determine, direct, or decide important matters affecting an entity (NDAA sec 1703).

14.5.3 Investor Legal Status

NDAA explicitly recognizes foreign investors contribution to domestic economic development and R&D (NDAA sec. 1702(a)(3)) and even recalls Dwight David Eisenhower's warning against losing from sight mutual advantages of international economic cooperation and its contribution to the "internal strength of the American economy" in the haste of emergencies (NDAA sec. 1702(a)(6)). Hence, the US should continue to "enthusiastically welcome and support foreign investment, consistent with the protection of national security" (NDAA sec. 1702(b)(3)).

The national security constitutes a very flexible basis for CFIUS intervention (as there is no legal definition of national/homeland security, sec. 1703), as it may include availability of human resources, products, technology, materials, and other supplies and services, (NDAA sec. 1702(c)(4)). It thus seems worth to point out that NDAA at least stipulates that investments should not be reviewed in the national interest absent a national security nexus (NDAA sec. 1702(b)(9)).

In terms of transparency, NDAA imposes upon CFIUS robust reporting obligations. *Prima facie* significance of these obligations are of indirect and limited importance to individual investors, however, it remains to be seen, what will be the actual practice, and to what extent it will have a disciplining effect upon the Committee.

Arguably, the most important provision concerning risks of arbitrary use of NDAA powers is that respective actions and findings of the President are not subject to judicial review NDAA sec. 1715 (50 U.S.C. 4565(e)). Other civil actions challenging an action or finding by CFIUS can only be brought in the US Court of Appeals for the District of Columbia Circuit. This may be worrying in light of limited transparency in terms of screening criteria and pending/completed reviews.

Whereas CFIUS discretion to screen transactions is very large, NDAA also seeks to mitigate regulatory burdens. The Committee can exempt certain transactions, create streamlined filing procedures for summary screening, and most importantly maintains, in general, voluntary nature of filings.

14.5.4 International Coordination

NDAA calls upon the President to urge and help allies and partners to establish processes that are similar to CFIUS for screening foreign investments for national security risks and to facilitate coordination (NDAA sec. 1702(b)(6)) and to lead a collaborative effort with allies and partners to strengthen the multilateral export control regime (NDAA sec. 1702(b)(7)).

14.6 Conclusions

Emerging normative trend of establishing investment screening mechanisms requires broader consideration in terms of possible impact both on international investment law and, more broadly, future of democracy and free-markets.

Ratio legis of screening mechanisms for "policy or security concerns" (the EU) or "national security" (the US) does not appear controversial. Paradoxically, history makes full circle, as the current normative trend in respect of investment screening mirrors discredited neo-Marxists and dependency theorists approach to incoming investments.[44] From a practical perspective, as technologies can be harnessed for various purposes, especially in case of so-called critical technologies, actual screening practice will involve the impossible task of differentiating between economic purposes and possible security implications of technology transfers.

On the one hand, screening bodies are thus endowed with broad, discretionary powers. This seems in line with the notion of an inherent right of self-defence, as enshrined in art. 51 of the UN Charter, but also with self-judging formulation of the majority of clauses on essential security interests.[45] On the other hand, this opens space for arbitrariness serving economic or political ends. For instance, NDAA covers "emerging technologies that could be essential for maintaining or increasing the technological advantage of the United States over countries of special concern with respect to national defense, intelligence, or other areas of national security, or gaining such an advantage over such countries **in areas where such an advantage may not currently exist** (bolded MJM)." One can recall here the ease of Donald Trump's administration with which it imposed tariffs against long-time allies, on the security grounds, while tightening relations with somewhat surprising partners.

---

[44]Vandevelde (1998).

[45]Rose-Ackerman and Billa (2008).

From a narrow perspective, the risk of hidden protectionism is both economically doubtful (for consumers), and also will have a chilling effect on innovation. Free circulation of ideas spurs innovation and a general ban on exports of a possibly fundamental technology will be more suffocating than the most stringent IP regimes.

In terms of international legal order, the more economies move towards knowledge- and services-based, the greater significance of these emerging institutional arrangements for undermining protection offered by international investments law. Screening mechanisms also inevitably politicize the process, which contradicts the very foundations of international investment law. Rather than carving out exceptions, states could rely on treaty interpretation and revision tools (notably essential security clauses) and, as an secondary means, necessity exception under international customary law. One could recall for instance number of, somewhat inconsistent, arbitral case law on economic necessity with regards to Argentinian economic crisis. Also the International Court of Justice confirmed in *Nicaragua Judgment (Merits)* that 'the concept of essential security interests certainly extends beyond the concept of an armed attack'.[46]

While states will not renounce their power in respect of national security, it should not be used as a blanket exemption from international economic commitments. In their current shape, the EU/US framework show hardly any reminiscence of the rule of law standards. In terms of possible internationalization of investment screening, or at least international scrutiny thereof, international investment law could only exceptionally provide avail in the pre-investment phase (somewhat more likely to offer protection in case of increasing already acquired shares, as reflected in *Eureko* award). While the security concerns are subject-specific, and certain information will be sensitive, it is important to insist upon coordination of screening efforts, which could also serve the *peer review* purposes.

However, as screening mechanism are likely to become important regulatory barriers, they present both a challenge and an opportunity for regulatory governance.[47] If States decide to move to the subsequent step of integration within the "technology development and application zones", as advocated in this paper, the emerging economic area will play a major role in international economic order. As a result, because of costs efficiency, such a zone could play the role of transnational regulator *de facto*.

Moving to broader democracy and free-market concerns, the changing cost-benefit ratio brings us ever closer to supra-national integration. However, as there are vested interests in a nation-state framework, the possible transition will meet resistance, mutually reinforced with social unrest caused by profound socio-economic shifts. As an alternative to a state-led process, supranational consolidation could be driven by companies.[48] The mentioned above technology risks can even

---

[46]Military and Paramilitary Activities in and Against Nicaragua (Nicaragua v. U.S.), 1986 I.C.J., para 224.

[47]Menkes (2017b).

[48]Dugain and Labbé (2016).

more easily serve corporate interests of technology developers. Another possibility is that the very same technologies will play a self-defeating role ("technology trap") and allow to wreak chaos and instability among democratic societies, leading to political disintegration. This seems to be the case, for instance, of Brexit driven by misinformation and emotional manipulation. Yet, unless humanity renounces science and technological development, the pressure will mount again.

Once the cost-benefit ratio enables integration, the first to use this opportunity will exponentially gain economic advantage over rivalrous power centers. Hence, the states are faced with two possibilities.

They can approach new technology sector as yet another mode of economic activity and try to restrain its circulation with regulation. Given current incapacity to control or to tax transnational companies,[49] such an attempt seems unlikely to succeed in the long-term. History of the original Bretton Woods order, blown up by capital markets despite capital control efforts, is a telling warning. Also, as the popularization of screening mechanisms may undermine international (investment) law, states thus diminish their regulatory powers over companies in the long run.

Alternatively, economic dynamics favoring integration could be met with coordination integration efforts by states, actively co-shaping the process. Such a scenario requires normative reconceptualization of technologies. International law ought to provide new "property rights"[50] to foster innovation and sustainable growth. This implies a common approach to the rule of law and reduction of regulatory barrier, at least, within "technology development and application zones". A more advanced package could include a streamlined approach to the protection of intellectual property rights. Cooperation surplus available to states—i.e. economic gains to be shared between companies and participants of such zones—could facilitate overcoming non-cooperative behaviors in respect of international taxation of transnational companies.

Yet safety has also non-economic, security component (including cybersecurity[51]). Coordination-integration in this respect is mutually reinforcing-dependent with economic cooperation. The greater safety within zones offered, the lower technology development and application costs. Yet again, this requires new approach to technological sovereignty transcending nation-state border and, as one scholar suggested, possibly restoration of somewhat duty notion of self-determination.[52]

Perhaps the greatest paradox of the emerging normative trend in respect of foreign investment screening is that it reminds us the hard learned lesson of World War II. First, international peaceful coexistence needs to rely upon political, military

---

[49]Menkes (2015).

[50]In the economic sense of property rights i.e. exclusivity of enjoyment (use and taking benefits) and the right to alienate, whether formally in a form of property right per se or not, North and Thomas (1973).

[51]Snyder (2018).

[52]Ohlin (2017).

and economic pillars. Second, one can hardly imagine building mutual trust, necessary for complex social interactions,[53] neglecting any of them. To this extent the emerging normative trend in respect of investment screening could be the first step towards restoring communitarian thinking about international law. This way we make sure that political structures serve public purpose and not the other way round.

It remains to be seen, whether we manage to harness the opportunities of technological advancements or fall into a trap of our own making.

Acknowledgments The author thanks the Kosciuszko Foundation for the support of research at Cornell University.

References

Bauman Z (2000) Ponowoczesność jako źródło cierpień. Sic!, Warszawa

Brower CHI (2003) Structure, legitimacy, and NAFTA's investment chapter. Vand J Transnatl Law 36:37–94

Brower CN, Schill SW (2008) Is arbitration a threat or a boon to the legitimacy of international investment law? Chic J Int Law 9:471–498

Cassese A (2006) Diritto internazionale. Il Mulino

Cheng T-H (2005) Power, authority and international investment law. Am Univ Int Law Rev 20:465–520

Chimni BS (2004) International institutions today: an imperial global state in the making. EJIL 15:1–37

Chung O (2007) The lopsided international investment law regime and its effect on the future of investor-state arbitration. Va J Int Law 47:953–976

Dugain M, Labbé C (2016) L'homme nu - La dictature invisible du numérique. Plon

Franck SD (2005) The legitimacy crisis in investment treaty arbitration: privatizing public international law through inconsistent decisions. Fordham Law Rev 73:1521–1625

Freud S, Hitchens C, Gay P (2010) Civilization and its discontents, Reprint edition. W. W. Norton & Company, New York

Fromm E (1994) Escape from freedom. Holt Paperbacks, New York

Fukuyama F (2006) The end of history and the last man, Reissue. Free Press

Hayek FA, Caldwell B (2007) The road to serfdom: text and documents--the definitive edition, 1st edn. University of Chicago Press, Chicago

Marx K, Engels F (1932) The German ideology

Maupin JA (2013) Public and private in international investment law: an integrated systems approach. ID 2144019

Menkes MJ (2015) The divine comedy of governance in tax evasion matters. Or not? J Int Bank Law Regul 6:325–329

Menkes MJ (2017a) 200 lat Kongresu wiedeńskiego: od harmonii sił do siły harmonii. In: Cała-Wacinkiewicz E, Menkes J, Pęksa W, Staszewski W (eds) Idee, normy i instytucje Kongresu Wiedeńskiego - 200 lat później - perspektywa międzynarodowa. C.H. Beck, Warszawa, pp 257–269

Menkes MJ (2017b) Regulatory cooperation under TTIP. If you can read this, you're too close. In: Czarny E, Kuźnar A, Menkes J (eds) The impact of the transatlantic trade and investment partnership on international cooperation. Peter Land, Frankfurt am Main, pp 55–63

[53]Sztompka (2007).

Menkes MJ (2019) Rule of law in international monetary and financial law: new(ish) solution and old mistakes. Eur Yearb Int Econ Law

North DC, Thomas RP (1973) The rise of the western world: a new economic history. Cambridge University Press

Ohlin JD (2017) Did Russian cyber-interference in the 2016 election violate international law? Tex Law Rev 95:1579–1598. https://doi.org/10.31228/osf.io/3vuzf

Rose-Ackerman S, Billa B (2008) Treaties and national security. N Y Univ J Int Law Polit 40:437–496

Sauvant KP, Alvarez JE (2011) International investment law in transition (introduction). In: Alvarez JE, Sauvant KP, Ahmed KG, del Vizcaino GP (eds) The evolving international investment regime: expectations, realities, options. Oxford University Press, New York

Slaughter A-M (2005) A new world order. Princeton University Press, Princeton

Snyder T (2018) The road to unfreedom: Russia, Europe, America. Vintage Digital

Sztompka P (2007) Zaufanie. Fundament społeczeństwa. Znak

Vandevelde KJ (1998) The political economy of a bilateral investment treaty. Am J Int Law 92:621–641. https://doi.org/10.2307/2998126

Waibel M, Kaushal A, Chung K-H, Balchin C (eds) (2010) The backlash against investment arbitration. Perceptions and reality. Wolters Kluwer

The manufacturer's authorised representative in the EU is Springer Nature Customer Service Centre GmbH, Europaplatz 3, 69115 Heidelberg, Germany. If you have any concerns regarding our products, please contact ProductSafety@springernature.com

Printed and bound by CPI Group (UK) Ltd, Croydon, CR0 4YY
30/09/2026
02225648-0007